TURNING POINTS

TURNING POINTS

The Detroit Riot of 1967, A Canadian Perspective

18/10/03
To Robert,

For your interest
in history.
Enjoy!

HERB COLLING

NATURAL HERITAGE BOOKS
Toronto

Published by Natural Heritage / Natural History Inc.
P.O. Box 95, Station O, Toronto, Ontario M4A 2M8

www.naturalheritagebooks.com

National Library of Canada Cataloguing in Publication

Colling, Herb, 1953-
Turning points : the Detroit riot of 1967 : a Canadian perspective / Herb Colling.

Includes bibliographical references and index.
ISBN 1-896219-81-0

1. Riots—Michigan—Detroit—History—20th century. 2. Detroit (Mich.)—Race relations—History. 3. Detroit (Mich.)—Public opinion. 4. Public opinion—Ontario—Windsor. 5. Detroit (Mich.)—History—20th century. 6. Windsor (Ont.)—History—20th century. I. Natural Heritage/Natural History Inc. II. Title.

F574.D457C64 2003   977.4'34043   C2002-903978-9

Cover and text design by Sari Naworynski
Edited by Jane Gibson

Front cover image by "Spike" Bell
Back cover images courtesy of *The Windsor Star*

Printed and bound in Canada by Hignell Book Printing, Winnipeg, Manitoba

Natural Heritage / Natural History Inc. acknowledges the financial support of the Canada Council for the Arts and the Ontario Arts Council for our publishing program. We acknowledge the support of the Government of Ontario through the Ontario Media Development Corporation's Ontario Book Initiative. We also acknowledge the financial support of the Government of Canada through the Book Publishing Industry Development Program (BPIDP) and the Association for the Export of Canadian Books.

This book is set in Cartier. It is a typeface named after the explorer Jacques Cartier which was designed by Carl Dair, a Canadian graphic designer.

To Anne

Love to the Nth

"I will let no man drag me down
So low as to make me hate him."

– BOOKER T. WASHINGTON

Contents

Acknowledgements   viii

Explanatory Note From the Author   xii

Introduction   xiv

Chapter 1:   The Riot: The American Story   *1*

Chapter 2:   Windsor Firefighters Join the Brigade   *40*

Chapter 3:   Canadian Newsmen   *56*

Chapter 4:   Caught By the Riot   *72*

Chapter 5:   The Border Is Closed   *91*

Chapter 6:   Relief   *109*

Chapter 7:   Emancipation and Human Rights   *117*

Chapter 8:   Slave and Racial History: Windsor   *139*

Chapter 9:   Racial History: Detroit   *178*

Chapter 10:   The Quebec Question   *207*

Chapter 11:   Post Riot: Detroit   *226*

Chapter 12:   The Aftermath: Windsor   *250*

Appendix I: AN ENTERPRISING SOCIOLOGIST: BENJAMIN SINGER   *271*

Appendix II: A TRIBUTE TO LIGHTFOOT   *280*

Sources by Chapter   283

Bibliography   290

Index   294

About the Author   306

Acknowledgements

My uncle opened my eyes to racial discrimination in the 1980s as we drove from Sacramento, California, to Ontario in a 1967 blue Ford Mustang. It was early Sunday, and we were travelling through a run-down area, which my uncle dubbed the "black district." There wasn't a soul in sight and I asked him how he knew it was Black. He said, "Because it's run-down," to which I replied that it could be poor Whites, Hispanic or any other poverty-stricken group.

That started an argument about Blacks in America, about discrimination, slavery and racial hatred. When I suggested that the problem is socio-economic because Blacks have not received equal opportunity or education, my uncle replied that Blacks simply "don't have the grey matter." He said that Blacks are not as intelligent as Whites, which prompted me to name every successful Black I could.

I was supposed to be navigating but, in the heat of the argument, I missed a turn. When I realized my mistake, he looked at me and said, "How could you be so stupid?" I threw up my hands and replied, "I must be Black!"

Once on the right road, I said that his attitude kept the black man down, prevented the development and integration of the race in America. He immediately replied, "If that's how you feel, then why don't you do something about it?" I didn't have an answer for him then, but I do now, and this is it.

I hope this book casts some light on racism, and outlines solutions, just as that trip opened my eyes, made me revisit my beliefs, and those of the people around me. It was quite a journey, one that I will never forget and, for that, I am thankful. I am also thankful for the help I received from friends and colleagues along the way.

TO THE PEOPLE WHO WERE THERE

Jennifer Beaudoin; Bob Bingham; Bill Bishop, photographer, *The Windsor Star*; Ann Bondy; Donald Bondy; Vicki Bondy (nee Fox); Lieutenant Colonel

Dan Bonner; Grant Bowbeer; Tim Burton; Bernice Carlan; Bob Cassler; Katherine Clark; Charlie and Gene Colling; Jim Colling; Kevin Conrad; Inez Coxon; Barney Crichton, Windsor Police Department; Ron DiMenna; Madelyn Della Valle, Windsor's Community Museum; Ted Douglas, *The Windsor Star*; Jeanne Drouillard; Bob and Carol Ferguson; Robert Ferguson, Windsor Fire Department; Dave Fields, Chief, Windsor Fire Department; Garnet Fox; Cheryl Garrod; Dorothy Gascoyne; Jeanne Godfrey; Sue Goerzen; Lloyd Graham, Windsor Police Department; Ken Hull, *The Windsor Star*; Juergen Hendel; Dennis Hinckley; Ruth Hirtenfeld (nee Colling); Sister Immaculata; Bill Jackson, Windsor Police Department; Bob Jones; Layne Katzman; Steve and Denise Kristof (nee Belisle); Lieutenant Colonel Phil Labelle; Dave Lane; Jack Leopold, Windsor Fire Department; Les Mather, *The Windsor Star*; Walt McCall, *The Windsor Star*; J.A. "Pete" McGarvey, Wordsbilt Productions; George Mooney; Gail Oliver; Dino Paniccia; Rachel Parent; Rosalind Peck (nee Ward); Lieutenant Colonel Garnet Ryan, retired, Essex and Kent Scottish; Benjamin Singer, Professor, University of Western Ontario; Dick Smyth, CKLW Radio; Dick Spicer, *The Windsor Star*; Joe Suchan; Hal Sullivan, Reporter, CBC Radio; Bill Taylor; Jim Travis; Ivy Vander Zanden; Jim Van Kuren, News Director, CKLW-TV; Allen Walls; Dr. Bryan E.Walls; Charlie Weston, Windsor Police Department; Ted Willis, Windsor Police Department; Bill Willson; Rick Wynants; and Eileen Zuccaro.

TO THE PEOPLE WHO PROVIDED SUPPORT:

Irene Arseneau; Lillian Beckett, Tour Guide, North American Black Historical Museum (NABHM); Tim Berthiaume, Windsor Fire Department; Janet Brown, Archives, Windsor Public Library; Gail Brownell, Production Assistant, *Ideas*, CBC Toronto; Bob Carroll, Photo Editior, *The Windsor Star*; Linda Chakmak, Archives, Windsor Public Library; Lillian Charette, Administrative Assistant, (NABHM); John Doig; Margaret Douglas; Sister Rose-Marie Dufault, Hotel-Dieu Grace Hospital; Margaret Evans; Eleanor Gignac, Archivist, Marsh Collection Society; John George; Anne Gooch; Joanne Haines, Administrator, Windsor Police Department; Tim Halford, formerly Hôtel-Dieu Grace Hospital; Kevin Hart; Barry

Harvey, Manager, Early Morning Productions; Gerry Head, CBC TV; Steve Hecnar, Retirees Association, Windsor Police Department; Fred Johnstone; John Kearn; Larry Kulisek, Professor, University of Windsor; John Laycock, *The Windsor Star*; Sister LeBoeuf, Hotel-Dieu Grace Hospital; Lisa Lewis, Archives, Windsor Public Library; Mary MacDonald, Coles Books, Tecumseh Mall; Jennifer MacLeod, Archivist, Marsh Collection Society; Owen McPherson, North American Black Historical Museum; Joan Magee; Mary-Elizabeth Marentette, Windsor Community Museum; Joan Mavrinac, Human Resources, Windsor Police Department; George McFee, Windsor Police Department; Bob McLean; Susan McMullen, Info Services, Windsor Police Department; Yvonne McRobbie; John Metcalfe; Patience Nauta, Detroit Historical Museum; Janice Paniccia; Sherie Penner; Gary Percy, Fire Rescue, Windsor Fire Department; Hendrika Ruger; Pat Ryan, Technician, CBC Radio; Erin Semande, Windsor Community Museum; Ken Schmidt; Phil Smith, Windsor Police Department, retired; Stephanie Smith, Events Assistant (NABHM); Thom Smith; Fred Sorrell; Bob Steele, CBC Radio; Mary Sweet; Heather Taylor, Tour Guide (NABHM); Michael and Philippa Taylor; Ed Tellier, Junior; Ari Varsa; Madelyn Della Valle, Windsor Community Museum; and Jim Winter, Professor, University of Windsor; and, of course, to my former publishers: Carl Morgan, Norm Endicott and Caroline Walker; and to my current publishers: Barry Penhale and Jane Gibson, who made it all possible.

Special thanks to Ana-Maria Sydor, Librarian at the University of Windsor, for getting me started; the LaSalle Mariners Yacht Club, good friends who put up with me; to Ken Farrow, Windsor Police Department, retired, for a delightful afternoon going through scrapbooks; to the Marsh Collection Society in Amherstburg for allowing me to get underfoot; to Elise Harding-Davis who regaled me with interesting stories, and to her staff at the North American Black Historical Museum and Cultural Centre for giving me the virtual run of the place; to Sarah and Bill Jarvis for the spicy bits and their local knowledge, support and encouragement; to Laurie Smith for providing "insight"; to the Walls family for giving me perspective, especially Shanse and Winston for being "conductors" on the

Underground Railroad; to Howard McCurdy for providing contacts; to staff at the CBC for their local knowledge, especially Gino Conte, Bill Baker, and Sandra Precop, who had no idea why I asked so many questions; and to former Record Librarian Beth Hebert for her repeated trips to the CBC archives.

An extra-special thanks to photographer Spike Bell for his stories, pictures and critical read; to Nicole Raposo (nee Rivest) who saved me oodles of computer time with one welcome and important hint; to Nicole Mahler who graciously read and helped edit the manuscript, gave me an incentive to keep going when I needed it most, and who helped me more than she may know; and, finally, to Anne Colling who gave me the freedom to work, and without whom there would be no point.

Some on the list may scratch their heads and wonder, "Why is my name here? I didn't do much." If your name's included, then you did. Whether a two-page story, a paragraph, a tip or two, a phone number, or name, even a gentle word of advice, it all helped make this book what it is: a series of reminiscences and impressions of what the Detroit riot meant to people in Windsor in terms of their racial consciousness. If I've inadvertently forgotten anyone, I apologize. I am grateful.

And finally, by recognizing the many who contributed so much, I must acknowledge, however, that the responsibility for accuracy rests with me. Any errors brought to the attention of the publisher and myself will be addressed in future editions.

Explanatory Note from the Author

I used the word "Black," recognizing that it's a dated reference with negative connotations. "Coloured" and "Negro" were more common, preferred by some who felt the terms provided "societal elevation"; but the words were falling out of favour because of an association with "bias and distortion" on one hand, and racial epithets on the other. Not used universally, "Black" was gaining prominence in 1965 and was preferred by Blacks by 1967 as indicated by the expression: "Black is beautiful."

Black is also questionable because it's a colour, not an ethnic delineation. It is opposite to White, is associated with the occult or evil, and is described in the dictionary as "dismal, sullen, horrible or foul." White is considered good, pure or simply Caucasian. One implies the absence of colour, the other a combination of colours. Both are inaccurate and inappropriate. As one person said, "colour is incidental." We should look at people as people, recognize and celebrate our differences.

Elise Harding-Davis, curator of the North American Black Historical Museum in Amherstburg, says "Negro" derives from Black in Latin, but that "nigger" is a corruption of the River Niger, which was used for shipping during the slave trade. The latter is negative and demeaning. Harding-Davis laments that Blacks are the only group not dignified by their place of origin. There are Poles, Ukrainians, Germans and French; and there are Blacks. Having said that, she prefers African-Canadian or African-American; not "afro" or "afri." "Afro" is a hairstyle and "afri" is a misnomer. There's no such thing. Personally, Harding-Davis describes herself as a "Canadian black woman" with the stress on "Canadian," not "American."

I capitalized the word "Black," giving it the status of a proper noun because it is common with most writers who talk about race or black history. I didn't stray from the norm, even though capitals seem affected and look strange to me on the page. I also capitalized "White," even though the words are adjectives, misused as nouns. As I've pointed out, they are not adequate and don't deserve prominence, but who am I to rebel against convention. I've never seen a truly black man, just as I've never seen a white one. They're opposite ends of the colour spectrum, but most people fall somewhere in the middle.

When I was young, my sister asked about her own pigmentation. "What colour am I?" Mom did a double take and laughed. "Well, what colour do you think you are?" My sister looked at the back of her hand and said, "Kinda brown!" to which Mom replied, "And don't you ever forget it!"

For my family, that was a turning point in our lives. Hence, the title of this book. The Detroit riot marked a turning point for the city of Detroit, and for its black community, its white police force and government. It marked a turning point for Windsor, both in its relationship with Detroit, and with its own black community. It marked a turning point for other black communities in places like Chatham, Amhertsburg and Dresden. It was a turning point for Windsor firefighters who repaid a debt, for a Windsor police officer who volunteered and furthered his career, and for Windsor journalists and journalism. In short, the Detroit riot was a turning point for anyone who found themselves caught in the event and its aftermath.

In writing *Turning Points*, I did not try to soften the blow. The vocabulary is sometimes rude and crude. At times, the subject matter is brutal. It's the kind of material that many people try to avoid, try not to address. Some readers may think some of the words offensive, and may suggest that they are not politically correct. Those readers may be right.

In chronicling the stories surrounding the Detroit riot, I had no intention of being politically correct. I'm afraid that too many authors restrict or shape their writing into material that is likely to be accepted—an approach that I don't believe is appropriate or wise. In fact, I think we're too politically correct and not direct or truthful enough about issues that concern us.

I hope this book will be straightforward and will help break the colour bar.

Introduction

People remember things for many reasons. If you're old enough, you remember where you were when U.S. President, John F. Kennedy, was shot in Dallas, Texas, on November 22, 1963. You remember Apollo XI and the first moonwalk by Neil Armstrong in July 1969. "One small step for man, one giant leap for mankind." Canadians remember October 1970, when government troops moved into Quebec during the FLQ crisis. Terrorists killed labour minister, Pierre Laporte. Martial law was declared with tanks and troops on the streets. For Canadians, it was shocking, unbelievable, but it happened and left an indelible impact on our identity. And what adult alive today will forget the events and repercussions of September 11, 2001.

The summer of 1967 is a time to remember. An average person made $5,500 a year, and you could buy a Ford Mustang for $3,300. The best picture was *A Man For All Seasons* and Disney's new animated feature *Snow White and the Seven Dwarfs* cost 50 cents for kids. Musically, *Light My Fire* pushed The Doors to the top of the charts and there was a controversy as to whether a book called *Fanny Hill* should be banned.

1967 was also the year that troops from Israel and Egypt skirmished on the banks of the Suez Canal, Biafran soldiers made a bid for independence from Nigeria, and Communists in Vietnam attacked the Da Nang airbase. In North America, a new book called *The Wasp* was published in the United States. It told of intolerable conditions in the ghetto. As one reviewer said, "... it was one long, high-pitched scream of rage."

Domestically there were ominous clouds on the horizon, but it was also a time of celebration in Canada. It was our Centennial. The Pan Am Games were underway in Winnipeg, and Expo '67 was being held in Montreal. Based on the theme, Man and His World, Expo was dominated by an enormous U.S. pavilion, a geodesic dome designed by R. Buckminster Fuller. It was also highlighted by Habitat '67, a multiple housing project that stressed the increased urbanization of the world's population.

This emphasis on city life and the United States was appropriate. It reflected what the summer of '67 was about: the Civil Rights Movement, black identity and pride, racial consciousness and discrimination. American Blacks were documenting injustices in their quest for equality. They lived in squalid, crime-infested cities with poor educational and recreational facilities, few jobs and even fewer prospects. They wanted better housing and social reforms. They wanted racial justice, but the authorities weren't listening – the impetus for unrest and anger. Many Blacks were poor and militant, aware and impatient. They wanted something better and they were determined to get it by any means possible.

Dozens of race riots erupted throughout the United States. In April, 200 Black youths smashed windows and looted stores at a shopping centre in Omaha. In May, skirmishes in Chicago resulted in over 50 arrests and several injuries. In Jackson, Mississippi, the National Guard finally restored order after two nights of rioting in which one student was killed. In Houston, Texas, a police officer was murdered and several people injured. In June, Blacks in Tampa, Florida, stormed the streets, smashed windows and set fires after white policeman shot a burglary suspect. In Boston, 100 people were injured and 73 arrested during four days of rioting. The resulting damage cost millions.

As the summer of discontent continued, violence spread. In Atlanta, Georgia, demonstrators protested the shooting of a black youth by police. One person died and three were injured. In Prattville, Alabama, snipers exchanged gunfire with police after black activist, Stokely Carmichael, was arrested for disturbing the peace. At the end of June, violence in Buffalo, New York, left 100 people injured and another 240 arrested. In Cincinnati, Ohio, one person died, six were injured and 365 were arrested. Violence flared again on July 3 to 5, when 19 more people were arrested. By mid-month, ten other American cities were paralyzed by rock throwing, fire bombing and looting. In Fresno, California, one man was shot and 30 people arrested after 200 black youths refused to leave a park at closing.

I was only 14 and not particularly interested in world affairs. For me, the summer of '67 was typical Georgian Bay: blue skies, cool water, green trees and sunlit days in the small town of Midland, Ontario, north of Toronto. The United States, Vietnam, the Suez and Biafra were far removed, and yet, an awareness was stirring. I remember my parents discussing something in hushed but anxious tones, and I knew something was wrong.

It was Monday, July 24, the second day of a riot in Detroit, Michigan, across the border from Windsor, Ontario. It was described on television as a war zone with looting, vandalism, shooting and fires. Blacks were out of control, and Detroit police were watching it happen. The National Guard had been called, and an appeal was issued for federal troops to keep order.

Because of the Vietnam War, we were used to watching military conflict, but the fighting had never been so close. It was important for us because our cousins lived near Detroit on the American side, and my parents were afraid for their safety. It looked as though the entire country was on the brink of civil war. My parents offered our home as a refuge. Nothing came of it. Our cousins were safe in the suburbs, well removed from danger but, to me, the whole scenario emphasized that all was not right with the world.

I would not think about Detroit again until 12 years later when I moved to Windsor in the spring of 1979. It was my first time in the city and I was surprised at the proximity of Windsor and Detroit. Located on the toe of the boot that is Essex County, Windsor is the southwestern tip of Ontario. Detroit is less than a mile across the river that serves as an international boundary, and the only division between our two cities. It is the largest American city to sit directly opposite a major Canadian city on the longest undefended international border in the world.

Windsor is connected to Detroit by a railway tunnel, a vehicular tunnel and the Ambassador Bridge, but it's also connected by its psyche. Many Windsorites are close to their U.S. cousins and seem more American than Americans. Some have even developed a Michigan accent in their speech. They shop, go to restaurants and bars in Detroit; their favourite sports teams include the Detroit Tigers (baseball), the Detroit Lions (football), the Detroit Red Wings (hockey), and the Detroit Pistons (basketball). Windsorites are more likely to watch American football than the CFL, and are as familiar with the *Star Spangled Banner* as they are with the Canadian anthem. Local businesses encourage U.S. dollars. Some even prefer them.

Many people from Michigan also come to Windsor for fun. It could be slot machines and horses at Windsor Raceway; a proliferation of strip bars, bingos and nightclubs; or even Casino Windsor, which caters to Americans. You're more likely to see buses from the American Midwest than anywhere in Canada, and blue Michigan license plates are as common as Ontario tags on cars. Some Michiganders live in Windsor because it has a lower crime rate, and thousands of Windsorites have green cards, which allow them to work in Detroit. Many Canadians go to school in the U.S. while American residents do the same in Windsor.

When people from Windsor travel, they often describe their town in relation to Detroit so other people will understand where they live. It's fitting, since the two places seem to merge. There's an unusual visual phenomenon, almost an optical illusion, for visitors driving to Windsor. It's the impression that Windsor's downtown is a large metropolis, since you can see skyscrapers from Detroit while not actually being able to see the border. It gives the idea that those buildings are part of Windsor and that the downtown is grand. As a result, some people joke that the best thing about Windsor is the view of Detroit.

Many Windsorites read *The Detroit News* or *Free Press* as well as their local paper. They tune to American TV, and they identify with American culture generally. The local radio station is a prime, if not peculiar, example. CKLW is a 24-hour broadcaster licensed to serve southwestern Ontario. It has offices on Ouellette Avenue in Windsor and is governed by Canadian regulations. It's owned by Canadians, but to make money, the station beams into Detroit. Canadian content is required by law, but it's buried beneath terms and references American.

In its heyday, in 1967, CKLW was known as the Big Eight, and was located on Riverside Drive with a view of Detroit. It highlighted American news and music, and even used American pronunciations to reflect its major market. Rich, noisy, and brash, the station discovered hit songs that Americans paid millions to hear. In fact, CKLW knew what Americans wanted better than Americans themselves. It was Motown from Windsor, and it featured the music of American Blacks: Stevie Wonder, Smokey Robinson, Diana Ross and the Supremes. The station's dual citizenship reflected a uniqueness, but it also emphasized Windsor's identity crisis.

An automotive town, Windsor developed as a branch plant economy of the United States. It grew with The Big Three, Chrysler, GM and Ford, all of which established factories in Canada in order to sell to the British Commonwealth. As industry evolved, so did Windsor's empathy with the American way of life. Tool and die, mold and other companies increased in size because of their dependence on American technology. Pharmaceutical companies established in Windsor because of the proximity to Detroit.

Windsor's relationship to Detroit is exactly what gives the city much of its appeal. Windsorites enjoy a cosmopolitan American city while living in a small, provincial, Canadian town. There were 192,500 people and a tiny black community in Windsor in 1967, compared to Detroit which boasted a population of 1.6 million, over a third of whom were Black.

Given the social relationship and geographical proximity, it's no surprise that a major event in Detroit had a huge impact on Windsor. Prior to the riot, Windsorites spent a lot of time in Detroit. After, that all changed. Windsor treated Detroit with more caution, perhaps even suspicion or fear. Residents went over, but only in company, to areas that were well-lit and policed. They knew where they were going, and went there directly without making sidetrips, staying too late or deviating from their usual path.

Prior to the riot, Tim Burton, a lifelong resident of Windsor, would ride his bicycle over the Ambassador Bridge to shop at Hudson's, the United Shirt Store, or Flagg Brothers Shoe Store. On Sundays, he'd head downtown to Sanders Ice Cream Parlour and the Vernor's plant at the foot of Woodward Avenue to watch bottles being filled with ginger ale. He'd enjoy a float, sundae or large glass of Vernor's at the marble counter. Burton admits he was careful, but he was never afraid. After the riot, he was no longer so sure. He still went over, but he didn't spend time downtown. Instead, he'd head for the shopping malls and bars in the white suburbs where he felt safer.

Elise Harding-Davis has a similar feeling about Detroit. As a Canadian black woman, she remembers residential areas where people in shirtsleeves sat on porches, drinking and joking. She thought nothing of going to the Fox Theatre to see Motown revues but, after 1967, she became more cautious. The areas were more tense, not as friendly. Seeing burned-out buildings and devastation was traumatic and she no longer shopped in Detroit or went over alone.

By Thursday, July 27, 1967, the riot was winding down, already overshadowed by other news. Pat Whealan, as an editorial writer for *The Windsor Star*, had his finger on the pulse of the area and wrote Detroit's epitaph. In his article, he lamented the passing of a town that was once near and dear to his heart. He talked about buying roasted peanuts for a dime at a stall outside Mariner's Church, or buying a novel at the Michigan Book Exchange to read on the Boblo boat as it churned downriver toward the amusement park near Amherstburg. He frequented the Quickie Donut Shop for good coffee and newspapers pinned to the wall so patrons' hands were free to eat.

The Detroit that Whealan loved was casual and leisurely, a bit down-at-heel, but a much friendlier town with spirit. He gave spare change to street people, but there was no real threat, no fear. He spoke fondly of downtown bars like The 509, The Golden Eagle, and The English Tavern, which offered Canadian dollars at par. If you heard a loud voice in those places, it was usually a Canadian and probably someone you knew.

To Whealan, Detroit was changing, but in subtle ways. Urban renewal was altering the pace of the city. It was faster, more jostled. Whealan complained about the glittering new Detroit and lamented "the good old days." He also expressed fear for the future. "It will survive because it has a solid foundation, but it will never be the same." Whealan felt the heart going out of the city. The riot was just the stake to finish it off.

Jeanne Drouillard, a French radio commentator, introduced me to the highlights of Detroit and, especially, its theatre. On our way home one night, the usual route along the John Lodge was closed for repairs and we had to detour into a dark section of the city. We tried to follow signs, but became hopelessly lost in an industrial zone of warehouses and low-rises. My first reaction was to stop and ask directions. Jeanne's was to lock the doors and speed up, a direct result of fear instilled by the riot in 1967. It was a panicky situation until we spotted the Renaissance Centre, a tall hotel and business complex downtown. The development looks like large grey oil drums, but it set our course and we quickly headed back into the light. With genuine relief, Jeanne entered familiar territory, eventually crossing the border to the comparative safety of Windsor.

Jeanne's paranoia was contagious. A year later, I was driving from Sarnia to Windsor, using a short cut on the American side. Entering Detroit, I missed the signs to the tunnel or bridge and suddenly found myself on a sunken stretch of highway with nothing but grey walls on either side or overpasses above. I knew I was heading the wrong way, probably toward Toledo, Ohio, but, eventually, I noticed an Amoco sign above an off-ramp and decided to ask directions. I drove into a run-down area and was already out of the car before I realized the service centre was closed and boarded up. Off to the right, and across the parking lot, was a van with people inside. Map in hand, I walked over to the vehicle, smiled at the two black men and told them I was lost and trying to get back to Windsor. They'd heard about Windsor, that it was a really nice place, and they seemed impressed. When I asked where they were from, they said Detroit, but they'd never crossed the border. They gave me directions and I headed back to my car.

As I went, I couldn't help feeling uncomfortable. I had a strange fear that what I had done was stupid and dangerous. The fear was irrational, but I'm positive it developed since coming to Windsor. For me, Detroit represented a different lifestyle and culture, an awareness that there are places in the world that are close to home, but aren't as innocent and easy. My feelings toward Detroit were also changed – indirectly – by the riot.

Many people in Windsor remember exactly where they were on Sunday, July 23, 1967, when the riot broke out. Rachel Parent was only 12 years old and she recalls walking along the riverfront with her father, listening to the guns. She was too young to know what was going on, but she remembers the "pops" like firecrackers on the 1st, or 4th, of July. Lloyd Grahame also spent time by the river. He was a Windsor police officer and he sat in his patrol car, listening to the machine guns and helicopters, thankful to be on the Canadian side of the border.

As a black man, Bryan Walls was employed at the GM Trim plant in Windsor, and he remembers being singled out by his colleagues who were confused and wanted to know what was happening. Because of his skin colour, they felt he knew, but they were wrong. As a Canadian, Walls didn't understand, or share, the American Black experience. He says that, in Canada, he wasn't really aware that he was Black, and the riot made him focus on his own racial heritage.

Gail Oliver watched Detroit burn. A nurse on the afternoon shift at Windsor Western Hospital on Prince Road, she remembers the rosy haze in the sky, and was reassured by the fact that the violence was over there, across the river, somewhat removed from her world. The water was a moat, the dividing line between two cultures and Oliver was thankful because it made her feel safe. Oliver used to dine or shop in Detroit and never thought twice about it, until afterward. Then, she went in groups, but never alone.

The Detroit riot was a wake-up call. It made Rosalind Ward's father load his World War II pistol, afraid that Blacks might invade Windsor. Ward was in her teens, and she remembers a friend's father, a Detroit police officer. He didn't come home for the duration and his family was afraid, until he called to let them know he was okay.

For Cheryl Garrod, the riot settled an argument with her mother. Garrod had fought for three months over whether she could go to a Monkees concert at the Detroit Olympia at the end of July. She was crazy about the rock group, but her mother didn't share her enthusiasm for the music or the city. Cheryl's mother eventually put her foot down and won the debate because of the riot. She said, "See. That's why I didn't want you to go." As it turned out, the concert was cancelled anyway.

According to *Windsor Star* reporter, Walt McCall, Detroit was smug prior to that summer. There were racial disturbances in other American cities, but Detroit was exempt. Race relations seemed pretty good and the city kept the lid on. After the riot, McCall says, the smugness was gone. Municipal officials realized that they had the same problems as any large American city.

Steve Kristof was only six, and one image sticks in his mind. It was a field trip to the Detroit Zoo, and they were travelling up Woodward when he saw a pair of legs sticking out of a garbage can. It was a mannequin damaged in the many fires that plagued the city. That, to him, represents Detroit and the riot. It gave him an impression of danger, of evil, of what Detroit and the rest of the United States must be like.

In later years, Kristof realized his first impressions were false. He's travelled extensively through the United States and found many areas of lasting beauty, peace and harmony. Despite that, Kristof's wife, Denise, locks her car door the minute she hits the border. As Windsor poet Laurie Smith suggests, "get to Traverse City and outside Detroit, they're just like us: No different." Smith says, Detroit is the big urban myth, with a culture all its own.

For people who didn't live through the riot, there's no concern about Detroit but, for those who remember, there is still some trepidation. Garnet Fox is from Amherstburg and he has no great fear; but he won't go to some areas of the city. Some people no longer cross the bridge or tunnel unless it's absolutely necessary, or they enter Detroit, but only to well-lit haunts or safely guarded suburbs. Katherine Clark is a teacher in Essex County and she's among that number. She remembers shopping in Detroit before, but not after the riots. For her, July 23, 1967, is a date she won't forget. It's a time that changed her perceptions of an American city.

This book will explore those perceptions and what happened. It will look at the Detroit riot and how it relates to Windsor in an effort to understand the conflict, our cities and perhaps even ourselves.

Chapter 1

The Riot: The American Story

It's 6:30 on a Sunday night in 1967. Five cars are in a traffic accident on the corner of Twelfth Street and Clairmount in the heart of the black district in Detroit. There aren't enough ambulances to take people to hospital and a pregnant white woman is selected over a bleeding black man. A second ambulance is delayed. A crowd develops and 200 people – mostly Black – don't like what they see. Angry comments lead to pushing and shoving as racial tensions erupt. Police lose control after the first brick is thrown. By 9:00 p.m., windows are smashed. There is looting, arson and sniping. Simply put, the white police force bungles it.

This hypothetical scenario is presented to 15 rescue personnel on Thursday, June 20. It's a mock riot, a test for community services, the police and fire departments, and the Michigan Civil Rights Commission. Their job is to analyze and diffuse problems during the long hot summer. Officials are convinced that Detroit must be prepared but, when participants hear details of this pretend disaster, they shake their heads in disbelief. For the next two hours, they discuss their actions, but consider it so unlikely, it's hard to take seriously. The rescuers are supposed to develop a plan, but are convinced there's no hurry. It's a ridiculous exercise. No one even takes notes. They don't believe it can happen. Yet, ironically, it does – one month later – one of the most destructive, and deadliest, riots in the history of the United States.

SATURDAY, JULY 22, 1967

It's a hot, sweaty night as police attempt raids on five seedy "blind pigs," or after-hour drinking and gambling establishments. One of the blind pigs is called the United Community and Civic Action League. It's located in a second-floor apartment above a vacant print shop in a dilapidated building on the corner of Clairmount and Twelfth Street in Virginia Park, one mile west of Woodward on Detroit's west side.

Frequented by prostitutes, pimps, drug pushers and "out-of-towners looking for some action," the blind pig is an important part of life in the ghetto. There are dozens of these juice-joints in a four-block area known as "The Strip" or "Sin City." The illegal operations began with prohibition, but survive as private watering holes. Initially, they served middle-class Blacks who were banned from white-only bars and restaurants, but they flourish in a black slum that has seen better days.

A hot spot for night life and entertainment, the strip boasts all-night restaurants that serve soul food: pig's feet, mustard greens and baked yams, washed down with cheap red wine. All for just under $2.00. Diners listen to the music of Motown: Aretha Franklin, Otis Redding and the Miracles. Night owls hit jazz clubs and pool halls, as motorists cruise the streets, radios blaring. Pimps, in gleaming white Buicks, promote their $10 tricks, as high rollers scout their next game and junkies look for a hit. Plainclothes officers mingle with bar patrons, trying to make a statement. They want to clean up the district.

The United Community and Civic Action League was raided twice in June. Ten people were arrested and, in the second blitz, 28 people were rounded up. To area Blacks, it's a form of harassment. Of 4,600 policemen, only 200 are Black, and many people feel the raids have more to do with racial discrimination than law enforcement.

Just before 10:00 p.m., two black undercover officers – members of the Detroit Vice Squad – try to gain access to the club by masquerading as basketball players from Cincinnati. They plan to shut the place down for operating without a license. They have to prove a violation, but they don't make it past the doorman.

SUNDAY, JULY 23, 1967

At 3:45 a.m., police officers Charles Henry and Joseph Brown figure they'll give it another shot. Henry enters with three women. Once inside, he buys a beer. The club is open well past the 2:00 a.m. closing imposed by Michigan State law, and Henry settles down to wait, listening to the juke box and watching gamblers shoot craps on the pool table. As part of the drill, other vice squad officers wait for 10 minutes. If Henry doesn't come out, they go in. In this case, they smash a glass door with a sledgehammer and charge upstairs. When the patrons hear breaking glass, they know they're in trouble.

The police expect to find 24 people in the bar, but are surprised to discover a large party for two black servicemen who've just returned from Vietnam. Eighty-two people are arrested. The owners are charged with operating an illegal drinking establishment and the found-ins are charged with "frequenting." Police describe it as, "an average raid."

Normally, police take arrestees out the back door and into an alley away from public scrutiny but, in this case, the door is padlocked and the prisoners are herded into the street. Because of the large numbers, it takes over an hour to ship them to the police station. They have to wait for patrol wagons, which only take 14 people at a time. One wagon is delayed when it gets lost on the return trip to the precinct.

At first, there are only a couple of bystanders, but passing cars slow down to watch and, pretty soon, there's a crowd of 20 to 30 people flanking the building and loitering across the street. They're drunks and drifters, prostitutes and gamblers, as well as factory workers on their way to the plant. Detainees chat with their girlfriends, exchange jokes and comments. Hanging out in a blind pig is a $25.00 misdemeanor with no fear of a jail sentence. The fine is like a cover charge.

The crowd swells to 200 as the arrest drags on and, as numbers increase, so do tensions. One youth shouts, "Black Power. Don't let them take our people away. Look what they're doing to our people." Another says, "They wouldn't act this way in Grosse Point." A few bystanders threaten, mock and taunt police, trying to incite the crowd. There are rumours that white officers use excessive force, beat prisoners with a gun butt or nightstick when they fail to show I.D. There are complaints about fights, and people being "roughed up" when they resist.

Someone in the crowd shouts, "Let's get the bricks going" as a bottle lands at the foot of an officer. Ten squad cars are on hand as the crowd jeers and mills about. More beer bottles, cans and rocks are thrown. One officer says it's getting "hairy," as police move on two rioters protected by the crowd. At 4:40 a.m., the police finish loading. Twenty minutes later, the last cruiser rolls away as an empty beer bottle arcs through the air and crashes into the rear window. The cruiser keeps going. Police are ordered out of the area. They hope the crowd will leave too.

People on the street view the retreat as a victory. A litter basket is thrown through a store window. A black youth yells, "We're going to have a riot." The crowd flows like a river down Twelfth Street. There's broken glass as the first stores are looted. Rioters steal TVs, jewellery, guns, groceries and booze from pawnshops and convenience stores. It starts with druggies, pimps and hookers, "the Cadillac and silk suit crowd," but then teenagers and 20-year-olds join in and, finally, older adults. Some looters suffer cuts to their hands and legs while more experienced thieves wear gloves and hard-soled shoes.

Conrad Mallett Junior, 14, is a carrier boy for *The Detroit Free Press.* He always expects a sideshow on Twelfth Street, but isn't prepared for 500 to 600 people. There's a nervous expectancy, a pent up anger, and it's breaking loose. Mallett is urged to go home fast. His supervisor has already been mugged, his wallet stolen. Excited and concerned, Mallett bolts into his father's bedroom. "Dad, I think the riot has begun." Mallett's father is the man who designed the mock riot one month earlier, and there's a striking similarity between it and the real thing. Mallett's worst nightmare has come true.

Sunday is usually quiet for Detroit police. A tactical unit, which specializes in crowd control, went home around 3:00 a.m. Other officers can't be mobilized because they're fishing or hunting for the weekend. Had the raid occurred at 10:00 p.m., as planned, the force would have been at strength and could have handled it. As it is, there are fewer than 200 officers on the streets and only 44 in the 10th Precinct where the blind pig is located. At 5:20 a.m., Detroit Police Commissioner Ray Girardin is notified.

He immediately cancels his vacation, switches the police to 12-hour shifts, and calls Mayor Jerome Patrick Cavanagh about the bad news. Seventeen officers, from other parts of the city, are ordered into the riot area. The police station is flooded with calls. Burglar alarms wail incessantly on Woodward.

By 6:00 a.m., about 30 windows have been broken and the first looters arrested. Three squad cars – with four officers each – patrol Twelfth Street, but the police are outnumbered. When the Esquire Clothing Store is ransacked, a police car goes by with siren blaring. At least 50 looters cut and run. There are too many, so police keep going. Nearby, the owner of a shoe store watches helplessly as looters strip boxes from his shelves. Smoke billows from broken windows. Firemen arrive. People watch, some still in their nightclothes.

Twelfth Street is one of the most densely populated streets in the United States with 21,000 people per square mile, double the city average. Correspondingly, there's more unemployment and low scholastic achievement. Six to eight black families cram into apartments that were originally meant for two. Twenty-five percent of the housing is substandard and should have been torn down. Many houses are over 30 years old. Conditions are miserable, rancid and squalid. The blight of poverty includes rats, 'roaches and despair. Most people rent and landlord-tenant disputes are common. Blacks pay more than Whites. They know it, and that adds to the problem. The crime rate is twice as high as the rest of the city.

Originally, Twelfth Street was a neat, middle-class Jewish district. Then middle-class Blacks moved in. When nearby slums known as the "Black Bottom" were cleared for urban renewal, poor Blacks made the transition. For a while, it looked integrated until Whites moved to suburbs in Southfield and Oak Park, leaving a few white merchants behind. Twelfth Street became "an ugly neon scar," an unkempt commercial strip surrounded by a sedate residential district of sturdy brick homes and manicured lawns.

By 8:00 a.m., 17-armed officers form a "vee" and make their first sweep. The police were going to wait for reinforcements, but have to do something even though they're outnumbered. Someone yells, "The cops are coming!" and the crowd moves aside. Some people scatter into alleys, but the mob fills in as police pass. It's estimated that 3,000 people smash windows and loot. One officer is amazed by the riot, but Ed Bailey isn't. He's a black freelance photographer for *Time* magazine. He phones his office and says, "It's here, baby!" By mid-morning, 1,100 men – one quarter of the police department – have reported for duty. Half are assigned to the riot. One hundred and eight officers cordon off six blocks from Clairmount to West Grand Boulevard, and east and west of Twelfth Street. They do not use force or interfere with looters. They banter with people who've turned out to watch. They let people leave the restricted area, while preventing others from going in. News of the riot spreads like a festering rash.

People run in and out of stores, laughing and joking with police. The crowd has a feeling of superiority or, at least, immunity. There are few arrests and some looters taunt police or shove goods into their faces. "It's an epidemic of excitement, just like a holiday." White-owned shops are primary targets, especially ones whose owners treat Blacks with contempt. Some stores have hastily scrawled signs: "Soul Brother," "Afro all the way," or "Very, very Black." Their owners hope that rioters will leave them alone. In some cases, the signs are put up by Whites to protect their businesses. The notices work for a while but, soon, by-passed shops fall to looters as other stores are emptied.

United States Representative John Conyers Junior lives a few blocks from Twelfth Street. He's a shrewd, 38-year-old black attorney, well-known and respected. When he's told of the disturbance at 8:30, he attends an emergency meeting at Grace Episcopal Church along with 20 black clergy who fear that lives will be lost if police are used. Before noon, Conyers takes to the streets, driving around with community leaders, asking people to stay in their homes or disperse. The task force tries to dispel rumours and calm things down, but to no avail. Looters pay no attention.

The scene is vastly different from a similar disturbance on August 9, 1966, when another peace patrol kept order in the Kercheval district near Belle Isle on the city's east side. Blacks stoned cars driven by Whites and smashed windows for three nights. Riot troops were called to break it up, but it was a discreet show of force without one shot being fired. Police arrested key members of the Afro-American Youth Movement and maintained barricades while black leaders and ministers worked to "cool it." A black community group went door-to-door to keep peace in the neighbourhood. There was some looting, firebombing and arrests, but the city of Detroit remained relatively quiet and an explosive situation was neutralized. While it could have erupted into the first full-scale riot in almost a quarter of a century, it was confined to a small area and with Kercheval having a more effective police/community relations program, fewer stores and people, the operation worked.

Compared to Kercheval, Twelfth Street is high stress. Most residents are dissatisfied and want to move. One-third carry weapons. They feel that streets aren't safe, especially at night when beatings and muggings are common. On Sunday, July 23, the stress is acute. The temperature is 86 degrees, the humidity 79 percent. Add the oppressive social conditions and tempers are sharp in Detroit.

Conyers doesn't like what he sees. A woman with a baby in her arms curses "Whitey" for no apparent reason. A rumour spreads that a black man was bayoneted by police and left to bleed to death. Another circulates that officers kicked and pushed a handcuffed teenager down a flight of stairs. The crowd is belligerent and angry. At noon, Conyers grabs a bullhorn and climbs onto a car at the corner of Twelfth and Clairmount. He's confronted by a man he once defended in court, but who was jailed for civil rights activities. Extremely bitter, the man incites the crowd and challenges Conyers, "Why are you defending the cops and the establishment? You're as bad as they are."

Conyers urges the crowd to stay cool and stop rioting. In return, he'll ask white police to leave. "We're with you," he shouts. The crowd replies, "No! No!" One man yells, "We don't want to hear it, Uncle Tom." A rock lands next to Conyers. Another rock hits a policeman in the head, drawing blood. Newsmen are pelted with rocks and bottles. Conyers gives up and leaves. Ironically, many people consider Conyers the most popular black leader in Detroit, but as one black man explains, "He ain't never been hungry." The police chief comments that black leaders "were practically White when they came back." Girardin's officers complain they've lost an hour waiting for the task force. They could have acted to control the riot and prevent it from escalating.

Across the city, key installations are under police guard, including the National Bank of Detroit, Chrysler headquarters, the Parke-Davis Pharmaceutical Company, Detroit Edison, the water treatment plants and public utilities. Courtesy of B.G. "Spike" Bell.

When a squad from a police commando unit blocks an intersection, their appearance draws residents into the street. The officers wear helmets with plastic face shields, and carry bayonet-mounted carbines. They are taunted and questioned for being in an area where there is no trouble. Conyers shows up and convinces the commandos to leave. There are mixed reports from police who say they are gaining, then losing control. They've never faced a riot before, and are ill-prepared, with no procedures on how to act. Officers stay behind sawhorses as looting continues. They remain as rioters pass, and they're still there after the street is quiet.

Later, when the Kerner Commission investigates, police say they had no instructions. They're angry and humiliated because they're told to show restraint rather than return fire or prevent looters. They're to standby with a show of force, supposedly to reduce deaths or injuries. They're powerless against looters and jeering hooligans. They believe it's a mistake to withdraw police, that a weak show of force is as harmful as no force at all, and that failure to exert control encourages deviant behaviour, and is a sign of weakness. Detroit police believe the tactic failed during the Watts and Tampa riots, and they should have clamped down sooner. The commission agrees that a firm hand could have prevented any escalation. "You're not supposed to wait until the town's burning." Even looters wonder why more arrests aren't made.

As chief of police, Girardin believes that a confrontation could have made things worse. "If we started shooting in there ... not one of our policemen would have come out alive. I am convinced it would have turned into a race riot in the conventional sense." Girardin says he could have used tear gas, but wind conditions prevented it. He also says gas masks restrict visibility and aren't readily available. He thought that the incident was a "pocket-riot" which would blow itself out. Girardin hoped that, once police lost control, they could wait for a lull in the action and break the momentum.

Some Blacks are disappointed that the riot doesn't become a full-scale revolt against Whites. "When I saw the first person coming out of the store with things in his arms, I really got sick to my stomach and wanted to go home. Rebellion against the white suppressors is one thing, but one measly pair of shoes or some food completely ruins the whole concept."

By 1:00 p.m. Sunday, the crowd swells to over 8,000, some drawn by police sirens. Stonings accelerate and some officers are injured by rocks, bottles and other objects. Blacks are defiant and threaten to kill white police. In one instance, a black man lies slashed and bleeding on the pavement with police standing over him. The crowd asks, "Why'd you cut him?" The officers say they found the man and will take him to hospital. The crowd cajoles. "We'll get you later." So far, the mob has not attacked and yet, it could easily overwhelm the small number of police.

Ironically, Cavanagh holds a press conference, confident that the situation is under control. He's told by reporters that it isn't. Embarrassed, the angry mayor requests another sweep of Twelfth Street, still unsure whether he has "a full-blown riot." Thirty helmeted police with rifles, shotguns and tear gas protect firemen, but there are too many looters, too many fires. An all-black fire-fighting team is placed under the command of Captain Marcene Taylor, but it's also pelted with bricks and bottles, and suffers even more verbal abuse than Whites. "We seem to be their favourite target."

A police sergeant with a bullhorn rides up and down the streets. "You are ordered to disperse." His vehicle is barraged with missiles and his rear window is smashed. One officer says it's like "trying to hold back the surf." The riot area is growing steadily. It's now three-and-a-half miles wide and extends from John Lodge Freeway, a north-south artery in the east, to Livernois in the west; and from West Grand Boulevard on the south, a mile and a half to Chicago Boulevard on the north.

The mayor meets 100 black civil rights and political leaders at police headquarters. Cavanagh says he used restraint, allowed rioters to blow off steam, and hoped calm would prevail. Reverend Hubert Locke and Councillor Nicholas Hood agree that force is needed, but Cavanagh hesitates to call Michigan State Police and National Guard because they're all White. He has no choice. "We don't want another Newark here." Councillor Hood deplores rioting and says responsible Negroes are not involved. He says his family has been threatened and is leaving temporarily.

Some people feel this is not a racial conflict, but a protest of authority; not a mass movement, but the actions of a few who are locked out of society with little chance of getting in – the "have-nots" against the "haves." "It's not a matter of civil rights," Hood says, "It's just lawlessness," the work of a disorganized criminal element which just happens to be in a predominantly black area. "The time has come to separate basically good people from the hoods and the punks," regardless of their colour. Conyers agrees, but says he didn't have much luck on the streets. "You try to talk to these people and they'll knock you into the middle of next year." Conyers says responsible people are in their homes on Boston and Chicago boulevards. Middle-class, wealthy, law-abiding black citizens, they strive for a better life in an affluent society. They're the people who give cars to their kids on their 16th birthday.

By 3:00 p.m., a request is made to bring in state police; 360 officers assemble at the armoury, the marshalling centre for "Operation Sundown." Several hundred National Guardsmen are also on hand. They're in the city for training but, by 4:00 p.m., they're committed to the "civil disturbance" with more on the way. Police officers protect Tiger Stadium where 34,000 spectators attend a doubleheader between the New York Yankees and Detroit Tigers. The cheering crowd doesn't realize that, only 10 blocks away, a disturbance has broken out. The Tigers lose their first ball game 4-2, but win the second 7-3. It's the fifth victory for the Tigers in seven outings.

Just before the second game, police announce which streets are safe and which to avoid, but without giving reasons for the diversion. When fans finally leave, they're confronted by the first signs of the riot. Detours and roadblocks steer people away from the stricken area. A hand-lettered sign says, "Peace on earth." Other signs on the sidewalk read, "Black Power." The familiar cry has been heard at civil rights rallies throughout the '60s, but has always been obscure, unclear to Whites. Scrawled in chalk on the sidewalk, the slogan has new meaning as a challenge to white America.

As arsonists step up their activities, there are too many fires to handle. In one neighbourhood, a man throws a Molotov cocktail into a business. The flames are fanned by heavy winds and, within minutes, showers of sparks explode like fireworks on the roof of a home next door. Residents spray the houses with garden hoses, but the fire spreads to two more buildings. Within an hour, the entire block is in flames. Ironically, the ninth house in the row belongs to the arsonist. The farmer's market is also set ablaze after being ransacked. By 4:30 p.m., all firefighters are called in, but they're pelted with bricks and debris before they can even run out their hoses. They watch from behind police barricades. As fires spread, black storeowners set up bucket brigades.

State Representative James Del Rio is camped in front of his building as two 10-year-old boys threaten to throw a brick through the window. Del Rio warns, "That building belongs to me." One boy replies, "I'm glad you told me, baby, because I was about to bust you in." Many black homeowners use rifles and shotguns to protect their property. Looters shout, "We're going to get you rich niggers next." Young people are, "dancing amidst the flames," destroying goods for no apparent reason. Children, riding two to a bike, have loot in their arms or hanging from their clothes. Looters in trucks are laden with everything from floor mops to furniture, price tags still dangling. Months after the riot, the goods are still being sold on the streets.

At 4:45 p.m., 68-year-old Krikor Messerlion, a white shoe repairman, is protecting his store on Linwood. He's a short, slight Armenian, known as

George or Koko by his friends. Despite his size, he's never been known to back down from a fight. Armed with a sabre, he chases looters who are carrying clothes from a dry cleaning store. One youth is nicked on the shoulder. Messerlion is knocked to the ground and beaten with a club. He dies four days later in hospital. His assailant, Darryl Curtis, a 20-year-old man from Alabama, is arrested for murder and sentenced to life.

For the past 13 years, Sandra West has lived two blocks from where the riot breaks out. She moved in with her parents in '54 because it was a nice neighbourhood, but now she's not so sure. A black reporter, West describes smoke so thick it smothers homes 20 feet away. The heat is so intense, it's felt for blocks. People cover their heads to protect themselves from falling cinders. Some families have been burned out of their homes. They struggle with suitcases full of whatever they can salvage. Their eyes are filled with tears from loss and smoke.

Rumours spread, but it's hard to get facts about the riot. Neighbours relay messages by telephone until the circuits are jammed. Many phones are out of order because the lines are down, telephone poles burned. Residents at Twelfth and Linwood pack their belongings and prepare to leave in the middle of the night, if necessary. West packs too. At 5:00 p.m., she closes the windows in her home to prevent smoke from filtering inside. An hour and a half later, the electricity goes out. There are no fans, so she opens the windows again. West heads into the street with her neighbours. A 12-year-old flashes a diamond ring he found on his lawn.

During the evening, a string of boutiques is looted in the "Avenue of Fashion," a five-block stretch near Livernois and Seven Mile Road. One dress shop is stripped of garments none of which sell for under $100. Walter Meyer has been in business for 16 years. "I've never seen anything like this in Detroit." In another store, mannequins are strewn on the floor, stripped and abandoned. Looters are brazen and dare police. "The fuzz is scared. They ain't going to do nothing." One boy smiles, "They won't shoot … The mayor said they aren't supposed to." Police use discretion. As one rioter says, he'd stop, if police pulled their guns. He believes police enjoy seeing Twelfth Street torn apart.

A reporter describes it as a thieves' paradise, "an eight block supermarket with no checkout counter." Cars pass with couches and carpets tied to the roof. A looter walks by with a refrigerator on a furniture dolly. Some thieves try to sell their goods for cash. Spectators scold them until they realize how futile it is and start looting themselves, grabbing the last of the merchandise from the shelves. It's a free-for-all. Both Whites and Blacks go after the spoils as looting becomes integrated, equal opportunity. Police call it a riot of thieves rather than race.

With the situation hopelessly out of control, officers begin making wholesale arrests. To bring order to chaos, a curfew is imposed from 9:00 p.m. until 5:00 a.m. It's impossible to enforce, but some streets are relatively quiet. Sandra West rummages for candles and flashlights as the sun sets. It's hot and humid. Shortly after curfew, the first sniper-fire is reported. A 16-year-old black boy is wounded. More gunshots are directed at a helicopter.

Floyd Shively, a photographer for United Press International, is snapping pictures when he hears three shots and feels something hit his leg. He thinks it's a rock, until blood oozes from a hole in his pants. His co-workers drive him to the Dearborn Medical Centre where he's treated for a flesh wound. Shively was a policeman for 10 years before he took up photography and he's never been shot. He figured he'd be safe with UPI. He's a victim of the most violent period of the riot. In one day, 17 people die.

The city in a state of siege. Officials fear that the riot has been organized by outside agitators and might spread. Courtesy of B.G. "Spike" Bell.

The governor declares a state of emergency. Police cars, trucks and jeeps speed past, laden with National Guardsmen who've been on the street since 7:00 p.m. It's expected that 4,000 Guardsmen will be mobilized by midnight, but they're too late for some looters. Willie Hunter, 26, and Prince Williams, 32, are the second and third people killed. The two men live and die together. They're short, dark, and could be brothers. Their bodies are found in a burned-out drugstore.

At 11:00 p.m., a 45-year-old white man, Walter Grazanka, is helping himself to groceries at the Temple Market. On his third trip out of the store, another white man – the 30-year-old owner of the business – drives by, firing a .22 calibre revolver. Grazanka is shot. He dies 25 minutes later in hospital. Along with the groceries, Grazanka's pockets are stuffed with seven cigars, four packs of pipe tobacco and nine pairs of shoelaces. He told his wife that he was just going down the street to check on the riot.

As Grazanka is dying, 23-year-old Sheren George, a white woman, is heading home, a passenger in the family car driven by her husband. They've just dropped off two black friends. Their car is picking its way along Woodward, slowed by a milling throng. A group of Blacks is beating a white man. George watches helplessly, as they manouevre through the crowd. There's a bang. Sheren George is shot at close range. The same bullet also wounds her husband. He immediately turns off Woodward, going the wrong way on a one-way street. They arrive at a fire station. Sheren George is transferred to Detroit General Hospital where she dies at 1:35 a.m.

Shortly before midnight, Mayor Cavanagh phones U.S. Vice President Hubert Humphrey and Attorney General Ramsay Clark. It's the beginning of a nine-hour debate involving municipal, state and federal governments as to whether the army can be called. The conversations are marked by anger, confusion and recriminations as a Democratic mayor and president wrangle with Republican Governor George Romney about the deployment of federal troops. None of the politicians wants to accept blame for the riot, nor does anyone wish to make the others look good.

There are no guidelines on how to approach the feds for support. Cavanagh figures it should be easy to call in the army, but by federal law he can't make a verbal request. It has to be in writing. It must say that this is not a "riot" but an "insurrection," and it must be accompanied by an admission that the local authorities can't handle the situation. The trouble, however, is local politicians not wanting to admit failure, and their lawyers advise that such a declaration could be dangerous. Admitting a "war or insurrection" could exempt or cancel millions of dollars in fire insurance for homes and businesses.

To make matters worse, Romney and Cavanagh have different backgrounds. Cavanagh is a fun-loving Irish Catholic, and Romney is a straight-laced leader of a Mormon Church. The two men don't see eye-to-eye. The problem is compounded by a rift between Romney and President Lyndon Baines Johnson. Romney could run against Johnson in the 1968 presidential campaign, so Johnson wants to prove that the Michigan governor is inept, unable to maintain order in his own state. Romney resents the squeeze and won't succumb to pressure. He "recommends" that troops be sent in, even though he's advised by federal officials that he'll have to use the word "request." Johnson is reluctant to commit federal troops. He doesn't want his political career tarnished by blame or racial hatred. His civil rights and anti-poverty programs are under fire, and Vietnam is going badly. His credibility is at stake. Critics say, "we cannot put enough people in Vietnam, so we go out and shoot civilians in Detroit."

Romney eventually gives in on the "request" of federal troops, but only to "suppress looting, arson and sniping." He refuses to call it an "insurrection." There are many hoops and hurdles, delays the city can ill afford. Meanwhile, federal officials are told by police that the National Guard can take care of it and federal troops aren't needed. Michigan officials don't want to be responsible for a wrong move or for over-reacting. Cavanagh, on the other hand, figures he needs experienced troops because he believes the National Guard is incompetent. As his aide suggests, "They are gutsy guys. But they have no more training for this kind of thing than a good troop of boy scouts."

As Sunday comes to an end, several hundred people are injured and 1,300 arrested. There have been 209 fire alarms, 85 more than normal. A mile of Twelfth Street, and 20 blocks along Grand River, are in flames. The riot covers 11 square miles. When Governor Romney flies over Detroit in a helicopter, he comments, "It looks like the city has been bombed."

Monday, July 24, 1967

At midnight, three young white men protect their apartment building on Alexandrine from fire. They're on the roof, armed with a shotgun and equipped with water buckets and blankets. Almost three hours later, National Guardsmen receive a report of "snipers." They surround the building and tell the boys to come down. As they descend, a National Guardsman thinks he hears shots. He shoots back, killing 23-year-old Clifton Pryor. The boy is on a second floor landing under the glare of a large lamp. The Guardsmen say they told him to stop, but other boys say no command was given.

Pryor's death indicates that the rules have changed. Tired, raw-tempered police and young, inexperienced National Guardsmen have been ordered to fire, if need be. Ready to retaliate, they no longer watch from the sidelines, giving rioters a free hand. As a result, there are more senseless deaths. Most victims have three things in common: they're unlucky, civilian and Black. To some observers, what began as a riot of Blacks against police has become a riot of police against Blacks. Some police seek revenge; vent their hatred in a lawless situation. One officer comments that Blacks "are savages."

Julius L. Dorsey is a 55-year-old black security guard hired to protect a market at the corner of Field and Lafayette. He's doing his job with his usual zeal when he's chastized by two men and a woman. They want the goods in the building. As the argument heats up, Dorsey tells a neighbour to call police. Hoping to scare his assailants, the guard draws his pistol and fires three warning shots in the air. A police radio reports, "Looters. They have rifles." A patrol car pulls up with three National Guardsmen who open fire as the looters flee. By the end of the skirmish, Julius Dorsey is dead.

A black youth and a National Guardsman are hit by snipers and four looters are shot overnight. Two of the shootings are accidental. One occurs during a struggle with a police officer. Another involves a private guard who shoots himself while pulling his gun out of his pocket. In the 13th Precinct, a sergeant is hit in the head with a cue ball. Hundreds of rioters are arrested overnight. They're kept in Recorders Court, herded into bullpens where they lie on the floor like cattle. Helicopters whirr overhead. Tourists huddle in the door of a hotel, afraid to come out.

At 2:00 a.m., 800 State Troopers and 1,200 National Guardsmen help 4,400 Detroit police, equipped with five tanks and two armoured personnel carriers. Together they resemble a small occupational force, but are not in time to prevent injuries to 20-year-old Mary Phillips. At 4:00 a.m. she's shot in the arm on North Burdick Street. Two officers try to help, but the mob moves in to keep them from her. The police are overpowered as shots are fired. The city is in chaos. Anarchy spreads.

Similar outbreaks are reported in the neighbouring cities of Pontiac, Flint, Muskegan, Saginaw, Mount Clemens and Kalamazoo. All have large black populations and roving bands hit the streets.

Pontiac is an industrial community of 90,000 people. Municipal leaders call for a curfew, similar to the one in Detroit where the National Guard is having trouble maintaining order. Just as they fix bayonets to bring one area under control, rioting breaks out in another section around Highland Park. Flames destroy fifteen blocks, but there are no firemen on the streets. National Guardsmen are manning barricades, but they can't be everywhere at once. Storekeepers shoot two more rioters. In all, 25 Blacks are arrested. Forty fires are burning by dawn.

Rioting in Grand Rapids results in 11 fires and hundreds of broken windows. There are 50 arrests and several injuries, mostly passengers in cars whose windshields are smashed by people throwing rocks. Police in Toledo report looting and small fires in a black section of the city. There are no injuries or sniper attacks. Sixty miles south, in Lima, Ohio, 21 youths are arrested after breaking three store windows and, in New York, police empty their service revolvers at Puerto Rican youths who are firing rifles and hurling bricks and debris from tenement roofs. Two people are dead as violence flares in the third day of rioting in Spanish Harlem.

In Detroit, the governor and mayor renew their request for federal assistance and are told, once again, that, unless a "state of insurrection," which cannot be handled by municipal or state police is in effect, no help is forthcoming. The two men rethink the idea. At 9:00 a.m. they ask again, suggesting that "time could be of the essence." Government officials tour the streets and, fearing a second night of rioting, send a wire to Washington. "I do hereby officially request federal troops to restore order in Detroit."

With daylight, residents gather on the streets, scowling at the debris and chatting. They lean on mailboxes or lampposts or furniture salvaged from a burned-out building as the occasional car snakes around the broken glass and bricks littering the street.
Courtesy of B.G. "Spike" Bell.

The city is like an armed camp or ghost town. Stores, schools, bars, offices, theatres and banks are closed, the parking lots empty. When it's discovered that service stations are selling gas in buckets and bottles, they're shut down to cut off fuel for firebombs. Liquor and gun sales are banned, airlines cancel flights to the city, summer courses at Wayne State and several colleges are cancelled, garbage collection and buses are halted, the zoo and Detroit Institute of the Arts are closed. Detroit Receiving and Memorial hospitals are designated to take care of riot victims. In Recorders Court, hundreds of prisoners queue up for justice as if it were an assembly line. One judge hears 600 not-guilty pleas in a 12-hour period. The judge posts a high bond to keep suspects off the streets. Of 2,000 people arrested, only 500 are white. Sporadic rioting continues. In one case, looters dismantle a porch and hurl bricks at police.

Some white shop owners sweep up. Others, whose stores haven't yet been touched, are out with shotguns. One sits at the front of his store in a rocking chair, a rifle on his lap for protection and a beer in his hand for comfort. A bold young man gets out of his car, walks up to a shattered window, grabs a wig from the store and gives it to his girlfriend waiting in the car. He smiles at shopkeepers who look on in amazement.

Thirteen blocks of Twelfth Street, from Bethune to Atkinson, are a mess. One quarter of the businesses are burned-out skeletons of brick and steel, the rubble still smouldering. Firemen are on the scene, hosing the ashes. A black man walks up to firefighters outside a grocery store and introduces himself. "I just want to get my kid some cornflakes," he says and then escorts his six-year-old inside the store. They come out several minutes later with boxes of cereal. Other looters fill shopping carts with bags of groceries. "How dumb can they get," one man asks. "Where are we going to get food tomorrow? Where are all these people going to work?" A rioter replies, "You take what you get, and get it while you can."

In a music store, looters clean out bins of jazz and sacred music. They leave the Lawrence Welk behind. Every piece of electronic equipment: guitars, amplifiers and phonographs have already been cleaned out. At a pawnshop, two men pry up the bottom of a security gate as another scrapes through on his belly. He reaches through the broken window and scoops watches in the display case. One-third of the liquor stores, and hundreds of small grocery stores, have been plundered.

Associated Press reporter, Justinas Bavarskis, and photographer, Al Quinn, are roughed up by rioters and then let go. William Serrin, a reporter with *The Detroit Free Press*, is struck on the head by flying glass. He runs from 50 black youths. Dick Tripp, a photographer with the *Free Press* and a former *Windsor Star* staffer, has his glasses knocked off and is cut in another skirmish. Several reporters, and at least 15 policemen, suffer similar injuries and yet, other scribes are not hassled.

At noon, President Johnson dispatches 5,000 paratroopers from Chicago to Selfridge Air Force Base near Detroit. They're members of the 82nd Airborne Division, Third Brigade, from Fort Bragg, North Carolina, and the 101st Airborne Division, Second Brigade, from Fort Campbell, Kentucky. Four hours after they're mobilized, they start to arrive. Since a number of National Guardsmen are in reserve, the politicians keep the paratroopers at the military base where they're on standby, ready to go into action.

When federal troops arrive, they clean streets, collect garbage, trace missing persons and end the confusion. Grateful neighbours provide lemonade, soup and sandwiches. Courtesy of B.G. "Spike" Bell.

Cyrus Vance is the special assistant to Secretary of Defence Robert MacNamara, and he's called to Detroit to see the riot first-hand. When he arrives, there's no sign of looting or sniping and the fires seem under control. In the early evening, Vance tours the city with Cavanagh and Lieutenant General John L. Throckmorton, a no-nonsense professional soldier who's seen action in Korea and Vietnam. It's Throckmorton's job to control the riot but, in driving through the city, it seems as if the rioters have gone for dinner and the two men wonder what the fuss is about. The only problem Vance sees is "a flat tire" and he figures local forces can handle it. Vance is irritable because he's suffering back problems and his mother recently died. He looks around and says, "It doesn't look too bad to me," to which Cavanagh retorts, "Usually the city isn't burning!" When rioting escalates and continues until dawn, Vance orders three battalions of Throckmorton's paratroopers to the fairgrounds on the north edge of the city.

Despite the afternoon lull, more people are killed by gunshots, most described as looters. Three are in the wrong place at the wrong time. Herman Ector is 30, a quiet, intelligent black man who dislikes rude and indecent language. He and a friend walk past a security guard in front of a grocery store as the guard curses and pushes a couple of looters. Ector tells his friend that the guard shouldn't treat people that way. The guard over-hears and challenges him. "Who you talking to?" The guard strikes Ector on the shoulder with his carbine and then shoots him. Ector dies before he reaches hospital. Murder charges against the guard are dropped. Ector's father goes berserk after his son's death, locks his family in the house and holds police at bay for 17 hours.

In another incident, Fred Williams is afraid that his home on Goodwin Avenue is about to go up in flames. Most of his block is already burning and he takes a few possessions down an alley to an empty lot. He figures they'll be safe but, as he watches, flames leap into the air and ignite high-tension wires on hydro poles above him. The wires drop, snapping and hissing as they hit the ground. When they hit Fred Williams, he dies instantly, still clutching his belongings.

Nathaniel Edmonds, a 23-year-old black man, is sitting on a porch after checking on relatives to make sure they're safe. A white man in a car stops and accuses him of breaking into a store. An argument develops and the white man points a shotgun. Edmonds, still protesting his innocence, is killed. Edmonds' parents can't believe it. "A lot of Whites just thought it was open season on Negroes. That's all there was to it." An all-White jury finds the killer guilty, but reduces the conviction to second-degree for "going on a hunting expedition that ended in murder."

Victims include National Guardsmen and police. Two women are injured by stray bullets, fired as police chase looters in a market. The women spend weeks in hospital. An eight-year-old black girl and a 14-year-old white boy are also injured in crossfire.

Throughout the havoc, one ghetto is exempt from rioting. Twenty-one thousand residents in 150 blocks on the northwest side have established a Positive Neighborhood Action Committee. They've organized block clubs and, when the riot breaks out, neighbours mobilize quickly. Youngsters stop traffic and only two small fires are set in the neighbourhood, one in an empty building. It's a small haven of peace.

At 10:00 p.m., there's heavy firing near Mack, Gratiot and East Grand Boulevard as tanks and infantry seal off the area. Twenty minutes later, the National Guard comes under fire at Southeastern High School and that section, too, is cordoned off. Four black men in a station wagon are flagged down at the checkpoint and are asked to detour on their way home. They come across another military jeep on Lycaste Street, between Charlevoix and Goethe. Thinking it's another checkpoint, they slow down just as a shot rings out. A National Guardsman is wounded in the ankle and falls. His friends believe the shot came from the car and open fire. Seventeen bullets riddle the vehicle. All five men are hit. One of them, 27-year-old Henry Densen dies. He slumps in the front seat with a bullet through his neck.

About two blocks away, firemen, police and National Guardsmen report a rooftop sniper with shots apparently coming from the southeast – the direction of Charlevoix and Lycaste. The officers shoot back. A young fireman, Carl Smith, is killed. An autopsy shows the bullet was fired at street level and probably came from the southeast. As the rioting continues, snipers shoot from rooftops and darkened windows to harass firemen and police. One firefighter suggests, "Those bastards aren't even trying to hit us ... They just want to see us jump."

At 11:20 p.m., President Johnson deplores the violence. He's convinced that federal paratroopers should be used and he federalizes the Michigan National Guard. In an impassioned speech, Johnson addresses the nation. He says that people in the U.S. seek more than the uneasy calm of martial law. They want mutual respect for each other and for law. "We seek public order, built on steady progress, to meet the needs of all people." There can be no lasting peace with troops. "Make no mistake," Johnson says, "Looting, arson and pillage are not part of the civil rights protest. No American has the right to burn, loot or riot, or fire rifles from rooftops. Those actions are illegal and will not be tolerated." Johnson advocates strong punishment and says the riot must be dealt with swiftly to protect the innocent. He's afraid the bitterness will take a long time to heal. Already, 4,000 people have been arrested and are now in detention.

Moscow also comments on the Detroit riot. The official news agency, *Tass*, claims Blacks are merely defending their rights. The Soviets blame police for using cruel measures against their citizens.

As trouble continues, 5,000 National Guardsmen are at work in the city, but they're tired, poorly trained, inadequately equipped, hastily deployed and ineptly led. Because of inexperienced officers, they have poor discipline. Some have been on duty for 30 hours after travelling 200 miles. Totally without riot training they were given on-the-spot instruction about mob control, only to find themselves ill-prepared for what they face – there are no mobs on the darkened streets. Two men are assigned to an intersection on Monday and are still there on Friday. In the confusion, some National Guardsmen even become lost in the city.

Two years earlier, in the Watts riot of Los Angeles, the National Guard learned restraint, didn't over-react or shoot unless absolutely necessary. That lesson was not passed on to units in Michigan. A newspaper reporter spends an evening in a National Guard command jeep, and tells about clumsy handling of loaded weapons and accidental firings. The Kerner Commission confirms that reports of snipers in Detroit are grossly exaggerated. Most of the shooting is done by Guardsmen whose lack of military discipline is dangerous to the public and to themselves. Even Commissioner Girardin warns against the Guard. He's seen them in action and fears a "slaughter." As Girardin points out, the Guard has a tendency to fire wild volleys into the night, shooting at phantoms or anything that moves, rather than wait for an identifiable target. In a feverish, near-paranoid hunt for snipers, the Guard ignores the safety of innocent bystanders, which increases the terror of haphazard gun battles.

When a Guardsman thinks he hears a shot, the patrol lays siege to an apartment building, thought to be occupied by a sniper. A tank commander shouts, "I'll give you 'til 10 to get out of the building." There's no response. Without authorization, the machine gunner sprays the tenement with .50 calibre bullets, which rip into the walls. Guardsmen rush into the tenement, but find it empty. Sometimes they fire into the darkness only to be answered by bullets from their own tanks.

Only 42 of 8,500 National Guardsmen are Black. As an all-white force, they are aggressive, intimidating, insulting and abusive. Detroit papers report that Guardsmen shout obscenities and fire over people's heads to make them obey. Some journalists are more threatened by Guardsmen than rioters. The performance of the National Guard is disappointing. They take several days to settle down, but by then the riot is over.

TUESDAY, JULY 25, 1967

At 2:00 a.m., 12 police officers guard firemen at the corner of Vicksburg and Linwood near Twelfth Street. Flames light the sky. Gun flashes come from two buildings and a sniper fires from an alley to the north. Detroit police officer, John Hamilton, fires a burst from his machine gun, but is cut down by another volley from the east. He's hit by four bullets. Two other officers are struck when they run to his side. Five suspected snipers are rounded up as more police and National Guardsmen arrive on the scene. They blanket the area in a hail of bullets.

The official death toll stands at 26 when Detroit patrolman, Jerome Olshove, is shot in the stomach. Olshove is only 32-years-old and has been on the force for eight years. His father was a cop and Olshove loves the job. He's received 20 citations and is a man with a future, until 3:00 a.m. Rioters are looting a grocery store when Olshove's cruiser pulls up. His partner, armed with a shotgun, jumps out of the car and is caught in a scuffle. Olshove assists, just as the gun goes off. Over 300 police from 26 departments, including Windsor, attend his funeral on Saturday. He's the only officer killed in the riot.

Four looters are shot and killed on Tuesday morning. Ronald Evans, 24, and William Jones, 32, are middle-class Blacks. They stay home during the first two nights of rioting, but are curious about what is going on. They're shot and killed by police after breaking into a cornerstore for beer. Arthur Johnson and Perry Williams suffer a similar fate. They're high school dropouts. They're at a pawnshop, a symbol of frustrated poverty. The place is empty, stripped bare. They're standing outside when a police cruiser comes hurtling down the street. The two men duck into the gutted store as police spray the building with bullets. Two officers go in and the boys don't come out.

At 4:00 a.m., federal paratroopers, under Colonel A. R. Bolling, arrive at Southeastern High School. The area is dark and still, and the colonel thinks he's in the wrong location. National Guardsmen crouch behind a

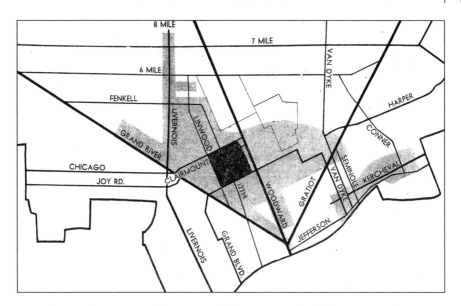

Map showing the riot area of Detroit as of July 25, 1967. The black square at the corner of 12th Street and Clairmont designates the "blind pig" where the riot began. The grey shadings denote the areas in which the riot spread and the extent of the city affected. Courtesy of The Windsor Star.

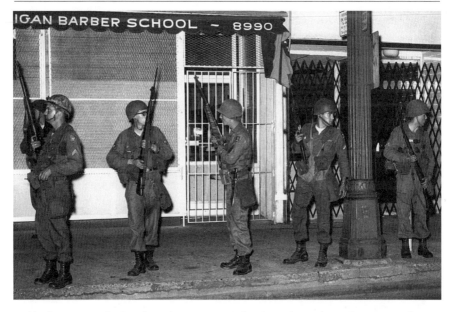

Federal troops are deployed on the city's east side where the rioting is less intense, but they're quick to establish an uneasy calm, maintaining a unified armed presence on the streets. Courtesy of B.G. "Spike" Bell.

wall, afraid of sniper fire. The colonel orders the lights turned on. All the windows of a nearby apartment building have been shot out and the walls pockmarked with bullets. Many residents spent the night on the floor and are relieved that the army has arrived and there will be no more shooting.

General Throckmorton believes the key to order is to "saturate the area with calm, determined, hardened professionals." He instructs his troops to leave their weapons unloaded and not to fire, except on the command of an officer and only if their target is visible. Soldiers are equipped with tear gas, M-16's and M-79 grenade launchers, but mass firing is prohibited. "We don't shoot just because something moves or somebody runs, but if there is a need for crowd dispersal ... they usually don't like to give a command twice." Throckmorton's philosophy works. During five days in the city, 2,700 army troops fire only 200 rounds of ammunition and only one man is killed by a soldier. At police headquarters, reports of sniper fire continue to pour in, but only 10 are from the army. No paratroopers are shot.

There's no comparison between the frightened, inexperienced and insensitive National Guard and the discipline, efficiency and self-confidence of the paratroopers. The 101st Airborne is successful because many soldiers are Black and have been under fire in Vietnam. It's an integrated force, and they know how to behave.

Throckmorton orders more lights turned on, but Guardsmen continue to shoot them because they're afraid of snipers. A reporter says he's pinned down by "sniper fire" when, in fact, Guardsmen are firing volleys to extinguish a street lamp. As Throckmorton orders barricades removed to return the city to normal, National Guardsmen order people off sidewalks, porches, and away from windows. Two people fail to respond quickly enough. They're both shot. One of them dies. He's Roy Banks, a 46-year-old black man, who was on his way to work. Witnesses say someone shouted, "Shoot the son-of-a-bitch." No warning is given, but Banks couldn't have heard it anyway. He's deaf. Police write him up as a suspected looter.

It's exactly six months to Christmas and Detroit freeways are almost deserted. They're usually packed with rush hour traffic. An occasional convoy of trucks, filled with paratroopers, joins a few cars moving along the John Lodge Expressway, which links Detroit with the suburbs. Blue-helmeted police drive by in squad cars, eight to nine vehicles at a time, cruising bumper-to-bumper, blue and red lights flashing, sirens wailing. The officers are armed with lever-action carbines and pump-action shot-guns, black barrels sticking out the windows. Residents say they hear shouted warnings. "You niggers get your black asses off the streets." As one neighbour complains, "It was like we were guilty of being Black."

National Guardsmen protect service employees who repair damage to gas lines around a burned-out apartment building. The Guardsmen report sporadic sniping. A tall white woman stands in front of her looted store on Grand River Boulevard. A hundred men, White and Black, backed a truck to the door and carried everything away. Hands on hips, Katherine Sandburg surveys the damage to her wire, rope and cable business. "It's so stupid. Who can this possibly help?"

Sniper fire ends by mid-morning and there's another lull. Government offices, banks and businesses re-open, but there's more talk than work. City bus service is also restored. GM and Ford open their offices and facto-ries, but only half of the employees at GM show up and only five percent at Ford. American Motors and Chrysler are in production. "Come and pick up two dead ones," a police radio crackles, referring to two looters. Police fear the riot will flare up again.

During the day, the Detroit Tigers postpone their night game against the Orioles. It's switched to Baltimore and will be played on August 11 in a three game series. Wednesday and Thursday games are also on hold. One has to be played in Cincinnati. Scheduled games for Baltimore on September 12th and 13th will be switched to Detroit.

In Atlanta, Georgia, Doctor Martin Luther King supports the use of fed-eral troops to stop rioting in Detroit, but he also calls for a massive pro-gram to end unemployment. King fears that rioting will spread if nothing is done. "Revolts come out of revolting conditions." Black leaders in Detroit also condemn the riot as the work of a small number of hoodlums and hate-mongers. The majority of Detroit's 550,000 Blacks don't support the violence, although they are unhappy with the lack of adequate housing, education and jobs. For his part, Mayor Cavanagh promises a massive clean-up, including the distribution of food to the homeless, neighbourhood offices to handle insurance claims and even a rat-killing program in areas ravaged by fire. Cavanagh makes the announcement despite a tight municipal budget.

Between 7:00 and 11:00 p.m., there are 444 reported incidents, mostly snipers. At 8:00 p.m., three white men, armed with a .22 calibre rifle, take over an expensive, three-storey house in an integrated, middle-class neighbourhood. They own the building and change the lock to protect it from tenants who are not home. The landlord is having trouble with the renters. When the tenants return, they're refused admission to the building and threaten to call the National Guard. About 9:00 p.m., 30 Guardsmen show up after hearing reports that snipers have taken over a building and evicted the legal occupants. A tank moves into position on a lawn across the street. A captain of the Guard hails the house, but receives no reply. He hears a shot and sees a fire-streak in an upstairs window. He orders his men to open fire. The hail of bullets is so intense that, within minutes, it causes $10,000 damage. Bullets ricochet off walls and a pair of stone columns is nearly shot in half. The three men surrender and are arrested as snipers. They're jailed at the Tenth Precinct and two are reportedly beaten by a police officer, attempting to force a confession. One man's skull is cracked, but he isn't taken to hospital until other prisoners complain that he's bleeding to death. Twelve days later, charges against the three men are dismissed.

Detroit courts work 'round the clock. Another 1,000 people are arrested for curfew violations, arson and looting. Looters are held on $25,000 bond. Snipers are retained on a $200,000 bond. Bail is set high to keep people off the streets, but it also creates problems. There are already 2,000 people in jail and conditions are crowded. Many prisoners are detained at a special centre on Belle Isle with the overflow sent to county jails in Washtenaw and Monroe, Michigan. Three men are detained in each six-by-eight foot cell meant for one person. Six buses, each with 40 prisoners, are sent to Jackson State Prison where detainees await trial in the sweltering heat. Others are shipped to primitive, hastily made cells at the Fort Wayne Induction Centre and the federal installation at Milan.

Hundreds of prisoners are rounded up indiscriminately by police. They're curfew violators, looters and anybody else who looks suspicious.

On Tuesday, July 25, federal troops relieve many National Guardsmen. They arrive in jeeps and patrol cars, their M-16s at the ready. Courtesy of B.G. "Spike" Bell.

They're brought into the Tenth Precinct where officers attempt to extract confessions. There are dozens of charges of police brutality as injured prisoners are taken to hospital. Discipline has vanished because the precinct commander has moved his headquarters to a riot command post at a nearby hospital. Prisoners request a phone call, but are told, "The telephones are out of order." Congressman John Conyers and State Representative James Del Rio want to establish a community patrol, but give up when they see the state of the department.

A young woman is told to strip while one officer takes pictures and another fondles her breasts. One of the Polaroids is fished out of a wastebasket and turned over to the mayor's office. Some officers remove their badges, cover license plates, and tape the numbers of their patrol cars. They don't want to become targets, nor do they want to be identified. In some cases, officers fire at fleeing looters, but make no attempt to determine whether they're wounded. Some are found dead or injured later.

A suspected arsonist, being questioned by police and National Guardsmen, tries to escape by vaulting over the hood of a car. An officer fires a shotgun, but the youth disappears. The police drive away, leaving the boy dying in an alley. The death is attributed to sniper fire. No police report is filed until several witnesses complain to a Detroit newspaper that the boy was shot after being told to run by police. Three weeks later, an officer admits firing the fatal shot, but the prosecutor's office refuses to file charges, citing discrepancies in the testimony of witnesses.

At 9:15, Jack Sydnor, a 38-year-old black labourer, arrives home from work, takes out his .32 calibre revolver and fires into an alley to see if it works. He's been drinking. Police arrive and force the door to Sydnor's third storey apartment. Patrolman Roger Polke is the first officer through the door. As he enters, Sydnor shoots Polke in the abdomen. The officer fires six shots as other officers join in. When the shooting stops, Sydnor's body is full of holes. The force of the volley has driven him backwards and through a window. He's dead. There are reports of "heavy sniper fire" and the National Guard shows up with two tanks, ready to flush out the shooter. Nearby, another police officer and a black man are struck by stray bullets, more "sniper fire."

Shots are heard throughout the night. A 19-year-old man lights a cigarette in a window of an apartment. A machine gunner on a tank is startled by several shots, sees the flash from the match and fires on the building. The bullets nearly sever the arm of 21-year-old Valerie Hood. Her four-year-old niece, Tonya Blanding, is playing on the dining room floor with a broken toy. She's killed – "a .50 calibre bullet hole in her chest."

WEDNESDAY, JULY 26, 1967

Most firebombing and looting are over, but there are 800 reports of sniper fire during the day. It's the worst shooting yet. Pressure mounts for police to restore order. Officers search homes on the flimsiest excuse. A Detroit newspaper says, "Everyone's a suspect in no-man's land." Anyone with a gun is liable to be picked up or shot. By the end of the day, there are fewer incidents of sniper fire and some indication that the city is returning to normal, but the death toll continues to rise as 10 people are killed.

At one roadblock, on Lycaste near Mack, National Guardsmen fire shots across the hood of a passing car. It's a white station wagon with five occupants. John LeRoy, 30, is shot and the driver, Charles Dunson, is hit and blinded in one eye. Another bullet rips into his wrist and leg. The men are ordered out of the car and told to lie in the street. It's an hour before an ambulance arrives. LeRoy dies three days later.

At another checkpoint, a Guardsman is killed when he's caught in a similar crossfire. Larry Post is a 26-year-old bachelor who believes in protecting the peace. He has little tolerance for people who don't follow rules or can't hold a job. He's shot by an unknown assailant with a machine gun. The official report suggests a car ran a roadblock. Three Blacks are charged with assault with intent to kill. They're taken into custody and beaten. One suffers a broken jaw and requires treatment in hospital. The charges are eventually reduced to violation of curfew. Two are given six months probation, the other receives a suspended sentence.

One of the most controversial shootings occurs at the Algiers Motel, a two storey, "U" shaped brick building which surrounds a swimming pool. The Algiers is a faded, two-star accommodation at Woodward and Virginia Park, a favourite hangout for entertainers, gamblers and girls. Three teenage black men, Aubrey Pollard, Fred Temple and Carl Cooper are partying with two white women. Cooper fires a starter pistol and the noise brings authorities to the hotel. By the time police leave, the three men are dead, shot repeatedly at close range. Two women are described as "mauled and beaten," and a black ex-paratrooper is roughed up. Witnesses say police beat the men, made racial and sexual comments, and fired their shotguns into the wall over their victim's heads. When one officer breaks his rifle butt over the head of Pollard, the officer says, "This nigger made me break my shotgun." Pollard replies, "I'm sorry."

Two patrolmen are charged with murder in a case, which drags on in both civil and criminal court for two years. The delay is partially caused by prejudice from a best-selling book called *The Algiers Motel Incident,* written by John Hersey and published in 1968. The police officers argue self-defence, but their statements are thrown out by a judge who rails against Hersey's book as "yellow journalism." There are a series of motions, counter-motions and other delays until only one officer is brought to trial. He is acquitted in 1969 by an all-white jury in Mason, a small town in Michigan. Despite the officer's plea, many people feel the victims were executed because they were Black and were partying with white women. Hersey goes further. He's convinced the deaths are an act of murder in a notorious and lethal game of harassment and terror, the result of racial hatred and a festering anger by police who seek revenge for the slaying of their fellow officer, Jerome Olshove, earlier in the week.

Six blocks from the Algiers at the Harlan House Hotel, a white business-woman, 50-year-old Helen Hall, is registered. It's 1:00 a.m. and the hotel is under siege. Visitors listen to gunfire from behind curtains in darkened rooms. Hall is on the fourth floor, consoling a young Canadian, 24-year-old Lisa Poirier from Montreal. Hall says there's nothing to worry about and, to prove her point, she opens the curtain of a floor-to-ceiling window. "Come and look," she says. "There's a tank across the street." As she speaks, Hall is hit in the chest by a bullet from a high-powered rifle. She dies instantly. More bullets slam into the building and another slug passes over Poirier who faints.

When George Talbert and a friend walk over to Twelfth Street to survey the damage, they run across a National Guard unit. A rifleman raises his weapon and fires. Talbert is hit. Before he's taken to hospital, a white priest from a nearby church administers last rights. The Guardsman claims he was confused, felt threatened, and is reprimanded for disobey-ing orders. Talbert dies 10 days later.

Three other men are also killed by accident. Willie McDaniels watches looters as police drive up and start shooting to disperse the crowd. McDaniels is shot in the head by a stray bullet. 26-year-old Julius Lust helps himself to car parts in a junkyard when police investigate. Lust runs. An officer tells him to stop, but Lust continues. The policeman fires. Lust's family hears of his death on TV. In the third case, Albert Robinson, 35, puts out the garbage as the National Guard storm his apartment. They believe that Robinson is armed with a pistol. They knock him down, bayonet and shoot him.

THURSDAY, JULY 27, 1967

Soldiers and Guardsmen in their fatigues shoulder rifles and machine guns, and watch as people stream back to work. Two stores are burning and there are gun battles near Hazelwood and Taylor. Officials in Detroit hope that the riot is over. Governor Romney lifts the 9:30 to 5:30 curfew only to re-impose it because too many gawkers are taking pictures, sightseeing and hampering the clean-up crews. Gatherings of more than five people on the street are forbidden. Liquor sales are suspended and gas sales restricted to five gallons. Entertainment places remain closed. Bus service has been cut in half and there are no buses running after midnight.

Merchants increase prices on milk, bread and other goods in their stores, sometimes by as much as 200 percent. In one store on the west side, the owner is charging $1.00 for a quart of milk and 75 cents for a loaf of bread. He says he needs more because there are no deliveries, and he's afraid of losing his store if he doesn't make money. He's already hired two security guards to protect himself from angry customers. Governor Romney objects to this blatant "profiteering" and Mayor Cavanagh passes an emergency ordinance against price gouging by "unscrupulous individuals." The new law calls for penalties of 90 days in jail and a $500 fine.

The UAW pledges funds for cleanup from 600,000 Detroit union members, and President Johnson offers food, drugs and hospital supplies. As well, the president endorses a national day of prayer to condemn terrorism, and mourn victims. "We pray for strength to build together so that disorder may cease." Johnson believes the riot is the result of poor people fed up with their status. "It's not Civil Rights and it's not racial. It's just people who want something for nothing. They just want to steal." A black minister says, "It's a mess created by people who won't work." Johnson sets up an 11-man panel to study the riots, while Cavanagh appoints a six-member task force to rebuild the city.

Politicians talk of rebuilding, but also of blame. Questions are raised as to whether politicians were properly informed and whether delays in sending troops were political. A poll by *The Detroit Free Press* suggests that law enforcement officers should have exerted more authority from the outset. In the same poll, 34 percent of respondents are convinced that Governor Romney handled the situation well, but only 12 percent are in favour of Mayor Cavanagh's performance. The Detroit Bar Association feels the police should have used force, and that there was too much emphasis on listening to middle-class black leaders who didn't represent their people or the poor.

An Episcopal Bishop believes that the riot is not really a race riot because it didn't erupt in interracial warfare – Whites against Blacks. Instead, it's more a fight against poverty. The strife may have started as a Black reaction to an all-white police force, but it degenerated into wholesale theft – poor Blacks and Whites, trying to grab as much loot as they can. Control of inner-city crime would control the problem.

Many Whites believe that black Detroiters watch riots in other cities and feel that insurrection in Detroit is inevitable. They say it happened because a few reckless and angry young black men began trashing and looting. Thousands of others were just caught up in the heady sensation of power and the eagerness to get something for nothing.

The rhetoric doesn't help 19-year-old Willie Dalton. A restless young man, he lives in a poor section of the city and hates it. He's stopped on the street after curfew and is accused of a violation. Police believe he's been looting and burning. They push him against a tree, then march him to an alley where he's shot in the stomach at a range of ten feet. Police claim they were under fire from snipers and couldn't conduct an investigation. There are no reports of snipers, National Guard, or other police activity in the area. Dalton's mother, Ethel, is advised to join a secret Black Power movement to avenge the deaths of black youth by police. She refuses. "It wouldn't bring Willie back."

FRIDAY, JULY 28, 1967

Officially, the riot is over. It lasted from 4:00 a.m. Sunday to midnight Thursday, a 92-hour rampage of exhilaration and despair, greed and madness. President Johnson names the Kerner Commission to probe the causes of the riot as urban unrest is expected to continue. In Detroit, the ban on liquor sales in the suburbs is dropped, so people scurry into outlying areas for a drink. The curfew stays in place and police continue to crack down. Twenty-seven people are charged with sniping, but only three go to trial.

More than 7,200 people have been arrested; 6,400 are Black. The youngest looter is ten years old, the oldest 82. Most detainees are incarcerated in makeshift jails. Some are members of the press whose credentials were ignored. Many prisoners are kept up to 30 hours on buses, which reek of urine, garbage and sweating bodies. Others spend days in an underground garage without toilets. A couple of prisoners are lost in the system when they can't post bail or the bailiff can't remember where they've been sent. Eventually, bail is reduced and half the prisoners, those without criminal records, are released on their own recognizance to relieve overcrowding. Only three percent of those arrested ever come to trial and half are acquitted.

Detroit police stations are inundated with loot, everything from baseball bats to bathtubs. As the riot subsides, the paratroop regiment is ordered out of the east side, which is turned over to the National Guard. Forty-seven hundred soldiers remain in the Detroit area until Sunday, but they have been told to stand-down. The last of the troops actually leave the city on Wednesday, August 2, a week after they arrived.

SATURDAY, JULY 29, 1967

The curfew is finally relaxed as 1,000 National Guardsmen are sent home. The rest are still heavily armed and on the streets. They're to be off Sunday night, with the curfew lifted by Monday, July 31. That's also when liquor sales resume. Detroit police and firemen are paid overtime with $12,000,000 raised from the sale of a new bond issue. Federal relief funds are tough to get because Detroit has never officially been declared a disaster area. Many people also turn to small business loans to put their lives in order.

As the riot winds down, it also claims its last victim. Ernest Roquemore is a 19-year-old from a poor black neighbourhood. When police pull up in front of his apartment, they're looking for loot. They start shooting. Roquemore runs up the stairs and out the back where a paratrooper is waiting. As Roquemore runs past, someone shouts, "He has a gun." The soldier shoots. No pistol is found. Police say the guy with the gun got away. A youth says officers mistook his shiny transistor radio for a revolver. Several people are wounded, including two teenage girls and a boy who has his leg amputated. Police recover loot in Roquemore's apartment and the death is ruled: justifiable homicide.

Aftermath

The Detroit riot is the bloodiest urban riot of the century, a week of fire and rage in which more lives are lost, more damage done than in any riot to that time in any American city. That includes the Kensington riot of 1964 in Philadelphia, the Watts riot of 1965 in Los Angeles or the Hough riot of '66 in Cleveland. Officially, 43 people are killed in Detroit. Thirty-three are Black, ten are White. Most deaths are ruled accidental. It's estimated that at least 18 people are killed by Detroit police, most described as looters. Nine are killed by National Guardsmen; at least five are innocent bystanders. Six are unconfirmed kills by either the National Guard or police, and four of those are innocent. Three people are killed by private citizens, two by storeowners, two by downed power lines and two more in a fire. The army is involved in only one death. One police officer, one Guardsman and two firemen are dead. Only a handful of snipings are actually confirmed and yet hundreds were reported.

Many people are convinced that the death toll is much higher and that police are hiding the actual numbers for fear of reprisals and renewed rioting. Some people say official figures are just the tip of the iceberg and the real count may never be known. An ambulance driver says, "The morgue was filled with victims of the police ... They were stacking bodies up like cordwood." Wayne County Medical Examiner John Burton says, "We hear that stupid story over and over again and it just isn't true." He says the rumour is generated by people who want to keep things stirred up. Reporters give the law the benefit of the doubt, but black civil rights leaders say some police shootings are deliberate executions that will never show up on police blotters. Fifteen cases of Whites shooting non-Whites, many involving police officers, go before the courts. All are ruled justifiable homicide, despite unusual circumstances.

Some people call the Detroit riot a race riot, a spontaneous anarchy against an affluent, but unresponsive administration, a seething anger of the oppressed against the oppressors with black citizens in an untenable social condition being harassed by white police. On the other side are people who call it civil disorder: the poor against the rich because of that same uncaring regime. Ronald Reagan, Governor of California, calls it the work of "mad dogs and lawbreakers," thieves who rampage for personal gain and plunder. In a national address on television, Mayor Cavanagh blames Congress for the riot, for failing to deal with social problems in large American cities. He feels that people died because of hatred, incompetence and bad judgement and, he says, it's lucky that more people weren't killed.

There are those who believe that the original raid on the blind pig should have been aborted because the crowd was too large to handle. Police were ill-prepared to round up prisoners who should never have been left on the street. Instead, the police should have sent everyone home with a warning. Critics say that an inept police force violated rules of crowd control, precipitated the riot and contributed to the strain. Many Blacks felt the raid was a double standard. It probably wouldn't have happened if the participants in the bar were White. Others discount this idea. Given the volatile relationship between police and the black community, something else would have triggered a riot anyway.

Some people, including police, don't believe the riot was caused by racial hate and inequity. They say it was planned in advance by professionals, outside agitators and conspirators, perhaps black nationalists, militants or even Communists brought in from out-of-state. It's felt that they encouraged looting by a small segment of the black population who were upset by their own poverty and desperation, and that there was a pattern, plan, and direction to the shootings, designed to keep the whole thing rolling.

Police made much of the fact that they saw a young black man in a green shirt and pants who seemed to be a leader, agitating and inciting the crowd. Police nicknamed him "Greensleeves" because of his outfit. They spotted him in several places, including the blind pig, shouting orders at looters, jeering at police and throwing beer bottles. The FBI investigated, but could not find any proof, and the Kerner Commission discounted the idea. The belief that outside forces were at work is a paternalistic attitude, which suggests, "Our good Negroes couldn't be guilty of these dastardly things."

There was even a belief that militant black leader, Malcolm X, orchestrated the whole thing. After a riot in Cincinnati on June 11, a black activist in Detroit was heard to say, "We already had our riot and we're here to show you how it's done." FBI sources said young Blacks had Molotov cocktails ready for use against "White credit stores on Detroit's west side," and the riot began three weeks later on Detroit's west side.

Known agitators were involved in other riots and, in a controversial move, President Johnson promoted legislation to stop them moving from state to state. The new anti-riot bill was passed by the U.S. House of Representatives and imposed a $10,000 fine with sentences of five years imprisonment for demonstrators who crossed state lines or used interstate mail to incite riots. The new law prompted demonstrations, not the least of which was a protest by 30 young people at the U.S. Consulate in Montreal. They carried French and English signs: "U.S. troops get out of Newark and Vietnam," and "Anti-riot or anti-poverty act?" The protesters passed out flyers, which complained that the government had launched a campaign against black people in the United States.

One positive result of the riot was a reappraisal of the performance, training and procedures of the National Guard. It was apparent that the Guard had to be taught not to load weapons or fire them indiscriminately. The FBI emphasized that the most effective way to eliminate snipers was with counter-snipers, equipped with high-powered, telescopically sighted rifles, one-on-one. It would eliminate National Guardsmen shooting at each other and endangering the lives of others.

A good chunk of Detroit was reduced to ashes but, contrary to popular belief, the city was not torched from end to end. The riot stretched from Livernois on the west, as high as Eight Mile Road on the north, past Woodward, to Gratiot and Van Dyke in the east and then into the Kercheval and Jefferson areas in the south. It resulted in millions of dollars damage, with many commercial and residential pockets requiring large-scale urban renewal, but estimates of that damage varied greatly. Preliminary estimates were grossly inflated at over $500,000,000, then dropped to $250,000,000, then dropped again to $22,000,000, excluding damage to contents, churches and institutions. Insurance claims were pegged at $32,000,000 and covered approximately 65 percent of the losses.

It's estimated that 657 people were injured and hundreds more were left homeless, but even those figures are hard to quantify. Many participants didn't come forward for fear of incriminating themselves, so the number of injured could have been higher. Early reports of the homeless were as high as 5,000, but one month after the riot the final tally dropped to 388. Early reports suggested that 1,300 buildings were destroyed, but *The Detroit Free Press* pegged the figure at 412, with 682 fires and 1,700 lootings.

Hundreds of people were left without jobs because of the number of businesses destroyed and yet, some rioters felt their actions were justified. They destroyed businesses that bilked Blacks, and where credit was easy to get because it cost too much. Regardless of the rationale, the lost man-hours in retail stores and the auto industry, the psychological hurt and human suffering, may never be known.

In short, the Detroit riot scarred the city's soul. Some say the riot was triggered by chance, but the wounds had been festering and it only took one incident to set it off. The disturbance continued because of ill feelings between police and rioters. Ironically, when it was over, the police released 61 of 82 people arrested at the blind pig. No charges were laid. *The Detroit Free Press* calls it "the most expensive pinch in history."

Chapter 2

Windsor Firefighters
Join The Brigade

For the first time ever, Windsor firefighters join their colleagues in Detroit to fight fires on the American side of the river. The Detroit Fire Department virtually begs for help, but it isn't necessary; the Windsor crew are anxious to answer the call. They're proud to volunteer as repayment of a 118-year-old debt, dating back to the day when Detroit saved Windsor.

Just after midnight on Monday, April 16, 1849, sparks from the steamboat *Hastings* ignite cedar posts in Windsor's harbour. High winds whip flames into a fury and, soon, much of the village is ablaze. Fire leaps across Ferry Street and one wooden building after another catches. Windsor's Fire Department sets up a bucket brigade, taking water from the Detroit River and passing it hand-to-hand, but the effort is futile. Windsor's 300 residents simply do not have the equipment, and they're facing the worst fire in the history of the town.

An alarm sounds from the tower of the old Presbyterian Church in Windsor and Detroit's entire fire department – six men – muster at the foot of Woodward Avenue. Only a year before, the two communities had signed an agreement to help in the event of fire. The Americans watch as a large brick warehouse in Windsor is engulfed in flame, but they have an agonizing wait. Ferryboats are nowhere in sight. And when one does appear it takes over an hour for the *Hastings* to voyage to the American side so the detachment can cross the river.

Initially, there is a dispute with the captain of the vessel. He's concerned about waves on the river and doesn't want to load both fire engines, two hose carts, and the men. As it turns out, one fire engine is too tall to fit below deck and so, only one is loaded with its cart. Just as the boat is about to leave, Detroit fireman John Owen suggests that both carts be taken, providing an extra 250 feet of hose. His foresight saves the day.

By the time Detroit firefighters make it to the Canadian side, an acre in the town is burning. The fire has jumped a main street and is threatening the rest. Flames are licking the front of the Windsor Castle Hotel and it's just a matter of time before they catch. Within five minutes of landing, Detroit firemen have a stream of water soaking the old hotel. They stand in the middle of the street, battling for two hours with flames behind and in front. With extra hose, they're more flexible and fight from two sides. Their hats are nearly burned to cinders, their hair and whiskers singed. Their faces and hands are blistered, but they eventually triumph and their valiant efforts contain the blaze.

The losses are great, but could have been double, if not for the fire brigade from Detroit. The blaze destroys $30,000 worth of real estate in the business district, including four barns, two warehouses, two dwellings, a dry goods store, hardware, customs office, restaurant, Queen's Hotel, bakery, schoolhouse and several outhouses. Saved are the Windsor Castle Hotel, two nearby residences and four barns. The fire is halted and the remaining town is no longer in danger.

Windsor residents are exceptionally grateful; they provide food, coffee and cigars and, at 5:00 a.m., heartily cheer their rescuers as the Detroit firemen, grimy and tired, head for home aboard the ferry *Ariel*. As a result of the fire, Windsor purchases its first hand-drawn, hand-operated pumper engine, widens its streets as a firebreak, and installs fire hydrants. A few months later, July 2, 1849, a delegation from Windsor, complete with a German band, arrives in Detroit to present American firefighters with a silver trumpet. It's a speaking-trumpet or megaphone inscribed with a fire engine, a description of the event and the coat of arms of the United States and Great Britain. The inscription reads:

"Presented to the fire brigade of Detroit by the inhabitants of Windsor and Sandwich as a testimonial of their gratitude for their able and generous conduct in crossing the river under the direction of Mr. Duncan, the chief engineer, during the intensely cold night of the 16th of April 1849, with their engine, by means of which, under their unwearied exertion and management the destruction of Windsor was mainly prevented."

Only 14 inches long and 6.5 inches wide, the trumpet is a small token of appreciation. But it is an important symbol of mutual support and respect to be acknowledged during the Detroit riot when Windsor is finally given a chance to show its gratitude.

On Sunday, July 23, 1967, beleaguered firemen in Detroit cannot keep up. There are too many fires. Attempts to control them are hampered by attacks and interference from rioters. The first major fire breaks out in mid-afternoon, Sunday, at the Starbright Market on the corner of Twelfth and Atkinson. The building has been ransacked and firemen are pelted by

A National Guardsman guards a Detroit fire truck with a smashed windshield to protect it from further damage, July 25, 1967. Courtesy of B.G. "Spike" Bell.

rocks, bottles and debris. As they're beaten back, they pick up garbage can lids as shields. Firemen on aerial ladders are afraid of snipers; they feel like sitting ducks.

Police are supposed to provide an armed guard in accordance with the riot plan, but they too are understaffed. Their forces are split between protecting firemen and tightening a cordon around the riot area. In some neighbourhoods, residents show up with guns, knives and clubs, or set up their own rifle squads, but the fire department is simply overwhelmed. Firemen complain about the lack of protection and are told by radio to pull out and let the fires burn if they have any trouble. "This is Engine 42 over at Linwood and Gladstone. They are throwing bottles at us. We are getting out." At 4:30 p.m., exhausted by heat and futility, Detroit firemen are forced to withdraw.

The Detroit Fire Department is one of the smallest in the United States for a city of its size, and the increasing number of fires presents a formidable problem. Seventeen hundred men have to protect a city of 139 square miles. That compares to Newark, New Jersey, where a force of 1,000 men cover only 16 square miles. In Detroit, there are no mutual aid agreements, so the city can't call reinforcements quickly. It's 9:00 p.m. before help arrives from 45 fire departments in surrounding communities.

When Windsor Fire Chief Harold Coxon hears that there's trouble, he's ready. After all, when Windsor has a waterfront fire, the Detroit Marine Division aids in rescue operations, and the Detroit Fire Tug is often dispatched. Similarly, Detroit police and fire departments assist during Royal visits and parades on the Canadian side of the border. Detroit rarely asks for assistance, and generally restricts its requests to fire departments on American soil, but Coxon has a good rapport with Chief Charles Quinlan and the Detroit fire brigade. And he's anxious to extend a courtesy, show the co-operation that, he feels, border communities should enjoy. He's never had an opportunity before, so he's happy to assist, and he expects the same of his men.

Coxon is blue-eyed, blond-haired, stocky, but muscular and solid. He's an ex-navy man and proud of it. Community-minded, Coxon is a dedicated career fireman who loves his job – "a firefighter's firefighter." He runs a close-knit department and his men depend on each other, on the job and off. When somebody moves, or there's work around the house, members of the department are on hand to get the job done.

In his 50s, Coxon has four children, from 25 to 17 years of age. He's a jovial man, but his job comes first and his wife knows it. When Coxon's mind is made up there's no talking to him. He'll do what's necessary. Eventually, Coxon obtains the official "okay" from Windsor's mayor and is on his way to fight fires in another country, another world. It's a dangerous situation, but it's as if Coxon is leading his troops into battle.

When the fire bell goes, Inez Coxon is alert and ready. She doesn't eat or sleep all the time her husband is in Detroit. She stays home, watches the riot on television and wonders what her husband is doing, hoping that he's okay. The anxiety comes with the territory and is something that every fireman's wife experiences.

Initially, Coxon's crew of 10 volunteers take the number two and number seven water-pumping fire engines, a Chevrolet station wagon as a command car, and Coxon's own personal vehicle. The last two automobiles are laden with extra gear and clothing. It's the first wave of support that lasts for the duration of the riot and sees 95 of Windsor's 249 firemen volunteer in Detroit. It's a significant contribution, especially since several Michigan companies refuse to answer the call. Their detachments are either too small, or they're afraid of the danger and liability to their insurance coverage.

Detroit has 92 pieces of firefighting equipment in service, leaving only four engine companies to protect the rest of the city. Fifty-six trucks and cars are brought from neighbouring communities. There are 209 fire alarms on Sunday, double the usual number for a July day. Syndicated columnist Jimmy Breslin describes the sky as a "red glow, bitter with smoke and cinders." The whole city seems on fire. Some families are burned out as flames spread from shops to homes. Many fireboxes in the riot area are inoperable from repeated use or are damaged by heat and flames.

Captain Robert Ferguson is a veteran with the Windsor department, but he's never seen anything like this. His crew reports to headquarters in Detroit and is escorted to its first fire, a raging inferno in a furniture store at Grand River and Lincoln. Ferguson has no idea where he's going, but when he arrives, he knows his job. It's the worst blaze in a part of the city

These two pumpers, manned by Windsor firefighters, battled numerous major fires in Detroit during the riot in July 1967. Engine 7, a 1959 Elcombe is on the left, and Engine 2, a 1965 Mack, is on the right. Fire Chief, Harold Coxon, left, and Captain Roy Gibbs, stand in front of the trucks. Walt McCall took this photo from the roof of the Windsor City Market downtown. Courtesy of Walter M.P. McCall.

where violence has been contained, at least for now. "We must have passed thirty fires on the way. We wondered when we were going to stop."

Central dispatch tells Ferguson to do his best, allow the fire to burn itself out, while protecting buildings on each side of the inferno. His first blaze involves two apartment houses and a whole block of stores. It's a tough job. The threads of Canadian fire hoses don't fit American hydrants. There aren't enough adaptors and connectors, and the pumper truck only has 150 gallons of water in its tank. It's barely enough to battle fires that, in Windsor, would be considered a general alarm with many more fire trucks on the scene. "These aren't ordinary fires ... They're firestorms ... We never stopped." Ferguson describes it as a nightmare, like being to hell and back.

Ferguson is constantly looking over his shoulder for snipers in neighbourhoods he doesn't know and under conditions he's never experienced.

If residents become too rowdy, if bricks and rocks start flying, then he's to shut down and get the hell out. Windsor firefighters hear the occasional rifle shots, but nobody throws anything. As a precaution, Windsor firemen tape the windows of their trucks. They don't want glass shattering, if they're hit by stray bullets. Eventually, fire engine number seven takes a couple of hits from snipers. Says Ferguson, "I never thought human beings could turn like that."

At 8:00, Monday morning, acrid smoke boils over the skyline as Windsor firemen return to Pitt Street on the Canadian side. They're covered in soot, and exhausted. They've been battling fires all night, and they're relieved by the next shift which works until 4:00 p.m. Coxon is quiet when he comes off duty, keeping much of what he's seen inside. He doesn't get emotional or involved, just does his job. He won't talk about it, and for good reason. So far, Windsor firefighters have been lucky. There have been only two cases of smoke inhalation. It could have been worse.

That morning, Coxon is directing operations at a fire in a large warehouse on the corner of Lafayette and Connor when he hears a scream from above. Detroit fireman, 24-year-old John Ashby, is working a high-pressure hose on an aerial ladder. A 4,800-volt electrical wire snaps and falls and hits Ashby's metal helmet on the way down. A skilled firefighter, Ashby always goes by the book. He insists on wearing his helmet against the advice of the older guys. Ashby figures it will provide better protection, but he's wrong. He suffers burns to his head, chest and shoulders. The ladder is quickly lowered and Ashby is unbuckled and brought to the ground. Coxon says, "most of his scalp remained inside the helmet when we took it off. His skull was too hot to touch."

The eyes of the injured firefighter turn milky white. Coxon covers him in a blanket and starts mouth-to-mouth, while a Detroit fireman applies an external heart massage. The injured fireman comes to, but he's barely breathing. They place him in an ambulance and send him to hospital. Coxon knows it's touch-and-go, but he doesn't have time to follow up. He is too busy fighting fires. Ashby dies in hospital a week later. He is young, has a family and his death is tough on Windsor firefighters. They try not to dwell on it, but it could have been any of them. Shaken, Coxon attends the funeral to say a quiet farewell.

The next shift immediately heads across the border and, for the second day in a row, Windsor firemen are working side by side with Americans from Royal Oak, Grosse Point, Flint, Lansing and Toledo, Ohio. The men work as though they have always known each other, always been a team. The firemen are forced to let some buildings burn while they concentrate on others. At noon, they're fighting a blaze at Dexter and Waverly. They call for police protection because they're being pelted by bricks and bottles. Shadowy figures in dark alleys tell them to get out and stay out. At 1:30 p.m., engine number two and number seven call for support again. They've stayed at their posts and continue to work with no police in sight. They're ordered to withdraw immediately if attacked by rioters. They eventually receive an armed guard, which stays with them for the duration.

A couple of firemen report sniper bullets whipping by, but it's hard to be sure in the heat and confusion. One Windsor firefighter was in the military and remembers basic training when riflemen fired over the heads of troops in the field to get them used to battle. He knows the sound of those bullets, but never heard anything like it in Detroit.

At 3:34 p.m., during the height of firebombing, Windsor engine number two leaves one blaze to fight another in a six-storey apartment on Twelfth Street near Clairmount. Windsor firefighter Bill Tate says flames are rolling 15 feet out of the windows and setting fire to buildings across the street. The hydrant is on the other side of the wall of flame. On a cue from a Detroit firefighter, the Windsor crew guns the motor of their pumper and drives through the fire. "The heat was unbearable. Then I heard a God-awful roar and shouts from the back of our truck ... The entire building collapsed into the street behind us. We missed the falling wall by two seconds."

By 9:36, Windsor firefighters are battling a blaze in a row of stores at Lysander and Trumble. As night descends, rioters overrun the area and firefighters come under a barrage of rocks, bottles and debris. The pressure is intense and firemen are forced to withdraw. They don't even have time to unhook their hoses from fire hydrants. They abandon them, leave them, lying in the streets. When they come back next day, their hoses are still there, ready to use.

By late Monday, 1,000 Detroit firemen have worked for 24 hours without a break. They're exhausted. Five men have suffered heart attacks, or fatigue, and have collapsed. At times, racial tensions run high because most Detroit firefighters are White. There are only 40 Blacks in the whole department. Some white Americans shout for the National Guard to shoot rioters. "Kill the black bastards ... Control those coons. Shoot 'em in the nuts!" Despite the abuse, some black bystanders grab hoses and spray their burning houses. They stand out against the all-white crews. As one suggests, "No matter what colour someone is, whether they are green, pink or blue, I'd help them if they were in trouble." It's significant that, years later, a black rioter becomes a Detroit fireman.

Some black residents give firefighters cold lemonade while others stand back with tears in their eyes. Tate says older Blacks are more likely to help, while the younger ones are more likely to loot and bomb. Windsor firefighter Jack Leopold believes that some Blacks want to help because it's their only hope and yet, he fights fires on one side of the street while looters strip stores and break glass on the other.

In some cases, rioters try to sell things to firemen. Leopold watches a Detroit fireman haggle over a pair of shoes. The fireman dickers the looter down to half price only to find that he's purchased two left shoes. In another instance, a guy backs a truck up to a building and calmly fills it with televisions. Leopold watches in awe, helpless to stop him. Sometimes looters hand Canadian firefighters bottles of stolen liquor. Tate says, "We saw 14-year-old girls struggling with a case of whiskey under each arm. Nothing was too big or too small to take away."

At the end of the shift, Windsor firefighters console each other to relieve their eight-hour stress on the debris-strewn street. They're breaking new ground, fighting fires in a way they were never taught in school. They have no time to clean, roll or pack the fire hose as they would normally. They just throw the bulky, wet hose on top of the truck and head to the next blaze a few doors down. "It's unreal, terrifying. You just forget everything you learned about fighting fires."

Tuesday provides a breather, a feeling of hope, as an uneasy peace stretches over the city. It's a deceptive calm because the killing and fires are far from over. At 1:40 a.m., a rioter throws a brick. It strikes a Windsor firefighter hard in the shoulder, dropping him in his tracks. Lieutenant

Gurney Garnet is rushed across the border to Windsor's Hôtel-Dieu Hospital for treatment. Despite the assault, only three Windsor firefighters are injured, none seriously, and they're feeling more confident because soldiers are riding on top of the fire rigs. In some cases, machine guns are mounted on sandbags as a morale booster. The soldiers will shoot, if necessary. They sit quietly with loaded weapons beside firemen who've climbed onto hoses to sleep between fires.

At 7:33 p.m., Windsor engines number two and seven head back to their home base. They've been operating for 40 hours and require an extensive mechanical inspection. They're relieved by two fresh pumpers – engines five and nine. Coxon says his firefighters will remain on American soil as long as their services are needed. As the two trucks leave Detroit for the last time, they encounter some unusual hostilities, surprisingly, at the border itself. The crew in number two is confronted by an arrogant young tunnel employee who demands that firefighters pay the toll. This is the second time the truck has been stopped. The command car, carrying an officer and six tired men, is charged $1.20 – 60 cents for the car and 10 cents for each of the passengers. When a firefighter explains that they are on official business to provide emergency protection in Detroit, the toll collector snarls, "Give me the money and I'll give you a receipt."

Star reporter Walt McCall picks up the story and, for the next two years, the Windsor Fire Department receives mail from angry U.S. citizens who want to cover the cost. "There are envelopes with dollar bills and the letters read: just so you don't think we're all cheap sons of bitches over here." McCall's story makes national news. "Harold Coxon was mad as hell," McCall explains. "Someone made a poor decision, no question about it." Later, McCall joins Coxon in the command car on a trip to Detroit. They meet the same toll collector who shoves back into his booth and says, "I don't want to talk to you guys." They continue through the tunnel without paying the toll and, from that time on, Windsor firemen are exempt from charges whenever they cross the border. Coxon says tunnel officials apologize and the employee is disciplined. They call it an unfortunate mistake and hope that a wrong has been righted.

By Wednesday, "order from chaos" emerges. Detroit's Assistant Fire Chief Arthur Seymour says, "We only had 21 fires from midnight to 8:00

o'clock." Everything is calm. In some cases, firefighters are called to blazes that they've already extinguished. They flare up because the men are over-worked and don't have time to do the job properly the first time. Coxon describes it as "cramming years of fire fighting experience into a space of less than three days and under conditions that defy everything in the training manuals." Coxon figures his crews have attended 200 fires, most of them serious.

Detroit expects to return to normal by Friday, so out-of-town depart-ments return home. In all, 45 communities provide 924 men and 88 pieces of equipment. While some crews remain on duty until Thursday morning, Windsor's two pumper trucks and 15 firemen head home at 2:00 p.m. Wednesday, leaving Detroit still-smouldering. They've been relieved of duty after spending more than 60 hours battling fires. Volunteer and off-duty firemen have logged a total of eight, eight-hour shifts and they have an unwritten promise to return, if needed. It's estimated that the extra duty will cost the Windsor Fire Department $2,400 in overtime, but Windsor absorbs the bill. As Coxon says, "You can't charge a friend for favours." Detroit officials are so grateful, they're prepared to answer any S.O.S. from Windsor within one hour. Meanwhile, the city of Warren, Michigan, actually bills Detroit more than $4,300.

On Thursday, Detroit Fire Chief Charles Quinlan has nothing but praise for the heroic actions of the Windsor detachment. The Detroit Board of Fire Commissioners is also overwhelmed by the generous response. The board extends its thanks, as does Michigan Governor George Romney who is gratified by the prompt emergency service provided by his Canadian neighbours. Overwhelmed by the praise, Windsor firefighters settle down to their usual routine at home. They answer six calls including a grass fire, a truck fire, an overturned flare pot, two false alarms and some wires struck by lightning. It's easy work, considering what they've been through.

In sorting through their equipment, the Windsor department recovers several extra lengths of hose and a nozzle. It also has a 24-foot extension ladder and two fire axes, which belong to the Detroit Fire Department. Two of their own axes and a ladder are missing. A couple of hose adaptors have also disappeared. Detroit fire halls set up a lost and found for mis-placed equipment, so the problems are easily solved.

Forty Windsor firefighters have another duty over the weekend. They attend the funeral of 30-year-old Carl Smith of Detroit's Engine Company Number 13. At 11:30, Monday morning, Smith was fighting fires on Mack Avenue. There were reports of sniper fire and the National Guard shot back. The firefighters hit the ground, waiting for the barrage to end. During the hour-long battle, Smith was separated from his truck. He made a dash for it, but was hit in the head in the crossfire. His death is ruled accidental. Officially, he was felled by a sniper. Unofficially, it could have been a Guardsman.

Delegates from at least 30 fire departments from as far away as New York, Chicago and Cleveland attend the funeral at 11:00 a.m. Saturday. Half an hour after the eulogy, the funeral procession moves from the fire station at the corner of Fort and Elmwood to the Elmwood Cemetery. Windsor's Phil Murphy is a member of the Detroit Fire Department Band and he's in the entourage. A fire engine draped in black leads the cortege

B.G. "Spike" Bell of Tecumseh, now a Master of Photographic Arts, was working as a freelance photographer for The Detroit Free Press *in 1967 when he took these and other shots of the riot. Detroit firefighters work to save a building already consumed by flame. It's just one of the hundreds of buildings that they work to save over the dire days of rioting.* Courtesy of B.G. "Spike" Bell.

Many efforts by firefighters are futile, as buildings are quickly consumed in flame and smoke. Note the protection by police and military units. Courtesy of B.G. "Spike" Bell.

followed by 15 muffled drums. On Smith's gravestone, there are two engraved trumpets, the traditional symbol of the firefighter.

By Sunday, July 29, Detroit has responded to over 1,600 fire alarms, an average of 231 per day, compared to 119 normally. There have been fires on 132 streets, covering 50 square miles, or about a third of the city. Molotov cocktails have set half of the fires. The number of buildings destroyed ranges from 300 to 1,100 depending on whether you talk to the city engineering department, the newspapers or the insurance companies. The fire department estimates that 412 buildings are destroyed, with 282 damaged, mostly commercial buildings, including furniture and grocery stores.

According to the Kerner Commission, fire damage is more significant in Detroit than 23 other riot-infested cities. It's estimated that 200 homes are burned and 600 people left homeless. Only 34 arsonists are arrested and only 13 prosecuted. Twelve hundred workers lose their jobs because their place of business is destroyed. In all, two Detroit firemen are dead, and 60 injured, 10 seriously.

Because of dry conditions, fires spread easily. In many cases, there's no insurance, so losses aren't covered. Shortly after the riot, burned buildings are bulldozed. Years later, those empty lots are neglected and covered with weeds or made into small parks. One of those areas is the original blind pig, which was engulfed in flames. In many alleys, scarred furniture and scattered clothes are left behind, a testament to the Detroit riot.

For the Windsor Fire Department, the ordeal is over. When Coxon talks about it, he speaks mostly about people rampaging and throwing Molotov cocktails. Coxon is amazed that they wouldn't back down and let him do his job. He's convinced that the riot could have been avoided. In the final tally, Windsor firefighters had to withdraw 283 times, but they performed their duties well and escaped mishap.

Walt McCall, a fire buff himself, describes it as one of the proudest moments of Windsor's civic history. The mouse is finally given a chance to help the elephant simply by crossing an international border. As McCall puts it, "Howard Coxon's goodwill in responding to the plea for help is remembered to this day. Windsor is so well regarded that, if anything happens, the Detroit Fire Department is here in five minutes."

An official expression of gratitude is made in a formal announcement in *The Windsor Star* and, eventually, a Detroit fire station is named in Coxon's honour, complete with a bronze plaque. On the 20th anniversary of the riot, the Detroit Benefit Fund decides to issue red, white and blue ribbons to Windsor firefighters who served. Administrators want to issue medals, but they are prevented by Detroit's first black mayor, Coleman Young, who refuses to concede that 1967 is a riot. He calls it an "insurrection."

In 1996, the Windsor Fire Department uses its celebrated trumpet at opening ceremonies of the International Freedom Festival, a huge party thrown in July by the cities of Windsor and Detroit. The instrument has been on display at the Detroit Historical Museum since 1928 and must be returned, but it's a demonstration of mutual support. The annual Freedom Festival recognizes our friendship and, in front of a huge crowd, firemen cross aerials of a Detroit and Windsor fire truck, lower the two

At a special ceremony in the middle of the Ambassador Bridge, Detroit Fire Chief, Charles J. Quinlan, gives the silver trumpet back to Windsor Fire Chief, Harold Coxon, in a symbolic gesture that Windsor has finally repaid its long-standing debt to Detroit.
Courtesy of The Windsor Fire Department.

national flags and exchange the silver horn from one department to the other.

To Windsor Fire Chief Dave Fields, the gesture recognizes the significance of the speaking trumpet and keeps its symbolism alive. Fields has a personal reason for the ceremony. In 1967, he's a 19-year-old rookie who volunteers for Detroit. As a new recruit, he's green, but eager. Unfortunately, his father – a captain in the fire department – is in charge of volunteers. When he sees his son's name on the list, he pulls it, and doesn't let his boy go over. The gesture by an anxious father afraid for his son's welfare creates a rift between the two men. Fields now realizes his father only tried to protect him, but he still wants to show he was ready to help. It's a gesture of support that lives in the tradition of firefighters in Windsor.

At the Fireman's Field Day at the old bandshell in Jackson Park, a special "Thank You" is extended to Windsor from the City of Detroit. Windsor's 95 volunteers receive certificates of appreciation. At the same ceremony, the young widow, of Detroit fire fighter John Ashby, and Earl Berry, president of the Detroit Fire Fighters Association, present Windsor Fire Chief Harold Coxon with a certificate of appreciation and a gold watch for his services. On stage front, l to r: unknown, Mrs. Ashby, Earl Berry, Harold Coxon. Courtesy of B.G. "Spike" Bell.

Chapter 3

Canadian Newsmen

At 8:55 a.m. Sunday, the United States wakes up to the first reports of a disturbance. The story runs nationally on ABC, but there's not much impact because of the small audience. At 10:00 a.m., the Michigan Civil Rights office appeals to managers of Detroit TV stations, WJR radio and *The Detroit News* and *Free Press*, asking them not to carry inflammatory reports of violence for fear of blowing everything out of proportion and escalating the riot. Authorities are afraid that too many people have already heard about it. They hope they can stop coverage and control it.

Initially, the media cooperates with police, backs off or downplays the riot, but that only adds to the confusion. The blackout doesn't last long because stations outside Detroit hear rumours of looting and send their own reporters. The embargo ultimately breaks down because the event is too large to conceal.

The first local report is broadcast by a TV station in Windsor at 2:00 p.m., ten hours after the riot began. Jim Van Kuren is director of the tiny newsroom at CKLW - TV, working with a writer, announcer and two cameramen. Just before the broadcast, Van Kuren receives a call from an old friend, Ray Girardin, Police Commissioner in Detroit. Girardin is a former newspaperman who's worked with Van Kuren before. It's getting harder to keep the lid on and, since Girardin is an old drinking buddy, he provides the inside track.

Van Kuren knows he has to get something on-air but, without visuals, he has a problem. He wants to send a cameraman, but one of his technicians refuses to go because he's afraid. Finally, Van Kuren gives the assignment to his other shooter, Don Grant. Van Kuren hasn't heard about the riot from any other source, but he knows it's a matter of time, and he still needs pictures. CKLW is located at the corner of Riverside Drive and Crawford on Windsor's waterfront where the view of Detroit is panoramic. Van Kuren jockeys his studio cameras onto the front lawn of the station and his announcer, Irv Morrison, gives details with smoke from the first fires showing in the background. Morrison simply explains that an incident has occurred in Detroit, a police officer has been "hit by a rock and one man stabbed as hundreds brawled for five hours."

There's a lot of confusion during those first hours, and nobody understands the enormity of it. It doesn't take long, however, for other cameramen and reporters to show up from London, Toronto, Toledo and Cleveland. Eventually, there are journalists from all over North America. WXYZ - TV reports falsely that a policeman has been killed, and WWJ - TV alarms thousands of viewers by reporting that riots have spread to the suburbs. Meanwhile, announcers on black-oriented radio stations try to calm their listeners and convince them not to riot. By 7:30, CKLW is on top of the story: "Fires were blazing as far as three miles from the core of the riot activity. The fire department was forced to pull out because rioters stormed firemen as they tried to get to the scene." Van Kuren goes over on the second day when things are pretty quiet. People sit on porches and smoke cigarettes in doorways. Some American newsmen try to convince kids to throw rocks or smash windows so they can get visuals. Van Kuren just sticks to the facts, doesn't speculate or embellish.

As a newsman with *The Windsor Star*, Walt McCall figures he missed the chance of a lifetime when the riot broke out. McCall is in his '20s, and is building a reputation as a reporter. Early Sunday, he receives a call from a fellow fire buff that something is up on Twelfth Street. He turns on his scanner and listens at home. As the riot escalates, he knows it's unusual, so he heads into the office. Excited reporters and photographers discuss what they're going to cover and how. There's not much to go on, but they know there are big problems in Detroit.

Late in the afternoon, McCall goes over to the headquarters of the Windsor Fire Department at 254 Pitt Street where they're on standby. By suppertime, Detroit is begging Windsor and other areas for help. It's something that has never happened before. Fire Chief Harold Coxon tells McCall they have two trucks heading to Detroit with room for one passenger. "Would you like to come along," he says. "We're leaving about 9:00 - 9:30 and there's a seat for you."

"Sure. Great," says McCall proudly, "but I have to check with the office first."

McCall knows that this is his big break and he's anxious to get started, but he heads back to *The Star* to confer with the boss. While he's there, Norm Hull, the executive editor, announces that, "Nobody, absolutely no-one, is to set foot in Detroit on fear of dismissal." Hull is concerned about the safety of his staff and about insurance coverage and liability, especially if someone is injured or killed. Many reporters have young families, and he doesn't want anything to happen to his people. He has eye contact with McCall who knows that he shouldn't have waited. McCall drags himself back to the fire hall and watches the volunteers head for the tunnel without

Another reporter, John Larke, interviews National Guardsmen for one perspective of the Detroit riot of 1967. Many reporters say they had no difficulty doing their jobs at the time. Courtesy of J.A. "Pete" McGarvey.

him. He agrees to meet them next morning when they come back, but it's a sad parting. McCall wants nothing more than to be on that truck.

Les Mather is also flabbergasted by the edict. Night editor at *The Star*, he's been on the golf course and has no idea what's going on until he sees smoke. The police are still calling the riot "civil disobedience," but every reporter knows that this is major and they're upset. They line up to volunteer, anxious to go where the action is. They know that it's getting dark and there is danger. They recognize that they have to be careful, "but that's the risk … the job."

Mather is ex-army and figures he can look after himself. He has a heated argument with Hull. "Are we a newspaper or fish wrap?" Mather wants to go to the police station in Detroit where it's relatively safe, but where they can get some first-hand news. Instead, he's assigned to the border to talk with people coming through about what they've seen. He knows that a second-hand account is second best and it's no way to cover news, but he has no choice.

McCall also feels cheated because the story has national implications. It's the biggest Windsor story since the war, and he can't believe that not one reporter will be sent. Their professional pride is hurt because other news agencies already have teams in place. Journalists are arriving in Windsor, wanting help on where to go and who to see, and McCall knows they'll have a head start, a better handle on what's happening. "To sit there in your newsroom while reporters from *The Toronto Star* and *The London Free Press* are scooping you in your own backyard, that was pretty hard to take." It was demoralizing. McCall pleads with Hull, but eventually realizes that he can't change the editor's mind. There isn't much point in arguing and reporters go by the rules, but the agitation continues. "When can we go?" McCall says. They're like children anticipating a trip to the beach.

Years after, reporters call it the disgrace of the newsroom, an embarrassment, an eternal shame. It's still talked about by reporters who weren't even there. There's even gossip that the decision drove a wedge between a father and son. Ken Hull was the education reporter at *The Star* and son of the executive editor. Reporters believe that Ken was so upset with Norm Hull's decision, that he deserted Windsor and the paper, even though Ken says those claims are false. He admits he was upset, and did leave the paper for *The Calgary Herald* several months later, but it was not because of his father. He applied for the position long before, and Norm wasn't even aware that his son was looking for work until *The Herald* phoned to say that Ken got the job. By then, Ken was in Detroit covering the riot and couldn't take the call. Norm reached his son on the two-way radio: "What's this about a job in Calgary and you're leaving?" Ken tries to explain, but his father interrupts. "I'll talk to you when you get back." Ken says his dad is angry, primarily because he doesn't want his grandchildren to go west. Ken has a three-year-old daughter and a one-year-old son, and Norm Hull will miss them.

Like other reporters, Ken doesn't like his father's decision, but he respects and understands it. *The Star* is a Canadian paper, which does not make a habit of reporting events in Detroit. It has access to American coverage through a reciprocal arrangement with its U.S. counterpart and that is sufficient. An exception is made for sports, Hull says, but not Detroit politics, racial strife or even murders or traffic deaths. Coverage of a Detroit event is only allowed if it has a Canadian angle or an impact on Windsor. Hull says a riot in Chatham or London is more likely to make the paper than anything across the border.

McCall admits it would be reckless to allow reporters to go with so many unknowns, especially when law and order is suspended, and someone could be shot. It's especially difficult in the early hours when the news blackout is on. There is just no way of knowing how bad it is.

When the border is closed, *Star* news bureaus in Chatham and Sarnia ignore the edict and send reporters across on the Bluewater Bridge to Port Huron, Michigan, and then to Detroit. They're warned not to call or they'll be told not to go. They write stories and take pictures, but *The Star* refuses them, so they're freelanced to another paper. Some reporters are in Detroit on their off-hours, visiting friends or relatives. They claim they're caught in it, and simply write columns about their experiences when they get back.

On each anniversary of the riot, McCall says, there's soul-searching in the newsroom. Reporters wonder whether they should publish a retrospective. It's a sensitive issue because they're afraid it might trigger more violence. The trepidation lasts well into the 1970s and '80s.

Reporters, National Guardsmen, police and federal troops crouch beside cars, in door-ways, and behind any cover they can to duck sporadic gun fire from snipers on rooftops and alleys. Courtesy of B.G. "Spike" Bell.

By the end of the second day, Norm Hull changes his mind and allows reporters in. On Tuesday morning, McCall teams up with *Star* photographer Bill Bishop. The reporters are warned away and have to convince police at the tunnel that they have a legitimate reason for being in Detroit. When they insist, they're allowed through the barriers and, once they're in, it's awesome. "You can smell the destruction, see the carnage." Despite blue sky and a gorgeous summer day, they can sense the panic, smell the smoke and charred wood; hear the sound of sirens and helicopters. There are blocks of burned-out buildings: three-storey shells of brick, interiors reduced to cinder and ash, walls toppled, nothing left. On one street, a Buick has been run over by a tank, crushed like a tin can.

McCall says there are gangs wandering the streets, burning buildings indiscriminately. He feels sorry for the victims who watch helplessly as flames approach. They have minutes to collect their belongings before arsonists cave in their windows, throw Molotov cocktails, and burn houses to the ground. "What sense is that," McCall wonders. The madness of looting and arson is beyond him. The liquor stores go first, then grocery and shoe stores. "They trash the place, empty it and then burn it down. It's anarchy." Bishop watches broken gas jets burn on residential streets, flames shooting into the night like Olympic torches. The gas companies can't shut them down, and there are too many to cap. "Another waste."

Bishop and McCall turn a corner and run smack into a paratrooper with an imposing weapon. They ask politely if they can continue into an area where fires are burning. The soldier just looks at them and says, "Negative." McCall decides not to press it. He knows these guys are under pressure. They've been up for hours, so he bites his tongue. They watch a five-storey furniture factory burn out of control. No firemen are on the scene.

The two newsmen monitor their radio for hot spots. They take cover from snipers, but have no idea whether they're a target or just in the line of fire. "You see the National Guard firing back and you stay the hell out of the way. They are dangerous." Many are 19 to 20 years old, "weekend soldiers" with no real training or experience. McCall figures that the Guardsmen are trigger-happy amateurs, so he keeps his distance. At dinnertime, they watch an unusual sight, a catering truck selling food and drinks to burned-out residents.

Bishop says many Detroiters are dazed. "I think they're in shock, like they can't believe they're doing it to themselves." After several hours, Bishop and McCall head back to the station to write stories, process film and meet their deadline as the next shift crosses the border. McCall says

Reporter Pete McGarvey carrying the tools of his trade at burned-out stores on 12th Street in Detroit on July 24th. Courtesy of J.A. "Pete" McGarvey.

McGarvey talks to frightened, hungry children like David, a grade six student who says he saw a baby shot. David is afraid of being outside and thinks "bad men," who started looting, should pay for the damage and then be shot too. As McGarvey comments, "It's a sad introduction to the cruel world of an eight-year-old on the streets of Detroit." He wonders what impact the riot will have on those children as they grow.
Courtesy of J.A. "Pete" McGarvey.

the staff pulls together, "doing one hell of a job." Not just reporters and photographers, but the guys on the desk who have to edit and balance local and national coverage.

By the end of the week, reporters still have to be careful. It's terrifying. The body count is rising and there are pockets of resistance. McCall is going on vacation in Kapuskasing and he's glad to get out. "You can't get much further away than that and, I'll tell you, it feels nice." He's like a war correspondent, but he can escape at night, flee to the comfort and security of his own home, his own bed in Windsor. McCall says it's one of his best experiences as a journalist.

Dick Smyth is news director for CKLW Radio and he's one of the first Canadian reporters across on Monday. He's 33 years old, "full of shit and vinegar" and this is his first time in a "war-zone." His station is owned by RKO General in the U.S. It has reporters in Detroit but, as the action heats up, Smyth figures he'd better take a look. He views Windsor as a suburb of Detroit, and figures it's his job to keep his listeners informed.

Rumours are rampant. Overnight, Windsor police are swamped with crank calls about firebombs downtown. There are reports that boatloads of armed Windsorites are heading for Detroit. There's even a rumour that Blacks have seized the Boblo boat and are sailing to Canada. Police have to investigate the calls, but it's so ridiculous that Smyth wants to know what's happening first-hand. He doesn't want to allow the craziness on-air, so he recruits Bert Allen, a technician at the station, and they drive across the border. Smyth figures Allen will be useful because he has a military background and will know what to do in an ambush. He's also Black.

The colour of Allen's skin has never been a factor at the station before. He's just one of the guys, does his job like anybody else. Smyth says it doesn't make much difference on this occasion either, but reporters remember it years after the riot. Van Kuren says that Allen was raised as a middle-class Canadian, and probably doesn't even realize he's Black. There's not much difference in the way he talks or acts. Van Kuren is concerned about Allen's colour. It could be an advantage with rioters on the street, but a disadvantage with police. He could be killed for no reason. Police do give him a rough time until they realize he's Canadian.

Smyth is too excited to feel threatened, but figures he made a pretty good target. They're in a Dodge van with the company letters on the side. They cruise Twelfth Street and then head over to Grand River where they're pinned down by sniper fire. They get out of the vehicle and crouch beside it, using it like a shield. There are shooters behind and in front, so they stay put until things settle down. Smyth has the presence of mind to keep his tape recorder running to capture the sound. For a few dramatic seconds, you can hear bullets banging into the pavement. Despite the intensity of Detroit, Smyth insists that other news and baseball scores be covered on his station, so that people will have a rounded view of what's going on. He's in constant touch with his home base, filing reports over the telephone. He wants balance, so he talks about what he sees. Smyth says the police are praying for rain to dampen the flames, but also to quench the fire for looting. Police say, "Rain is the best cop on the beat."

Smyth says many Blacks are arrested and detained without food or water on buses in front of city hall. Some are looters, but others are innocent. Jesse Powell has been hauled out of the garage where he works for no apparent reason other than the colour of his skin. He's detained nine days in the bathhouses on Belle Isle, which have been turned into a temporary jail. He isn't fed for two days and his family has no idea where he is because he can't contact them. Smyth is concerned that prisoners aren't being properly treated, but he tries not to overreact.

Like the shooting in Detroit, Smyth's reports are dramatic, staccato-style, rhythmic, punchy and sensational. CKLW is known for its rapid 15-second stories that have more to do with mood than substance. No newscast is longer than four minutes. "Gore on the floor of the liquor store," as one reporter describes a shooting. Five to ten-minute commentaries, the job of understanding or interpreting the riot, is left to others. When Smyth charters a helicopter and flies over Detroit, the pilot says they're under fire, and that a bullet has ricocheted off the Plexiglas. Smyth doubts it, but doesn't say anything. It's a status symbol to be under fire.

Smyth collects lots of tape, which doesn't fit the AM format. It's too good to waste, and he decides to run it on FM. It's some of his best work, and it is recognized by his peers. CKLW is the only radio station in Canada to win a Radio and Television News Director's Association Award for responsible, thorough and accurate coverage of the riot. It's a great career builder, but Smyth is humble and philosophic about his role. He looks on it as a unique, team-building exercise. In 1968, he's picked up by CHUM in Toronto at a salary to match his coverage but, he says, there's still a bond between the guys who were there.

One of those guys is Hal Sullivan, 26, a reporter for CBC Radio in Windsor. On Monday night, Sullivan compares notes with Smyth over the telephone. Smyth says he doesn't want to go back. "I don't have a cement head, you know." Sullivan understands the feeling. Before he goes over, he watches the fires with family and friends from the roof of the ten-storey Security Building which houses the CBC station downtown. Riot watching is a common pastime. Reporters with *The Windsor Star* even have lawn chairs on top of their building. Sullivan spends a day covering the riot. He drives over at 9:00 a.m. after Windsor police wave him through the border with a warning. "You're doing it under your own responsibility."

Usually, the border is choked with cars, but only three or four are going through. Sullivan cruises streets that are devoid of people and full of paper. It's bewildering, like one of those grade 'B' horror movies after an alien invasion or nuclear holocaust. Sullivan hunches over the steering wheel, looks at the tops of buildings, and watches for snipers. He drives his own car, a '64 Chevy Impala, which he parks on the street, knowing that he won't be ticketed. He just hopes it will be there when he gets back.

The pressroom at police headquarters on Beaubien is where Sullivan spends most of his time. Once you go in, he says, the police keep you there. Reporters go out, but at their own risk. Sullivan isn't sure whether it's for their safety, or so police can keep an eye on them. Scribes mill about, chat, compare notes, and telephone their newsrooms. Periodically, someone makes a statement. It's the mayor, police chief, or head of the National Guard and it's the official word of what is happening. Many reporters are reluctant to leave. They're either afraid of bullets in the streets, or of coming under fire from their editors if they miss something.

Sullivan keeps his eye on a female columnist from *The London Daily Express*. She's particularly striking because she comes from Fleet Street, straight from the airport with no time to change. She's wearing a bright yellow mini-skirt and, to Sullivan, it's incredible. "It takes everybody's mind off the riots." Male reporters are wearing khaki, military fatigues, or something akin to battle attire, but her outfit reminds Sullivan of the times. "Swinging London, the Beatles and so on." Only a week before, 3,000 Hippies, "Flower Children, the Beautiful People" as they are called in the English press, campaign in London's Hyde Park for the legalization of marijuana. They wear flowers in their hair, chant and sing, "make love and be happy." They dance barefoot in the grass. The female reporter looks at Sullivan and says, when they flew over Detroit, they could see the city clearly. The pilot announced over the intercom, "If you look out, you'll see one of the saddest sights in the history of America."

Initially, the local CBC feeds the network in Toronto but, on Tuesday, when editors in the provincial capital finally realize that the riot is major, they send one of their own reporters. Sullivan says the national reporter doesn't know the territory, or even where Detroit is in relation to Windsor, and it rankles the local boys. All national reports are filed with his voice and yet, they shepherd him around. Sullivan figures local reporters do the work, provide the contacts, but the national takes the credit. He's convinced that local reporters can handle the story.

The national reporter is Tom Leach and, in one of his stories, he crouches under a jeep as dozens of National Guardsmen fire hundreds of rounds at a lone sniper on a rooftop. A black marine says, "Just put a few rice paddies down there and it will be the same as Vietnam." Stores and offices are closed, but Leach finally finds a place to eat. "The cafeteria at the Statler-Hilton serves lunch to a line of people coiling up the stairs from the basement counters and out onto the street." Food is scarce in Detroit. Vehicles are scarce too. Leach says there are fewer cars in the Motor City then since the Model "T" first rolled off the assembly line.

Chatham station CFCO also covers the riot, even though it is 40 miles from the border. The station has a news exchange with a couple of Detroit stations and, in return for Canadian news, it has a pipeline into everything happening on the American side of the border. Initially, CFCO cooperates with the blackout and refuses to mention the riot. Then, it refers in vague terms to a skirmish with police, but does not go into detail. As other media report the story, the pressure mounts to provide first-hand coverage.

Many people think reporters are crazy for going over, but Pete McGarvey, 40, is anxious for the opportunity. He's the news director in Chatham and it's his first time for anything like this. He links up with Doug Arbour of Arbour Ambulance Service in Chatham because Arbour is a native of Windsor and knows Detroit well. He figures Arbour can drive because he's cool and calm, a good guy in a tight spot. The two men cross on Tuesday and spend three days in Detroit.

McGarvey is apprehensive as they drive through the streets, but he soon settles into his mission. He talks with Father Joseph Potts who stresses the need for clothes and medical emergency relief so that people with no transportation have access to doctors and prescription drugs. Potts says that, over the first three days of the riot, he helps 2,500 people at his church with housing donated by parishioners. The federal housing agency offers 50 homes, and a local hotel offers 200 rooms. Even white suburban families open their homes for temporary housing. "I haven't seen the extent of this kind of passion before. It is inspiring."

Potts is optimistic about the outcome of the riot. In a lengthy interview, he suggests that, to rebuild, the government must work with the people. The poor may not be articulate, but their needs should at least be heard. Patronizing Blacks has not worked, and Potts believes it's time for innovative ideas. He is confident that new committees will help, as long as the government spares no expense and pours as much money into the problem as it takes out. Only then, can men be men again. The first problem,

Potts emphasizes, is to deal with employment because male Blacks are not making enough to care for their families.

People say they don't condone rioting, but can understand why it is happening. There's high unemployment. The government ignores housing applications from the most needy, and only responds to violence. As one black man says, it's the only way of making officials listen. "The Negro now feels he's ready to take over, and the tension is getting worse ... We like to wear white shirts too ... we just want to be treated same as everybody else." The man says Blacks have some equality, but not enough, and he hopes the riot will mean more respect. "People don't treat you right, not as a person." He identifies Cavanagh as progressive, "but he's not worth a Chinese quarter." Troops can stay in Detroit but, when they leave, the riot will start again.

McGarvey says there's no hostility from looters, and it doesn't appear to be a White-Black confrontation. McGarvey says it's mostly a problem of urban poor. People treat him with goodwill; they answer his questions thoughtfully and candidly. When he tapes his reports, there's a tremor in his voice as he sets the scene, describes the action and captures the feel of what it's like. He stands beside a U.S. army tank with "Mission Impossible" scrawled on the side in chalk. There are 12 men on the carrier, each with a rifle, their eyes on buildings two storeys and higher. They're poised, as if for battle, staking out a sniper near Woodrow Wilson Avenue.

When McGarvey approaches an intersection at Clairmount, he meets soldiers. "You are asked to move quickly along and you don't need a second invitation." It's Wednesday afternoon and rain is threatening. It begins to fall as he enters the city. "Not a heavy, steady downpour, just a few drops of rain, not enough to cool off tempers. Not enough to make any difference to the tension of this riot-wracked city of Detroit." As he describes people on their verandahs, someone in the background yells, "Yankee go home." McGarvey talks about his feelings of relief as he leaves Clairmount and turns onto the John Lodge Freeway. Throughout his reports, the sound of sniper fire is heard in the background.

While other reporters are caught up in the excitement and fear of the riot, Spike Bell has time for the humorous side. As a Windsor photographer, working for *The Detroit Free Press*, Bell looks for the offbeat and finds it.

Hard at work doing what he does best, talking to people, Pete McGarvey interviews two National Guardsmen on July 25 about what they've seen and done during the riot.
Courtesy of J.A. "Pete" McGarvey.

Windsor firefighters are trained to use all the bells and whistles, make as much noise as they can every time they move their rigs, but they're eventually told to turn their sirens off by Detroit firemen who are fed up with the constant sound, the blaring noise. On one street, Bell sees a general sitting beside two riflemen and a machine gunner in an armoured personnel carrier. A couple of shots ring out, and the general buries himself in the bottom of the half-track under the other soldiers.

Late at night, Bell is pinned down by sniper fire near Twelfth Street. It's pitch dark because many of the streetlights have been shot out by police. Bell can hardly see, and there are only two sounds – the sporadic crack of rifle fire and someone cursing nearby. Bell wants to know what's going on, so he crawls on his stomach toward the sound of the swearing. When he's close enough, he sees a Detroit police officer sprawled on his belly on the pavement. Bell says the man is wearing a huge, British-style, World War I army helmet. It's two sizes too large and, every time the cop moves, his hat falls down over his face and covers his eyes. It causes great consternation and another colourful outburst.

The sight reminds Bell of helmeted police that afternoon. They were given white helmets, which were easily spotted and made the men feel like targets. Bell says some officers took them home and covered them with dark material or even their wife's bloomers to prevent them from being so obvious. The new creations look ridiculous, but the men feel safer even though they're "razzed" by their fellow officers. Bell says it's hilarious, but he empathizes. He's been under fire. He's been told not to use the flash on his camera for fear of being shot by snipers.

Bell also had his share of rifles pushed into his face at roadblocks and checkpoints. Sitting in his car on Grand River, there's not a soul in sight and it's dark. The windows are rolled down, and he's just about to pull away when he hears a gruff voice whisper, "You move that car and you're dead." He looks into the barrel of a rifle. A police officer hauls him out, makes him spread-eagle with hands on the roof. Two other officers have shotguns. Bell explains who he is and what he's doing, and struggles for his ID. The officers apologize and talk for a few minutes. They've just been shot at by persons unknown, and they're edgy.

During the month of August, tensions in Detroit run high, perhaps fuelled by the media. There's a great deal of hostility toward reporters. A black newspaper warns readers to be wary of interviewers because of a network TV show in the United States, which featured sensational conversations with alleged snipers. Speculation runs rampant as to what caused the riots, whether they were inspired by outsiders, and who did what to whom, but the situation is best described in a personal account by *Windsor Star* reporter Cec Scaglione.

As a white Canadian, Scaglione says, "You can understand the Negroes' problem if you wander into riot-ridden ghettos. You understand because you become the intruder, the outsider, the one who is different." The desecration is unbelievable, but the frustration is understandable as you drive through poverty-stricken slums. Scaglione describes sweat dripping down his sideburns. His hands are dry and his breathing short with apprehension. He keeps his eyes straight as he watches for a policeman. He feels like a target for snipers. "Your back grows to 400 feet." The mood of the crowd alternates from inflamed, sullen, to unconcerned. No one knows how hot it is, how long it will last, or what rioters want.

Reporters live, eat and sleep the riot. When it's over, they sigh with relief, analyze their coverage, pat themselves on the back, and move to the next story. Generally, an event is forgotten as other assignments take its place. That's how it usually works, but this riot is different. It's the story that reporters talk about, agonize over. They clip bylines, save newspaper cuttings and relegate photos and negatives to their bottom drawer. It's the story worth savouring. It's the story they'll tell their grandchildren. It's the story they'll always remember.

Chapter 4

Caught By the Riot

To Kevin Hart, the news blackout is scary. From Windsor, he sees smoke and hears sirens, but doesn't know why. Some people are afraid that a rebellion is underway. Rumours spread, but people are in the dark. The problem is even worse for Canadians caught by surprise in Detroit. Because of the blackout, it's over twelve hours before they know the truth.

Betty Day lives on Larkin Road in Windsor, but she's trapped at her job in a Detroit florist shop on the first day of the riot. She seeks refuge at a friend's on Eight Mile and Livernois, a couple of houses away from buildings that are torched. Some Windsor mothers and their children are stranded in downtown Detroit with bullets spraying around them. They've been window shopping and are stuck at a bus stop on Woodward Avenue, five blocks from the tunnel. Bus drivers make U-turns after they clear U.S. customs and refuse to go up that far. Police cruisers scream past. Looters pour through the area unchecked.

John Lavis, who lives on Ouellette Avenue in Windsor, is also caught at the bus stop. "It's worse than the London blitz," he says, referring to German bombing during World War II. Lavis herds the women from bus stop to bus stop in the direction of the border. Occasionally, they take shelter while crowds careen past. Detroit police order them back to the tunnel, but refuse to help. Lavis watches as looters storm Sam's Department Store, Cunningham's Drugs and the downtown terminal of the Greyhound

Bus Company two blocks from the tunnel. He finally makes it to the border and safety.

On Sunday afternoon, Rick Wynants and his friends head to Detroit not knowing that the riot is underway. They're amazed by what they see and immediately return to Canada. When he's stopped by customs, Wynants realizes he doesn't have his citizenship papers and has a few anxious moments. He's questioned about where he's been and why he went, but his friends intervene and, on the strength of his Ontario driver's license, Wynants is eventually allowed back into Canada. Over the next few days, he watches the riot from the windows of a Windsor mold shop where he works on Riverside Drive. The flames change his attitude toward Detroit.

Allen Walls is at a barbeque at his girlfriend's house just down the street from the action. They want to see what's going on, so they walk to the corner where looters break into a furniture store. Walls says a cab drives up, a guy gets out, grabs a TV and gets back into the vehicle as it drives away. Other men push a safe down the street, trying to break into it as they go. A policeman points an assault rifle at some kids and a tank drives over a neighbour's front lawn. Walls says many people watch. They're hard-working, law-abiding people who can't understand what it's all about or how anarchy can reign. Walls has a hard time too. A 19-year-old carpenter from Amherstburg, he's Black, but he's lived in Maidstone township all his life and it's impossible to relate. He knows there's deep-seeded racism in Detroit. He also knows that looting is a form of survival in an urban jungle, a human response to frustration and fear.

Spiros de Bono is visiting his brother-in-law on Curtis Street between Six and Seven Mile roads in the northwestern part of Detroit. He ignores reports of the riot until after Governor Romney announces his curfew at 9:00 p.m. Afraid to go back to Canada, he beds down on the living room floor, but can't sleep. De Bono's six-year-old son nudges his father and says, "What if some Negroes walk in. What would you do?" De Bono replies, "I would offer them a cup of coffee and ask them to leave." "What if they don't," his son asks. De Bono doesn't know how to answer. The next day, the police tell de Bono to return to Canada by way of the Bluewater Bridge between Port Huron, Michigan and Sarnia. It's an hour's drive – and then two-and-a-half hours back on the Canadian side – but it's safer than the riot-torn area of Detroit.

As a columnist with *The Windsor Star*, John Lindblad writes about what happened to him in his column in Monday's paper. He has dinner, Sunday, at a friend's house in West Bloomfield with no idea that the riot is underway. He describes his drive through the slums of Detroit. "Black men and women with nothing to do, nowhere to go, in a section of the city where welfare, unemployment, illiteracy, vice and crime are high." Conditions are low, he notes, and then came the luxurious white suburbs. It's the American dream – big cars and homes, drinks on the patio, good education and jobs, safe and secure.

Lindblad says Blacks in Detroit are better off than other U.S. cities because many have jobs in the auto industry, but it's still a far cry from the lavish white world. He describes a frustrating, and purposeless condition, and suggests that the riot is merely an example of unsheathed anger, the senseless tearing down of society. He's not surprised by the riot. For months, there have been rumours that Detroit would be next. Lindblad chastises the conservative, black middle class, which is more interested in helping itself than dealing with problems of the poor. He also blames black militants for setting the Civil Rights Movement back a decade or more and losing the sympathy of a new white generation, which, he claims, is more tolerant and willing to help. He admits that the white man in Detroit is going to have to come half way, but so is the "Negro."

Knowing about the riot on his return trip, Lindblad is happy to be heading home, feeling lucky to live in Canada. He describes listening to the police radio in the newsroom at *The Star*. It's a one-channel police band with a crystal control, but there's cross talk on the same frequency from the Windsor police and the National Guard. Windsor calls are routine and quiet – a barking dog, a car accident with no injuries. Detroit radio, on the other hand, is hot with riot information: looting and shooting. To Lindblad, it's quite a contrast, which shows the difference between Canada and the United States, and yet, riots aren't unknown in Canada.

Two days before the riot in Detroit, there's a small skirmish at a carnival in Wallaceburg in Kent County. Just after midnight, Friday, an angry mob of 75 young people swarms the midway. Described as a "violent nightmare," it's tame compared to Detroit. "Rioters," between the ages of 16 and 30, avenge the alleged beating of one of their friends by "carnies" earlier in the day. Wallaceburg police say the mob, "tore into the midway and ripped everything to pieces. They were carrying everything from chunks of pipe to bicycle chains." Armed with tear gas, 40 reinforcements from the Ontario Provincial Police restore order at 3:00 a.m. One loaded rifle is seized, and over $5,000 damage done to six games, before seven people are arrested and 27 charges laid, including rioting, possession of an offensive weapon, assault, willful damage and illegal consumption of alcohol by a minor. Three men are taken to hospital, one suffering a concussion and scalp lacerations. The others sustain cuts and bruises. The carnival is closed and sent on its way to prevent further outbreaks.

When the cases are heard in court on Monday, charges against two carnival workers are dismissed because they are defending themselves and their property. Charges against three local youth are remanded to August 8th. When the young men appear in court again, they're sentenced to six months in jail plus a $300 fine. One of the accused is only 19 years old. The incident prompts town council to ban carnivals and recommend that the Wallaceburg Police Department purchase equipment to control mobs. As riots go, it's small potatoes compared to Detroit.

At 6:00 p.m. Sunday, Canadian Dave Lane is heading down the John Lodge with his girlfriend, Eileen Zuccaro, and a couple of friends – Bob Paz and Diane. They were at the beach at Camp Dearborn north of Detroit, and are heading home. As they drive, they're amazed there is so little traffic. Eventually, they see smoke, turn the radio on, and can't believe their ears.

Paz lives with his parents on Livernois not far from the riot. His parents are elderly and alone, and the four friends go there to make sure everything is all right. The atmosphere is tense. Lane is at the front door armed with a baseball bat. Paz stands guard at the back door with a loaded bow and arrow. He steps onto the porch when he hears a loud noise in the alley next to the house. It's 2:00 a.m. and dark. He sees the shadowy figure of a man moving through the yard. Paz takes aim but, just before he fires, he realizes it's the janitor on his way home from work from the bakery on the corner. Shaken, Paz heads into the house and unstrings his bow. Nobody sleeps. They listen for gunshots. They watch the National Guard cruise the streets in half-tracks. The radio is on, and they listen to the play-by-play.

The vigil lasts until morning. Lane's girlfriend lives in Detroit, but he takes her back to Canada. He telephones the tunnel and is told that it's under heavy guard by police with machine guns. They drive past tanks parked on the side of the road. The freeways are closed, but police and National Guardsmen wave them through. There are trucks with smashed windows. At the border everything is quiet, but they have a tough time getting through. Americans are turned back. Because Lane is Canadian and the car has Ontario plates, they're finally allowed to cross. They spend the rest of the day in safety, watching the action on television.

Ron DiMenna and four of his buddies have a similar experience. At 7:30 p.m., Sunday, they're on Twelve Mile Road in Detroit at a neighbourhood bar called the Coral Gables. Detroit is a popular drinking spot for Canadians because the bars are open longer. In Ontario, the pubs close at midnight, but they're open until 2:00 a.m. on the American side and many watering holes offer Canadian dollars at par. DiMenna is a 24-year-old resident of Kingsville, Ontario, and he and his friends are looking for girls. They've just settled in for the evening when Michigan State Troopers burst in and close the place down. Police round up two more cars of Canadians and escort them on back roads toward the bridge. DiMenna figures the officers know exactly where Canadians hang out and are making checks throughout the city.

At Six Mile Road, two jeeps pick up the convoy with three National Guardsmen in each. The men are in uniform with side arms, rifles and a mounted machine gun. One jeep leads, using detours to avoid hot spots. At first, DiMenna can't see anything. It's quiet, and he wonders what all the fuss is about until he hears gunfire. Chatter on a walkie-talkie tells him that the tunnel to Canada is chaotic.

The convoy heads toward the bridge, which is already blocked by saw-horses. A dozen armed soldiers stand near a tank and another soldier leans against a .50 calibre machine gun. One trooper takes down the barrier and they drive through to Windsor. They immediately head for a friend's apartment on the eighth floor of a high rise on Goyeau Street where the view overlooks Detroit. They watch as tracer bullets streak the sky on the American side. DiMenna says the border remains closed but even when it opens, he doesn't go back for six to eight months, and then the trips are infrequent because they're not fun anymore.

Before the riot, people went over almost daily for shopping at the big downtown department stores. At Christmas, the windows in Hudson's and Kern's held huge festive displays much like the T. Eaton Company and Simpson's windows in Toronto. There were dances at the Surfside Dancehall on East Jefferson in Detroit where new recordings were released every Saturday night and, for music and theatre, there was the Fox, Olympia, Masonic Temple, Music Hall and Fisher.

For Garnet Fox and his family, driving to St. Clair Shores and back to visit friends in the suburbs is a regular event before the riot. It's a routine jaunt through Detroit, almost a mini-vacation but, on this trip, things are different. Fox is on his way home to Amherstburg in his old blue Chev station wagon. His wife and an elderly friend are in front, six kids in back. Some off-ramps have been closed and, as they drive under the pedestrian overpasses, people throw garbage cans, rocks and debris onto the road. Fox has to weave all over the highway to avoid hitting anything. At times, the smoke is so thick that it obstructs vision. Fox finally turns on the radio and learns that there's a riot and they're about to close the bridge. He thinks of turning back, but it's getting dark, he's close to the tunnel, and he figures he's committed.

As Fox nears Porter Street, he sees a car approaching on the other side of the median. A man is hanging out the window with a rifle or machine gun. Fox isn't sure which, but he isn't waiting to find out. His heart in his mouth, he orders the kids onto the floor and guns the motor as the two cars pass. Fox breathes again. As he nears the tunnel, a car full of men pulls in front and stops. The men get out. They're yelling, but the windows are closed, and Fox can't hear what they're saying. He doesn't want to hear. He pulls around, speeds up, and keeps going. "Canada never looks so good," he thinks as the blue station wagon clears the tunnel.

Fox's daughter, 11-year-old Vicki, says, "It's scarier and scarier" as they head downtown. "Seeing the whole city on fire is like watching the world come to an end." Vicki has lived all her life on King Street in Amherstburg. She has many black neighbours, but she's not familiar with prejudice or discrimination and can't understand the anger and bitterness. She doesn't appreciate the significance of the border, the difference between races, or between American and Canadian Blacks. Over the next few days, she watches the riot on television. If not for the drive through Detroit, she wouldn't have paid much attention.

Windsorites often cross the border on a Sunday evening to catch the boats which head down river to the amusement park on Boblo Island off Amherstburg on the Canadian side. Four Chatham teenagers are on such an evening, starting with dinner in downtown Detroit. They're halfway through their meal when a waiter tells them they'll have to leave. One teen, 18-year-old Jeff Beuglet says, "We just couldn't believe it." Beverley Kee agrees. "There isn't a car in sight. There were only a few Negroes walking down the street." The teens are parked seven blocks away and can't hail a cab, so they run back to their vehicle. It's just before curfew, and a police officer warns them to get off the street or he'll arrest them.

Barney Crichton knows how they feel. He caught the Amherstburg ferry to take his family to Boblo earlier in the day, but has to return around 4:00 p.m. when the island closes early. No reason is given, but Boblo caters to a large number of Americans, and officials are afraid for their safety, and their liability, even though they're reluctant to lose money.

When the curfew goes into effect, the loading docks for Boblo are closed. To be on the safe side, the captains decide not to return to Detroit. One boat anchors at Amherstburg, the other makes a brief stop for fuel at Dieppe Gardens at the foot of the main street in Windsor, then berths in Canadian waters with 30 crew members on board. A spokesman for the company says the boats will not run to the island amusement park until the curfew is lifted. It's Tuesday before they return to their berths, and Friday before they resume their regular runs. Because of the riot, Boblo suffers a 65 percent drop in attendance for the summer.

The riot is an amazing contrast for another group of Canadians. Juergen Hendel, Curly Ellis and George Mooney are ghosting along the American shore of Lake Huron in a Mark II sailboat called *Rakaia Three*. They're slowly heading home from the annual Sarnia To Alpena Yacht Race, a 165-mile sailboat regatta, finished the day before. They're just off Saginaw Bay in northern Michigan on a 40-mile stretch, travelling close-in. There's an offshore breeze and they can smell the pine trees on land. It's great to be alive and under sail.

The three friends have been celebrating another first in their class, but now Hendel and Ellis are below, catching some shut-eye. Mooney is at the helm, listening to tunes on a radio program called: *Night Flight 760* on "WJR – The Great Voice of the Great Lakes." The show is hosted by J. Roberts and, after awhile, the music gives way to talk. Mooney wakes his friends. "You've got to listen to this. I'm not sure what's going on, but there's trouble in Detroit." A reporter is on the scene. You can hear gunshots. "It's shocking," Hendel says. "Unbelievable," says Mooney. "It's a glorious night, without a care in the world and yet, this is going on." For the rest of the trip down the St. Clair River and across Lake St. Clair, the radio is their constant companion. When they finally reach the Detroit River, it's 2:00 p.m., Monday. They hug the Canadian shore, giving Belle Isle a wide berth. They're curious, but they don't want to be shot either. They can see smoke and fire, but aren't sure what they'll face down-river.

Sue Goerzen has a similar apprehension. She's American, originally from Oklahoma. She teaches family studies to grade 12 students at a school on Twelfth Street in the heart of the riot area. She's married to a Canadian and lives on her husband's homestead near Harrow, Ontario. School officials are trying to keep classes open in Detroit in the hope it will take black kids off the streets. Goerzen wants to go in anyway because she loves, and is devoted to, her students.

Police are inside the school when Goerzen arrives. The doors are locked and Goerzen has to show her ID before she's allowed in. Once inside, she's told to lock the door of her classroom. Attendance is poor and there's a great deal of tension. Goerzen knows that some teachers keep a steel rod in their desk for protection, but she doubts she'll need one. She has the trust and confidence of her students, and views them as her friends.

Goerzen talks about the riot to give students an understanding of the problem. Some favour looting, but she tries to dissuade them and keep them out of trouble. Goerzen is White, but she doesn't feel there's a colour bar. She has faith in her students, and in God. Her husband, Gerhard, shares that faith and encourages her to go to school if she must. When it's time to go home, 10 of Goerzen's students walk her to her car. It's their way of protecting her, but she doesn't go back for the duration.

Ivy Vander Zanden, 29, is visiting her mother in Windsor when the riot breaks out. She's Canadian, but lives and works in Detroit. She's a medical technologist at Grace Hospital between John R. and Brush near Beaubien. She knows the riot is on, but her sense of duty compels her to drive over anyway despite her mother's protests. She figures her home in Canada is closer to the hospital than the homes of her American co-workers in the suburbs, and she can probably get there faster and easier. Police are turning cars back from the border, but Vander Zanden convinces them that she provides an essential service and is needed at the hospital. They tell her not to stop for lights, traffic signals or even people; just head straight for the hospital and stay there. As soon as she leaves the tunnel, she realizes just how alone she really is. She says it's terrifying, the longest seven minute drive of her life. In one instant, the streets are deserted; the next, there are people looting and running. She's shaking by the time she arrives.

Vander Zanden spends the next five days at the hospital. She never leaves. Interns sleep on the floor or crash at desks in the auditorium. It's as if they're under siege. National Guardsmen are posted throughout the building, and there are patrols outside. Anyone entering or leaving has to show ID and only emergency patients are admitted. Some people are questioned and searched for weapons. Even lunch bags are opened. One-tenth of the staff make it to work and so, when Vander Zanden is finished blood testing in the lab, she helps feed patients, or works in housekeeping and the cafeteria. She also helps a 19-year-old black girl, a student nurse who is shaking and crying uncontrollably, demanding to speak with her mother who lives in Alabama. Vander Zanden figures she's having a nervous breakdown. They finally reach her mother on the telephone and they talk for a long time until she's calm. Vander Zanden never asks, but she believes the girl is afraid for her life, that police or Whites in the hospital might harm her.

In their off-hours, the staff watches the burning and looting from windows on the upper floors. Vander Zanden sees a black man run from a drug store with his arms full of loot. A police officer in riot gear raises a rifle to his shoulder and shouts, "Stop or I'll shoot." Oh, my God, she thinks, they're going to kill that man. It brings goose bumps to her flesh. The man doesn't stop, but the officer doesn't shoot. He lets him go.

At times, nurses crawl past windows on hands and knees. They smoke cigarettes in closets, sitting on the floor to avoid being shot. They congregate on the roof to eat their lunch, catch a few rays, and watch what's happening, until a helicopter hovers overhead. A police officer on a bull-horn shouts, "Clear the roof, or we'll shoot." They all head downstairs in a hurry. When it's over, they're shocked at the devastation in the streets and can't imagine how it happened.

When it's time for Layne Katzman to go to work, she is reluctant, but she has a clause in her contract that stipulates she'll be available during emergencies. Katzman is a microbiologist at Henry Ford Hospital on West Grand Boulevard. She lives in Windsor and, to make it easier, her boss sends a car to escort her across the border. She presents her ID at the hospital, and walks past armed soldiers who guard the front doors, bayonets fixed. Katzman says the hospital is a madhouse. The emergency room is full of shooting victims and there's terror in the eyes of the patients. Some stare, some cry and some vent their anger. There's a rumour that a sniper is loose in the hospital, which adds to the paranoia, a feeling of doom. Katzman stays at her post and does her job. She knows that no one is after her, but she is afraid that rioters might find their way to her office or that she could be held hostage. There's so much craziness, she figures anything can happen. When her work is done, Katzman is relieved to be heading home, even though she realizes she'll have to return the next day. She feels threatened, and hopes that this is as close as she'll come to a war zone.

As a chief technologist with the American Red Cross, Bernice Carlan is also needed at work. A Canadian living in Windsor, she has a special form attached to her green card which allows her to cross the border in emergencies. There are three cars at the tunnel when she arrives, but she's the only one with a permit and the only one allowed through. She isn't aware that the border is closed. "Lady, are you sure you know what you're doing?" the guard asks. "Yes," she says, but begins to have doubts as soon as she clears customs. The National Guard stops her as she attempts to drive up Brush. She's re-routed to Woodward, Detroit's main street. "It's safer," a Guardsman says. Carlan is afraid of guns, and thinks she'll faint when the soldier approaches her car. She keeps her cool and does what she's told. She parks next to her building and runs in the front door. She intends to be home before dark.

In her mid '30s, Carlan has a 13-year-old daughter at home who cries each time her mother leaves the house. She's convinced that something terrible is going to happen, that her mother is going to be shot. Carlan says there's near panic on the first day of the riot when there aren't enough nurses to do the job. If not for Canadians, the clinic could have been in trouble. To appease her daughter, Carlan car pools with other Windsor women who work in Detroit. After all, there's safety in numbers.

Despite her daughter's fears, Carlan enjoys her job and the team pulls together. Black workers have a tougher time gaining access to the building, but there's no tension between races. "Everybody says hello to everybody else." Carlan is used to racial prejudice and doesn't think about it. Her husband calls her "Dark-White." She's Ukrainian and her family lived on the east side of Drouillard Road in Windsor. She says the principal at Walkerville Collegiate made it clear they were from the wrong side of the tracks. When they moved to a new neighbourhood, a petition was circulated against her father to prevent a "foreigner" living on the street.

During five days of rioting, blood is collected at mobile clinics in Dearborn and sent downtown for processing. It's a frantic job. The blood has to be sorted by type and matched with local hospitals, which require transfusions. Two armed police officers are constantly on the run, delivering blood where it's needed most. Emergency facilities at Detroit Receiving and Memorial hospitals are open to riot victims, and hundreds of people are treated for heart attacks, gunshots, knife wounds, cuts and abrasions from broken glass. To its credit, the Red Cross collects over 5,000 pints of blood. The normal amount is 1,800.

Carlan receives a commendation for her service from General George Marshall, the head of the American Red Cross. A week after the riot, shop girls and lunch counter workers return to the downtown core. Most are Black and they call Carlan "Mrs. Lab" because they know where she works, but don't know her by name. They're happy she's okay.

Heroic efforts are common by people who are committed to their jobs in the border community. Bill Jackson is caught in the riot, but not by surprise, by choice. As with the Windsor firefighters, it's because of a debt owed.

Jackson is a Windsor police constable and fingerprint technician. He offers his services and volunteers in response to news reports that the Detroit police are backed up and overworked. They're under stress, virtually camped in their offices, slaves to their job, unable to go home for a

When the Identification Branch of the Detroit Police can't keep up, Windsor constable Bill Jackson offers to identify hundreds of people being arrested. The prisoners have to be fingerprinted, cross-referenced for previous convictions, and their information filed. Photo by Spike Bell. Courtesy of Bill Jackson.

rest. Jackson goes over on his own time, on his own recognizance, without thought for personal safety. In so doing, he goes above and beyond the call of duty, eventually winning a medal and praise for his involvement.

Well before the riot, Jackson graduated from the fingerprinting course at the Institute of Applied Science, and was still taking courses to further his career. An avid police officer in his early '30s, Jackson was on a quest for knowledge, and just couldn't get enough. Always willing to learn, he knew that Detroit had an extensive library with information that he couldn't access anywhere else and so, just prior to the riot, he approached the department for extra books, equipment and expertise to continue in his chosen field. If the Detroit police didn't have what he was looking for, they searched until they found it. Jackson met several people on the force who supported his quest for knowledge. In fact, the guys were so good to him, so helpful and accommodating, that he was proud to return their favour when the riot broke out. "I felt obligated, so I made the telephone call and they were more than happy to have me." His new friends were intrigued by his offer and the top brass gave the okay.

Every day at 5:00 p.m., four plainclothes officers, armed with shotguns and rifles, drive across the border to pick Jackson up at the tunnel entrance and take him to the police station at 1300 Beaubien Street. It's Jackson's own personal bodyguard. They're in an unmarked car and they travel past National Guardsmen, personnel carriers, armoured cars, barbed wire and barricades. Generally, the officers flash their badges and have no difficulty getting through but, one time, somebody phoned to warn about a car with five men armed to the teeth. The group is stopped and has some fast explaining before they're allowed to continue. When they arrive in Detroit, they drop Jackson off in the basement of police headquarters where another armed guard escorts him to the fourth floor offices of the Identification Branch. There, Jackson works diligently for eight hours or more, before being escorted back home.

Fingerprinting and classification is tedious. It requires precision and detail. "It's like needing glasses and trying to read a newspaper without them. It's awful taxing on your eyes." Jackson has an advantage, though. Because he's from a relatively small police department, he's done all aspects of the work. The Detroit police are specialists. One man dusts for fingerprints, or takes the print, another classifies it, and yet another files it. Jackson figures it takes seven American officers to do the work of one man in Windsor where the workload isn't as heavy.

Detroit police officers are surprised and pleased that Jackson is so versatile. Initially, they watch him like a hawk because, if he misfiles one card, it could take years to find it again. There are thousands of fingerprint records in dozens of metal cabinets around the office, but Jackson quickly picks up the procedure and is soon unsupervised. He relieves each officer for an hour or two, which allows them to sleep at their desk or grab some sandwiches and coffee. Jackson spells officers who've been on the job longest. Some are double and triple shifting.

While Jackson does most jobs, he never actually fingerprints living suspects, even though he has done that in Canada. His job is to categorize fingerprints for distinguishing marks, search the files and then, if a match is found, check for fictitious names, previous convictions or criminal records. Every card has a series of fingerprints with symbols and numbers on the top, which describe the characteristics of each. It's a complex system, not unlike shorthand. The symbols describe whorls, bifurcations, islands, indents, scars, arches, loops and ridges on the finger, and the numbers correspond to the amount of each characteristic. Jackson simply takes his sample and compares it with 1,000 other file cards, which describe that type of fingerprint. He usually narrows his search by concentrating on an unusual or striking feature like a scar, before getting down to specific details in the match. Jackson says experienced officers can isolate six or seven similar prints within minutes and then, using a small magnifying glass mounted on a tripod, they find the exact match. Fingerprints are like snowflakes with no two alike. The natural characteristics never change and they're formed before we're born.

Initially, Jackson is given 1,500 prints to match. He's led to believe that the FBI returned them because they were too blurry. If no match is found, Jackson assumes the individual has no prior arrests or record, the card is classified and becomes a new entry in the file. The police keep them for future reference, even though charges are never laid in some cases. It's illegal, but Jackson doesn't think about that. "All I know is that they would set a big pile of them down in front of me and I would go to work." He turns the matches over to the supervisor and the department takes it from there.

As Jackson makes new contacts in the department, he's assigned to jobs with greater responsibility. One task is to fingerprint bodies in the morgue. A gruesome assignment, but it's all in a day's work for an experienced officer. The morgue is several blocks from the precinct and Jackson heads into the empty streets where he can hear gunfire and see troops. He zigzags from doorway to doorway with a wary eye on rooftops and windows, trying to avoid being shot. He never sees anybody, never actually comes under fire, but he isn't taking chances. As a police officer from a neighbouring country, Jackson has no official status. He's in civilian clothes, unarmed and feeling vulnerable. If anything happens, he's on his own, just another person on the streets.

At the morgue, bodies are tucked away in metal cabinets or placed on gurneys and slabs. They're suicides, murders, accidental deaths, plus the overflow from the riot. Jackson is assigned to corpses with no identification, and no way of notifying the next of kin. He takes their fingerprints using a sensitized inkless paper, which he carefully rolls onto the dead person's digit. The finger is soft and deteriorating and he gently, but firmly, presses it into the indented portion of a cadaver's spoon. A chemical reaction on the paper causes the fingerprint to appear automatically, much like a photo from an instamatic camera. Jackson numbers the picture to correspond with the individual's toe-tag. He's pleased when he makes a positive ID and can name a body. At least the family will know what happened.

Jackson spends four hours in the morgue on two separate occasions, taking 20 sets of prints. Fingerprinting doesn't take long, but Jackson doesn't work steadily. He spends some time in the fresh air. "It was eerie. I didn't like being in there by myself … If you've ever been in a morgue, it's not the nicest place to be, especially if the air conditioning isn't working."

Throughout his sojourn in Detroit, Jackson's wife and teenage son are at home watching the riot on television. Despite his assurances, they're petrified that something terrible might happen. Jackson never thinks or worries about it "until one night we're sitting on the fourth floor, doing some work right next to a window and, all of a sudden, there are gunshots going off and the P.A. system: 'everybody hit the floor!'" No windows are broken, but they spend a tense 15 to 20 minutes before they can resume work. Jackson isn't sure if the building is actually under fire. "All I know is, we're ordered down and down we went." He doesn't talk about it until a week later when he tells his wife what happened. That's when he begins to realize just how far he'd stuck his neck out, and how close he might have come.

The Windsor Police Department can't sanction, condone or support officer volunteers, but it doesn't object either. Charlie Weston is an inspector in charge of Number Two Precinct and he says workman's compensation and the city's liability insurance won't cover volunteers in the event of injury or death and so, it's too risky for the department to get involved. Besides, Windsor police aren't armed to the same extent as their American neighbours. They don't have enough riot gear, or gas masks, and they have their own jobs in Windsor. No other Canadian officers volunteer, but some head across the border in their spare time to see what's going on. Jackson says the men are torn about going over. "They wanted to go, but they didn't want to go. I decided I was going, regardless of whether they liked it or not."

Bill Jackson, left, receives the Detroit Police Commissioner's Citation from Detroit Police Superintendent Eugene Ruter, right, while Windsor Police Chief Carl Farrow, centre, and other officers in the background look on. Courtesy of Bill Jackson.

It's a major commitment. In the course of a week, Jackson puts in 40 hours of work on his regular shift in Windsor and then another 60 hours in Detroit, often cruising on four hours of sleep a night. For his efforts, Jackson is called into the office of his immediate supervisor in Windsor. It's September 28, 1967. He figures he's done something wrong, but he's told that he has an important assignment. He's to meet Windsor Police Chief Carl Farrow in his office at 8:30 the following morning. He's to wear civilian clothes, and drive the chief to Detroit. When Jackson arrives on the fourth floor of the police station on Beaubien, he's pleasantly surprised. He's greeted by all the men with whom he worked during the riot, and is presented with the Detroit Police Commissioner's Citation for valuable, outstanding service. It's the 108th medal ever given out, and it's the first time in 100 years that it has been presented to anyone other than a member of the Detroit Police Department. It's a real honour.

There's a big bash at the Stroh's Brewery and the Americans even ask

Jackson with his citation and medal, a small gold-coloured octagon, engraved with the picture of a police officer. The medal is attached to a ribbon with the colours of the Detroit Police Department – alternating stripes of blue, gold, blue, which compliment Windsor's gold, blue, gold. Courtesy of Bill Jackson.

Jackson if he'd like a job. They're prepared to offer him a green card and citizenship if he accepts. Farrow intervenes and says there's no way Jackson can stay in Detroit. As Jackson put it, "I said thanks, but no thanks. I'm quite happy where I am."

When they arrive back in Windsor, the chief keeps Jackson's medal. For the next week, he shows it to everyone who goes by his office. "He was just beaming with it," Jackson says, smiling. On October 6, the young constable is called to a meeting of the Windsor Police Commission where he's officially thanked for his contribution to the Detroit force "which brought credit to the Windsor Police Department." He's also given a cheque for $100. It's an honorarium, a small token of esteem.

Meanwhile, the situation in Detroit has raised the question of just how well Windsor is prepared to quell a riot. It's a thorny issue, a dilemma for Police Chief Carl Farrow, Magistrate Gordon R. Stewart and Judge Bruce Macdonald. They're the three members of the police commission and they're reviewing the adequacy of their emergency equipment and officer training. The commission eventually authorizes the purchase of additional gas masks and canisters, riot clubs, high-powered rifles with telescopic sights, shotguns and a newly-developed helmet which provides protection to the ears, neck and face as well as the head. The department also buys a new weapon called mace. It's a non-lethal gas to control personal attacks. Farrow says the materials are to be issued in the case of an emergency, and officers will be trained in their use.

The commission also recommends that additional courses be provided at the Ontario Police College. A seminar on crowd control is offered in the spring and four officers go, so they can pass information on to other officers in the department. The Windsor police also work in conjunction with the OPP to report on crowd control, eventually recommending that a local plan be developed in the event of an emergency. It includes the closure of service stations, liquor stores, taverns and gun stores. It also imposes border restrictions.

Police preparedness is an important concern, but for some members of the black community it doesn't go far enough. Racial discrimination always lingers below the surface in Windsor, but it intensifies during the riot in Detroit and is brought home to one Windsor resident, in particular. Gale Bost is caught in the riot in a frustrating and frightening way, through no fault of her own. She isn't looking for trouble, but it finds her anyway. Bost is Black and she complains that white males yell at her during the riot. "Your house is on fire. You'd better go home." It's just one example of racial prejudice and it upsets her.

Bost wants something done about "attitude," concerned that Whites blame Blacks whenever an incident occurs. They don't consider the frustrations and anxieties that build up to create the situation, so it's no wonder that Blacks react. Bost says she's proud of being Black, despite having to fight for decent jobs, houses and education beyond grade eight. She's afraid that the violence will continue until Blacks realize equality and until Whites realize that Blacks are every bit as good as they are. She's so incensed about her situation that she writes a letter to the editor in the Windsor paper, imploring the white community to do some serious soul-searching.

To put it in perspective, *Star* reporter Ken Campbell talks to a black man in Detroit who says simply that, "you have to be a Negro to understand why the riot started." The man says it's frustrating trying to find a job when the colour of your skin is against you. It's hard buying food when you know that the prices at the white stores in the white districts are cheaper than the prices in the white stores in the black slums. "It's the kind of thing a white man wouldn't even notice." The situation may not be as severe in Windsor, but there are instances of a subtle form of racism that the black community would like addressed, and the sooner, the better.

As the riot continues, Windsor commuters express their increasing bitterness toward Blacks for disrupting their lifestyle, preventing them from their jobs and confronting them with racial tension and fear. As the frustrations become more evident, *Star* editorialist Pat Whealan tries to deal with it. "It was Negroes who did the rioting," he writes, "but you can no more blame Negroes in the mass, than you can condemn all white men as murderers because Hitler and his Nazis were White." Whealan says a comparatively small number of Blacks actually participate in rioting in Detroit. They are the uneducated and poor at a time when the United States is rich and booming. Their hatred of slums is building, reaching intolerable levels. Whealan implores Whites not to see all Blacks as rioters. He's afraid that stereotypes are being reinforced and perpetuated, rather than dissolved through understanding. It's a situation that catches all Windsorites, whether they're aware of it or not, in the Detroit riots.

Chapter 5

The Border Is Closed

For most people in Windsor, July 23 is a normal summer Sunday with church attendance, swim meets, backyard barbeques and picnics in the park but, by afternoon, the reality of racial turmoil is literally burned into the Canadian consciousness. At 2:00 p.m., the first smudges of black smoke in Detroit are visible from Windsor. As darkness falls, five major fires burn several blocks apart; their flames reflect orange and pink off the clouds.

All afternoon, Windsorites congregate in waterfront parks on the border to watch the smoke and listen for sounds of the riot. Teenage boys sit on the hoods of their cars or lean against break walls as they hug their girlfriends protectively. They gossip with picnickers and fishermen, point and exclaim every time they see a new disturbance. In Canada, the riot is a uniting force, a powerful draw for a shocked people with a morbid fascination – a horror on one hand and yet an excitement that something significant is happening in their own backyard.

The riot hits home for Wilfred Ouellette, sales manager for National Grocers in Windsor. His brother-in-law, Don Chauvin, operates a grocery store at Grand River and Stanley, near Olympia in Detroit. Six weeks ago, two black men robbed the store and stuck a gun into Chauvin's ribs. In the struggle, Chauvin was shot in both legs. Ouellette says he won't be out of hospital for at least two months. In the meantime, the grocery store is boarded up. To Ouellette, it's just another example of trouble in Detroit.

Windsor residents at the border can see the fires burning on the American side as the riot continues in Detroit. Courtesy of *The Windsor Star.*

Surprisingly, life goes on in Windsor within sight and sound of the turmoil. In Dieppe Gardens, a small crowd spends a tranquil evening at an outdoor band concert with a panoramic view of Detroit. Guests at a banquet in the Skyline Room on the second floor of the Cleary Auditorium also watch as Detroit burns. Carloads of people cruise Riverside Drive hoping to see something. By nightfall, there's a traffic jam from Ouellette to Huron Line. People crowd vantage points at the foot of Caron Avenue where leaping tongues of orange flame burst forth on the American side and then settle back into a dull rosy glow on the horizon. It's reminiscent of other riots during "the summer of fire in the U.S." but, this time, Windsor has a front row seat.

Windsor resident Bob Steele is on the Ambassador Bridge, watching people flee Detroit like refugees. Cars stream across the border, laden with bags, boxes, mattresses and furniture; and kids are piled into the back on heaps of clothing. Everything is hastily thrown in or roped down. An impressionable young man, Steele can't believe it.

One anxious young person is 23-year-old Carol Zeni. She's waiting for her 73-year-old father who is returning from a trip to St. Thomas, Ontario. Zeni is American and she wants to head her father off before he goes back to the U.S. Zeni lives in Highland Park, a suburb on Detroit's east side which is only 15 blocks from the riot. The nearest fire is only two blocks away. Zeni says they're the only white family in the area and, when trouble started, they spent hours in their home, afraid to go outside. During a lull in the action, the family packed up and fled. With her five-month-old baby in her arms, Zeni screens every car. Her other baby, an older sister named Juliana, a German Shepherd, and a cat remain in the car. There's an assortment of knives in the glove box for protection. Eventually, Zeni finds her father. They spend the night in a Windsor hotel and return to their home in daylight.

Doreen Johnson's car is also loaded to the roof. She's Black, and she's had it with the United States of America. She can't stand the fear and suspicion against her race. Johnson is one of the last people through the border on her way to her parent's home near Buxton, just outside Chatham, in Kent County. That's where she stays for the duration. The riot has changed the way she views Detroit and, eventually, she comes back to Canada for good. When she arrives at her father's place, he telephones an elderly relative in Detroit, asking if he should come and get her. The answer is no. The woman has lived state side for over 60 years and she's not going to let a riot disturb her now.

Many hotel rooms on the Canadian side are already full of Americans. It's estimated that seven percent of middle-class Blacks, 15 years of age or older, leave Detroit for safer locations. The owner of a Detroit apartment shows up at his cottage near Harrow. His building in the U.S. was destroyed by fire and he's winterizing his cottage, planning to stay in Canada permanently. He's disgusted by the riot, doesn't feel safe in his own country anymore. He says that some black people try to get ahead, improve their situation, but are restricted by others who are jealous and destroy everything. Some people say they want jobs, but then they won't work. He complains that a number of people look for work at his apartment building, stay for the day, but once they receive their pay, never come back. He says those kind of people create problems and make it harder for everybody else.

Pat Walker has an amusing anecdote about the riot. She's secretary of the Windsor Clippers, a senior 'B' team with the Ontario Lacrosse Association. They're scheduled to play an afternoon game in Orangeville on Sunday, and they're waiting at the bus depot in Windsor for a couple of players from Mount Clemens, Michigan. The Americans slept in but, under league rules, if a team shows up short-handed or late, the group is fined a dollar a minute until the full team arrives. The Clippers are an hour late and face a $60 fine. At this point, they're not aware that a riot has occurred in Detroit. Later, when Walker writes league officials to explain the team's tardiness, she mentions that a couple of players came from Mount Clemens, Michigan, and adds, "as you know, it was the first day of the riot." She didn't lie. She never said the players were delayed because of the riot, but the league waives the fine anyway. As an amateur team, the Clippers had no extra money, and had to sell tickets just to pay for the bus. To this day, Pat Walker feels she saved her team!

There are many interesting stories about the riot and its affect on Canadians. Debbie Gascoyne and her friend Nickie spend Sunday afternoon at Colchester Beach near Harrow. They're enjoying the cool summer

Early morning on West Grand River. Sniper fire pins down police and army units. There's nothing to do, but wait it out. Courtesy of B.G. "Spike" Bell.

breeze from Lake Erie when a dozen black people claim part of the beach. It's not unusual. Many black settlers came to Colchester in the 1800s and their ancestors are still there. Many black families from Detroit also own cottages along the beach. In this case, though, they spread a blanket, turn on a portable radio and then sit quietly, listening intently. Gascoyne knows something's wrong. Usually, when people come to the beach, they're in a holiday mood, but nobody in this party is running, swimming, playing ball or even dressed for fun. There's such a stillness that it gives Gascoyne a strange feeling. She can't figure it out until she heads back to the car, turns on the radio and hears the first reports of the riot.

For the next few days, Colchester Beach is a popular spot as the clandestine meeting place of smugglers. Rowboats, laden with boxes of merchandise, pull up on the sand in the dark. The contraband is for sale to cottagers, "no questions asked." It's a cheap place to pick up a radio, TV or small appliance.

For three hours on Sunday afternoon, the Bell Telephone Company in Windsor brings in staffers who are normally off-duty. The phone lines to Detroit are jammed. Most calls are to relatives and friends from pay phones as word filters down that a riot is underway. It's a stressful, frantic time, knowing that loved ones may be in danger, but not being able to get through. Because of the backlog, operators are eventually told to take emergency calls only. D.A. Noble is the district traffic manager for Bell and he says direct dialling equipment is taxed to the limit on Sunday and Monday with over 175,000 calls, almost triple the normal number. Long distance calls dialled by an operator double to 15,000 on Monday and Tuesday and continue above average on Wednesday and Thursday. People are encouraged to dial direct, rather than tie up an operator. Telephone service doesn't return to normal until Friday.

About 32 kilometres outside of Windsor on the shores of Lake St. Clair, there's a small town called Belle River. It's a sleepy little farm and cottage community, and Bill Taylor has lived there all his life. On Sunday, he looks out his window and sees carload after carload of black men and women passing his home, heading toward the lake. "There are at least 50 cars." He considers it unusual, but doesn't give it much thought until he hears about the riot. He figures they're all heading to the Belle River Surf Club or

Joe Louis' place where the former world heavy-weight boxing champion is a familiar sight, jogging along the railway tracks while training for the title. He's set up a private resort where middle-class Blacks from Detroit can get away from it all. They're doctors, lawyers and teachers who enjoy fancy cars and fine clothes. They like dinners and dancing and that's exactly what the Surf Club has to offer.

Just east of the Ruscom River, on Surf Club Drive off old Tecumseh Road, the club features 184 acres, lots of sandy beachfront, and a large bar in a 26-unit motel. As a focus of high society life for Blacks, it's a reaction to Whites-only clubs in Detroit. Some Belle River residents have been invited to the club for drinks or fishing, but there's still a lot of secrecy about the place. Members just want to be left alone to enjoy family and friends. Jim Travis is a regular, and he says there's nothing special going on, but admits that many members congregate there on Sunday. The owner of a gas station on Highway Two says carloads of Blacks ask him for directions to the club. Fed up, after the 15th time, he sends them south in the wrong direction.

At 9:00 p.m., border crossings at the bridge and tunnel are severed except for police, fire and emergency vehicles. There's a rumour that they're shut down for political reasons after two youth in a car careen past firefighters at the station on Pitt Street. One boy yells, "You're not doing anything now, but you soon will be. Windsor's going to be next." Truth is, a curfew is on in Detroit in an effort to quell the riot. All public areas are closed and many people are turned back by Canadian customs at the request of U.S. immigration. American citizens are still allowed in to the United States, but they're warned to steer clear of riot areas. Buses, travelling from Detroit to Windsor are running late because drivers must be checked by police.

On Monday morning, thousands of Windsor commuters are turned back as they go to jobs in Detroit. American officials enforce the ban, but Canadians merely warn travellers that they won't be allowed in. Al Broderick is a lieutenant with Windsor police, and he talks to motorists at the bridge, turning back those who just want a closer look. As one official says, "We're letting in Americans and emergency people only." That means doctors, nurses and newsmen. Tunnel buses aren't running, and

The military style jeeps of the National Guard are in sharp contrast to the Ford Mustang and the boy on a bicycle on July 24 in Detroit. Courtesy of J.A. "Pete" McGarvey.

some people are angry that they can't go over. "The only people we are permitting to leave Detroit are those who have planned vacations and those on business. Otherwise, they don't get out." Many families, visiting friends or relatives for the weekend, are stranded, unable to leave.

Nine tourists are turned back as they try to enter the United States, including three South Americans and six French who are on a See America Tour. It's almost 7:00 a.m. and they're heading to Chicago. They're forced to backtrack at their own expense, to Leamington, a Canadian town about 45 minutes away from Windsor, where they catch the 4:30 ferry to Sandusky, Ohio. Frindel Raymond of Strasbourg, France, says "Everything was wonderful until today." He wanted to see an automobile factory and the Detroit Institute of the Arts. He also wanted to see the riot. He was in a similar situation between the Arabs and French in Morocco and he wanted to observe relations between the races in Detroit.

Many Canadians bypass Detroit, using ferries on the St. Clair River at Sombra, Port Lambton and Walpole Island. Port Lambton reports a record of 1,500 vehicles, 20 times more than usual. The Bluewater Bridge in Sarnia also reports more business. Normally, the bridge handles 7,000 cars, but 14,000 are expected. Customs offices generally close at 5:00 p.m., but stay open 24 hours a day to handle all the trucks. Sarnia buses connect from Detroit, Toronto and Hamilton.

In the meantime, Windsor is a haven for other "refugees." Twenty-six large boats dock at Anchor-In-Marina. There are 15 more at the Rendezvous. Some are worth $40,000 and are equipped with air conditioning, colour TV and well-stocked bars. They come from Keane's and Sinbad's in Michigan. One belongs to a Detroit fireman. He drops off the boat in Canada, and drives home with a friend to fight fires that forced him to move. As one boater explains, "Let's just say I'm taking a vacation." Many black families also use their boats to flee. They stay with friends or live on their vessels in snug Canadian harbours. Five Canadian boats from Chatham, enroute to Detroit, seek anchorage at Adam Martini's Marina in Windsor until the strife is over. Other travellers are also displaced. There are rumours that rats are swimming across the border and invading Windsor to escape fires in America.

Jerry Provencher is an American student at the University of Windsor and he stays on campus where he listens to the crackling sound of rifle fire. It's a different world being safe in an academic institution free to do whatever he pleases, while martial law is declared in his hometown only a mile away. Provencher contacts his wife by phone, then bunks down in residence. The school has no problem with their new guest. He can stay as long as he likes.

When Gordie Howe, star of the Detroit Red Wings hockey team, hears of the riot, he cancels a speaking engagement in Toronto and flies back to Detroit to get his wife and four kids out of the riot-torn city. "The riot is only three miles from our house now and that's too close," he says as he heads for summer camp and safety.

A carnival air persists in Windsor. It's like a circus, or drive-in, as hundreds of motorists and pedestrians cram riverside parks with lawn chairs, beer and 'burgers to watch the show. Ken Hall is a reporter with *The Windsor Star* and he says it's weird. People listen for gunshots as a city collapses in front of their eyes. The only traffic in Detroit is fire engines, with soldiers and machine guns sandbagged in back. Helicopters with searchlights and C-130 military transports fly above, laden with troops to be bivouacked in a military encampment in Grand Circus Park and Cadillac Square downtown.

Windsor taverns do a brisk business as thirsty patrons fill bar stools and tables. The only conversation concerns the riot. Other businesses aren't so lucky. The Windsor Chamber of Commerce says, "Things are definitely slower all over the city." Shows at the Top Hat and the Metropole Supper Clubs are cancelled. One show is staged at the Killarney Castle, but only eight people show up. Usually, 75 percent of the crowd is American. At the Elmwood Casino on Dougall Road, Diahann Carrol was supposed to sing, but she's replaced by the Lindsay Sapphire Dancers and comic magician Don Allen. Manager John Brezsnyak is concerned that Americans still won't come and he'll lose business. A similar problem exists across the river. Conferences have been cancelled, and hotels are feeling the pinch. The Pontchartrain loses $50,000 for the months of August and September.

Windsor industries are also hit by the crisis. Chrysler Canada sends 525 workers home only three hours after the beginning of their shift. Parts, to be shipped from Detroit, are held up because of traffic restrictions at the border. They finally arrive in time for the afternoon shift. The GM Trim Plant fears a similar slowdown. Ford and McKinnon Industries are not affected because they're shut down for summer vacation.

Freight still comes through the railway tunnel, and ferries are not affected, but truckloads are carefully inspected by U.S. customs. Canadian trucks only proceed with a police escort in convoys of four and five. Still, truckers are hit by rocks and bottles, roll up their windows and lock their doors. "I just kept going, praying to God nothing would force me to stop." Drivers slow for red lights and signs, but then drive through, one hand on the air horn.

Two British warships – the missile destroyer *HMS Hampshire* and the supply ship *HMS Tidepool* – are scheduled to stop in Detroit for public tours in a gesture of goodwill. Concerned about security, the captains dock in Canada where their vessels attract thousands of visitors. By Thursday, they're in company with a U.S. Coast Guard training vessel, which was supposed to stay in Detroit to provide shore leave to its sailors, but also opts for the tranquility of Windsor.

This street scene in Detroit on July 25 is deceptively calm. The photo could have been taken at any other time than during the worst riot in 1960's Detroit. Courtesy of J.A. "Pete" McGarvey.

On Thursday, August 3, two vessels with the Royal Canadian Navy cancel a three-day visit to Detroit. Instead, the *HMCS Nipigon* and *HMCS Kootenay* tie up at Dieppe Gardens in Windsor and open for tours. There's supposed to be a USO party Thursday night at the Veteran's Memorial Building in Detroit, a Navy League Ball at Grosse Isle Friday night, and a reception at Mayor Cavanagh's home on Saturday, but those events are cancelled. To compensate, the crews tour Windsor factories, Hiram Walker's Distillery and attend a series of baseball games before they head to Sarnia on Sunday. The two ships are part of Canada's Centennial and are on a visit to 32 Ontario ports with a courtesy call to Detroit. The vessels are equipped with anti-aircraft guns and a nine-ton Sea King helicopter. The equipment is impressive, and prompts wry comments from Windsorites: "Where were you when we needed you?"

As a result of these disruptions, Windsor residents are thankful when border restrictions are eased and Detroit struggles back to normal on Tuesday, July 25. Generally, about 5,000 commuters cross the border each day to go to work, but most have not seen Detroit since they left their jobs on Friday. Grim and shocking sights confront them as they filter back.

Khaki-clad militia look strangely out of place with rifles or machine guns slung over their shoulders. They patrol in front of Hudson's and protect car lots from looters. They're also stationed on rooftops. Barricades block entrances to side streets and police cruisers snake through rubble-filled alleys. Just off Grand Circus Park, there's a plundered jewellery store, a burned-out gas station and the still-glowing shell of a large furniture store. Many people travel to their jobs only to find that they're closed or destroyed.

Three buses are in operation by 7:15 a.m. to carry passengers downtown. Most buses are half-full with about 15 people each. A company spokesman says, "Everything is back to normal," but it isn't true. As the buses travel through riot-stripped sections of the city, a subtle change is taking place. Prior to the riot, commuters on buses say hello to one another and talk on the way to work. After, they don't. White commuters sit stony-faced and mind their own business. They stiffen when a black man gets on. As one rider suggests, "You never know whether they'll do you in with a knife or something." It takes a long time for scars to heal. Larry Affleck is a tunnel bus driver and he says, "I've been shuttling people over to Detroit and then taking them back again a couple of trips later." Affleck doesn't blame them for going home. "They couldn't pay me to go there."

Jennifer Bondy says her dad, Mark, never misses a day of work and he's not about to let a mere riot stand in his way. Bondy lives in River Canard just outside Windsor, but works as a bodyman at Downtown Collision in Detroit. After he crosses the border, he drives down Michigan Avenue, the only car in sight. Two tanks bear down on him, so he makes a quick U-turn and beelines back to the border. Jennifer never lets her father live it down. The story of his stubbornness becomes a standard family joke.

Another commuter is Michael Taylor from Belle River. He works at Austin Engineering on the fifth floor of a building on the corner of Grand Boulevard and Second, about ten blocks away from Twelfth Street. He parks his car in Windsor and takes the bus across, but still has to walk partway. Fearing snipers, he makes his way uptown, flitting from doorway to doorway, dodging military jeeps with soldiers and live ammunition. The offices of General Motors are next door, and are heavily guarded by three helmeted soldiers, two with M-1s, the other with a side arm.

Produce dealers and florists in Windsor and Chatham breathe easier with the opening of the border. Some vegetable markets close when supplies of fruit and vegetables from the U.S. are barred from entering Canada. Local merchants are afraid of a shortage of watermelons, plums, oranges, cantaloupes and raspberries if the trucks can't get through. Detroit markets are afraid to buy fruit and vegetables to supply the Canadian market for fear that looters will steal the goods. Much of the produce for Windsor comes through Detroit, but the Union Produce Terminal at the Eastern Market is destroyed by fire. Silverstein's Produce on Chatham Street in Windsor is buying citrus from Toronto, shipped from the United States through Niagara Falls.

A group of 50 vegetable growers from River Canard, near Windsor, is also relieved when the border returns to normal. They've been shipping produce to the Detroit market for years and rely on it for their livelihood. Don Bondy is one of those growers. He has 40 acres of peppers, parsley, onions, radishes and celery, much of it ready for market. Every two days, Bondy and his father, Dan, vie with 1,000 other vegetable growers from Michigan, Ohio, and Ontario for a chance to sell to corner stores, or wholesalers who sell to hospital, restaurant and grocery stores. The two Bondys usually go to market at 2:00 a.m. to get a stall, but some dealers camp in their trucks overnight to be there first in the morning.

It's hard to cross the border because of the curfew in Detroit, so some Canadian dealers call their buyers and tell them to meet on the highway halfway between Port Huron and Detroit. Windsor growers drive over the Bluewater Bridge at Sarnia and down on the American side to make the exchange, transferring their produce from one truck to the other on the side of the road. In Bondy's case, he and his father are determined to make it to market and, on the second day, decide to take their chances. They load their two-ton truck and talk their way across the border by playing dumb, saying that they didn't know there was a curfew and insisting that they have to make a delivery of perishable goods.

When they park at the market, the doors of their rig are flung open by two National Guardsmen with rifles and fixed bayonets. They poke their guns under the arms of the two Canadians, tell them not to move, and ask what they're doing in Detroit. Don Bondy doesn't breathe when he feels

Gutted buildings stretch for 100 blocks on both sides of 12th Street. Firefighters were forced to withdraw to wait for police at the height of the riot. Courtesy of B.G. "Spike" Bell.

that knife blade next to his ribs and he's quick to explain. The guards are pretty rough, but Bondy figures they'll ask questions before they start shooting. He knows soldiers can do whatever they like but, out of the corner of his eye, he sees one of them wink, so he believes that they're just having a little fun, trying to scare the Canadians. It works.

The Bondys' are hauled out of the truck. They roll back the tarp to show their load of lettuce and radishes. The two guards simmer down and tell the vendors to go to their stall and stay there. The Bondys are anxious to comply. Despite the confrontation, they continue going to market, even though it's tough, and they return home each day with unsold produce.

Staying away from Detroit would probably have been a good idea for a 70-year-old man from Belgium who arrives at the airport on Tuesday afternoon. Theofiel Dokx has never been in the U.S. before and he trembles as he's ushered into the terminal building and told he can't leave. Dokx knows nothing of riots and insurrection, guns and soldiers. He's to be picked up by his sister, Mrs. Alphonse Von Goethem of Chatham, whom he hasn't seen for 20 years. Dokx is alone and frightened and speaks no English. He waits three hours. He's told that his sister can't get over the border, but arrangements have been made to fly him to Port Huron, Michigan, in a small plane chartered by Standard Airways of Detroit. When he arrives, he's met by happy tears. Dokx smiles hesitantly and, through a translator, explains that he just wants to visit Niagara Falls. Meanwhile, the airport in Detroit is closed and planes re-routed to Windsor.

The riot disrupts plans for many travellers in Windsor, but some people are determined to go back and forth anyway. Aunt Ruby has been visiting Elise Harding-Davis on the Canadian side of the border, but now she's anxious to go back to her job as an executive secretary at the J.L. Hudson Department Store. As a black woman, she isn't thinking of the Detroit riot as an international or global incident and hasn't even considered its impact on her city. She's aware that friends and family might be in danger, but it's unbelievable to her. She just wants to go home and make sure her children and property are okay. It's slow crossing the bridge at the border, but she has no trouble getting through when she explains that she's going home. It's a little shocking to hear gunshots, but they're far off. When she arrives home, her neighbourhood is quiet and still. Her children are under the dining room table, afraid to come out.

Windsor resident Joe Suchan also has a visitor during the riot. It's his cousin, Sister Immaculata, a nun from Edmonton, and she has a peculiar request. She convinces Suchan to drive her across the border to a post office in Detroit. Suchan knows the city well because he owned a camera shop downtown. It's the third day of the riot and the streets in Detroit are empty, but for soldiers and guns. Burned-out stores look ominous with their smashed and gaping windows. Sister Immaculata buys a postcard with a picture of Detroit and mails it to her home in Edmonton, so she can prove to her friends that she was actually there.

When they return to Canada, Suchan stays up at night and listens to the riot from the safety of his home. He lives on Fairview at Riverside Drive in Windsor, just across from Belle Isle in Detroit. As he watches, occasional tracers light up the sky. At 3:00 a.m., helicopter gun ships circle the Motor City. Spotlights flash from rooftop to street, illuminating trouble spots. The brilliant beams bolt from one area to the next like giant fireflies, a surreal sight in an urban Vietnam. The sound of gunfire reverberates off the tallest buildings downtown.

Suchan can hardly believe he drove willingly into the maelstrom. He remembers the sound of metal chains on the tracks of tanks as they rumble along. When they stop, there's the "boom, boom, boom" of gunfire as they search for snipers. It's a sound he'll never forget. He talks to people as they walk past his house on the riverfront. Surprisingly, some are Americans. They're from the suburbs of Detroit and they've driven all the way to Port Huron in Michigan, across the Bluewater Bridge and into Sarnia on the Canadian side, then down to Windsor just to see what's going on. The trip takes several hours, but it's safer than driving in Detroit.

Carol Ferguson and her entire wedding party also end up stateside during the riot. They go over by choice, but for a different reason. Good friends, Doctor Norm and Ruth Bowbeer, are planning a bridal shower at their waterfront home on Grosse Isle several miles downriver from Detroit. They're boating buddies who swim, picnic and water ski together every summer, and their common love of the water forms a bond between them that transcends any boundary. Because of the riot, Grosse Isle has been cordoned off, the swing bridges left open and under police guard to prevent anyone going onto the island by land. It's a precaution to protect wealthy white residents. Since the Fergusons can't go to their

A One-Star General protected by Federal troops on Grand River East in front of the Riviera Theatre just before they're pinned down by sniper fire. Courtesy of B.G. "Spike" Bell.

party by car, they change their plans and ferry cakes, pastries, presents, decorations and all 25 Canadian guests to the island by boat. The unconventional bridal shower is remembered for a lifetime and yet, there is pause for uneasy reflection.

Just before the party, Ferguson's father is trapped in his car by Detroiters who throw sticks and stones at motorists. Ferguson escapes unharmed, but it's traumatic. It makes the family appreciate the safety of Grosse Isle. As guests laugh about their flotilla of boats, smoke drifts over Windsor, an ugly pall that settles like a shroud over the heart of the city.

The Windsor Star reports that 100 blocks in Detroit have been destroyed by fire. Eventually, border restrictions are lifted, but guards warn motorists to stay out of trouble spots. Sightseers are turned back at the border at the whim of the customs officer, but some spectators cause traffic jams in riot-torn areas of Detroit. Curfew violators are also "handled with discretion" as tourists scramble to return to Canada.

The riot generates a lot of controversy in Windsor and, at times, emotions are out of control. At 6:00 p.m., Thursday, Gordon Hurner is involved in a fight, following an argument over what caused the riot. He's taken to hospital where he receives 63 stitches to his face and neck. A 28-year-old Windsor man is held by police, pending charges. Meanwhile, some Detroiters are determined to "drink Canada dry" which is not so much a slur on the slogan of the well-known ginger ale as a comment on the number of Americans crossing the border for a brew, many for the first time in years. It reminds Windsorites of their rough and tumble past – the old rum running days of prohibition when the city was wide open to blind pigs and gambling dens. Americans curse Michigan's governor, a teetotaller who banned liquor sales and doesn't seem to care about the drinking habits of his voters. Many bleary-eyed bar patrons wryly suggest that Romney "is a riot." The ban on booze closes all 7,300 bars in Detroit for seven days. They don't open until Monday, July 31.

The problem of American drinkers comes to a head on Friday night when 25 Windsor officers are ordered to disperse an angry crowd at the St. Clair Tavern. Two hundred people, mostly from Michigan, are involved in a brawl when they refuse to leave at closing time. As one sergeant says, "This is their nearest outlet for booze." Police block Wyandotte Street East between Ouellette Avenue and Dufferin for an hour and use nightsticks to break up the fight. Two people are charged with creating a disturbance. Police tell bridge and tunnel authorities to screen cars with Michigan plates for "troublemakers." Customs officials say, "Anyone without a legitimate reason for crossing the border won't be allowed in."

As the vigil continues, anxious and curious Canadians continue to gravitate toward the waterfront. Garnet Ryan lives on Moy Avenue, only six houses from Riverside Drive, and he takes a kitchen chair with him when he walks to the river to watch. He's a lieutenant in the Essex and Kent Scottish and he wonders how the riot will affect him. He's in the reserve and he wonders if his unit will have to go. It might be interesting, but he doesn't know if he wants it. He sits by the river and thanks God that Canadians are different from their American cousins. He thinks it's because of our early abolition of slavery or because of the Underground Railroad and the escape to freedom of countless American Blacks who made their home in Windsor, Amherstburg, Harrow, Blenheim and LaSalle. "If not for Canadians, a lot of Blacks wouldn't have their relatives now. It's an altogether different concept." He believes that Blacks have more rights in Canada than in the United States.

Ryan hears rumours that the Royal Canadian Regiment is on alert in London, ready to deploy to protect Canadians should the riot spill across the border. There's talk that the army can be called at a moment's notice, and soldiers are said to have their gear at the end of their beds, ready to move. It's rumoured that 500 men in the unit – four companies of fighting troops – are ready should the government give the okay. Ironically, the army isn't even aware of the rumours. Lieutenant Colonel Phil Labelle is the Commanding Officer of the RCR and he says his troops are not on alert. He says the riot is an American problem, a non-event from a Canadian military point of view. Labelle says his troops are just like everybody else. They watch the riot on TV.

When all is said and done, Windsorites are unanimous on several points. They feel lucky to have a border and a river between themselves and Detroit, and they're convinced that a riot must never happen here. "If anyone thinks that rioting can solve anything, let him take a look at Detroit," says one Windsor man caught in the riot on Thursday. "Everybody suffered. Nobody gained." *The Windsor Star* says there's little likelihood of a riot in Windsor, but the paper hopes the Detroit experience spawns inter-racial cooperation and goodwill, just in case.

Chapter 6

Relief

Interracial cooperation and goodwill do emerge from the riot as the people of Windsor rally to a charitable cause. Windsorites are known for their generosity and proud of it; and, in 1967, they have a chance to prove that their reputation is justified. Charitable groups don't analyze the causes of the riot or assess blame. They don't even consider that the United States is a different country or that Detroit is a different town. All they know is that people have been burned out of their homes. They've lost food, shelter and clothing. They need help, and Windsor can provide it. When the call goes out for assistance, church groups, service clubs and individuals in Windsor are there. The relief effort extends well into Essex and even Kent counties of Southwestern Ontario.

By Wednesday, July 26, there are no stores open in the riot zone. There's no meat or milk, no baby food or diapers, no fruit or vegetables. People with very little to begin with are deprived of basic comforts. There isn't even electricity. It's a desperate situation. For the past three days, people have been afraid to come out except in large numbers. They're still reluctant, but they have little choice. They surface, survey the damage to their lives and scrounge for whatever they can. Children, babies and the elderly have to be fed and clothed.

People in Detroit open their homes to hundreds of riot victims. Schools, churches and municipal buildings also provide shelter. A disaster relief headquarters is set up and Detroit churches collect money, food,

Father Joseph Potts complains that people can't get groceries and can only be fed by checking in to his church as the riot shuts down the neighbourhood. Courtesy of J.A. "Pete" McGarvey.

clothing and medicine. By Friday, 38 distribution centres are established in the city. The U.S. Department of Agriculture sends 86 tons of food from the Flint and Wayne County general hospitals for distribution at schools. A supermarket donates five tons of canned goods and another company provides eleven crates of breakfast cereal.

Windsor is one of the first neighbouring communities to help. The Windsor Relief Committee is established as an inter-faith organization chaired by Reverend Roland Janisse. A loose-knit coalition of local church groups, it arranges its first shipment of canned goods, clothing, diapers, sleeping bags and tents to send on Wednesday afternoon. Even customs and excise officials get into the charitable swing of things by allowing items to cross duty-free. UAW Local 444 in Windsor donates $1,000, and another $2,000 comes from the World Relief Fund administered by the Anglican Church to defray the cost of trucking.

Movement of goods is coordinated by Reverend Libby, the director of St. Leonard's House, an Anglican rehabilitation centre in Windsor. Reverend G. Emmett Carter, Bishop of London, and Reverend Hans Zegerius, the chair of the Windsor Council of Churches, both appeal to Roman Catholic and Protestant churches for donations. They ask that a special collection be taken up on Sunday. Joseph Eisenburg, the executive director of the Jewish Community Council, also appeals for cash.

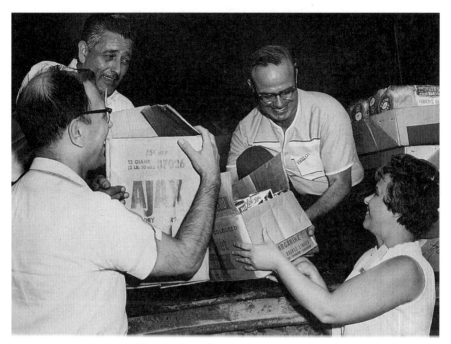

Twenty tons of food are collected in Windsor for riot victims in Detroit. Rev. Roland Janisse (left) organized the food drive, along with John Walker, Rev. William Kidnew, and Mrs. Howard Soulliere. Courtesy of *The Windsor Star.*

The relief effort extends beyond Windsor's borders with the help of Reverend Murray Masecar of Park Street United Church in Chatham who organizes a similar collection in his parish. He's looking for clothes in good repair, food and especially powdered milk, but no medicines or perishable goods because of border restrictions. Masecar describes the response as amazing, "beyond all my expectations." Female parishioners volunteer to box food and sort clothes and a Detroit couple, vacationing in Kent County, even drops off five cartons of powdered milk. Chatham Motors and Western Freight provide trucks to ship two loads from Chatham on Wednesday and another load on Thursday.

Initially, the Basilian House of Studies, at 2990 Riverside Drive West in Windsor, is used as a collection point. Eventually, the St. Vincent de Paul Centre, at 357 Pitt Street East, and the Central United Church and Jewish Community Centre, both on Ouellette, are recruited to assist. Officials, at St. Paul's in Detroit, figure it will take until Friday to reach many of the

More than 250 loaves of bread and hundreds of pounds of canned goods and vegetables leave Windsor on July 27 to help the homeless in Detroit's riot area. Omer Soulliere of Windsor (right) hands a box of bread to Michael Williams of Detroit on behalf of the Basilian House of Studies.
Courtesy of *The Windsor Star.*

hungry families. "There are so many calls for help, we hardly know where to start." The relief effort needs more trucks and volunteers.

Despite the problems, 70 cases of milk, 250 loaves of bread, hundreds of pounds of canned goods and vegetables are delivered on Thursday. Omer Soulliere is a volunteer driver and he says ten tons of food have been shipped from Windsor. While the latest truck is being unloaded in Detroit, there is a report of a sniper in the neighbourhood. Fifty federal troops arrive to evacuate an apartment building, but no rifleman is found. Hungry children line up for food. Because their homes have been destroyed by fire, they're wearing the only clothes they own. They've only eaten scraps in the past three days and there are tears of joy. Their parents know little of Windsor, but they express their heartfelt thanks. "Boy, you people from Windsor must be good people."

As head of the Windsor relief effort, Janisse says, "The scriptures are pretty clear about feeding the hungry ... it's part of our religious responsibility." It's also easier for church groups because they're motivated by compassion. They have volunteers and can easily overcome red tape to move massive amounts of aid, even though it's hard to keep up with demand. It's estimated that the homeless need 1,400 quarts of milk per day. Janisse keeps up the drive until Friday when he closes the doors to the Emergency Relief Centre and appeals to the city to set up its own relief fund or have regular agencies take over.

A little red wagon, laden with food, clothing and bedding for riot victims in Detroit. Four Windsor girls collected the provisions: 10-year-olds Catherine Desramaux and Mary Catherine Mongeau, and 11-year-olds Anna Gomes and Jackie Anderson.
Courtesy of *The Windsor Star.*

Some churches remain open for donations. The First Lutheran Church works directly with the Greater Detroit Lutheran Council Relief Fund. Combined with that effort, Windsor, Essex, Leamington, Tecumseh, LaSalle and Chatham all contribute ten tons of bedding and $300 to buy drugs for children. With its last shipment on Saturday, the Basilian House alone has delivered 40 tons of food.

The spirit of giving is contagious. On Friday, four girls from the Roselawn area of Windsor collect food, clothing and bedding for riot victims. Catherine Desramaux, 10, and Jackie Anderson, 11, say they meet the nicest people as they pull their little red wagon from house-to-house. As 11-year-old Anna Gomes points out, they work in two teams, each taking a side of the street. "We got something from just about every home." Ten-year-old Mary Catherine Mongeau says, "We plan to keep going at least until Saturday." The Mongeau garage fills up fast as the girls wait for a truck from Assumption Church where a *Windsor Star* photographer takes their picture. In a similar gesture, three boys from the Walkerville area collect 300 cans of food and 15 pounds of powdered milk over the weekend. Twelve-year-old Claude McGraw, 11-year-old Michael Kos, and 8-year-old Mark Kos work all day in the rain. Their mother, Eli Kos says, "They're pretty tired and I think they just about picked the area clean."

By Tuesday, August 1, Windsor City Council has set up an emergency relief fund with the help of the Emergency Measures Organization. It takes over the relief effort in Essex County and raises a total of $13,000. In Lambton County, the Sarnia and Port Huron Jaycees establish their own cross-border fund and collect four large boxes of canned food, powdered milk, bread and cash. Everything is non-perishable, no fruit or meat. The two efforts remain open for two more weeks, collecting at fire halls, public libraries and city hall.

In an editorial, *The Windsor Star* comments on this outpouring of community spirit and applauds the Canadian relief effort – the rallying of churches to grapple with problems, especially the deprivation of countless American citizens. The paper editorializes that Canadian charity knows no bounds or boundary, which is commendable since Windsor is across the border, and not directly affected by the riots. To *The Star*, it's an indication that white people do want to help their black brothers. It's a demonstration of compassion and kindness, which rises above hatred and prejudice and diminishes the bitterness between races. The local paper complains that too many people in the U.S. are laying blame for the riot, while not doing enough to recognize the problem as a national tragedy. *The Star* concludes that the U.S. government is ultimately responsible for solving the housing crisis and must take charge to rehabilitate, rebuild and restore order but, until then, humanitarian aid from Canada is an inspiration. It provides hope.

The Canadian relief effort is coordinated by the Detroit Interfaith Committee through its Interfaith Emergency Centers, which collect and distribute goods to riot victims who need them most. Over the past few years, Detroit churches decided that they must speak out, in unison, if they are to claim moral leadership, and act forcefully and quickly in emergencies, especially in inner-city areas where racial problems predominate.

To that end, they meet regularly, have developed close ties, established a friendship and trust, and set up communication links to create a firm working relationship not evident in other riot-torn American cities. Churches are recognized by the mayor's office as the only operational and effective communal response during the crisis. IEC volunteers are given permits from the police and National Guard to travel during the curfew, while other American relief agencies are forced to close or are mired in red tape during the riot.

Church officials call their parishioners to monitor the extent of the disturbance, assess damage to church property and provide help. They talk about racial issues, ghetto poverty, job discrimination and low-cost housing but, on this occasion, when told of looting and arson, they urge their priests and reverends to go to the streets in their clerical garb to help restore order. Alternately, 25 church officials hold a meeting at 3:00 p.m. Monday afternoon. They're told that the city isn't providing much more than police and fire protection. They realize that a call for order isn't sufficient, that something is needed to solve the crisis. They set up an information centre run by seven volunteers who answer phone calls from people who need help and from others who want to assist. The calls start coming in after 6:00 p.m. Monday, after announcements are made on local radio and TV stations. At first, volunteers refer calls to other community service groups, but they receive so many that they establish temporary shelters in three large Catholic churches and two public schools. Until now, the homeless have been sleeping on sidewalks. Suburban churches are notified to bring food and clothing to inner city areas and 25 collection centres are linked with 21 distribution centres throughout Detroit.

The Wayne County branch of the UAW provides volunteer drivers with trucks donated from major companies in the metropolitan area. The police handle emergency requests, and keep in touch with walkie-talkies. At one distribution centre, a woman phones to say she's run out of formula for her four-day-old baby and is afraid to leave her home. In another call, a diabetic runs out of insulin, and a blind person is disoriented and frightened. To help, volunteers work day and night. As the riot continues, more people line up for donations at Grace Episcopal Church on Twelfth Street which is located in the midst of the heaviest burning, sniping and looting. The church stands out because it is untouched. No windows are broken. There are no fires. It's spared because it is the meeting place of the relief effort. Similarly, delivery trucks, clearly marked with large signs, are left alone, accepted as distributors of humanitarian aid.

Many young people volunteer their services, not worrying about personal strain or fatigue. Community leaders see this "welding together" as a positive sign. They recognize that people care and hope that mistakes can be avoided in the revitalization. There's only one complaint. The church is criticized for giving food to anyone without determining need. Critics say this encourages fraud and prevents an early return to normal. The IEC recognizes that some people take advantage, but feels it can't allow the majority with legitimate needs to go hungry. Also, it has to distribute perishable goods like milk, butter and vegetables quickly, so that they don't go bad.

To alleviate some concerns, the IEC agrees to halt its activities when there's no longer a need, or when commercial or traditional enterprises are back in business. By Saturday, July 29, church groups in Detroit gradually phase-out the distribution of food, which allows municipal agencies to kick in. The withdrawal takes four days, but the Interfaith Emergency Center continues working for four more months to help victims put their lives in order and deal with emotional stress and shock. It also re-unites people with their families and friends, and finds alternative housing and jobs for victims who've lost their homes and businesses and can no longer pay their bills. By November 19, 1967, the crisis is over and church relief disbands.

Chapter 7

Emancipation and Human Rights

While the relief effort demonstrates the more charitable side of Windsor's character, there's also a darker side. The outpouring of community spirit is laudable, but does not go far enough. In 1967, many people in the city are afraid that the riot could spill across the border, that American Blacks could wreak havoc on Windsor. That fear ultimately cancels an annual black celebration, and drives a wedge between the black and white communities. The dispute involves city council, the police, the Ontario Human Rights Commission and, eventually, the Supreme Court of Canada.

Every year, during the first weekend of August, starting in 1938, the Emancipation Day celebration was held at Jackson Park in Windsor. It was a huge party in honour of the abolition of slavery in the British Empire in 1834, fully three decades before slaves were freed in the United States. The event would last from two to five days, attracting thousands of people from Ontario, Michigan and Ohio. There was a religious service, devotional music, a parade, carnival, picnic, speeches from local dignitaries, a beauty contest, sporting events, including baseball and soccer, and a few card games, as well. It also featured the presentation of the local Freedom Award, which recognized an outstanding contribution to the cause of interracial harmony and equality.

One of the earliest references to Emancipation Day is in a black newspaper published in 1851 by Henry and Mary Bibb of Sandwich (now part of

Emancipation Day Parade, Amherstburg, Ontario, 1890s. Archives of Ontario, McCurdy Collection AU5442.

Windsor). *The Voice of The Fugitive* invited people to celebrate the birth of liberty in the village of Sandwich with guest speakers from Detroit. On August 1, Blacks marched to the town docks to welcome friends from the United States and other Canadian cities. Then, they headed to the park for games and songs. The Jubilee Singers sang spirituals and, at night, the annual ball was held at the town hall. In 1859, to coincide with the 25th anniversary of Emancipation, a major celebration was held with "fugitive slaves and other coloured persons residing in Canada and Detroit." Then, in 1865, a three-day holiday began at Prince's Grove in Sandwich. On the first day, there were speeches, river excursions and band concerts. The second day was proclaimed Lincoln Day with banners, a parade and picnic to commemorate the emancipation of 3,000,000 slaves in the United States Then, on day three, the celebration ended with a grand ball.

After being held in Sandwich and Amherstburg for many years, Emancipation Day was reinstated in Windsor in 1905, but it gradually deteriorated into drinking bouts and quarrels. The event was resurrected in 1932 when Walter Lawrence Perry took it over. Perry wanted to renew the festival's glory as "the greatest freedom show on earth." Born in Windsor in 1899, Perry was the great-grandson of slaves and a former athlete who

Photographs capture the celebratory nature of Emancipation Day, for young and old alike. Photos by Herb Colling from promotional material.

held Ontario records in the broad jump and the 100-yard dash. A cigar-chomping hustler with a ready smile, he was a popular, good-natured man known as "Mr. Emancipation." A promoter, who played to his audience, Perry brought in big-name speakers, including: Joe Louis, Reverend Martin Luther King, Mahalia Jackson, Jesse Owens and even Eleanor Roosevelt. He was also known for his annual pilgrimage to council to ask for favours and promote his show. Every year, he appeared, carrying several huge trays heaped with barbecued ribs slathered in what he called his "secretive sauce."

For area Blacks, Emancipation Day was the place to be, and to be seen. In 1953, the National Film Board made a movie about the celebration to represent the life and freedom of Canadian Blacks and to highlight their accomplishments. A year later, there was even a wedding for a Detroit couple in front of a crowd of 4,000. As the local newspaper quipped, the groom was too much in love to understand the irony of being married on Emancipation Day, a celebration of freedom.

During the annual talent contest of 1959, a 15-year-old singer named Diana Ross debuted with her group – the Primettes; who later became the Supremes. Originally, they sang at union halls in Detroit, but saw Windsor as the big time. They begged their parents to go, but almost missed it when the bus to Windsor was delayed. Competition was stiff and it wasn't until they sang *There Goes My Baby* that they finally won the $75 prize and took the first step toward Motown and eventual stardom.

To a young Elise Harding-Davis, Emancipation Day was a family time with great parades, a chance to stay up late and meet interesting new boys. It was also one of the only opportunities for young Blacks to have a summer job and get paid. As a young woman, Harding-Davis counted money and made out bank statements for the festival. She gained a work ethic and established her first bank account with money that she earned from Emancipation Day. Her father was an electrician and he wired the park every year for which he received free tickets to the rides. It was another reason she pinned her whole summer on the August 1 holiday.

To the black community of Windsor, Emancipation Day was the highlight of the year, bigger than New Year's Eve, maybe even Christmas; but to the white community, there was a growing apprehension following the riot of 1967, a concern that something terrible was about to happen.

W.L. Clark, a columnist for *The Windsor Star*, captures that fear in an article on Monday, July 24. He expresses the concerns of white shopkeepers that the riot could lead to civil war in the U.S. and that an influx of angry American Blacks to Canada could mean violence on this side of the border.

Clark maintains that American authorities could have prevented problems by doing something about poverty and squalor. Without actually saying it, he gives voice to thoughts of the white community. Walter L. Perry and his friends may not cause trouble, "but what of those who are not his friends?" Some people feel that Emancipation Day follows too closely on the heels of the riot, and there's concern that something bad is going to happen, simply because the event involves Blacks.

Clark's warning causes Windsor City Council to take action. At a meeting that lasts over two hours, a committee presents an ultimatum to Perry: Shut Emancipation Day down, or council will close it down. Council hopes it will not be forced to act, that festival organizers will concede. It's a tough stand, made tougher when council refuses to commit to the resumption of Emancipation Day in 1968 or any year thereafter.

Georgina Montrose is the acting mayor of Windsor and she points out that the city has received many letters and phone calls from taxpayers who are alarmed at what might happen if the event goes ahead. Downtown businesses are afraid that a large black crowd could jeopardize public safety and cause unnecessary property damage. Residents, near Jackson Park where the festivities take place, are petrified, as are home-owners and merchants along the parade route. Six council members, including John Wheelton the mayor, are attending a three-day municipal convention on adequate housing at Expo '67 in Montreal, but they've been in touch with Montrose by phone and agree with her actions. She's advised to err on the side of caution, even though the decision could create hard feelings in the black community.

Windsor police and fire officials have already met to discuss Emancipation Day. They've heard rumours about the Black Power Movement and a possible disruption this year, and they're concerned about what a handful of "trouble-makers" can do. The celebration generally attracts 50,000 visitors, half from the United States. There are no controls on people coming across the border and the police are not equipped, nor do they have the necessary personnel to cope with a major disturbance in Windsor. The nearest support from the military would have to come from London, which is several hours away. The police admit that the event is generally peaceful, but there have been arrests for drinking and other offenses. In

1966, festival organizers asked for off-duty police to patrol Jackson Park, but the request was denied because they expected the city to pay for them. Eventually, the festival hired 13-armed Blacks from the United States as private security guards. Canada Customs took away their revolvers at the border and police took their nightsticks in Jackson Park.

Perry has been working on the festival for the past ten months and has lots of time and money invested. Most preparations are already finished, and he's upset by council's decision. This is also Canada's centennial year and the festival's 35th anniversary. Emancipation Day is to be the biggest ever, but Perry has little choice. He has until noon, Friday, to make up his mind. After that, council will force cancellation. Perry says he has a contract with the city to use Jackson Park, but the city says the contract is void because he hasn't prepaid the fees, and hasn't provided proof of insurance and other guarantees. Insurance experts doubt it's possible to obtain coverage because of the riot.

It takes Perry almost a day of soul-searching before he finally cancels. He's upset, but hedges his bets for the future, making it clear that, "we're already starting to work on the 1968 Emancipation Day celebrations." As soon as Perry announces the cancellation, he receives a call of support from Paul Martin, the minister of external affairs and MP for Essex East. It's a sigh of relief from the white community and it demonstrates the distance between the two races.

Perry is also under pressure to call off a jazz concert and dance at the Windsor Arena. Manager Sedo Martinello says the dance is not directly associated with Emancipation Day, although it is held in conjunction with the big event. He admits there has been trouble and it's another bone of contention. In 1960, for example, the dance was oversold with 4,500 people in attendance, most from Detroit. Many people with tickets weren't allowed in. During intermission, a crowd developed outside. Tempers flared on that hot summer night, as some people tried to force their way in. A brawl broke out and some participants pulled switchblades. People threw chairs and bottles, and fought in the stands. The melee spilled into the street with more pushing and shoving.

Constable Bill Jackson was moonlighting as a security guard and he says the event was supposed to continue until 3:00 a.m. but, at 1:30, he called police. Before the first officers arrived, several people had been stabbed and, when police tried to break up the mob with riot sticks, more police had to be called. An officer was knocked down, and another slashed on the hand. One youth was rushed to hospital, suffering chest wounds. It took police 30 minutes to gain control as police carted the offenders off to jail to make them think twice about causing trouble in Windsor. Seven people were charged with assault, using obscene language, carrying an offensive weapon and attempted murder, but the cases never went to trial. When the men were released on bail, they skipped across the border and never came back.

The Windsor Star described the skirmish as a riot, but police constable Ken Farrow denies that there were racial overtones. He believes the problem started as a grudge between rival gangs from Detroit, and the whole thing was blown out of proportion. "The Windsor event only provided an occasion for a few people looking for trouble to get together and find it." Jackson agrees. He commends Windsor police for "nipping it in the bud" and views it as a good exercise in crowd control. In total, 15 people were injured, including seven police officers.

Many Windsor Blacks think it's ridiculous that Emancipation Day is cancelled for something that Canadian Blacks didn't take part in. To them, it's an insult, but those feelings aren't reflected in The Windsor Star. The paper quotes local Blacks who agree with the cancellation. Clifford Walls is the manager for Ascon Construction and he's not a great fan of the Saturday jazz concerts. He says they promote rowdy and sometimes-violent behaviour. He supports the church service to attract a different type of clientele, "those not looking for excitement," but he doesn't mind the cancellation of other events.

Howard Watkins, a black police detective, will miss the parade, but he doesn't want to take a chance on the event. The parade is a big hit with as many as 20 bands and 60 marching units from all over Ontario and the northeastern United States but, as Watkins explains, "If a wrong element were to attend, it would besmirch the fine record of Emancipation Day." His sentiments are echoed by Henry White, president of the Windsor Civic Softball League and a staffer at the Canada Manpower Centre. "It's too close on the heels of the rioting." White recommends postponing the

ceremony to the end of the month until the courts deal with Detroit rioters and establish penalties as a deterrent to others. Bernie Smith is the
director of the children's A Cappella Choir and he supports postponing
Emancipation Day until next year. "What would we think if a carnival celebration had been held within a week of President Kennedy's death."

Howard McCurdy is a black biology professor at the University of
Windsor and he's not surprised that the event has been cancelled, but he
doesn't like the way it was done. He says the system could not understand
the depth of feeling of Blacks in the community. He admits the dances are
always troublesome because they draw a different crowd than the rest of
the celebration, but most of the regulars to Emancipation Day are relatives and friends from Michigan. They number in the thousands and are
eminent leaders of the black community. Well-spoken, they hold good
jobs and are upwardly mobile: doctors, lawyers, dentists, tradesmen,
storeowners and auto plant workers. McCurdy supports the event in principle, but is concerned about its economic viability. "People from Detroit
would be too preoccupied with conditions over there to come here."

Eugene Steele is the only dissenting voice in *The Windsor Star* article.
He's concerned that the city is overreacting, being too negative. He's a
black fireman who volunteered to serve in Detroit and he sees no reason
to cancel. "There is too much emphasis on fearing fear itself. If the Detroit
riots had happened before Thanksgiving, you wouldn't cancel
Thanksgiving, would you?" Some Windsor Blacks want to become more
involved in planning the celebration, to make it "more representative of
the history and future of the Negro people" and to ensure its success. As
Bernie Smith suggests, it's positive, adds value to the community and
should be continued, but only if it pays for itself.

By way of protest for the cancellation, Perry publishes the Emancipation
Day program, an elaborate magazine called *Progress,* which features advertisements and articles about the annual event and includes information
about the guest speaker. The program in 1967 is Canada's Centennial edition with the Confederation logo, a stylized maple leaf, on the front. It
comes complete with two scathing editorials about the cancellation.

In the first article, Perry complains that the city is trying to kill his event
in favour of the International Freedom Festival, a similar annual celebration

organized by the cities of Windsor and Detroit. Perry says Windsor gave $59,000 to the Freedom Festival, but not one penny for Emancipation Day and yet, his program brings more people to the city than all other events staged during the year. Perry says Emancipation Day has been around for 125 years, longer than Canada has been a country, and he accuses the municipal government of being unfair to Blacks because it charges for the use of Jackson Park. In the second article, Irma Kelly, one of the organizers, complains that Emancipation Day isn't even supported by the Windsor Chamber of Commerce. Kelly says that the chamber looks on Emancipation Day "as a fish fry and clam bake, something straight from *Tom Sawyer* or *Uncle Tom's Cabin.*"

In 1967, Perry is organizing three extra prayer services in Jackson Park with more than 100 clergymen. He even plans to discuss riots with guest speaker Doctor William Holmes Borders, a civil rights activist from Atlanta, Georgia, whose topic is "Riots are Rooted in Ruins."

To compensate for the cancellation, the Canadian Council of Churches organizes a national day of prayer on Sunday, August 6. In Windsor, it's held in conjunction with the Emancipation Day Sunrise Service, which takes place at 6:00 a.m. at the First Baptist Church on Mercer Street. Sparsely attended by only 15 parishioners, it's the only Emancipation Day event of 1967.

During the ceremony, the annual Freedom Award is presented to Genevieve Allen Jones who started the Sunrise Service in 1954. As one parishioner bravely suggests, "They can't stop us from praying." The service is similar to one being promoted by President Johnson in the United States. It's a common plea for sanity against riots, which plague the nation. Even as churchgoers congregate for their ecumenical services, another riot erupts in Milwaukee, Wisconsin.

On Monday, July 31, Walter Perry surprises council with a bill for $25,000 to cover his expenses for organizing Emancipation Day. It includes $4,000 for himself, a $1,500 honorarium for his wife, $1,500 car allowance and $1,500 for each of his directors. The bill could go as high as $30,000 and prompts a letter to the editor in the local paper. The writer suggests that the demands are ridiculous and that it's ludicrous to expect taxpayers to pay the tab for a private enterprise. Tongue-in-cheek, the author says, it would be cheaper to have a riot than to pay Perry. "At least then we would know where the money went." The writer believes the city should cover Perry's fixed costs, but not stipends to his wife and staff. If Perry profits at taxpayer expense, it would make Emancipation Day a business. The author respects Perry, but questions his gall, attempting to deceive the people. Council orders a full investigation into Perry's bill.

Many people in Windsor have trouble understanding how Perry finances his annual venture. He keeps details in his head with little time for traditional accounting. The festival has a history of red ink and yet, there's no admission charge. Bands and speakers are paid, and there are cash prizes for contests, including $200 and a watch to "Miss International Sepia," winner of the annual beauty pageant, which started in 1941. Some money comes from the sale of advertising, the rent of concession booths, the midway, the sale of refreshments and donations, but there are also rumours that some cash comes out of Perry's pocket.

Ironically, the people of Windsor soon discover Perry's source of capital. Two weeks after the riot, "Mr. Emancipation" enters hospital, suffering from hepatitis. He dies on August 17, 1967, at the age of 68. He has $28 in the bank, and debts of $11,000. He's buried at Windsor's Grove Cemetery and, during the procession, the band plays *When The Saints Go Marching In* and *Birth of the Blues*, according to Perry's last request.

Perry never said why he organized Emancipation Day, especially at such a personal cost. He never touted the accomplishments of his race, or said that he wanted to help young Blacks attain a place in life. Embarrassed by the question, he'd only smile broadly, and say he loved a parade, or that he got a thrill from music and laughter.

Throughout the winter, Windsor City Council consults the police commission on whether Emancipation Day should be held. On February 19, 1968, council discusses the use of Jackson Park in August. It's a thorny issue, but council defers any decision until the next police commission meeting. On March 9, the police recommend that a license for the carnival and parade be denied because the event is both a private and commercial affair. The recommendation is one of the most contentious issues of the season, and causes the black community to erupt angrily with cries of racism.

City of Windsor

HARRY O. BRUMPTON
COMMISSIONER

STANLEY WILLIMOTT
DIRECTOR OF RECREATION

GERALD W. DAWSON
EXECUTIVE ASSISTANT
COMMISSIONER OF PARKS & RECREATION

DEPARTMENT OF PARKS & RECREATION

CITY HALL
WINDSOR, ONTARIO

PHONE 254-1611,
EXT. 277

November 10, 1967.

Mr. Edmund Powell, Vice-Chairman,
Walter L. Perry & Associates,
1122 Marentette Avenue,
Windsor, Ontario.

Dear Mr. Powell:

I have been directed by the City Manager's office to answer
your correspondence of September 4, 1967.

I am pleased to confirm the following dates, Thursday, August 1
to Monday, August 5, incl., as requested for the use of Jackson
Park for the 1968 Emancipation Day celebrations, under the usual
terms of an agreement to be prepared by the City of Windsor.

Yours very truly,

G. W. H. Dawson,
Executive Assistant,
Parks & Recreation.

GWHD:mf
cc: Commissioner
re: 1968 Emancipation Day Celebrations

*Letter from Windsor Parks and Recreation Department dated November 10, 1967,
confirming the use of Jackson Park for the 1968 Emancipation Day Celebrations – a
confirmation that was later rescinded by the Windsor Police Commission.*
Courtesy of Howard McCurdy. Photo by Herb Colling.

On April 1, 1968, the city is notified that a formal complaint has been lodged with the Ontario Human Rights Commission. Edmund Powell is the new chairman of Emancipation Day, and he complains that he's been discriminated against because of the recommendation. He says he asked Gordon Preston, the deputy police chief, for the parade and carnival license some time ago, but the commission didn't process the claim. Powell says he didn't find out about the denial until he read an article in *The Windsor Star* on March 23, and he feels the decision was made because the participants are Black.

The problem is compounded by the assassination of Civil Rights Leader Martin Luther King Junior on April 4, 1968. Detroit erupts in a mini-riot to protest the shooting. Two days later, a delegation of Emancipation Day organizers appears before the police commission in Windsor. Powell is

CONCILIATION PROPOSAL
RE: 1968 EMANCIPATION DAY PARADE AND CARNIVAL

The Ontario Human Rights Commission respectfully suggests that the Windsor Police Commission review its decision in respect to the above noted matter and give conditional permission for the celebrations on the following grounds:

A) That as a service to the City of Windsor a series of on-going reports be prepared and submitted to the Windsor Police Commission and the Mayor respecting the extent to which Windsor might be affected by the racial situation in Detroit;

That in respect to the carnival and parade the following Detroit organizations be consulted with a view to having them submit reports well in advance of the celebrations for the guidance of the Mayor and the Windsor Police Commission:

1. Detroit Neighbourhood Service Organization: a Voluntary social agency doing direct work in the Negro Ghetto. Mr. Harold Johnson, M.S.W., a Canadian and former Windsor resident, was already consented to advise the Provincial Government on this matter

2. The City of Detroit Commission on Community Relations, Mr. Barry Marks, Director

3. The Michigan State Civil Rights Commission, Mr. Burton Gordin, Director

4. The Detroit Police Department

B) That while recognizing the responsibility of the Windsor Police Commission to cancel the celebration if there is immediate danger to the publics safety, nevertheless, the Commission requests that, in the interest of better community relations, all reports be studied and assessed with the Mayor, the Ontario Human Rights Commission and the Police Commission—and discussions held with the aforementioned Detroit Civil Rights Agencies and responsible leaders of the Windsor Negro Community—if the celebrations are to be, again, cancelled.

April 11, 1968

Conciliation proposal for the 1968 Emancipation Day parade and carnival. The Ontario Human Rights Commission asks the Windsor Police Commission to review its decision. Courtesy of Howard McCurdy. Photo by Herb Colling.

accompanied by Ralph McCurdy who represents the South Essex Citizen's Advancement Association, and his nephew Howard McCurdy who represents the Guardian Club in Windsor, a unique organization, predominantly Black, whose sole purpose is to fight discrimination. The meeting is held privately in the chambers of the police commission. Ralph McCurdy enters first, shakes hands and sits next to Magistrate Gordon R. Stewart. None of the three black men is introduced which sets the tone for the heated exchange to follow.

Howard McCurdy opens the discussion, lobbying for Emancipation Day, asking that the commission reconsider its decision on the carnival and parade with the understanding that the events be cancelled if there's another riot. McCurdy says he has an arrangement with black groups in Detroit that Emancipation Day organizers would be notified immediately of any disturbance on the American side. Judge B.J.S., (Bruce) Macdonald is chairman of the commission, and he refuses to consider it. "If you think that this commission is going to permit 10,000 Negroes to come across the border for the purpose of creating civil disorder, then you have another thought coming."

McCurdy explodes. He finds the comment presumptuous and offensive and suggests that it demonstrates the "mentality that makes it possible for someone of King's stature and leadership, with his capacity for reconciliation, to have been shot." Outraged, he explains the reasons for unrest in the United States. and expresses his concern that only black affairs are being cancelled. He complains that there is no attempt to ban the International Freedom Festival or a Fireman's Field Day, which both have carnivals and attract American visitors. He says they're similar, but with one subtle difference – they're sponsored by Whites.

Macdonald and Stewart say they know what kind of conduct they can expect from Whites, "but we're unable to anticipate the conduct of coloured participants." Stewart even suggests that he's been threatened with violence in his courtroom by a young "coloured person" accused of an offense. McCurdy explains that they have no intention of holding the celebration if it proves dangerous to the people of Windsor to which Macdonald replies that the commission is not going to listen. "The commission tells people what to do and does not permit people to tell it what to do." The statement illicits more fireworks from McCurdy who complains about the arrogant, controlling attitude. He insists that he will be heard, at which point Macdonald becomes even angrier, refuses to compromise, and threatens to evict McCurdy.

Ralph McCurdy describes Macdonald as rude and discourteous, behaving as if he were the only member of the police commission. He wonders if it is a reaction to their complaint to the Human Rights Commission, which was filed five days earlier. McCurdy admits the move was unfair, premature and unwise, and that the petition should have been kept in reserve and filed afterward, pending the outcome of the meeting with the police commission.

Ralph's nephew, Howard, is angry that the system is incapable of responding in ways that make sense. He doesn't think Blacks are the problem, and he can't understand why Macdonald is making statements against them. McCurdy feels that Canada is a land of racial dignity and fair play, more civilized and less racist than the United States, so it's nonsense to think that Blacks could come here and cause trouble. McCurdy says white racists from the U.S. are more likely to cause problems, considering the deep-seeded racism in Detroit. McCurdy concludes that the issue has not been settled satisfactorily.

Windsor police concede that chances of a major insurrection are remote, but they want to be prepared. Gordon Preston is the new chief of police, replacing Carl Farrow who retired on March 31. Preston has learned, through the Intelligence Branch of the OPP, that problems may develop from the Black Power Movement if Emancipation Day goes ahead as planned, even without the carnival. As a result, Windsor police are trying to figure out how to call for extra police or army personnel, how to close the border as well as liquor and gas bars, and how to impose a curfew, if the need arises.

The Windsor Star applauds the city's efforts, but suggests that council should go beyond Windsor police and look at provincial and national forces, since there's nothing similar to the National Guard in Canada. "The knowledge that plans are ready for any emergency would reassure the public and discourage the outbreak of any riot."

All this talk about being prepared is discouraging to the 3,000 members of Windsor's black community. As McCurdy suggests, the police are even thinking about buying a half-track or tank. He figures the department is "racist to the core" for even thinking about it. He's concerned he's being labelled an instigator of civil unrest.

Preston advises the city that 150 uniformed officers, over and above the regular force of 66 men, will be needed on standby during the four-day festivities, but he is concerned about the expense. Looking at his budget for the year, he figures it would cost $18,000 for the local detachment and, if 100 OPP and military police are also brought in, it would mean an additional $20,000. Preston says the troops could come from London within hours, but the request would have to be issued from the mayor to the Attorney General of the province. Lieutenant Colonel Johnson of the Essex and Kent Scottish says his regiment would have a minor role of handling equipment and transportation, but the event would still require the cooperation of military and police forces.

Meanwhile, Windsor's solicitor advises the mayor that he has no authority to refuse the parade permit. The police commission says it will issue the permit, but Powell must apply for it properly with a formal decision to be made at the next meeting on April 20th. When the mayor meets with Daniel Hill, the chairman of Human Rights, and Michael Marentette, a local representative of the commission, he's advised, "that the Windsor Police Commission should reconsider its decision." Human Rights suggests that the black community has no desire to put the white community in danger, but there's no way of knowing in March what might happen in August, and there's no reason to believe that American Blacks are more likely to riot than American Whites. Human Rights also takes Judge Macdonald to task for his statements. "As the police commission realizes, disorderly conduct is not a monopoly of any one racial group."

Human Rights recommends that conditional approval be given to the Emancipation Day ceremonies while a series of reports is prepared about the affect on Windsor of the racial situation in Detroit. Human Rights also recommends that the Michigan State Civil Rights Commission, the City of Detroit Commission on Community Relations, the Detroit police and the District Neighborhood Service Organization be consulted before determining if the event should be cancelled. The commission reiterates, "Let such a decision be based on multilateral consultations rather than unilateral fiat. Let it be based on evidence rather than conjecture. Let it apply to all celebrations which attract Americans, not simply Negro-sponsored celebrations."

When Powell appears before the police commission again, he's told that a decision on the carnival application will be deferred until he proves he has support from the black community. The board also wants to know how the black community will police the event. Powell figures it's an impossible task, and tries to allay the commission's fears by suggesting that police reinforcements could be made available at a moment's notice. The mayor replies that there's no guarantee that would eliminate the danger of a disturbance, and the carnival license is denied unanimously. The mayor moves that a parade permit be issued for Sunday, August 4. The motion carries with only Magistrate Stewart in opposition. By the end of April, Powell withdraws his application for permits and the city rescinds permission for his group to use the park.

Black organizers complain that the city approved a carnival sponsored by the Canadian Legion, a group "composed primarily of white people." Because of that complaint, the city defers issuing a carnival license for the Fireman's Field Day from August 30 to September 2, pending the resolution of the Emancipation Day dispute. Eventually, the license is granted when the commission decides that the risks are not the same. The event of the previous year was held shortly after the riots with no racial overtones, and there's no indication that large numbers of Americans attended.

Windsor's solicitor James Watson, QC, is studying the validity of the complaint about Emancipation Day, and he's convinced that the city is acting properly. Watson graduated Osgoode Hall in 1937, was appointed assistant city solicitor in 1947, and took over the top job three years later. In 1955, he became Queen's Council. He's Black, but he believes that police are within their rights to grant or deny a license without providing any reason for their actions. To Watson, decisions of the police commission, with regard to licensing, do not come under the purview of the Human Rights Commission, but are governed by the Ontario Municipal Act. He also determines that the decision is not subject to a review in a court of law except to an appeal by a judge of the Supreme Court whose decision is final. Watson says he can find no case on record in which this has actually happened and, in a letter dated April 30, 1968, he makes his findings known to Judge Macdonald, a member of the Windsor Police Commission.

Macdonald responds that Powell did not apply for licenses prior to lodging the Human Rights complaint and so, the police commission could not be accused of discrimination. Powell filed his complaint on April 1, but did not apply for licenses until April 8, and the issue was not dealt with until April 20 at which time the carnival license was refused, but the parade license granted. Macdonald feels the licenses had been granted for 30 years, and the police commission cooperated fully with Walter Perry, the original organizer of the event. As a result, Macdonald believes the complaint is invalid, and the refusal to issue licenses cannot be considered racially motivated. As the presiding judge, Macdonald is under no obligation to explain his position, but he does as a courtesy to the inquiry, and because of the controversy, which has generated public interest.

As chairman of the Human Rights Commission, Daniel Hill says that the town cannot legally issue and then revoke a license, regardless of the situation in Detroit, unless public safety is in question or a riot is imminent. "We believe that sensible prevention is better than a cure." Hill believes that, if civil disorder exists, it is the city's responsibility to prevent it within the limits of its legal powers. He says that riots are explosive, unpredictable, spontaneous and irrational, so who can predict what might happen. "Only a month ago, further disturbances occurred in Detroit, as a result of which the border was closed, the military was called in and a curfew and other restrictions were imposed." To Hill, it's evidence of continued unrest which cannot be ignored. Hill also says that the decision does not deprive anyone of the right of assembly or freedom of speech. Jackson Park can still be used for Emancipation Day, even though the carnival and parade will not be held. Hill suggests he cannot incur unnecessary risk just to allow a commercial operation. In defence of the police commission, Hill says, theirs is a reluctant and regrettable decision, which should stand for this year. In dismissing the complaint against the police commission, Hill hopes Emancipation Day can be re-instated in future.

As soon as Powell is informed of the decision, he enlists the aid of Alan

CANADIAN CIVIL LIBERTIES ASSOCIATION · 62 RICHMOND STREET WEST · SUITE 903 · TORONTO · TELEPHONE 363-9661

April 15, 1968.

Judge Bruce J. S. Macdonald,
Chairman,
Windsor Police Commission,
Municipal Courts Building,
Windsor, Ontario.

Mayor John Wheelton,
Member,
Windsor Police Commission,
City Hall,
Windsor, Ontario.

Magistrate Gordon Stewart
Member,
Windsor Police Commission,
Municipal Courts Building,
Windsor, Ontario.

Gentlemen:

RE: 1968 Emancipation Day Celebration

I am writing this letter as Special Counsel for the Canadian Civil Liberties Association; the Association has been requested to represent the Guardian Club, South Essex Citizens Advancement Association, and Mr. Edmund Powell, in regard to the proposed ban against the Negro sponsored Emancipation Day Celebration.

The Canadian Civil Liberties Association fully supports the validity of the complaint filed by Edmund Powell under the Ontario Human Rights Code. To the extent that the parade and carnival were to be held in a public street and park in the City of Windsor, the setting qualifies as "a place to which the public is customarily admitted", within the meaning of the Ontario Human Rights Code.

To the extent that the Emancipation Day Celebrations might be treated differently from similar events convened by white citizens there would be a basis for concern about discrimination by reason of colour.

Support by the Canadian Civil Liberties Association for Emancipation Day celebrations in 1968, dated April 15, 1968. Courtesy of Howard McCurdy. Photo by Herb Colling.

Borovoy, general council of the Canadian Civil Liberties Association, who launches an appeal to the Supreme Court, which is heard in Osgoode Hall, Toronto, on May 14 at 11:00 a.m. The city is required to provide documentation of the riot in Detroit, including the number of casualties and the

City of Windsor

R. BALA,
~~SECRETARY,~~ SECRETARY

BOARD OF COMMISSIONERS OF POLICE

P.O. BOX 607,
Windsor, Ontario

April 24, 1968

Mr. Edmund L. Powell, Chairman,
1968 Emancipation Celebrations,
1122 Marentette Avenue,
Windsor, Ontario.

Dear Sir:

RE: 1968 EMANCIPATION CELEBRATION

This is to advise that the following action was taken by the Board at its meeting of April 20th, 1968, with respect to your request to the Chief of Police under date of April 8th, 1968 for a parade permit and application to the Board under date of April 9th, 1968 for a carnival licence:

(1) The Chief of Police was authorized to issue the necessary parade permit for Sunday, August 4th, 1968.

(2) The application for a carnival licence for the period August 2nd, 3rd and 5th, 1968, was refused.

Yours very truly,

R. BALA,
SECRETARY.

RB/cl

cc -- Chief of Police

The City of Windsor authorizes the parade permit for 1968, but refuses the carnival license with no reasons given. Courtesy of Howard McCurdy. Photo by Herb Colling.

amount of property damage, which resulted in the cancellation of the Emancipation Day celebration in 1967. It also has to forecast the problems with policing this year, the need for outside assistance from the OPP and military, and the cost to the taxpayer. A battery of Toronto lawyers is hired by the city to defend its case. The issue is finally settled on June 17 when Justice Stark dismisses Powell's appeal. Based on that decision, the Ontario Human Rights Commission also dismisses Powell's complaint, finding no discrimination.

On August 1, 1968, a eulogy is held for Emancipation Day and civil liberties in Ontario. It's described as a lament for racial equality. Borovoy discusses the decision of the court, which upholds the Windsor Police Commission under the Ontario Municipal Act which, he says, includes the power to grant and deny licenses while denying the rights of one group because of the illegal activities of another. The eulogy for decency is delivered by Dennis McDermott, head of the UAW in Canada, as a show of support by labour for the Emancipation Day celebration. McDermott emphasizes the interest of organized labour in human rights and civil liberties and the event ends with folk songs about freedom and civil rights.

It's generally thought that the controversy has been laid to rest, but there is another contentious issue to be resolved. In the August 10 edition of *The Windsor Star*, an article quotes Michael Marentette as saying that the cancellation of the festival was discrimination against the whole Negro population of the city, discrimination of a race by the police" and that "the Ontario Human Rights Commission fought the police commission decision, but lost." Marentette is the local representative of the Human Rights Commission and he's attending a convention at the First Baptist Church in Chatham. The article is short on attribution, but refers to the Emancipation Day debate as an example of discrimination, and complains that many instances of racial prejudice go unreported and fester because people don't want to press them. It suggests that a man's dignity can't be maintained through repeated insult, and it urges people to exercise their democratic right since those who complain to the Human Rights Commission can't be labelled as troublemakers. The story also blames the police for not granting a carnival license, despite the approval of the use of the park for Emancipation Day. Marentette is quoted as saying, "This act reminded me of the states where you see instances of the police commission making decisions for people rather than civil authorities."

The police commission immediately cries foul, saying the allegations are untrue. The City of Windsor also questions the accuracy of the report and complains that the charges merely inflame the black population, arouse their hatred and disrespect for a decision of the court. The city calls Marentette's statements shocking and intemperate. Daniel Hill, as chairman of Human Rights, is also incensed, suggesting that the story should be brought to the attention of D.A. Bales who, as minister of labour, is responsible for the Ontario Human Rights Commission. Hill recognizes that there are often inaccuracies in reporting, but he believes that Marentette must have made the remarks.

The city writes an official protest to the minister, challenging him to investigate the actions of members in his commission. "Had the statement been made by a private citizen in Windsor, its affect would have been minimal … but statements by a government official cannot be seen as anything but correct." The city says it did what it felt was right even though it was difficult and unpleasant. It felt it had to protect the safety of the public while not depriving the right and privilege of free speech, demonstration or assembly. The town says it allowed the use of Jackson Park for other festival functions while restricting a commercial carnival. The letter is signed by the three members of the police commission: the mayor, Judge Macdonald and Magistrate Stewart; and it asks for a public retraction and apology.

Marentette denies making the statements, but resigns from the Human Rights Commission. He says the comments were made by someone else not connected with the commission. In a letter to *The Windsor Star*, the commission concurs that the story is short on quotes, and protests the errors. The controversy seems innocuous, but demonstrates the difference in attitude between Blacks and Whites. It brings to the surface the insecurity some Whites feel because of a large influx of Blacks to the community, and it leaves many white Windsorites sighing with relief that the Emancipation Day celebration won't be held. There is also relief that the Detroit riot is over and, as time passes, will be less likely to cause a backlash in Windsor.

Emancipation Day is re-instated in 1969 and lasts until the 1980s, but McCurdy says it was never the same. Some people believe Ted Powell was too forceful, and may not have been as well understood or liked as Walter Perry who had a long-standing, quieter relationship with the city. Perry was less business-like, more warm and friendly. The event was less political and there were fewer chains of command. In 1976, the carnival was transferred to Mic Mac Park in the city's west end and the parade was no longer held on Ouellette Avenue, Windsor's main street.

The change in venue prompted Powell to complain that the city was trying to destroy the festival, "just when I've got it going good." He accuses several aldermen and city employees of being racist and, over the next year or so, blames council for the continued drop in attendance. In retaliation, officials at city hall complain that Powell is a "slap-dash" organizer. Powell responds that Mic Mac Park is out of the way and lacks proper facilities. He suggests that his celebration is hampered because it's too far from the downtown core and he complains that Blacks aren't given equal rights by Windsor police or the city. Repeatedly, over the next few years, he threatens to take his case to the Supreme Court of Canada – if only he could raise the money. He even threatens to move his show to Detroit.

In 1976, the International Freedom Festival – a big celebration between Windsor and Detroit – also uses Mic Mac Park, but moves downtown again after doing poorly. By 1982, the Freedom Festival has taken over as the main summer event in Windsor and it grows as quickly as Emancipation Day diminishes. In 1983, Powell finally moves Emancipation Day to Amherstburg and expands it. It's a gala event to commemorate the 150th year of the abolition of slavery.

To Howard McCurdy, Emancipation Day was the product of segregation in the 1940s and was in decline even before 1967. As early as 1956, the event was plagued by four days of rain. Attendance dropped again a year later when the 50-year-old grandstand in Jackson Park burned down only 16 days before the event. Emancipation Day organizers lost sound and lighting equipment that was never replaced. A temporary stage had to be constructed with bleachers and folding chairs for seats. Emancipation Day suffered another setback when Jackson Park itself was split in two for the extension of Ouellette Avenue. In 1958, the parade was cancelled because of a $5,000 deficit and, in 1960 there was the "riot" at the Windsor Arena. People stayed away in '61 for fear of a repeat performance. The zeal also seemed to go out of the affair when its primary advocate and supporter, Walter Perry, died in 1967. By the end of the Civil Rights Movement in the '60s, some racial barriers were coming down and Blacks had more alternatives. McCurdy says the need may have been less, but there's no doubt that the riot in Detroit played its part in the demise of Emancipation Day in Windsor.

Chapter 8
Slave and Racial History: Windsor

To think that a riot could spill over to the Canadian side of the river is as ludicrous today as it was in 1967. The idea was fueled by editorials and seemed real, but many people lost sight of the fundamental differences between Canada and the United States. For one thing, our slave histories are not the same and our racist attitudes, though present, are different.

The French brought slaves into Canada in the 1600s and the tradition continued with the British, but the degree of slavery was different. It's estimated there were 500 to 1,500 slaves in Upper Canada in the 1700s, compared to thousands in the southwestern states. Individual Canadians owned 20 to 40 slaves, compared to some 100 or more held individually in the U.S. As such, Canada's slave history is not as extensive, extreme or nefarious, but did exist.

American plantation owners needed cheap workers for large acres of labour intensive crops like cotton, rice and tobacco but, in New France, the farms were small and could be worked by the landowner and his family. The short, cold growing season ruled out plantation crops. It was also expensive to house, feed and clothe slaves through the long unproductive winter. As a result, slavery in the North did not become a prop of the economy, simply not profitable. Black slaves were also more costly in the Canadas. The French landed gentry kept two or three slaves per household as domestic servants and agricultural workers, but it was fashionable, more a symbol of status and wealth than a source of inexpensive labour. Owning a slave in New France was to show that an individual "had made it" in society.

The first black residents in the Windsor/Detroit area were slaves who arrived in 1701 with 100 French soldiers and settlers under the command of Antoine de Lamothe Cadillac, the fur trader and explorer. Because of their skin colour, black slaves were convenient and easy to trace. They helped build Fort Pontchartrain d'Etroit, the first settlement of what is now the city of Detroit on the "strait" of the Detroit River.

Often it is assumed that slaves were treated better in New France because they lived like other servants. In the United States, many slaves were often kept in ignorance, fear and poverty but in the Canadas, in many cases, slaves were given medicine when they were sick and generally thought of as children to be looked after. Many were baptized into the church and shown the way of God and, with the death of the master, were often handed down to family members who were charged never to sell their slaves, but to keep them like any treasured heirloom. Slaves were allowed to marry with the owner's consent and most families stayed together. In the Canadas, there were no slave breeding farms or slave breakers, nor were there as many whips and chains. Some slaves were trained in skills and became dockhands, valets, butlers and drivers. Slavery was perceived as "softer" and yet, as slaves these were people not free and periodically they revolted, ran away or murdered their owners.

Canadian slavery flourished in the 1700s and the numbers increased, especially after the British conquest of the French in 1759. By the articles of capitulation in the following year, the British took control of Detroit where there were 33 slaves in a total population of 450. Within 20 years, there were 127 slaves in Detroit. The British left captured Indian and black slaves in the hands of their original French owners, and then added some of their own. British society not only condoned slavery, but also reinforced it.

There was only one restriction against slave owners, which, once again, set the Canadas apart. Punishment of a slave, for improper behaviour or disobedience, became the right of the state and not the individual master. Police captured runaway slaves and returned them to their original owner who then had to appear in court to lay a charge while the magistrate imposed and carried out the sentence. The slave was tied to the whipping post and lashed the requisite number of times by the state. The master was not free to whip slaves directly which tempered slavery and placed controls on slave ownership. As time went on, it became harder for owners to get slaves back. Judges often dismissed the cases on the slimmest technicality.

After the American Revolutionary War in 1776, some 3,500 former black slaves, who fought for the British, came to the Canadas as free men. Most were not escaping the slave owner's whip so much as the oppression and prejudice of American society. Many settled in the Maritimes, but some came to Upper Canada, the shores of Lake Erie, and to border communities around "The Ferry," Assumption Parish or Sandwich which later became Windsor. Included were men such as Thomas and James Fry and William Lee who settled in Colchester township and Fort Malden. The border communities were accessible and convenient, located at the narrowest part of the Detroit River where many of the boats put in. As a result, Essex and Kent counties developed a higher concentration of black residents than other parts of the province.

The Gem, a ferry owned by William Campbell, helped transport fugitive slaves from Detroit to Windsor, circa 1858. The ferry is shown at the Windsor dock.

Reproduced courtesy of Windsor's Community Museum, Windsor Public Library, P5435.

Free Blacks were highly visible because of the colour of their skin, but it was difficult to distinguish them from slaves. They intermingled, dressed much like everybody else and were often seen in the streets going about their daily business. Because of their presence, it became difficult to enforce slavery. Free Blacks lived in their own communities with their own churches and schools and it was hard to stop slaves from running away to these black settlements and effectively "getting lost." There was always room for one more, and free Blacks did not mind harbouring runaways, sometimes as many as 13 or 14 at a time. With such a refuge available, it was a challenge to determine which men were slaves and which were free. One of the main tenets of slavery was unravelling – that a man cannot be enslaved unless he is perceived as different or inferior. Increasingly, it became harder to equate skin colour with servitude.

With the ordinance of 1787, the Americans passed the first anti-slavery law in North America, which abolished slavery in the Northwest Territory (now the states of Indianna, Ohio, Michigan, Illinois and Wisconsin). It was supposed to apply in Detroit, but the region was considered a wild frontier where government authority was blurred. In 1760, the British acquired the territory as part of the French concession but gave it up to the Americans in 1783 with the Treaty of Versailles. However, while Americans laid claim to it, the British governed it until 1796. As such, the land was both "free American territory" and British "slave" country at the same time. British slave owners ignored American laws and retained ownership of their charges, but slaves appreciated the law, took advantage of the ambiguity, fled the British, and sought freedom with the Americans. Although it lasted for only a short period, it was one of the most incongruous situations in American and Canadian slave history.

As time went on, sentiments toward slavery changed on the British side. Many Canadians became indignant about the ill-treatment of slaves and the separation of black families when members were sold. It was no longer acceptable to sell men, treating them no better than cattle. In June 1793, two years after the province of Upper Canada was formed, a bill that eventually led to the abolition of slavery was drafted by Chief Justice William Osgoode and introduced in the Legislative Assembly. It was read by John White, the first attorney general, but inspired by John Graves

Simcoe who some people feel was the Abraham Lincoln of Upper Canada. Simcoe was the first lieutenant governor, an M.P. for St. Mawes, Cornwall, and a soldier who led the Queen's Rangers in the American Revolutionary War. In his view slavery was anti-Christian, an evil institution that went against the British Constitution and he wanted to stamp it out.

Simcoe's new bill was fashioned after similar legislation presented two years earlier in the British House of Commons by political reformer and abolitionist William Wilberforce. His new law gave Upper Canada the distinction of being the first British possession to actually legislate against slavery. Simcoe, however, wasn't entirely happy with the bill because it was not a total ban. It was instead a compromise to accommodate wealthy and powerful slave owners. While not actually outlawing slavery, it prohibited the importation and purchase of new slaves and was a start toward the abolition of slavery throughout the colonies. It allowed owners to keep slaves, but they had to feed and clothe them properly. Children of slaves were freed when they reached 25 years of age, and their children were born free. Escaped slaves were also freed, and it was up to the original owner to make sure they did not become wards of the state.

Even though nine members of the Legislative Council or Upper House were slave owners, or members of slave-owning families, passage of the bill was made possible because the majority of the 16 legislators "kept only one table" which meant they ate with their servants and treated them equally. Still, it wasn't easy. The bill passed "with much opposition, but little argument" and, within five years, it was tested in the legislature when another motion was put forward to import slaves. Nothing came of it, however, which was yet another indication that the tide had turned in Canada. Slavery was on its way out, once and for all.

The new law was a calculated affront to the Americans, and an example to other slaving nations, as it recognized the democratic principle that human beings, regardless of the colour of their skin, were still human beings. The law was an act in support of human rights and it was hoped that it would change Canada's attitude toward slavery. A degree of freedom not enjoyed in the United States was being established and, because of this fundamental difference, the Canada/U.S. border became even more symbolic as thousands of Blacks crossed it in hope of finding freedom.

Between 1793 and 1815, about 1,000 refugee slaves came through Ohio to Upper Canada, but it took the War of 1812 for many American Blacks to realize that Canada was a free haven. A year after the war began, Kentuckians and militiamen from other slave states invaded what was to become Southwestern Ontario, only to encounter a force of 500 black troops who hated American slavery and wanted to protect their freedom and their homes. The Blacks served with the British army under the command of an Indian chief and were determined "to defend everything they called precious," to avoid being drawn back into slavery.

Word of Canada spread quickly between plantations, handed down in stories and songs with hidden meanings, so the white owners wouldn't understand. "Got one mind for the white folk to see, 'nother for what I know is me." *Away To Canada* was one such ditty, sung to the tune of *Oh Suzannah.*

I'm on my way to Canada
That cold and distant land.
The dire effects of slavery
I can no longer stand –

Farewell old master,
Don't come after me.
I'm on my way to Canada
Where coloured men are free.

Since slaves couldn't read, they were told in song to "follow the North Star and the side of the tree the moss grows on to find Canada – the land of freedom." The "drinking gourd" or Big Dipper led them on. Since white slavers rarely listened to black songs and the slaves could confidently follow these coded directions. It's estimated that the first refugees made it to Essex County and settled in Colchester township near Harrow as early as 1816.

Escape from slavery was encouraged by the establishment of the "Underground Railroad," an important symbol of freedom, the first time that Whites and Blacks worked together for racial justice and equality. The railroad, a metaphor for an escape route, was set up in 1804 by free Blacks, a few white Quakers and Methodists and other American abolitionists who, while not well organized, were devoted and sincere.

Although abolitionists comprised only two percent of the American population, they were dedicated to helping Blacks find food, shelter, transportation and clothing during their escape to freedom. Incensed by the brutal treatment of black people and the shooting of runaway slaves, Quakers actively demonstrated that slavery went against their religious teachings and their pacifist nature. They lobbied for social reforms, despite the threat of fines and imprisonment. Under their guidance and with the assistance of black "railroad conductors," many slaves travelled on foot, hid in steamer trunks, boxes and crates, secret compartments, false-bottomed wagons, under cargoes of vegetables, manure or lumber.

In the Niagara Peninsula, the most famous "conductor" on the Underground Railroad was Harriet Tubman, a former slave born in Maryland, who helped nearly 300 other slaves escape to freedom, including her own parents. From 1851 to 1855, she lived intermittently in the St. Catharines area, making almost 20 trips into the United States, for which she earned the nickname "the Moses of her people."

Tubman's counterpart in the Windsor area may well have been Laura Haviland, a white, Canadian-born Quaker who was called "The Super-intendent of the Underground Railroad." Haviland worked in Detroit, Michigan, to help slaves cross into Canada. Later, she was the first teacher at the Puce River Settlement School near Windsor. She stayed about a year, during which time she organized a "mixed" church, which reflected the different backgrounds of her parishioners.

Ironically, many slaves chose to escape and many remained on the plantation, skeptical about the Quakers and fearful of the unknown. There were rampant rumours, no doubt supported by slave owners, that abolitionists were cannibals and no one survived the journey. It was said that crows would pick out their eyes, that the river was 3,000 miles wide or that Canada was "a freezing hell" covered in ice and snow. The fear of death kept many Blacks at home.

For those who did take the chance, the trip was dangerous and difficult. Blacks left their friends and braved the unknown, the uncertainty

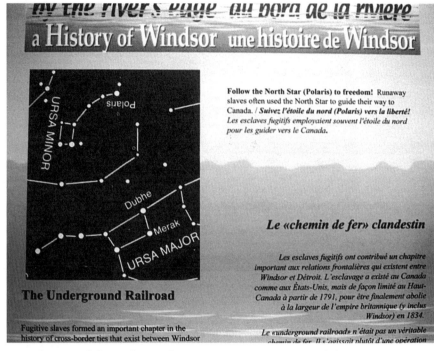

Part of a 2002 exhibit at the Windsor's Community Museum entitled "by the river's edge, a History of Windsor," explaining the Underground Railroad and the escape of slaves to freedom. Courtesy of Windsor's Community Museum. Photo by Herb Colling.

and sorrow, travelling at night through mosquito-infested swamps and across fields, hiding in woods, barns, cellars and attics during the day. They zigzagged from place to place, doubling back to elude hunting dogs. Most fugitive slaves came from North Carolina, Tennessee and Kentucky and Maryland, voyaging over 600 to 1,200 kilometres of rough terrain, subsisting on biscuits and water, or eating roots and berries along the way. They changed their names to avoid capture, and worked their passage north by harvesting wheat, chopping logs. To cross rivers and streams they stowed away on ferries, built rafts, stole canoes or swam. Often not knowing which way to turn, they relied on their own initiative and resourcefulness. No one could be trusted, not even other slaves.

The Railroad became a powerful and yet, misunderstood symbol. It followed secret routes through southern slave states including Tennessee, Virginia and Missouri. It was "underground" because it was secret, but the image was so effective, so graphic, that many people believed a real train, which had only recently been introduced as a mode of transportation in the United States actually ran through a subterranean tunnel. The mystique was enhanced by courageous and resourceful people who masterminded the escapes, using disguises and camouflage to avoid detection and defy the law. It was pure espionage. A lantern in a window or a coded letter indicated safe or secret houses. The misconception was supported by a code of railroad terms with double meanings to confuse the public and throw slavers off the scent.

Blacks were called "cargo, freight, packages or merchandise," as in "four large kegs of dark ale and one small one" which referred to four adults and a child. "Conductors" were people who helped "passengers" on their flight to freedom. "Stations" described safe houses 20 to 30 miles apart along the "line." "Depot agents" manned the stations and "stockholders" donated food, clothing and money. Refugee slaves were "new arrivals" to "the terminal" which was Canada. Blacks settled as free men in accessible towns including Amherstburg, Harrow, Windsor, Sandwich, Colchester, Puce, Marble Village and Little River in Maidstone township.

The Railroad has been highly romanticized in fact and fiction, "enlarged by popular opinion and exaggerated by legend," but it did exist and is a moving tribute to the human spirit. From 1817 to 1822, abolitionist Captain Charles Stuart reported that 150 refugee slaves came to Amherstburg. He helped them settle on small plots of land in town, "equal to any class labourer in the country." Many others died or disappeared enroute, but the Underground Railroad helped create pockets of black settlement as far north in Ontario as Owen Sound and Collingwood, and ultimately throughout Canada.

To emphasize the commitment to freedom in Upper and Lower Canada, there's the story of an ex-slave named Andrew who, in 1830, was working as a farmhand for the Baby family in Sandwich. The family had liberated its slaves, but Andrew's former owner tracked him down, and tried to buy him back for $2000, saying that Andrew had stolen a horse. When Andrew proclaimed his innocence, Baby refused to sell. The owner, along with five other men, tried to kidnap Andrew while the Baby family was at church, but with the help of neighbours, the slavers were stopped.

Baby collected enough money to send Andrew away to York, now Toronto, where it was felt he would be safe.

Attitudes were changing and, by 1833, most slaves in Canada were free, but it was still a slow process. In August of that year, the Abolition of Slavery Act was passed, 30 years before a similar act on the American side. The British bill was implemented in 1834 to abolish slavery throughout the Commonwealth. Notices were sent out, but some owners were reluctant to tell their slaves. Blacks on the farm of Colonel Elliott in Malden only found out by accident and were among the last to be freed in Canada.

Abolition had a profound effect on many visitors. In the winter of 1834, Reverend Jermain W. Loguen, who was born in Tennessee of a white father and slave mother, rode his horse across the frozen Detroit River. As one observer suggested, "Freedom touched his heart and it leapt for joy. Cold, cheerless and unpromising as everything looked, he felt the divine hand within him." Public opinion generally supported black refugees and prompted one group of Windsor Blacks to thank God for the "laws of this adopted country and for the easy conditions offered us in common with other settlers." There were some injustices and hardships, but conditions were generally better in Canada than on the plantations of the south.

When Levi Coffin, the "president" of the "Railroad" came to Sandwich in the 1840s, he was gratified to discover a thriving black community, and was pleased that a man's colour did not make much difference in the courts of this country. When a black man was accepted for jury duty, some Whites refused to sit in the same box. They were reprimanded by the judge, fined and then imprisoned. In another case, a white man was on trial for luring a slave from the Canadian side into the hands of his master. The offender was found guilty, imprisoned and fined, because "the moment a fugitive sets foot on British soil, his shackles fell off and he was free."

Slavery was abolished by degrees in Canada as attitudes changed. Blacks enjoyed a degree of civil rights and equality before the law, but their chances of success were curtailed because of their limited education and because of racial prejudice. Having been deprived of education, most Blacks were largely illiterate and some Canadian landowners took advantage, especially homesteaders in the southern part of the county. They convinced Blacks that, if they cleared and worked the land for ten years, it would be theirs. Because former slaves couldn't read, they took the landowner at his word. At the end of their ten years, the landowner took the land and evicted the Blacks. They had worked for nothing. Their trust was betrayed.

Success or failure was driven by circumstance or chance. Gabriel Timberlake was born on a Kentucky plantation in 1825. He fled the lash and arrived in Canada in 1844, walking up to a farm on the Gore Road near Harrow. The farmer called to his wife that there was a "strange coon" in the yard. Timberlake asked for some food and the farmer put him to work chopping wood. Timberlake worked for years, eventually making enough money to buy his own home.

Freedom in Canada was a delivery, but also a displacement and at times a disappointment. Ninety percent of the refugees to Canada received no outside help or charity and many were poor, hungry and emaciated. In 1848, the Canada Mission was established at an old military barracks, erected during the Rebellion of 1837 in Amherstburg. Designed to help immigrants, the mission was soon filled with 17 ragged families, including the sick and poor – men, women and children who needed food, shelter, clothing and jobs.

In the early days, black poverty was criticized by some Whites who characterized Blacks as inferior, "ignorant, lazy or both." There were few jobs because of the influx of labourers from the British Isles and, as black people competed for those jobs, the seeds of racism were sown. Although Blacks tried to isolate themselves from the hatred and humiliation by Whites, they were kept from better jobs, schools and, in some cases, land.

By the mid-1840s, local black residents were encouraged to live in model communities, planned settlements with Blacks-only churches and schools. These enclaves were developed, in part, through choice, but also through necessity when many Canadian Whites refused to associate with Blacks. With the help of abolitionists in Detroit and Toronto, black societies purchased large blocks of land, which they sold to black families. The little colonies helped former slaves buy land and earn an honest living "without being dependent on the charity of others."

A watercolour sketch of Mary Ann Camberton Shadd, educator, lawyer and first black publisher of a newspaper in North America, on display at the North American Black Historical Museum in Amherstburg. Shadd's motto was "Self Reliance is the True Road to Independence." The local artist is known only as B.W.
Courtesy of North American Black Historical Museum. Photo by Herb Colling.

These societies recognized that black people were willing to work, but needed to be educated. Their mandate was to reduce illiteracy, promote religious and orderly conduct, raise funds and provide jobs, and to alleviate the hardships that Blacks faced getting established. However, most were short-lived through a combination of financial problems. The Refugee Home Society was established near Windsor in 1851, but it was destroyed less than three years later, largely because of internal differences between two black leaders, both newspaper editors in the community.

Mary Ann Camberton Shadd was the editor of *The Provincial Freeman*, and she suggested that Blacks should develop self-reliance and financial independence, but integrate to reduce prejudice. She was opposed by Henry Bibb, editor of *The Voice of the Fugitive*, who believed in segregation, that Blacks should remain apart from the white population to develop their own independence and dignity. Bibb believed that Blacks needed a protected environment so they could learn to read and write and pick up a trade before assimilating into the mainstream of Canadian life. He feared that Blacks would lose face if they couldn't cope, but hoped that they would ultimately reduce their dependence on Whites. Devoted to black freedom, Bibb worked to create a more sympathetic climate and gain acceptance for the black man.

Henry Bibb

A pencil sketch of Kentucky-born Henry Walton Bibb, from the formal photograph of him taken for the frontispiece for his published bibliography, Narrative of the Life and Adventures of Henry Bibb, An American Slave, *published in 1849. This work done by local artist, Catherine Kersey, in 1983, is on display at the North American Black Historical Museum.*
Courtesy of North American Black Historical Museum. Photo by Herb Colling.

Ultimately, Bibb looked forward to the end of slavery in the United States and to a time when Blacks could return to their homes in America and end their self-imposed exile. Shadd, on the other hand, wanted to get on with life in Canada and extolled the virtues and achievements of Blacks in her adopted country. She didn't appreciate impermanence and promoted Canada as her home and place of business, even publishing a book on the subject. Called *Notes on Canada West*, it documented the positive elements of life in Canada, including housing, employment and natural resources to counter the negative image portrayed by American slave owners.

Shadd worried about the constant bickering of black leaders, but opposed black colonies because the more Blacks segregated from society, the more intolerant that society became. Shadd believed that separate churches and schools prevented the races from mixing, which impeded the goal of integration. A forceful writer, Shadd complained that all black

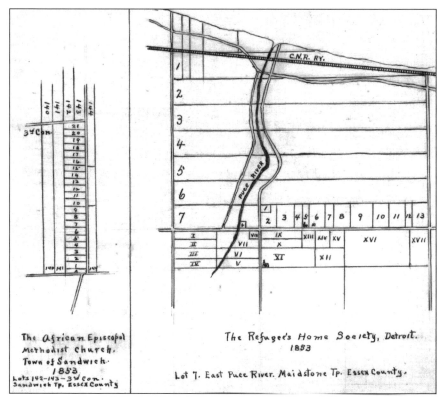

Henry Bibb helped to establish The Refugee Home Society. The intention was to promote the social, moral, physical and intellectual development of Blacks. This sketch shows plots assigned to black families, along the Puce River and Puce Road near Windsor, 1853. Courtesy of Windsor's Community Museum, Windsor Public Library M202.

communities depended on white philanthropy and she resented the implication that Blacks couldn't make it on their own without soliciting funds door-to-door or collecting old clothes to sell in fundraisers. She felt it was a demeaning form of begging, "materially compromising our manhood, by representing us as objects of charity." She also feared that settlers would never receive deeds to their land, or that they'd have to pay more for their properties.

Eventually, the grand experiment dissolved in a series of lawsuits over misappropriation of funds. Differing opinions and bad press continued, and the Refugee Home Society's finances were thrown into chaos.

It's ironic in Canadian society that racial tolerance can co-exist with intolerance. Ours is a subtle, understated form of racism, not as overt as the United States, but perhaps just as dangerous and debilitating. Racial tensions may not be as great, but many Canadians do have a deep-seeded prejudice, which often leads to discriminatory behaviour. As one historian wrote, "Black Canadians have been violated, ignored, limited to the lowest range on the social scale, all in an environment that insisted that they were free and equal, despite evidence to the contrary."

As a visible minority, black people became an easy target for discrimination by a white majority, and acts of discrimination increased according to the size of the black population or the scarcity of jobs. Some Whites feel threatened as the number of black people increases and Canada's sense of white superiority diminishes – a warped form of defence. Many white Canadians held a superior attitude toward black people, considering them inferior and only suited to menial work. Although such prejudices are rarely admitted in mixed company, racism perpetuates itself in private. Over time it has become institutional, accepted as normal and traditional, the custom in white society.

There are many examples of racism in our history. David P. Botsford, a local historian, talks about Irish immigrants in Amherstburg who, "under the influence," liked to play "practical jokes" on local Blacks. One incident involved a mock hanging that almost resulted in the death of a black man. Another involved a display of marksmanship from the porch of a local tavern, which destroyed Jim Simpson's clay pipe. "A bullet shattered the bowl and carried it away as he [Jim] was enjoying a smoke on his way home from work at Thomas's sawmill." Yet another black man is reported to have fallen asleep by the roadside after visiting too many saloons. When the Irish found him, they carried him home and filled his ears with candle wax. When he awoke, he could hear very little and was convinced that he was deaf before he discovered their prank. Harmless fun or malicious racism?

The most blatant example of racism made it into the political arena. When the Elgin Settlement – another black community and refuge for former slaves – was established, in Raleigh township near Chatham, by Reverend William King in 1848, not everyone endorsed it. The black settlers were hard-working and industrious and the community grew and prospered, but there were still critics. The stiffest opposition came from a white merchant named Edwin Larwill who believed that Blacks were inferior and irresponsible and that the town would suffer if they were allowed to stay. Concerned about declining property values, Larwill was openly hostile, convinced that white residents would move if the settlement remained. As he put it, "amalgamation is as disgusting to the eye as it is immoral."

Despite threats by vigilantes, King travelled to Chatham to make an impassioned speech in defense of his colony. A number of bodyguards, including one white man, protected him from the booing crowd. In 1854, Larwill became a member of parliament, but Blacks defeated him two years later. Politically astute, 300 members of King's community marched from Buxton to Chatham and voted as a block to defeat Larwill and racism. Larwill was replaced by Archibald McKellar, the white man who stood beside King years earlier as the crowd booed.

Although prosperous, with over 1,000 residents by the time of the American Civil War, King's settlement was finally disbanded in 1873 when the board of directors decided it had achieved its goals. The settlement had no debts so all the land was sold, and the stockholders and employees were paid. The church and school survived and some members stayed, and the community, although smaller, still exists today. As Canada's only self-supporting, all-black community, it is one of the few remaining original black settlements inhabited by the descendants of slaves, a testament to the ability of Blacks to progress normally when many people doubted their natural abilities.

Despite the willingness of black people to fit in and thrive, their inventiveness and perseverance, was not always rewarded or recognized by the white community. Delos Rogest Davis became the first black lawyer in Canadian history and, on November 10, 1910, the first black man appointed to King's Counsel. To become a lawyer, he was required to article in a law firm but, because he was "black," no one would have him and, for eleven years, he was unable take his final exams. In 1884, he appealed to the Ontario Legislature, asking that the requirement be waived. His request was eventually granted and Davis passed his finals on May 19, 1885, coming first in his class of 13. He was finally admitted to the Law Society of

Delos Rogest Davis KC, of Amherstburg, was the first black lawyer in Canadian history. Admitted to the bar in 1885, he became the first African-Canadian King's Counsel in 1910. He practised law at Mackenzie Hall in Sandwich near Windsor. Courtesy of North American Black Historical Museum. Photo by Herb Colling.

Upper Canada in November '86, after which he set up practice on Gore Street in Amherstburg as an authority in municipal law.

By settling in Canada, Blacks hoped to build a better life and, while they weren't openly prevented, there were minor skirmishes in stagecoaches, steamboats and hotels. Most Emancipation Day celebrations passed without incident, but some were marred by racism. On August 1, 1886, some 3,000 people "dressed in holiday attire" walked, drove, or travelled by boat from Sandwich and Windsor to Caldwell's Grove in Amherstburg to hear brass bands and speeches. They wanted to enjoy the picnic, baseball games and dancing and to offer thanks for freedom but, just as the passenger boat *City of Dresden* docked, an argument arose "between young Whites and some of the coloured boys." The white youths saw a pile of bricks on the dock and pelted the Blacks as they disembarked. Several people were injured.

Generally, black people comprised only one to two percent of the population. Since small numbers represented a small and insignificant minority, Blacks were either attacked or ignored by the white majority. Their stories were not told in history books and their rights were neglected. Since Blacks were not recognized as a significant group, they remained weak and powerless, demoralized, alienated and anonymous in an overpowering white society. Racism in Canada evolved differently from most other countries. Instead of being overt and obvious, it was either covert or outright blatant. Some Whites simply refused to have anything to do with Blacks. Since they didn't openly antagonize Blacks, they felt they could deny their own racism and not suffer the consequences of their actions.

Surprisingly, it took an American commission to document our subtle forms of racism. During the American Civil War in 1863, U.S. President Abraham Lincoln established the Freedman's Inquiry, led by Samuel Gridley Howe. It was to investigate the condition of black communities in Canada West as a means of determining the future of newly freed Blacks flooding into northern American states. Howe toured the black settlement in North Buxton, and was suitably impressed. In his final report, on December 31, 1863, Howe talked about good roads through the forest, 200 orderly cottages with several cultivated acres, an abundance of livestock, good fences and barns, a chapel and school with "no tavern or groggery"; all built within 16 years. He found no distinction between the homes of Whites or Blacks.

Howe suggested that these accomplishments were remarkable because of the dangers that former slaves faced as they fled the plantations of the south. He appreciated that Canadian Blacks owned property while 20 years ago they were slaves who had nothing. Howe said refugees survived years of toil, poverty and anxiety to enjoy comfort, hope and pride in their homes and possessions. An ardent reformer and abolitionist, Howe concluded that slavery was not necessary to the welfare of Blacks as many people in the south maintained.

Howe also recognized that, when Blacks came to Canada, the government did nothing to help them. Most fundraising was done privately and led to the establishment of communities or colonies. Trouble was, most of the money went to white agents with very little for refugees and Howe questioned the wisdom of that arrangement. He suggested that the "settlements were large in conception, but small in achievement" and he didn't feel they needed artificial encouragement because Blacks would congregate anyway. Howe concluded that colonies merely prolonged the dependence and servitude of Blacks rather than making them hardy, self-reliant men.

The commission noted that adult Blacks arrived in Canada with little or no schooling, but learned to read and write and had a strong desire that their children do the same. Blacks bettered their manners and morals, earned a living, built churches and schools and amassed property "not because they are picked men, but because they are free men." The report regarded the future of former slaves as hopeful and suggested that Canada could offer lessons to the Republic on how to deal with its own newly-freed Blacks. It concluded that "the Negro does best when let alone, and that we must beware of all attempts to prolong his servitude, even under pretext of taking care of him ... now let the Negro take care of himself."

Of course, the Freedman's Inquiry was significant for its conclusions, but also for another reason. It revealed a sinister and racial side to Canadian society. For example, the commission met a Canadian farmer who didn't like Blacks because they only worked if they were "looked after right sharp." The farmer said that Blacks didn't steal any more or less than Whites, but "Whites often got clear by saddling their sins on the backs of darkies." Anti-black sentiments were especially bitter after the American Civil War. As a man from Chatham complained, Blacks "are becoming so haughty they are looking upon themselves as the equals of Whites."

The report maintained that one "Negro" awakens sympathy, but that two awaken prejudice and antagonism. Captain Averill of Malden spoke highly of black sailors, for example. He said they were thrifty, drank less and saved their wages, but must be kept separate from whites. He never mixed firemen or deckhands, and said, "Never make them mates." As the report indicated, "freshwater sailors on the lakes and rivers shared the liberality of 'blue water salts,' and didn't object to 'coloured company' unless there was too much of it." Because of that white attitude, many Blacks rose to the challenge and proved that they could survive and thrive.

The town of Dresden, in the Township of Camden, Kent County, became known as "Nigger Hole" by those who opposed black settlement. Racial jokes were common in the local press and black businessmen were restricted from employing whites. Blacks were expelled from camp meetings, and The City Directory designated businesses and residences as Black-owned as early as 1850. Conditions were similar in Orford township "where no coloured man is allowed to settle." If Blacks tried to build a home by day, Whites would tear it down at night. In other areas, however, Blacks were allowed to coexist. In neighbouring Howard township, black families lived in harmony and were described as "respectable, religious, intelligent and clean .... Ministers of the gospel would actually call and take dinner with these people."

On the subject of mixed marriages, the commissioners learned that white women, who intermarried, were often shunned by society. As Mayor Thomas Cross of Chatham explained, "It is a very good trait in the characters of [black] people, that they do not regard it as any honour to marry a white person." The sentiment was echoed by Blacks who heard that a friend ran away with a white woman. "I always looked upon him as a respectable man. I didn't think he would fall so low as to marry a white girl." The commission concluded that only the most forlorn white woman would pursue "the most forlorn hope of all ... union with a black man." As a result, the commission concluded that there was no need for "anxiety upon the score of amalgamation of races in the United States." It was felt that Blacks would follow their natural affinities and marry amongst themselves. As Cross told the commissioners, "coloured people generally live apart" which, he felt, caused a strong prejudice against them. Blacks responded that they were forced to live apart because of prejudice.

The commissioners also noted a Canadian tendency to believe that prejudice was not a British, but an American attitude imported to the country. The feelings were especially strong with abolitionist Loyalists, but many Blacks didn't buy it. They maintained that, "when coloured people form a small percentage of the population, are dependent and not perceived as a threat; they receive protection and favours, but when they increase and compete with the labouring class for a living, and especially when they begin to aspire to social equality, then they cease to be 'interesting Negroes' and become 'niggers.' " The report concluded that Canadians protested too much. Saying that Blacks could hold office and have their rights protected did not make it so. In truth, their lack of education or culture disqualified them from posts they might have held.

Despite the boast of Canadian Whites "that their laws know no difference of colour, Canadian Blacks noticed signs of racial prejudice. While a few admitted that they would return "home" because of the cold, others referred to the climate of discrimination in Canada. They said they would gladly return to the United States if they had the same rights to freedom. It was a general feeling that racism was racism, no different in the United States or Canada. The commission recounts the story of a slave from Kentucky who, in the late 1700s, was captured by Indians and sold to a British officer in Fort Malden. The slave was so cruelly treated in Canada that he fled to Ohio. In another case, a woman from Virginia said she was anxious to go home because "the prejudice was a heap stronger in Canada." To her, most Whites believed that Blacks "weren't folks anyway" and, because of these attitudes, neither side had much to do with the other.

Once Emancipation was proclaimed in the United States, there was no longer a need for Blacks to stay in Canada, and many returned home. There had always been close ties between black churches, schools and families on both sides of the border, and it's estimated that at least half of the black families left Canada after the American Civil War. Only 15,000 Blacks remained in Canada, and many black communities dwindled. One hundred years later, there were fewer Blacks in Essex County than there were in the 1850s. In retrospect, it was a surprising exodus, an ironic twist to the quest for freedom for many Blacks, especially in light of race relations in the United States.

Many white people assumed that Blacks wanted to be left alone when they first came to Canada, but that wasn't necessarily true. Many refugee slaves were hard-working taxpayers who objected to segregation, but generally had no choice. They kept to themselves, in part, by necessity since integrated institutions were few and far between. Most white churches, for example, were united in their opposition to slavery in keeping with their Christian teachings, but were not as convinced about integration. As a result, segregation extended to all aspects of black society, including churches and schools. Many Whites were simply reluctant to mix with Blacks because they didn't like or understand their ways. Black Methodists and Baptists were too flamboyant and enthusiastic. They sang different hymns and spirituals and reacted differently to their sermons. As a result, mixed congregations were rare and white people made it known that black

Sandwich Baptist Church, built in 1851, is the oldest existing black church in Windsor. It was constructed of clay bricks, handmade by members of the church, many of whom were former slaves from the United States. Reproduced courtesy of Windsor's Community Museum, Windsor Public Library, P6205.

workshippers were unwelcome during services in white churches. Some white churches even forbade the burial of Blacks in consecrated ground.

Despite discrimination, black religions flourished. A belief in God motivated and sustained the flight to freedom, and helped Blacks overcome hardships in their new land. Christianity allowed Blacks an escape from bondage, and provided a sense of pride and self-worth. Even though they were ignored by the rest of society within the church they acquired a meeting hall and school, a cohesive, stabilizing and binding force, the only place Blacks could legally assemble. As Alvin McCurdy, a black historian, once said, "You made sure you got to church on time. Otherwise, you didn't get a seat." As curator of the North American Black Historical Museum in Amherstburg, Elise Harding-Davis says, the church was the centre of religious, cultural and social life for the black community, the one place to escape discrimination and find fellowship.

Another significant area of segregation was in the school system. Under the Common School Act of 1850, Blacks could send their children to common schools or, if sufficient numbers warranted, and twelve black families asked for it, separate schools could be set up. Trustees could not refuse admission to the common school and could not force Blacks to attend a separate school. "Coloured children have equal rights with all other residents to enter the school and to receive instruction, like the rest." The act allowed separate schools if Blacks wanted them, but not at the whim of trustees. Also, anyone, "laying hands on a coloured child, no matter how gently" and turning them out of school, was guilty of common assault.

The act was designed to prevent discrimination, but it didn't always work that way. The act was supposed to prevent the establishment of schools against the will of the people, but schools were often segregated. The act was meant to satisfy the wishes of the black community, but it was cleverly worded and subject to interpretation by each township, and actually invited discrimination. Trustees often refused to admit Blacks to white schools in direct contravention of the law. If Blacks were allowed in, they were forced to sit at the back of the class and were ridiculed. When black students enrolled in the common school, many white parents withdrew their children in protest. They didn't want their youngsters sitting next to black children, nor did they feel that Blacks should have the choice to attend a common school.

As the number of black students increased, the act was cited as justification for establishing separate schools, which generally provided second-rate instruction in run-down buildings. Often, there was no library, no furnace, no supplies, poor lighting, poor teaching and irregular attendance. Whites encouraged Blacks to set up their own separate schools and, once they did, they were not allowed to change their minds even though they recognized their mistake. Critics of the act suggested it was racist legislation that led to the widespread establishment of separate schools for Blacks whether they wanted them or not. An amendment allowed school boards to set up separate schools even if Blacks didn't request them, and black pupils were compelled to attend. Whites even set money aside to build separate black schools. Surprisingly, many Blacks didn't object, perhaps because of their acquiescence to the white man's world, or their strong belief in education, the belief that some schooling was better than nothing. Many black parents simply wanted an education for their children that they had been denied.

There was quite a distinction between common and separate schools. The idea of the public school was to integrate students to weaken the colour bar. Students from different races got to know each other, played, studied, became used to each other, whereas separate schools strengthened differences. A report on school conditions suggests, black students in common schools appeared as clean and bright and as decently clad as Whites and a touch more "mirthful and roguish," but their counterparts in separate schools "do not look so tidy; and are not so well-ordered." Separate school students were not so advanced in their studies because the supply and quality of teachers was not as good and they didn't spend as many years in school because their parents needed them for chores at home. Black children were set back, and kept back.

As late as 1840 in Amherstburg, there were no black schools and the black population was becoming larger and growing up in ignorance. They were too poor for schools of their own and not allowed into others, so a school was established for white and black children on an equal footing in an effort to do away with prejudice. Classes were taught by Robert Peden of the Glasgow Normal School. Many people believed the school would fail because no white children would be sent if black children were present, but it lasted six years as a tribute to the high-calibre teaching. Both white and black children attended, and the school was successful, although it never prospered because the fees were too low. Eventually, the building had to be sold and the teacher became a pastor of the Presbyterian Church.

In the Harrow area, near Windsor, black parents repeatedly went to court to attend white schools, but with no success. In 1852, Dennis Hill, a well-educated black farmer and landowner, wanted his children to go to the white school rather than travel four more miles to the black school. He went to court, but the judge ruled against him. Some Ontario boards of education even moved school boundaries so black neighbourhoods were not included. In 1864, teachers opposed segregation and discrimination at

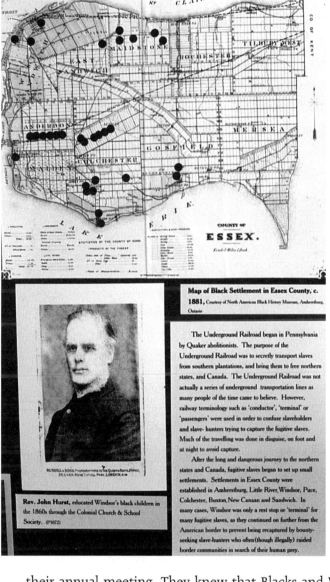

Map of Black Settlement in Essex County, c.
1881, Courtesy of North American Black History Museum, Amherstburg, Ontario

The Underground Railroad began in Pennsylvania by Quaker abolitionists. The purpose of the Underground Railroad was to secretly transport slaves from southern plantations, and bring them to free northern states, and Canada. The Underground Railroad was not actually a series of underground transportation lines as many people of the time came to believe. However, railway terminology such as 'conductor', 'terminal' or 'passengers' were used in order to confuse slaveholders and slave-hunters trying to capture the fugitive slaves. Much of the travelling was done in disguise, on foot and at night to avoid capture.

After the long and dangerous journey to the northern states and Canada, fugitive slaves began to set up small settlements. Settlements in Essex County were established in Amherstburg, Little River, Windsor, Puce, Colchester, Buxton, New Canaan and Sandwich. In many cases, Windsor was only a rest stop or 'terminal' for many fugitive slaves, as they continued on further from the American border to prevent being recaptured by bounty-seeking slave-hunters who often(though illegally) raided border communities in search of their human prey.

Rev. John Hurst, educated Windsor's black children in the 1860s through the Colonial Church & School Society. (P5072)

An exhibit depicting Reverend John Hurst, a local teacher of black children during the 1860s, through the Colonial Church and School Society. This organization helped establish black settlements in various parts of Essex County, as shown by the large dots on the map. Courtesy of Windsor's Community Museum. Photo by Herb Colling.

their annual meeting. They knew that Blacks and Whites were equally capable, but were ignored by the authorities. Black churches responded by setting up private, religiously-oriented schools while parents continued to protest. The new schools were better run, but were few and far between and did not last long because they were too expensive. These were called "Mission Schools" and were designed to right the wrongs of racism by providing a better calibre of education.

Surprisingly, the educational needs of black children sparked the establishment of Windsor's first hospital – Hôtel-Dieu of St. Joseph. In 1886, Father Dean Wagner, pastor of the Parish of St. Alphonsus Church in Windsor, expressed concern about the welfare and education of Blacks, and was determined to do something about it. Many black children were orphans, living in neglect, and Father Wagner wanted to establish a mission. He couldn't raise enough money locally, so he distributed pamphlets nationally. Mother Superior Justine Bonneau, of the Religious Hospitallers of Hôtel-Dieu of St. Joseph in Montreal, received one of those letters and was so touched by Father Wagner's devotion that she sent him a gold coin worth $2.50 and added that, if Father Wagner wanted to build a hospital, she would help.

There had been talk of building a hospital in Windsor, but there was a lack of funds and interest because some people were suspicious of hospital care. Father Wagner invited the Religious Hospitallers and, in July 1888, Mother Bonneau and Sister Josephine Paquet arrived in Windsor. They purchased six lots of vacant land on Ouellette Avenue and, on September 14, five sisters arrived from Montreal to care for the sick and the poor, and

Hôtel-Dieu Hospital was built in Windsor, in 1889, as a home for black children. After the school closed in 1893, and then the orphanage, the building became a hospital.
Courtesy of Windsor's Community Museum, Windsor Public Library, P6477.

to start a school and orphanage for black children. The construction of the building began one month later and it officially opened in February 1890, with 100 beds. Sister Josephine was the founder and first Superior of Hôtel-Dieu, which still exists today.

Over the next two years, 25 children were admitted to the orphanage, including eight boys and 17 girls with another 35 children at the school. Only six converted to Catholicism, however, and the mission failed. Irregular attendance, poverty, sickness and lack of proper facilities all took their toll. Also, the venture was not supported by wealthier members of the black community who objected to sending their children to a "benevolent school." They insisted on their right to attend the public system. The hospital remained open and expanded, but the day school closed on March 4, 1893, and the orphanage was slowly phased out.

Eventually, more and more black schools were integrated and there was no longer a need for separate schools. Segregation lasted officially until 1888, but it survived unofficially until the mid 1960s, not so much by law, but by geography and inclination. Until the 1950s, many professional schools in Canada would not accept Blacks. To become a medical doctor, for example, some Blacks had to go to the United States.

Ironically, the first doctor of African descent to graduate in Canada, in 1860, was Dr. A.T. Augusta of Virginia, who had been denied access to medical school in the United States. Following him, the first Canadian-born black to graduate from Toronto's King College Medical School in 1861 was Anderson Ruffin Abbott. In the course of his distinguished career, Dr. Abbott became the first black coroner for Kent County in 1874 and chair of the Kent County Medical Association in 1874. At the time, he, his wife, Mary Ann, and their family lived in Chatham where he maintained a medical practice in the Hunton Block on William Street.

Bill Willson was a lawyer for the Township of Colchester South and he remembers one school section near Harrow that was all Black. It was a two-room school, S.S. Number 11, at the Third Concession and Drake Side Road, and it had been segregated for 30 years prior to 1965. Black people moved to Harrow for jobs and land, but this school was in the worst building with the poorest education in the district, already condemned by public health officials when it was purchased by the school board. When they hired their own teacher, Whites withdrew their children and bused them outside of that school zone. The deplorable, unsanitary conditions were challenged in the courts as early as the 1940s, but the issue was lost.

According to one story, the township was concerned about conditions and legalities, but nothing happened until the central school system was introduced and school sections were eliminated. Local Blacks have a different recollection of events, however. They say that, in 1962, an arbitration board consolidated school boards in the township with a $240,000 school to be built the next fall. It was supposed to wipe out segregation and was applauded by the black community, but it took protests, intervention by the Ontario Legislature, and a series of meetings with the school board and minister of education, before the school was finally integrated.

S.S. Number 11 continued to operate for a year after white students were transferred to the new school, which, to the black community, was just one more indication of discrimination, another example of segregation by trustees. Black parents were humiliated and angered. They felt their children could be bused just as easily, since the black school was closer to the new school, or that white students could have been sent to S.S. Number 11 as other schools closed. Black parents felt that schools should have closed at the same time to avoid any appearance of favouritism, but the black school was left until last, as usual. Blacks felt their children suffered because they were disadvantaged, and thought it shameful that the situation continued for so long. Some white parents countered that the black school remained open, only because that's what the black community wanted.

During the fall of 1964, grades one to three were integrated in the new school and, by 1965, S.S. Number 11 was closed. Initially, the parents of black students rode the buses to ensure their children had an orderly transition to their new school. Leonard Braithwaite, the first black MPP in Ontario, was credited with forcing the closure of the last segregated school in the province, but the black community feels it was their collective strength and community involvement. They also say that the whole situation was just another indication that Canada provided freedom, but not necessarily equality.

As reporter Trevor W. Sessing once pointed out in *Saturday Night* magazine, it's ironic that some Canadians branded Americans as racist. It's also ironic that Canada is regarded as one of the better nations for its policies on race and integration. Racist policies extend to all aspects of life in Canada – from immigration to employment. Whites-only lunch counters existed in the early 1900s and there were Whites-only signs until the mid-1960s. In fact, segregation was practised in Canada throughout the first half of the 20th Century.

In 1911, Sessing says, a new, racist Immigration Act was proposed in the House of Commons to exclude Blacks by law. A letter from the Minister of the Interior to the Solicitor General suggested that Blacks be prohibited from entering the country for one year because they were "unsuitable to the climate and requirements of Canada." Some people expressed the belief that Blacks were poor farmers, undesirable and immoral, or that they didn't like the cold and could not adapt to it. As Elise Harding-Davis wryly explained, it was as if the legislators didn't realize that black people had been in Canada for over 200 years and bought hats, coats and boots just like anybody else. Sir Wilfred Laurier's Liberal government refused to allow the act and it never passed even though several members agreed with the idea in principle. To Sessing, it was a low-point in our history. It made Canadians look like hypocrites, negated Canada's stand against slavery and the treatment of Blacks in the United States. The act would have been the first such law in this hemisphere.

Meanwhile, immigration officials worried about how to be "functionally anti-Black," while not "appearing anti-Black." Sessing says border guards refused access to Blacks whenever they could. Other officials refused railway certificates, gave preferential rates to Whites, refused to pass Blacks on medical tests, required character screenings for new settlers, or refused to forward brochures to anyone they thought might be Black. As White hostility increased, thousands of Blacks were excluded from this country. Blacks were powerless to prevent this unofficial ban and black immigration did not begin again until after World War II.

Some municipalities in Essex County even had bylaws, which prevented Blacks from living within town limits. As a result, Blacks settled outside the municipal boundary. In Harrow, for example, a swimming

pool was never built because it would be open to Blacks. A popular watering hole in the county, The Meadows Tavern, refused to allow Blacks inside.
They could only be served in the rear at a small take-out window off the
parking lot.

In May 1921, Blacks in Amherstburg were officially banned, by written
proclamation of the local Sanitary Inspector, from a local theatre during a
smallpox epidemic. The edict supposedly had the sanction of the Medical
Officer of Health. It was as if Blacks, and only Blacks, were responsible for
the outbreak and spread of the disease. The black community complained
that the actions were unwarranted and unfair, that the spread of the con-
tagion had nothing to do with race. They felt that the decree had more to
do with malice and discrimination, and they petitioned the town for an
inquiry. They also suggested that only people exposed to the disease
should be placed under quarantine. The story received a small mention in
the local newspaper at the time, but was omitted from the official history
of the town written in 1996.

The most graphic example of racism appeared on a deed for a cottage
in 1926. The building was on Lakewood Drive in Malden township and the
deed stated, "No lot shall be sold to or occupied by any person or persons
other than those of the Caucasian race." Black people had to purchase
land through white friends because of restricted sales to minorities.

In 1951, legislation was passed in Ontario to ban discrimination because
of race, creed, colour, or country of origin, but it applied to employment
only. J.P. Salsberg, a Labour Progressive Party or Communist member, said
it was a step in the right direction. He expressed concern that large banks,
insurance companies and department stores were the worst offenders,
while newspapers were doing a good job of fighting discrimination.

Unfortunately, the new law didn't address other infractions and,
between 1949 and 1956, there were several incidents of racism in the town
of Dresden in Kent County. The town had a population of 2,000 people,
400 of whom were Black. It was a terminus of the Underground Railroad
and yet, residents voted five to one against a bylaw to require bar, restaurant and barber shop owners to serve anyone regardless of race, colour
and creed. At the time, Dresden Mayor Walter S. Weese said a municipal-
ity did not have a right to interfere in civil rights and suggested that, even

if the vote were upheld, it would be difficult to enforce. There was virtually no way for the town to compel a businessman to serve anyone. Weese
figured "coloured people in town are content," and he feared that a bylaw
with teeth "might start the ball rolling toward real discrimination." He
also suggested that a bylaw would require approval by the attorney general who had the final say in civil rights disputes.

Councillor Mike Fry said, "If coloured people can pay taxes, they should
certainly be entitled to the same privileges as white people ... I just want
to see everybody ... get an even break." As a compromise, he, and more
than 100 residents, signed a petition opposing racial discrimination in
Dresden, concerned that the town was "reversing its fine traditions." The
petition was never presented to council and so, a rally was held to protest
discrimination. As Rabbi Abraham Feinberg complained, "People brag
about Canada as a 'Christian country,' but treat their coloured neighbours
without the humility which is regarded as the essence of Godliness."

By 1956, Dresden was back in the spotlight. Two black men were
refused service and told to go to another establishment after ordering pie
and milk in a local restaurant. "We can't serve you here." When they asked
the reason, they weren't given an answer and were ignored for 20 minutes
until the owner came out and told them to leave. The owner said he
wouldn't mind serving the men, but was afraid that his other customers
would object and stop coming to his restaurant. He knew he was breaking
the law, but he "didn't want to lose business." The two men were
Trinidadian students from the University of Toronto and they were in
town to test the practises of local establishments, to expose racist attitudes and punish offenders. They knew the owner had been convicted of
the same offense two years earlier, but the decision had been reversed in
appellate court. They also knew of similar acts of discrimination against
Blacks at other restaurants and bars in town.

An inspector with the labour ministry eventually investigated after
another complaint was filed by another group of Blacks who were refused
service. A.R. Burnett, a Dresden carpenter, complained that he received
several threatening phone calls and letters after he made his concerns
public. When told to get out of town, he armed himself with a revolver for
protection. The dispute led to a court of inquiry, which was held at the

Dresden arena with over 300 people present. Town Council asked the court not to recommend prosecution because racial discrimination "could best be cured by educating people," not by legislation. The inquiry was the first test of the Anti-Discrimination, Fair Accommodation Practises Act of Ontario that had been passed two years earlier. It was also the first case of its kind in Canada, a test of the Department of Labour. The situation drew spectators and reporters from as far away as Vancouver who wanted to see if the department was strong enough to deal with the kind of racial discrimination that existed in Dresden for over 100 years.

When it went before the Ontario court, the constitutionality of the act was disputed by the defense as an infringement of the rights of the federal government. The defense said it was *ultra vires*, an attempt by the province to establish a Bill of Rights. It led to heated debate in court, fiery discussion in town council and raucous sessions in the provincial legislature. J.P. Salsberg, Labour Progressive member for Toronto-St. Andrew, said the discrimination was shocking. C.E. Janes, Progressive Conservative for Lambton East, replied that Communists and Detroit agitators were to blame for discrimination in Dresden and, if it weren't for people like Salsberg, "Whites and Negroes would be perfectly happy."

At the outcome of the trial, two Dresden restauranteurs were fined $50 and assessed court costs of $600. One owner still insisted he would cater black functions and sell candy, cigarettes and food to Blacks over the counter, but he would not allow them inside to eat. The case was appealed, but the verdict upheld. A Dresden hotel was also charged with refusing to serve beer to Blacks, but the case was dismissed for lack of evidence. By Christmas 1956, Blacks in Dresden were finally served in local restaurants.

During the 1950s and early '60s, calls went out for a Senate Committee to consider a Bill of Rights for Canada to be fashioned after the Universal Declaration of Human Rights of the United Nations. Supporters advocated a bill in recognition of freedom, justice, human dignity and equal and inalienable rights for all. The committee referred to Dresden, and a similar incident in Windsor, in which two black graduates were asked to leave a party in a suburban roadhouse because of their colour. The Bell Telephone Company was also criticized for not employing "Negroes, Japanese, Chinese or Jews."

In April 1957, the Board of Control in Windsor considered a clause in its bylaws, which required builders to sell houses without racial discrimination. Black Controller Roy Perry said he didn't think discrimination existed, but he felt the city should protect itself. City Solicitor James E. Watson said he knew of one buyer who was almost forced to take another lot "because he was coloured." Blacks were often intimidated into selling because they were not wanted. Petitions were circulated, threats made, or the black family was offered money to move. In some areas, property was not open to Blacks by "gentleman's agreement." Whites-only covenants confined Blacks to certain areas of the city, even though such pacts were no longer valid in Ontario. Residential segregation continued unofficially into the 1960s when a survey conducted by Blacks and published by the Guardian Club showed that 60 percent of Windsor landlords practised discrimination, refusing to rent to Blacks. Area golf courses also refused to allow Blacks to play.

In 1960, the Federal Government introduced the National Housing Act to prevent mortgage lenders from discriminating against property buyers by reason of race, colour, religion or national origin. It also provided a review of loan applications by an independent arbitrator. The law followed a complaint from a man who was prevented from purchasing a home by a Windsor realtor. The Ontario Human Rights Code, introduced on February 18, 1965, applied to houses with more than three dwelling units. A year later, black community groups asked that municipalities show indignation and contempt toward discrimination in housing, demanding that the code be extended to all communities and dwelling units.

The Ontario Human Rights Commission was established in 1961 and began operating a year later. In 1965, Windsor was the first city to have a regional field office in Canada. During the first fifteen years of operation, the commission dealt with over 200 complaints of racial discrimination in everything from employment and housing, to public accommodation. It covered Blacks who were refused service in barbershops, movies and restaurants; to doctors who refused to hire black nurses despite the fact they had the qualifications. Doctors had a common excuse. They said they wouldn't mind a black nurse, but their patients might. They also complained that Blacks didn't have the proper skills, but blamed their firing or failure to be promoted on job discrimination.

Banks and credit unions were also reluctant to lend money to black people. They justified their actions by saying that Blacks were in a precarious employment situation and therefore were insecure financially. Many bank officials feared that black businesses were doomed to failure. Some Whites also felt uncomfortable working for Blacks, or felt that Blacks wouldn't hire them because black employers catered to their own. Other Whites felt that Blacks had a chip on their shoulders and merely griped about racism instead of bettering themselves.

In 1965, the Human Rights Commission became involved with the newly established South Essex Citizen's Advancement Association (SECAA), a black coalition that responded to discrimination in Amherstburg. On June 6, five black teens from the United States and one from Amherstburg were beaten up at a dance hall on Boblo Island, by 20 white Canadians who were attending a Chrysler employee's picnic. The altercation started when a black boy asked a white girl to dance. He apparently made an indecent remark to the girl. A white boy tripped a black boy who responded by hitting the white boy. Foul language was followed by a shouting match, the girls were chased out of the dancehall and the fight was on.

The Chrysler employees were playing cards nearby when they heard shouting. They were told that black kids were beating white kids and decided to intervene. As one witness explained, when the men with white shirts and badges got involved, benches, sticks and broken bottles started to fly. One boy's arm was cut and required 15 stitches. There are reports that an American Black pulled a gun, but Whites wrestled it away. No weapon was ever found. The injured were taken to the first aid station as the police arrived. Testimonies differed. The officers couldn't verify who started it, or how. The black boys were turned over to Detroit police and told to stay out of Canada. No charges were laid.

The black community complained that witnesses weren't questioned properly and that the Amherstburg boy was not linked to the Americans. He was just an innocent bystander who happened to be Black and yet, he was knocked unconscious along with some of the Americans. Blacks also complained that some men were kicking a boy who was unconscious on the floor. The president of SECAA, George McCurdy, wanted a thorough investigation so that justice could be served. The police wrote a report, but McCurdy described it as a "whitewash" and was grieved by the incident. It was the first of several fights between Blacks and Whites that summer.

In the fall of that year, SECAA also raised concerns about a burning cross at Sinasac's garage at the corner of Sandwich Street and Alma in Amherstburg. It was a 12-foot by six-foot wooden cross in concrete, wrapped in burlap, soaked in kerosene and set alight after midnight on Monday, August 9. Witnesses say they saw two youths running from the scene. "KKK" was spray-painted in dark green on welcome signs to the town, and the front of the Baptist Church was defaced in crayon with "Niggers beware, the Klan is coming." Ralph McCurdy, George's brother, received a phone call that night from a man with a southern accent who complained that the McCurdy's were defending "niggers." He also remembered seeing a grey Ford station wagon with Michigan plates in the neighbourhood of the burned cross. Its occupants drove slowly around the neighbourhood and then followed McCurdy home before they drove off.

Only a week before, there were rumours that a card-carrying member of the Ku Klux Klan was in the area, but the allegations could never be substantiated. There was even a sensational article in a Toronto newspaper that the Klan was moving in, but there was never any proof. Three days after the fire, Robert Shelton, the Imperial Wizard of the KKK in Tuscaloosa, Alabama, denied that his group was active in the area. Police considered the incident a prank, rather than an example of racial hatred, because other places in town had been spray-painted in the same colours with slogans that were not related to race. According to the chief of police, the events were nothing to get excited about and he blamed the black community for bad press. The comments again distressed George McCurdy who felt the attitude was an insult to Blacks. He figured there were at least five suspects, including the son of a prominent citizen and four Chrysler workers. Later, the chief said he was misquoted and denied that he had made the comments. No charges were laid.

SECAA also complained about a minstrel show and textbooks, which the black community considered offensive at General Amherst High School in Amherstburg. The group asked the school board to look at education and how it portrays Blacks. It was most concerned about the word "nigger" in the course material, an epithet that black students consider offensive, slave-oriented, stereotypical, insulting and embarrassing. As members pointed out, the word merely added to white prejudice and created anxiety. They demanded that it be expunged from all material used in schools and that black history be taught to stimulate pride and understanding. The group also wanted human rights issues included in the curriculum, and it was prepared to press its case with the Ontario Human Rights Commission. All but one black adult and student in Amherstburg signed a petition, which was sent to the Department of Education in Toronto and then forwarded to the provincial legislature. The minstrel show was cancelled and the offending texts withdrawn.

Almost a year after the flaming cross, Amherstburg police investigated an attempt to burn an historic black church. The one-storey frame structure, at 105 George Street, was built in December 1849, as one of the first black churches in Canada. At 7:45 p.m., on May 19, a parishioner discovered the church filled with smoke from a partially burnt oilcloth on the newly installed floor. The fire burned a two-foot hole in the plywood before it guttered out. The intruder entered by a window, but left quickly by the door before the flames caught. Police said it should have been easy to torch the building, so the arsonist must have been an amateur. Police doubted that kids set the fire because the window was too high for children to reach, so it must have been a prank by hooligans.

The police chief and his wife received anonymous phone calls accusing them of being "nigger lovers," but the police determined that the incident had nothing to do with discrimination. Despite pressure from the black community, an intensive investigation, and a reward of $500, there were no arrests and the case went unresolved. Mayor Murray Smith admitted that anti-black sentiments had been expressed, but he felt they were minor and didn't consider them serious. He doubted a connection to the burning cross, or the fight at Boblo, and figured that the press exaggerated the problem. "Amherstburg is integrated as well as any town in Canada."

The chief was quoted as saying that the concerns of the black community were "frivolous," a comment he later denied. The police said that both the black and white communites were shocked and disgusted by recent events, but attempts to solve the case were frustrated. The fire was not reported until 12 hours after it was set, and crucial evidence, which might have led to a conviction, was cleaned by the caretaker before the police were called. The police chief insisted that there was no breakdown in law enforcement, and that Blacks enjoyed equal protection and impartial investigations. He said the Amherstburg police had a good record since its inception in 1957, with a notable decrease in crime.

The incident was followed by telephone threats from an anonymous caller to every black family in town. Blacks took the problem seriously, afraid that the KKK was involved, and that black homes might be next. They were concerned that a suspicious station wagon with Michigan plates was sighted near the church at the time of the fire, and they demanded a full investigation, convinced that the police weren't doing enough in cases of racial discrimination. They cited twelve similar cases that went unresolved. When the Criminal Investigations Branch finally launched an investigation, the Amherstburg police were criticized for their handling of the case. E.A. Duchesne, the crown attorney for Essex, described the police chief as "a good, old-style policeman," but one who didn't file adequate reports or seek proper advice. Despite the critique, the branch did not find discrimination toward Blacks by police.

The complaints prompted the mayor to canvas local business leaders and set up a series of meetings which not only led to better law enforcement and understanding between the two races, but also more employment opportunities and better housing for Blacks. The Human Rights Commission also looked into the hiring practices of several Amherstburg businesses, and an attempt was made to develop jobs for youth to get kids off the streets. It also investigated discrimination in employment at Boblo Island Amusement Park, which led to a change in policy there. A special committee was established to air the grievances of the black community and deal with the anger, bitterness and sometimes belligerence of black youths who felt they were being ignored. Local churches, schools and politicians also examined their attitudes which SECAA felt were "historically indifferent to the interests of Blacks."

Meanwhile, other incidents of discrimination were under investigation by the Human Rights Commission in other communities around Windsor.

One involved a complaint against the Mitchell's Bay Sportsman's Club which offered a boat rental service some 14 miles west of Chatham on Lake St. Clair. Alan Borovoy, the executive secretary of the Ontario Labour Committee, said the owner refused to rent to two black boys because he didn't have any boats available and yet, shortly thereafter, two boats were rented to Whites. The owner denied the charge. Daniel Hill, as director of the commission, said he wouldn't order a public inquiry if the club agreed to adopt a policy of non-discrimination.

On January 6, 1968, the first Citizen's Advisory Committee was appointed to the Human Rights Commission in Windsor to help immigrants and minorities train and find jobs, and to review complaints of discrimination. It was a free service to coincide with the 20th anniversary of the UN Declaration of Human Rights, and the designation of 1968 as International Human Rights Year. Windsor Councillor Georgina Montrose became committee chairperson, and Windsor Mayor John Wheelton was named honorary chair. It was an admission that discrimination was a problem in Canada, and that it had to be fought, not by hurling abuse at the system and crying foul, but by providing opportunities for the development of proper skills and education. Considering the racial history of the area, and coming only months after the Detroit riot of 1967, it was a fitting appointment.

In Canada, equality of races is accepted as reality. Overt discrimination is largely rejected by society and yet, covert discrimination still exists. Some Canadians still give the outward appearance of tolerance while, deep down, they are intolerant. The attitude is often evident at all-White gatherings. A speaker glances furtively around to make sure no Blacks are present before telling an off-colour joke at the black man's expense. If an individual comes off an unusual shift at work, he's told, "Oh, you're working white man's hours now." A smiling, cheerful sales girl attends to a white customer even though the black customer was there first. Overtly, she treats them equally, while covertly she discriminates.

A number of Canadians often hide behind the smug attitude that we don't suffer racial conflicts to the same extent as Americans. Incidents of racial strife are not as severe, or as pronounced, so we feel exempt and yet, racism remains, ever-present, just below the surface. Even today, many

Canadians don't like to admit that racism exists, but there is no question that discrimination is here, and that cultural prejudices have not been eradicated. Racism is less obvious and pervasive, perhaps because the black population is less obvious and pervasive. There simply are not as many black residents in this country. Racial inequalities, job discrimination and slums do not exist to the same extent in Canada, although some people think that this may change, is changing, and it is just a matter of time.

Canadian attitudes are deeply seeded, shaped to a large extent by history, but also influenced by American culture and our present reality. A key difference between Canada and the United States is our denial of slavery and racism. Discrimination is very much with us in Canada and, to a large extent, is still the great unspoken denial, as we continue into the 21st century.

Chapter 9

Racial History: Detroit

Discrimination may be bad in Canada, but it takes a more violent and virulent form in the United States. In 1833, fugitives from the first recorded riot in Detroit fled across the border to Windsor. On June 15 of that year, Lucie and Thornton Blackburn had been tracked down by slave catchers and arrested as runaways. As former slaves, the Blackburn's had fled Kentucky to live in Detroit. But as they were unable to prove that they were legally free, a Sheriff John Wilson kept them in jail while he decided what to do. His decision wasn't easy.

Blacks in Detroit were angry. They did not want the Blackburns returned to slavery and were determined to help. On June 16, Lucie Blackburn escaped to Canada by switching clothes with a visitor who remained in her place. The following day, armed Blacks stormed the jail and injured the sheriff while liberating Blackburn. He was immediately taken across the river to join his wife in Canada, where they were promptly arrested. They were, however, later freed and remained in Canada permanently, ultimately arriving in York (Toronto) in 1834 and settling there.

The incident may seem minor, but it increased racial tension on the American side. Whites demanded that black immigration be restricted, and Blacks responded by threatening to burn the city. The jail was set on fire on July 11 of that year and the situation remained volatile.

Michigan abolished slavery in 1838, but, like Canada, could not eliminate discrimination. There were several racial disturbances in Detroit:

direct, angry confrontations caused by the inability of two races to live together equitably. Each incident illustrated the problem facing, not only Detroit, but urban cities throughout the United States and, perhaps, to a lesser extent, Canada.

Although the American Civil War led to the freedom of thousands of slaves, it also caused a backlash against Blacks. Irish immigrants to Detroit blamed Blacks for causing the war. They also feared Blacks because of competition with them for labour and service jobs. The Irish saw black immigration as a threat to their incomes, occupational status and employment rates. Whites also complained that Blacks lived in poverty and, within Michigan, relief agencies were needed to provide food and clothing. Racial violence became directed against northern Blacks because of this aid and lynchings were designed to "put Blacks in their place."

During a riot in Detroit on March 6, 1863, Irish and German mobs tried to lynch a mulatto named William Faulkner. Faulkner had been convicted of molesting two nine-year-old girls – one White, the other Black. On his way to prison, soldiers protected Faulkner by killing one member of the mob and wounding several others. An angry white mob vented their rage on black Detroit. Two black men were killed and many others injured. Over 30 houses were burned and around 200 black people were left homeless. The infantry from Ypsilanti, Michigan, restored order while many white citizens condemned the actions of the mob and reimbursed Blacks for the damage to their homes. No one was charged and, seven years later, Faulkner was released when the girls admitted they lied.

Blacks in Michigan gained the right to vote in 1870 and racial divisions smoldered for the next 50 years. During the 1920s, the black population grew, as did the numbers of southern "Rednecks" and poor Whites from Dixie. Because of their life-long acquired hatred for Blacks, racism increased in the industrial setting of the north where the Ku Klux Klan flourished. The Klan harassed Blacks who tried to move to white areas, and forced them back to the ghetto.

In 1925, black physician Ossian Sweet bought a house on the corner of Charlevoix and Garland streets in a white section of Detroit's east side. Despite opposition, he was determined to move in and bought ten guns with lots of ammunition. With the help of two brothers and seven friends, he occupied his new home. The next night, a gang of white men surrounded the unlit building. A volley of stones smashed windows and Ossian and his friends opened fire, killing one man and wounding another. The police arrested everyone inside and charged them with first degree murder. The Blacks were defended by Clarence Darrow who maintained that they had a right to defend their property. They were acquitted by an all-white jury.

In 1940, Belle Isle, a recreation park on Detroit's east side, became the latest trouble spot. Two miles long and one mile wide, it's a grassy oasis located a half-mile off the north shore of the Detroit River. The park, covering almost 1,000 acres, includes baseball diamonds, tennis courts, picnic areas, a canoe shelter, skating pavilion and bathhouse. It was a popular haven for thousands of whites, but it was also one of the few recreation areas open to Blacks, and more and more were discovering it.

Belle Isle was conveniently located near the largest ghetto, a 60-block area bounded by Jefferson Avenue on the south, John R. in the west, Russell Street on the east and Grand Boulevard in the north. Called Paradise Valley, the ghetto included 3,500 decrepit houses with leaky roofs, crumbling staircases and outdoor plumbing. White landlords fought public housing and rented five-room shanties to five black families at the exorbitant price of $10 to $15 a month. Normally, the same houses rented to a single white family at half the price. Seeking some relief from the substandard housing and poor living conditions, black residents wanted an inexpensive way to relax, and were happy to head for the park to escape the city and enjoy the cool river breezes. Whites resented this influx of Blacks, however, because they felt they were being driven off the island.

On the evening of July 4, 1940, Detroit police arrested a young black men for stealing a canoe from a rental booth. Other Blacks responded by beating up the white operator of the concession. Three thousand Blacks surrounded the police station, hurling rocks and bottles at windows and yelling, "Turn him loose." Police barricaded themselves inside until reinforcements arrived and drove the mob away. Twelve policemen were injured.

Racial problems continued into 1941. A housing shortage in the city was accompanied by an unwritten code relegating 200,000 Blacks to squalid, overcrowded conditions. Recreation and cultural facilities were inadequate and Blacks were unable to break free of the ghetto until a new housing project was developed in an all-white neighbourhood. This site was called Sojourner Truth after an ex-slave girl who travelled north, preaching abolition and women's rights, and raising funds to aid fugitive slaves. Although the new homes were only drab green huts, "rejects from army housing," they promised a better life.

The buildings were completed in December, but remained unoccupied. On January 20, 1942, the Detroit Housing Authority decided to give the homes to Whites. A protest forced the city to reverse the decision, and Blacks were scheduled to take over the buildings on February 28. The night before, the Ku Klux Klan burned a cross on the site. Then, just as the black citizens were ready to move in, an angry mob of whites attacked with clubs, bricks and knives. The Blacks responded. Police intervened and arrested 104 people: two white men and 102 Blacks. The mob dispersed, after receiving assurances that Blacks would never live in the project, however they moved in two months later with an escort of 1,750 city and state police.

Blacks blamed the KKK for instigating the violence and were incensed when the two white men were never brought to trial. A committee blamed Detroit's racial problems on the housing shortage, on the police who kept Blacks down and on open hostility between whites and Blacks. It urged federal action to build 25,000 housing units, hire more black teachers, construct more recreational facilities and hire 10 percent more black police officers.

A series of sit-down strikes, along with a welfare crisis, made Detroit rife for a riot, but President Franklin Roosevelt refused to devote one of his famous fireside chats to the problem. Instead, he deplored race riots because they "endanger our national unity and comfort our enemies." The president's expression of regret merely added to black anger. Without federal help, nothing could be done about the housing shortage, or discrimination in factories.

By now, Detroit was the third largest city in the United States with over 3,000,000 people, and industry was booming. The Americans had finally entered World War II in 1941, and the battle was going well. Britain won a major campaign in North Africa and was preparing to invade Sicily. Thirteen million American Blacks were encouraged by the war. They equated victory in Europe with their fight for freedom at home.

In another positive move, the United Auto Workers opened auto plants to Blacks, especially where workers were in short supply. The union supported equal opportunity, but white workers did not. As one worker drawled, "I'd rather see Hitler and Hirohito win than work next to a nigger." Whites complained that Blacks had syphilis, and feared they'd catch it if they used the same machines.

Because of this rampant racism, Franklin D. Roosevelt promised an investigation. He also promised that federal war contracts would be cancelled if discrimination were discovered. A commission was actually set up, unable to prove anything, it was reluctant to cancel contracts important to the war effort. Use of black labour increased, but was still limited. Poor treatment of workers continued. Frustrated Blacks condemned the government and suggested that American soldiers should fight for democracy at home rather than overseas. In the long, hot summer of 1943, federal investigators warned Washington about the possibility of a riot. Detroit Mayor Edward Jeffries Junior campaigned to solve problems when he was elected in 1940, but those promises were on hold because of the war. Black hostility and bitterness increased.

On Sunday, June 13, 1943, over 500 people, including 200 sailors, start a brawl in Inkster, Michigan, an area heavily populated by black war workers. The fighting starts in a park where Blacks and Whites are cooling off from the summer heat. State and military police finally clear the streets. Two days later, police are called to a mix-up at Eastwood Amusement Park. Two hundred white servicemen and high school students try to kick 100 Blacks out of the park. There are stabbings, fights and altercations. On the domestic front, meat is in short supply because of the war. Gasoline and tires are rationed which makes it necessary to travel on crowded buses and streetcars. The stage is set for a full-scale riot as Whites and Blacks take to the streets to vent their frustration and anger.

Sunday, June 20, is bright and humid as Detroit police brace for trouble. The temperature soars to 91 degrees. One hundred thousand people, mostly Black, gather on Belle Isle to relax. There have already been a number of scuffles when a fight breaks out at a picnic and another at the pony stand. Two black women complain about harassment by a white man and woman. At 3:30 p.m., three 17-year-old Blacks: Aaron Fox, Raymond Thomas and "Handsome Harry" Mimmifield meet up with 20-year-old Charles Lyons and three of his friends. Lyons, a.k.a. "Little Willie," and Fox were chased out of the amusement park in East Detroit and they're looking for revenge. Lyons whacks a white boy with a stick and the boy runs off. Lyons and his friends come across a group of white picnickers. He strikes a man on the foot and proclaims, "Time to go home. Get going." They look at the seven black boys and start packing. The boys break up another picnic and steal the food.

At 8:23 p.m., police are called to break up a fight at the skating pavilion. A white boy, Earl Blaylock, is surrounded by Blacks who say he pushed through three lines of people waiting at a confection stand. They demand an apology. When he refuses, they knock him down twice and hit him on the head with a pop bottle. Some of the Blacks flee and police take Blaylock to hospital. He's the first of several hundred casualties over the next 24 hours.

In a skirmish on the ferry dock, people push and shove while waiting to board. The disgusted ferry operator slams the gate, and stops boarding until the crowd lines up. The ferry service and a $3,000,000 bridge are the only ways off Belle Isle and, when people want to leave, the bridge is congested. Drivers sweat and blow their horns in the traffic jam. Hundreds of people walk across the half-mile span to go home. It's 10:00 p.m. and Little Willie Lyons is with them. He bumps into Joseph B. Joseph and calls him a white son-of-a-bitch. Lyons knocks Joseph down and kicks him. One of Lyons' friends shouts, "Let's throw him over the bridge." A couple of sailors from the Naval Academy on Jefferson Avenue come to Joseph's aid as he struggles to his feet and takes off. Just two days before, two sailors were attacked and beaten. This time, 200 sailors join in. A mob of 5,000 Whites, some armed with knives, sticks and stones, gather at the bridge, picking on isolated Blacks. At 11:00 p.m., the mob attacks Gladys House and her date. They beat them up and chase after another young boy. "We don't want any niggers on Belle Isle." Police intervene and drive House to safety.

Rioting spreads one block west on Jefferson Street and four blocks north to Lafayette. It eventually covers Jefferson to Cass and St. Aubin up to Grand Boulevard. The violence escalates, fed by false rumours. Whites riot when patrons in a white night club are told that a white woman has been raped and murdered by Blacks. Blacks riot when a similar announcement is made in a black nightclub. Rumour has it that sailors have killed a black woman and her baby and have thrown them off the bridge. As the stories circulate, they become more and more distorted and the crowds go berserk. They pour out of nightclubs, looking for revenge. Two off-duty policemen in the white club ignore the fracas and simply go home. Later, they're convicted of neglect of duty and suspended for four months.

Black mobs loot and burn white-owned stores in Paradise Valley, the black section of the city on the lower east side. They also attack any white people who wander through. Looting continues on Hastings Street, the ghetto's main shopping district. Every window is broken for a distance of two miles, and everything from food and liquor to suits and shoes is stolen. Some looters pick up shopping carts and bags and leisurely choose their supplies. One of the looters is Little Willie Lyons. He's eventually picked up by police at a drugstore on Hastings.

At the corner of Forest, a black youth throws a rock at a passing white motorcyclist and knocks him down. The motorcycle crashes and bursts into flames. Six white passengers on a streetcar are stoned and the conductor and motorman are beaten with an iron bar. Blacks hurl stones at police until an officer shoots one of the rioters in the stomach. By midnight, Sunday, over 180 policemen are dispatched to make arrests and drive off the crowd. Three innocent bystanders: James Townsend Lee, a black bar owner; Ephraim Ashley, a black factory worker; and John Lewis, a black soldier in uniform are beaten up by police in separate incidents. None of the beatings is provoked.

The first knifing occurs at 1:40 a.m. A white man, Paul Haaker, is stabbed in the chest at the corner of Alfred and Hastings. Another white man is the first person killed. John Brogan, 28, is knocked unconscious and left lying in the middle of Brush Street where he's accidentally run over by a taxi. He dies at 4:50 a.m. The first black man to die is Sam Johnson, a looter who throws a brick through a plate glass window. He enters the store, but a piece of glass slices an artery in his leg and he bleeds to death.

About 7:30 a.m., 100 black rioters beat two white policemen. One of the Blacks is Carl Singleton. He throws a piece of concrete and runs. Another police officer yells at him to stop, but he keeps going. The officer shoots him in the back and Singleton dies before reaching hospital. A half hour later, ten patrolmen break up a crowd of 200 looters at a clothing store on the corner of Hastings and Division. Garments litter the street and police gather them up and take them inside. Most of the rioters back off, but not 23-year-old William Hardges, a former amateur boxing champion. An officer shoves him toward a patrol wagon. Hardges breaks loose, grabs an officer's gun and shoots two patrolmen. He's gunned down when four other officers open fire. Nine bullets hit Hardges, but one misses and kills Robert Davis, a black bystander in the crowd.

Late Monday night, a black man is in a parking lot next to a rooming house called the Frazer Hotel. He fires at police with his shotgun, hitting one officer in the stomach. An officer fires back, killing the young man immediately. More shots ring out. Fifty Detroit and state police fire pistols, deer rifles, shotguns and machine guns at the hotel. They pour 1,000 rounds of ammo into the building before tenants come out. Surprisingly, only one black person is injured. The residents line up against the wall while police search their rooms.

Before the riot is over, almost every store owned by a White in the ghetto has been smashed and ransacked, every shelf emptied. Steel grills, broken glass, clothing and paper litter the streets. Many rioters return home, afraid of lawmen who harass and beat black residents. They're also angry that, at curfew, police order Blacks off the streets, but not Whites. White police use force and beat black men, but they use persuasion to deter white rioters, or watch from the sidelines without interfering. Blacks complain about the double standard.

As Blacks riot on their home turf, whites riot in another part of town. On Woodward Avenue, white mobs attack Blacks on streetcars, throw stones at vehicles with Blacks, bounce rocks off the hood and windows, then beat up the drivers, and overturn and burn cars. One black driver loses control

Tuesday, June 22, 1943 – Detroit's bitter race riot continues. Members of the mob chase an unidentified black man (circled) through traffic, and across the street. Seconds later, the man's car (in front of bus) is overturned. Courtesy of *The Windsor Star.*

and slams into a safety island at a streetcar stop. When he gets out, he's kicked and punched by the gang. He escapes, but the mob rocks his car and tips it over. They open the gas cap, light a match, and torch the car. They do the same to 19 other vehicles. White police taunt one black driver to "get out and stay out." When other officers try to arrest white rioters, they're overwhelmed by the crowd and forced to let them go.

Early Monday morning, Blacks, leaving two all-night cinemas, are attacked and beaten by roaming gangs of Whites. Police say they entered theatres to warn and protect patrons, but a teacher at Wayne University says police stood by and watched. Some Blacks are even attacked by police or goaded into the street. Others remain in the theatre until 5:00 a.m. when they slip out quietly only to find that the mob is waiting.

A gang of 800 white men is on the streets by mid-morning. They storm trolleys on Woodward Avenue, looking for Blacks to beat up. In an effort to save his black passengers from a beating, a streetcar motorman refuses to stop. Another motorman grabs a metal switch bar and threatens a mob of 50 white men. He refuses to let them on the car and eventually scares them off. A white woman and her daughter hide a black man under their seat to save him. Once out of harm's way, he flees from the car and disappears down the street. As Whites surge through the front doors of the streetcar, Blacks leap out back doors or climb out windows and run for safety. Some make it, others don't. One black man jumps out at Davenport and is cornered against the wall by the mob. A white policeman forces his way through and puts himself between the black man and the crowd. One man shouts, "You're one of us. Why not just walk away and not get hurt." The officer pulls his gun and points it at the man. The crowd moves back and the officer tells the black man to "run like hell."

A black banker named Sam Mitchell is heading home for lunch when a mob of 2,000 Whites stops the streetcar. The motorman refuses to open the door, but a white man with a crowbar pries it open. They pull Mitchell off as something hits him in the side. Bleeding from a stab wound, he screams and runs toward two policemen who seize him and walk him down Woodward Avenue. White men run up and slap his face. An alert cameraman catches one on film. George Miller, a 31-year-old ex-con, is later sentenced to 90 days in jail. Mitchell breaks free from police with the crowd in pursuit. A squad car pulls up and more officers pull him inside. They push the mob back and rush Mitchell to hospital. He's released two days later.

Detroit Times reporter Robert Madigan helps another black man, takes his arm and guides him to a streetcar safety zone in the middle of the street. A white man yells, "Get away, nigger lover, or you'll get the same thing." The black man looks at Madigan and says, "You'd better go." Madigan backs away as the white man kicks the black man in the face. The crowd cheers. In another incident, a white clergyman and his son patrol Woodward in their car, stopping whenever a black man is attacked. The minister rushes into the mob, quoting scriptures or the U.S. Constitution while his son retrieves the victim. They drive the man to hospital. Other Whites try to help, but are threatened with beatings. The mob is armed with clubs, pipe and stones. The crowd reacts to reports that black soldiers are heading for Detroit to avenge their families. Five black soldiers try to seize ammunition and trucks, but they are arrested and thrown in the stockade.

Many cars were destroyed and burned as black drivers were caught in white districts, and white drivers were caught in black districts. Courtesy of *The Windsor Star.*

Detroit streets are littered with glass, sticks, bricks, rocks, overturned cars and empty tear gas shells as police drive the gangs back. "Just like Germany! Just like Hitler!" the mob shouts. A white man heaves a brick at a patrolman, knocking him down. Police form a flying wedge, beat a hole through the crowd with their nightsticks and seize the offender but when a black minister and his son are overpowered by the mob on Chene Street, other officers just watch. As one policeman explains, "Whites are doing the same thing to him that Negroes are doing to Whites on Hastings Street." When the reverend tells them he's a minister and doesn't mean any harm, the crowd backs off and police take him to hospital. By evening, the hospitals are overflowing with injured people. They come in every two minutes, 30 to 40 an hour. Most victims are alone or in pairs. A mob of 300 Whites tries to push its way into the black ghetto, but a weary line of Detroit policemen push them back, preventing an all-out war between Blacks and Whites.

By 6:00 p.m. Monday, Michigan Governor Harry Kelly declares a state of emergency, banning the sale of liquor, closing amusement halls and imposing a curfew of 10:00 p.m. He also pleads for calm, afraid that the riot will hurt the war effort. It's been hard to muster enough lawmen to keep order. Two thousand Detroit police officers are on duty, working 12-hour shifts. One hundred and fifty state troopers supplement the Detroit force, but it's still not enough. Kelly asks for 2,000 volunteers to help the National Guard, but only 32 are deployed because of inexperience and a lack of training. Mayor Jeffries also uses 200 black auxiliary police to handle traffic detail and patrol black areas. He neglects to tell white officers and, when the new recruits arrive with their helmets and armbands, they are mistaken for rioters. Police hand out extra shotguns and tear gas canisters before they realize that the men are not a threat, and before any shooting. The auxiliary is told to do what it can, but its members are helpless. They have no weapons and no power of arrest.

A request to use federal troops bogs down in bureaucratic wrangling while top brass decide if soldiers can be sent without a presidential decree. Mayor Jeffries and Governor Kelly regret that they've left it too long, but are afraid to ask the president to declare martial law because people might think they've lost control. They're also afraid to spend another night without the army, and they vow that they will never delay again should another outbreak occur. At 8:00 p.m., 45 minutes after troops are dispatched, the generals and politicians are still discussing the presidential proclamation, which is yet to be released. They won't receive the legal right to send in the army until midnight, when President Roosevelt finally signs the official approval. By then, troops have already restored order.

The soldiers are members of the 701st and 728th Military Police Battalions from Selfridge Field and Fort Custer. Members of the Ninth Infantry Regiment of Second Division are also called as reinforcements. They're bivouacked in parks, on library lawns and on high school athletic fields. Their most important function is to be seen. The first troops are immediately ordered to guard a retail outlet of the Defense Supplies Corporation, which sells pistols, shotguns and rifles to police and security companies. The firm has an inventory of 4,800 weapons and police fear they might fall into the wrong hands. The white police don't have the manpower to guard the facility, the army with its mandate is to protect property during an insurrection, does.

By 10:00 p.m., 350 military personnel are on the streets in combat gear, riding in jeeps, scout cars and trucks with guns loaded, bayonets fixed. They easily gain control and force the white mob, almost 15,000 people on Woodward Avenue, back into their homes. When soldiers are stoned and cursed by rioters, they respond with tear gas and rifle butts, showing tremendous restraint. Eventually, the army reaches a total force of 5,000 men and, by midnight, the situation is in hand. Sporadic looting continues until 4:30 a.m., but the military divides Detroit into four sectors to prevent a renewed outburst of violence. By Tuesday, the city is sullen but quiet. One thousand prisoners overflow city and county jails, housed in bull pens set up in the Armouries. The streets are deserted, the bars closed. Schools are open, but there are no students. Only half the factory workers show up for their shifts. Baseball at Briggs Stadium and horse racing at the State Fair Grounds are cancelled. People cower in their homes, afraid of the mobs. No food is available until the end of the week when grocery stores finally open with replenished supplies. Military troops remain in Detroit to keep order over the July 4 holiday weekend.

During the three-day riot of 1943, police kill 17 people, all black people. In total, 34 people are dead: nine White, 25 Black. There are 675 people injured, including 75 policemen. Half are Black, half White. Nineteen hundred people are arrested of whom 700 are released without being charged. The rest are charged with a range of misdemeanors to felonies including looting, carrying a concealed weapon and break-and-enters. Most serve a few months in jail. At least $2,000,000 in property damage is done, including several burned homes. In total, Detroit loses 1,000,000 man-hours of war production in a riot that shames the nation. It's estimated that 100,000 people participate, cheer or watch without attempting to stop the rioters. The Germans use it in their war propaganda in Europe. German-controlled Vichy radio tells the French that the riot is the result of "internal disorganization of a country torn by social injustice, race hatred, regional disparities, the violence of an irritated proletariat and the gangsterism of capitalist police." Radio Tokyo broadcasts a similar message. Cries go up that the Detroit riot is planned by infiltrators from Axis countries and Japan, but the FBI debunks those rumours.

The riot makes Blacks more anti-white and Black Nationalist than ever. As Louis Morin, editor of *The Negro Michigan Chronicle*, declares, "We have given up hope." Officials in New York, Chicago and Washington fear similar outbreaks and, when violence erupts in Harlem on Sunday, August 1, the mayor of New York mobilizes his police and calls on the army to put it down within 24 hours. No white mobs form and Blacks who riot are restricted to the ghetto.

The Detroit riot of 1943 is the last major outbreak in a series of summer riots involving racial discrimination throughout the United States for that year. In Mobile, Alabama, in May, 80 black people were injured in a bloody brawl when several hundred Whites protest upgrading of black workers in a local shipyard. In early June, servicemen in Los Angeles beat up "zoot-suited" Blacks and Mexicans, stripping them of their long jackets, pegged pants and pancake hats. In mid-June, 10,000 Whites in Beaumont, Texas, went on a 15-hour rampage when a white woman complains a black man has raped her. There is no proof, but that doesn't stop the mob from beating Blacks and burning their homes. Two people are killed and scores injured before state troopers restore order. Other riots are severe, but Detroit is the worst.

Once it's over, a sociologist prepares a questionnaire for 340 prisoners to determine why the riot takes place. A white social worker asks the questions with armed guards in the background. The Blacks claim they have steady jobs, suffer no discrimination and are ready to get back to work. The social worker is struck by how willing inmates are to cooperate. It isn't because of her skill as an interviewer. It's because of the armed guard and the compliance of southern Blacks to do what they're told.

A similar survey, conducted by black social workers, uncovers widespread complaints about abuse and brutality by police, and that white officers are in sympathy with white mobs. Critics say the authorities could have used equal force, but no Whites are killed by police. Riot hoses could have been used to spray brawlers but, instead, police stand by and watch or beat up, shoot and arrest Blacks. The police commissioner and mayor deny the accusations. They say the police department treats everyone alike. The police commissioner also responds to criticism that he didn't clamp down soon enough and allowed the riot to get out of hand. There is a suggestion from the white community that he should have ordered his officers to shoot to kill, that he treated Blacks with "kid gloves." The commissioner says he was understaffed, and counted on military support, which wasn't forthcoming.

There is a call for a grand jury to investigate the riot and the police, especially since the cause of 13 deaths is still unknown. The recommendation is never acted upon. Instead, the governor strikes a task force of the police commission. Kelly promises that the investigation will bring those responsible to justice, "so that such things never happen again in Michigan." The promise is never fulfilled. The investigation is hurried and superficial. The report blames the riot on attacks by black youth or "juvenile delinquents." The accusation ignores pictures of the riot, which show adults involved. By laying the blame on Blacks, the commission also ignores the fact that white gangs are roaming Woodward Avenue at the same time. The commission concludes that Blacks comprise ten percent of the population, but account for 70 percent of the crimes. It also blames black leaders for not keeping their people in check, and black newspapers for inciting the riot by dwelling on the need for black equality as part of the struggle for world democracy. The commission makes little attempt to prosecute Whites responsible for some of the beatings and killings, so Detroit is left with a legacy of suspicion and fear.

The idea that Blacks are "militant" is cited as nothing more than a provocation. *The Detroit Free Press* calls the report a whitewash and complains that the police commissioner could hardly be expected to investigate his own department. The paper says the report leaves too many questions unanswered and doesn't deal with the fundamental issue of black anger. It ignores the fact that the riot is an ugly reaction to the frustration of living in a white man's world where Blacks are regarded as inferior. The paper points out that Detroit's population has increased by 500,000 people without a corresponding increase in bus or social services.

A national committee is proposed by the attorney general to solve the problem, but he backs down in favour of a suggestion that Blacks be prevented from migrating to Detroit. The idea is to reduce congestion, but it causes a furor with civil liberties organizations, which says it's undemocratic to deprive citizens the right to move wherever they please. Again, the attorney general backs off. Instead, an interracial peace committee is formed to prevent another riot. It deals with racial discrimination in housing, employment and restaurants and is eventually linked to community groups interested in education and leadership. As it evolves, it lacks the power to resolve civil rights conflicts, and has to rely on, "negotiation and education" instead.

The mayor is also criticized for not mobilizing the police fast enough, for not calling the army soon enough, and for not making a plea for peace on the radio until well after the riot is on. After the riot, Mayor Jeffries could implement some social measures, but he lacks the political will and courage. In 1944, Detroit works out an agreement that makes it possible to coordinate Detroit police and state troopers, and to call federal forces quickly when, and if, necessary. A memorandum is developed, describing proper procedures to stop riots before they get out of control. Despite this, the problem is repeated in 1967 with many of the same mistakes. The government still has not learned how to secure federal troops, control rioters or process people who have been apprehended. The information is lost in the intervening years.

On Saturday, September 11, 1943, Detroit police struggle with a black man who is resisting arrest after fighting with his estranged wife. Five hundred other Blacks gather around and try to intervene. Police radio for help and twelve squad cars and a patrol wagon are dispatched. The crowd is broken up by 42 police officers using nightsticks and tear gas. No one is injured and only four Blacks are arrested, but the animosity continues. On September 13, 1948, a white mob is milling around, damaging two homes purchased by black citizens in an all-white neighbourhood. Hundreds of people are involved and yet, only three people are arrested. The charges are reduced from incitement to riot, to disturbing the peace. To the black community, it is one more example of white racism in the justice department.

The situation prompts Blacks to question the recruitment procedures of the Detroit police which is predominantly White. They complain that

Whites rarely fail the screening test and yet, candidates are blatantly racist. They conclude that the police are both discriminatory and prejudiced in their recruitment, hiring, assignment and promotion of officers. It is well known that Detroit police view people on the streets as an enemy or as criminals, especially in areas heavily populated by Blacks. Black men are subject to illegal arrest, indiscriminate and open searches, disrespectful and profane language, derogatory references to race and colour and violent intimidation against any protest of improper treatment.

The force is described as one of the "most bigoted" in the nation. As Judge George Edwards says, "there was open warfare between Negroes and police." By 1958, Blacks make up 23 percent of Detroit's population, but only three percent of its police force. White officers are segregated from Blacks unless they are being punished in which case they are confined to policing black districts. A Citizen's Complaint Bureau is set up to deal with disputes about the police, but it is ineffective.

Conditions settle into an uneasy truce until the '60s when Civil Rights Activist Martin Luther King Junior calls for non-violent protest. Once again, the black man's thrust for freedom, for his democratic right, makes white men cringe with fear and hatred. What begins as a peaceful process ultimately explodes into violence. Early on, many Whites admit being guilty of giving Blacks second-rate schools, menial jobs, poor housing, even robbing them of the most fundamental democratic freedoms, the right to vote. As President John F. Kennedy says, "The heart of the question is whether all Americans are to be offered equal rights and equal opportunity ... whether we are going to treat our fellow Americans as we want to be treated."

Trouble is, the black movement is becoming more militant. Blacks want change and, if "whitey" won't give it, they'll take it. There is concern that direct action by Blacks creates fear and hostility, which only hurts the black community since they are the ones that suffer most from violence when white power cracks down. The legacy from 1943 suggests that race riots paralyze efforts to attack racial problems. The black war on poverty, and toward equal rights, is just an expression of hope to share in the American Dream, and it would be tragic if that hope ends in violence.

In 1960, a wave of rapes and purse snatchings ends in the murder of a white nurse's aide, a 28-year-old mother of three. The government responds with 600 arrests, despite police reforms the previous year. Police work a six-day week to drive crime from the streets. They frisk prominent members of the black community, which causes complaints about the violation of civil liberties. The situation gives credence to a study at Wayne State University which indicates that race relations are a problem second only to housing.

Employment statistics are abysmal and the discrepancies are not being addressed. Incomes for Whites increase 71 percent during the decade to an average of $7,000. Incomes for Blacks increase only four percent to a level of $4,400. Surprisingly, education doesn't help. In fact, the more Blacks learn, the less they earn. Blacks and Whites with a grade seven education make the same, but Blacks with a high school education make $1,000 less. After four years of college, Blacks, working at the same job as Whites, make $2,600 less. Generally, they make one-third less than Whites hired for the same function.

Since Blacks are generally first to lose their jobs, black males are also more likely to be unemployed and their rate of unemployment increases faster because of a decline in auto and parts production and the flight of businesses to the suburbs. As a result, 11 percent of Blacks are unemployed compared to only three percent of Whites. By July 1960, 76 percent of black teenagers, 35 percent of Blacks in their early twenties and 21 percent of Blacks between 25 and 29 are unemployed. Most managerial jobs belong to white workers while twice as many waiter, janitorial and general labour jobs go to black workers. Throughout the '50s and '60s, three times as many Blacks are below the poverty line, all of which has an impact on black perceptions and attitudes as the violence continues.

On Tuesday, March 9, 1965, nine white youths are attacked and stabbed by Blacks as they walk home from a basketball game. A predominantly black school, Detroit Northwestern, loses by a score of 70 to 69 to a mixed school, Highland Park. Northwestern was previously undefeated and the black attackers are upset over the outcome. Violence and discrimination work both ways.

Ironically, before 1967, there are two trains of thought about Detroit. Some say a riot isn't possible. Others realize an explosion is imminent. As one writer puts it, you might not be able to pick the time and place, but it's long overdue. "In an odd way, everyone saw it coming and nobody believed it would really happen" and yet, Detroit is a main candidate for trouble. On July 23, *The New York Times* says, "Detroit probably had more going for it than any other major city in the North" but, despite efforts to build an international reputation, it doesn't have a patent on racial peace. Even Detroit's flamboyant Mayor Jerome P. Cavanagh expresses the fear that the city could explode when he appeals for federal, state and private aid to head off disturbances. Black Councilman Nicholas Hood denies the problem. "Only Whites are talking about it ... Detroit is far ahead of any major city in America."

From 1963 to '68, there are racial disturbances in 250 U.S. cities, but not Detroit. Many people believe that the Motor City is exempt as the most progressive city in America in terms of interracial cooperation and planning. It's an example to the nation, known as the city on the move, a model city, with a liberal administration that is finally dealing with racial discrimination in a positive way. It's thought that Detroit is becoming integrated, that there will finally be equal opportunity and justice for Blacks, but those dreams are never realized. They dissolve in the worst urban upheaval and tragedy in American history.

Given the riots in other cities, it is not surprising that racial turmoil erupts in Detroit. Many people see that violence is inevitable, and yet others are caught off guard. *The Detroit Free Press* says the city is the least likely in America to have problems because it works longer and harder to prevent them. Much of the credit for Detroit's perceived success goes to Cavanagh, a bright, handsome Irishman, who became mayor in an upset election in 1961 with overwhelming black support. Born in 1928, he worked through law school, served as sheriff, entered the mayor's race as a political unknown and won, despite all odds. Black voters backed him because they were fed up with the "Negro-bashing crackdown on crime" of his predecessor, Mayor Louis C. Mirioni who was supported by the city's power structure and the UAW.

Surprised by the upset, Detroit Blacks see Cavanagh's stunning victory as a show of political strength and a promise of much needed reforms, and Cavanagh is not about to disappoint his black electorate. He declares war on poverty, speeds up integration, and ends police excess. His administration becomes the model for race relations across the nation.

In the early '60s, Detroit is a city in decline, but it still enjoys better slums than most other cities. Housing is intolerable in some areas, but is superior to Chicago, New York and Cleveland. Detroit also boasts the largest black middle class in America, highly paid auto industry jobs with lower unemployment than other U.S. cities, and the largest branch of the National Association for the Advancement of Coloured People with 18,000 members.

Cavanagh feels he has a good rapport with Blacks. He believes he is helping to change attitudes in the city because of his responsiveness to the "needs in the streets." He appoints a more liberal police commissioner to improve relations with the black community and solicits federal funds to recruit more young Blacks to the department. The new commissioner is White, but he has the approval of black voters and, for the first time, Blacks are named to key municipal and city hall posts, positions with status and authority. Two school board trustees are Black. There is a black councilman; two Blacks are in congress, three on the judge's bench and 12 more in the Legislature. Faced with a huge debt of $19,000,000 in 1960, Cavanagh works to balance the budget within three years and, from '64 to '67, the city is also given federal grants to eradicate poverty. With a booming auto industry and new jobs, Detroit is facing a remarkable recovery, which alters the city's unfavourable national image. Cavanagh knows about racial divisions, but thinks he is moving toward a workable solution. He feels he has made progress since 1943 and, as an administrator put it, "To our credit, we have learned from our errors of the past."

There is a disturbance in the Kercheval District in 1966, a mini-riot, but Cavanagh figures the city quashed it bloodlessly and easily. Social scientists even travel to Detroit to learn how to deal with racial problems. Cavanagh receives "good press" as the "most glamorous" and best-known city mayor of the time, the Golden Boy, "the Dynamo of Detroit." His supporters think of him as a presidential contender, and his political aspirations go beyond the state to the White House. By the summer of 1967, Cavanagh firmly believes that progress is being made, but he is deluding himself. Cavanagh's optimism is based on discussions with middle-class Blacks who support his reforms and give the impression that all is well. Black leaders seem confident for the future, believing they can escape the racial disturbances of other cities during the "long hot summer." Trouble is, Cavanagh is talking to the wrong people.

Detroit's civil rights organizations are committed to a racially integrated society and seek to work with city leadership to achieve that goal. They consider themselves activists, benefitting from the Civil Rights Movement, but are more moderate in their rhetoric and more in tune with older, better-established and more conservative Blacks. In short, the black middle-class is more interested in its own upward mobility as it lunches and confers with white bosses. Middle-class Blacks feel they are on the road to the good life, despite discrimination by white racists, despite indifference by white moderates, and despite black extremists "who are against Negroes who have attained any success."

Middle-class Blacks may be closing the gap, but poor Blacks continue to fall behind. Socially, they are disorganized and suffer feelings of alienation, hostility and despair. Established black leaders do not represent the poor. As a result, the ghetto is leaderless, lacks a strong sense of community, and has no formal organization to which the authorities can relate. As one black man says, "The voice from the slums was never heard." As a result, Cavanagh is hopelessly out of touch with the ghetto masses where problems lie.

Race relations are deteriorating due to a growing separation between Blacks and Whites. Whites figure Blacks in Detroit are better off than those in most other cities, but Blacks don't compare their lifestyle to Blacks in other cities. They compare themselves to Whites, and they are far behind. Whites have more income, better homes, are more satisfied with schools, parks and police, and have better jobs which leads to strain, frustration and anger by deprived Blacks.

Detroit seems more integrated when, in fact, it's more segregated. The government proclamation of the '60s is: "fair housing for all" and, officially, the move is away from segregation. Blacks are encouraged to move into traditionally white areas, and it appears that integration is finally becoming a reality but, in fact, Blacks are more segregated in 1962 than in 1932. In the 1930s, 50 percent of all Blacks live in white areas but, by 1962, only 15 percent of Blacks are integrated. Between 1950 and 1960, 182,000 Blacks move into Detroit, but 363,000 Whites actually leave. The black population grows from 16 to 33 percent while the white population goes down by 23 percent.

Whites fear that the ghetto is overflowing, spilling into their areas of the city. They complain that real estate agents show houses to "anyone" and, fearing that their neighbourhood will be next, they decide to "sell before the panic." The agents are known as "block busters" because they're effective at selling one house in an all-white neighbourhood to a black family, knowing that all Whites will want to sell. The "unscrupulous" agent gains the commission. The area known as Russell Woods, for example, was 90 percent Jewish in 1955, but 90 percent Black by 1967. As black numbers grow, Whites leave for the suburbs, which most Blacks can't afford. It may appear that the city is integrating, but it's merely going through a transition from all White to all Black. Prosperous middle-class Whites are replaced by poor unskilled Blacks.

There are two exceptions to the rule. The first is in white minority areas where old neighbourhoods remain intact because residents don't want to lose their local ethnic institutions. Poles, for example, often remain in their traditional areas because of a church or a community centre. The other exception involves urban renewal. In Lafayette Park, for example, there is a pocket of white residents because of controls on residency, which restrict potential black owners. A study shows that 95 percent of affluent Whites are not interested in urban renewal if it is "open" to Blacks which gives credence to the phrase, "urban renewal means Negro removal."

In 1964, a vote on "closed occupancy" passes by a narrow margin of 54 percent, despite opposition by the church, UAW and Democratic leaders. Open occupancy only applies to the small percentage of the black community that can afford suburban housing. They represent fewer than 125,000 of 500,000 Blacks in Detroit. The comparatively low numbers are welcomed by the majority of Whites who simply oppose equality. They feel that Blacks are pushing too hard and they decide to push back. That same year, Wayne State professor Albert Mayer causes a furor by projecting that Detroit is becoming all Black and poor. It runs counter to the official optimism and is denounced even though it is true. Detroit is struggling against disinvestments, desertion and discrimination.

The gradual colour change causes major economic problems in Detroit. Whites who vacate are richer than Whites who stay or Blacks who move in. The city is abandoned by all but the poor who can't afford better housing and education. One-third of black children live in broken homes compared to only seven percent for white kids. Detroit becomes a city of dependents that require social and economic services, but on a shrinking tax base. Most of the money has to be diverted to the inner city, which prompts one official to say, "If the white middle class knew how disproportionate our expenditures in the inner city were, we'd probably have a white revolt on our hands." The city can't increase taxes because Blacks can't pay, and there are constitutional limits on tax rates. The city has to go to the state for financial relief and, as a result, it suffers a shortage of money for social programs. Detroit simply has too large a population on federal government assistance and cannot accommodate it.

As the black population rises, strain is put on the educational system to accommodate 300,000 school children, 60 percent of whom are Black. When an extra 50,000 students move into crammed elementary schools, the school board realizes it needs 1,600 more teachers and 1,000 extra classrooms. To relieve the problem, the board introduces busing and shuttles inner city students to suburban schools. White parents rebel by keeping their children home for three days and petitioning for the removal of school board trustees. They don't want anything to do with Blacks moving onto their turf.

Despite the controversy, more Blacks go to school. Unfortunately, their quality of education suffers. Inner city schools receive less money and personnel directors consider black diplomas less valid. As a result, more Blacks drop out in frustration. At one inner-city school, 90 percent of the graduating class is unemployed while 50 percent of the dropouts find jobs. By July 1967, unemployment on Twelfth Street is at a five-year peak: 12 to 15 percent for black men, and over 30 percent for black males under 25. Three times as many Blacks think their income is inadequate. Most are discontented, but have high hopes for their children. They want them to become professionals but, for Blacks, educational progress does not mean occupational or income progress, and the discrepancy creates more bitterness.

June 23, 1963, is the 20th anniversary of the riot in 1943, but many issues are unresolved. Blacks are impatient with the administration and their own leaders who fail to extract concessions from government officials. Demonstrations are held for better housing, education, employment, equality and opportunity. Blacks are making gains, but never quite achieve full racial autonomy. A group of black ministers plans a Walk to Freedom to protest problems. Wanting to make sure the demonstration is responsible and afraid that militant Blacks might incite a riot, Cavanagh participates and urges established black leaders to get involved. Martin Luther King, Governor George Romney and Walter Reuther of the UAW join the walk.

Over 125,000 people parade along Woodward Avenue to Cobo Hall. *The Detroit Free Press* calls it, "The largest civil rights demonstration in the nation's history." A "cheering, stomping, screaming" crowd of 25,000 packs Cobo Hall to hear King proclaim, "We want all our rights and we want them now." The rally is a triumph for black militants who denounce Detroit as "Upper Mississippi," and urge Blacks to, "get the white man off your backs." Because of actions by city and government officials, middle-class Whites are reassured during the walk, optimistic that Detroit is coming to grips with racial problems. Unfortunately, Whites who appreciate the seriousness of the situation are few and far between. Not many understand the frustrations of Blacks, or recognize the warning signs.

By 1966, a disproportionate ratio of Blacks to Whites exists on council, despite the fact that Cavanagh appointed black people to key positions in his administration. In elected positions, Blacks are still under-represented. Detroit has nine councilmen, but only one is Black. Of seven school board trustees, only two are Black. Thirty-nine percent of the population is Black, but they have only 11 percent representation in municipal government.

Council is not representative because most councillors are elected at large. White delegates come from a small district in the northwestern part of the city, a white enclave, where black candidates don't have a hope. As a result, black ghetto dwellers feel they have little political voice, and don't feel as committed to the community because they can't choose their leader. A third of city employees are non-white, which compares favorably to the overall black population, but only 22 percent hold management positions. The rest are labourers. A high proportion of ghetto businesses are owned by Whites. Business executives are White, and these elements create a highly volatile climate. As black minister, Charles Butler, wryly points out, "rebellion is proof positive that the Negro has grown weary of being the eternal afterthought of America."

In the 1960s, Detroit appears to have an affirmative action program. It requires companies, which contract with the city, to hire minority employees or risk losing their contracts but, by the time of the riot, the city has not cancelled a single contract as a result of this ordinance. The Committee on Community Relations is in place to promote open occupancy, equal employment and desegregated education, but it lacks enforcement power and the staff of 21 is too small to be effective. The committee communicates with government and business leaders, but is "out of touch with the community." Similarly, the Civil Rights Commission, set up in '64 to restrain the police, investigate discrimination and improve community relations, is ineffective. It sets up offices, but its eight members are reluctant to use their enforcement powers and never seek a court order against the police.

Even churches fail to address problems on the street. The Citizen's Committee for Equal Opportunity is established, but many white members are uninformed about race relations. Black church leaders try to provide leadership, to narrow the gap between disgruntled Blacks and contented Whites, to raise the consciousness of Whites, make them recognize their hostility and apathy toward Blacks, but they just can't do it. The churches have a good rapport and can mobilize in times of trouble, but they are ineffective in dealing with the malaise that grips the ghetto. Churches move middle-class Blacks into white middle-class areas to promote racial cooperation and harmony but, in so doing, they ignore inner city ghettos where the real problems lie. They fail to establish a working relationship with black leaders in the poorest areas and, as a result, cannot deal with the problems.

Blacks have high expectations, but are still below the poverty line, and their achievements aren't recognized and don't bring financial gain. Churches assume that racial divisions can be overcome by reminding Whites of their religious teachings and their moral obligations to their fellow man. Churches in white enclaves preach universal human dignity while their flocks live in a racially divided and prejudicial community. Blacks who live in white neighbourhoods suffer harassment, and black-only districts are encouraged by realtors, so focussing on moral issues and launching education campaigns is not enough.

A church conference in 1965 alerts the community to a rise in black crime in the inner city. It links cultural deprivation and alienation to criminal activities and yet, Whites are apparently not listening. The conference includes representatives of labour, academia, business and government, but Mayor Cavanagh is conspicuously absent. He's no longer accessible. As a national figure, he's running for governor and thinking of federal politics. His inattention leads to a void in leadership at city hall. As one organizer sniffs, "He simply could not be reached."

To a large extent, the riot, and the ensuing degeneration of Detroit, is Cavanagh's undoing, an indication that the city's reputation as an urban model is greatly inflated. Cavanagh's political future is on par with his own battered city. Once the brightest star on the Democratic Party horizon, Cavanagh's political future starts to fade. His bid to become the governor of Michigan in 1966 is unsuccessful and he also loses the nomination for a key seat in the Senate. Detroit's rising crime rate leads to a call for Cavanagh's resignation.

Cavanagh's downfall is as unexpected as his decline but, as his fortunes drop, so do those of his city. Cavanagh thought he'd gained the trust of Blacks in Detroit, but real progress is not being made in Motown. An ever-widening rift is developing between lower, middle and upper classes. There are warning signs: threats, bricks through car windows and skirmishes with police a month before the riot; but they are generally ignored. City officials don't consider the problem serious and do nothing to stop it.

Because of Detroit's poor financial straits, there is poor garbage collection and bad street lighting. In June 1967, the "blue flu" strikes the Detroit police during contract talks with the city. To protest low wages, 1,000 officers, who feel they no longer have the backing of the mayor and who are forbidden to strike, take sick leave and fail to report for duty. Once again, Cavanagh is under fire by his opponents. His only response: the city can't afford more policing or pay increases. Teachers are also expected to strike in September. They make about the same wage as a plumber's helper.

On the eve of the riot, old racial tensions, dating back to 1943, are still in evidence. Grocers and small business owners are arming themselves, and attending gun clinics, and a few people have been shot. To some people, it's a sign of anti-black sentiment, a long-standing grievance. Meanwhile, white police officers are convinced that the mayor is crazy, trying to improve relations with Blacks. They are convinced that most Blacks need a heavy hand. Police openly defy, and mock, the mayor's efforts. Blacks resent the attitude. They also resent the fact that the mayor and police commissioner are both White. Most black policemen hold lower ranks compared to Whites who have twice as much opportunity for promotion.

Rumours of police brutality and racism are a recurring theme and a thorn to the black community. Three weeks prior to the riot, there are rumours that vice squad officers beat up a black prostitute and pistol-whipped her boyfriend as part of a crackdown. The Police Complaint Bureau looks into the allegations, but can't come up with anything. The bureau finally rules that the woman was probably killed by her pimp. Soon after, another Twelfth Street prostitute is shot and killed near the United Community and Civic Action League. Area Blacks complain that members of the vice squad murdered her, but the police call it a mugging by local thugs who regularly rob prostitutes. A study suggests that the police are in a no-win situation because they can't shake their bad reputation. Even if the police were angels, there would be racial problems, primarily because economic conditions force Blacks into crime and the police are there to eradicate it.

Police aren't the only ones in conflict with the black community. Blacks feel that newspapers concentrate on negative stories, which deal with black crime rather than Blacks as victims. On June 24, Danny Thomas, a 27-year-old black army veteran, is killed while protecting his pregnant wife from sexual advances by several white males who shout, "niggers keep out of Rouge Park." The woman loses the baby, but the press fails to report the incident for fear of inciting a riot. No mention is made in establishment papers until after a story appears in a black newspaper. *The Michigan Chronicle* complains that, "the full story of the murder is not being told." The paper points to an irony. Blacks are marching to prove they can walk without fear in Mississippi, at the same time that the Thomas' lose their new baby. It indicates a double standard, which down plays stories of violence against Blacks while emphasizing black crime. Adding insult to injury, police arrest one suspect for murder, but not the whole gang, which prompts the black community to wonder why. They demand to know what would happen if the tables were turned and a white man was killed by a black man.

In a similar, but unrelated incident, an angry mob of 50 Whites tries to expel Ethel Watkins from her newly purchased home in the Bagley District, one of the neighbourhoods touted as a model of stable integration. Police protect Watkins, but no arrests are made. Hostile Whites demonstrate over several weeks and yet, newspapers ignore the story.

The riot of 1943 should have prompted government action, but it did not. The outbreak is symptomatic of a general malaise in society. The causes of the crisis are complex, clearly rooted in the wrongs, anxieties and conditions in Detroit. The riot in 1967 rips through Detroit's facade of being the calmest city in the United States. It demonstrates that problems run deep in black America. Blacks have been exploited for over 300 years and have heard promises for 100. Their impatience is rational, their anger justified as the normal channels for social change appear bankrupt. They watch the good life on TV and they want it, and their suppressed rage is finding a means of expression.

Unlike 1943, there is little overt white hostility or retaliation against Blacks. White and black looters work together in riot areas, just as some Blacks support white National Guardsmen and firefighters. *The Detroit Free Press* says it rules out racism. On July 28, the paper says the problem is just lawlessness in a permissive society, but the issue is racial to the extent that White/Black relations trigger the riot, and social and economic injustices fuel it. Discrimination and poverty alone do not start riots, but they do create a deep, festering bitterness. There are more opportunities for some Blacks, but, for most, life in America goes on as before, and the changes do little to alleviate basic grievances. Segregation still exists, as do subtle and not so subtle colour bars. There is a growing number of angry, young, lower-class Blacks, frustrated and with no way out.

Many Blacks consider the situation outrageously unjust, and don't need more proof of white brutality. Their attitudes are galvanized and they aren't going to take it anymore. The black man in Detroit is neither a full citizen, nor accepted no matter what he does. Degraded and feared, he lashes out to bolster his self-esteem and manhood as a way of gaining self-respect. On July 23, the rest of the world starts to realize just how adamant Blacks are about their plight in Detroit. To a large extent, the summer of 1967 marks the degeneration of the Civil Rights Movement into conflict and confrontation on the American side of the border.

Chapter 10

The Quebec Question

While racial conflict in Detroit emphasizes the difficulties ripping at the heart of American cities, a similar controversy threatens the heart of Canada. Several French-Canadian historians equate the conflict between Whites and Blacks stateside with the French/English question here. There's an interesting parallel between racial strife in the U.S. and the political situation in Canada.

In 1967, Quebec separatists are convinced that French Canadians face economic and political slavery. They compare that discrimination to their black counterparts in the United States. It's a peculiar time. Canada is celebrating Expo '67, the nation's showcase in Montreal. We're in the spotlight, under the microscope. We're front and centre in the eyes of the world, but so are our problems, and the cracks are showing, just as the cracks are showing in the United States.

The division between French and English has never been more pronounced. French Canadians resisted assimilation when New France fell to Britain after the battle of Quebec in 1759, and they are still resisting. French legal, cultural and language rights were supposed to be guaranteed when Quebec reluctantly joined the federation in 1867. It was a ploy to bring Quebec into the union, but it was an uneasy alliance with the new province demanding enough power to ensure the survival of its people. Quebec wants more and the split festers.

In 1967, many people in Quebec talk about equality and separation from the rest of Canada. They're fed up with the federal government, which controls the purse strings and prevents Quebec's self-determination. Similar to American Blacks, Quebeckers "want to survive as a people, and to be in charge of their own destiny." They do not want to be dominated politically and economically by Canada. They want to be free. With the upheaval of the '60s, the idea of a politically independent Quebec has never been stronger.

French President Charles de Gaulle lays the wounds bare on Monday, July 24. It's the second day of a state visit to Quebec, and of the riot in Detroit. De Gaulle is hosted by both the federal and provincial governments. Quebeckers want to assert their right as a nation, and demonstrate a kinship with another French-speaking country, but the trip is clouded. Federal and provincial bureaucrats squabble over who should roll out the red carpet. It's a carpet that both governments trip over in the rush to make arrangements for de Gaulle's tour.

During the height of black rioting in Detroit, de Gaulle plays upon this split in Canada. The 76-year-old general officially kicks off his five-day visit by speaking to 3,000 cheering French Canadians from the balcony of Quebec's city hall. In his speech, he encourages cultural and educational

"Vive le Québec libre." *French President Charles de Gaulle making his famous speech at Montreal's city hall on July 24, 1967.* CP/Source

ties between France and French Canada, and practically tells separatists to follow their own pro-French course. He salutes Quebec's will "to take its destiny in its own hands." He says there are two communities in Canada, and their status is not equal. He adds that France is not indifferent to that inequality and wants to help Quebec. "One always has the right to speak of liberty."

The flag-waving crowd applauds wildly. It's exactly what they want to hear. The frenzied masses are overjoyed when de Gaulle wraps up with "*Vive Montréal. Vive le Québec. Vive le Canada français. Vive le Québec libre. Vive la France!*" Separatists struggle with police to get near the general. Thousands demonstrate in the streets.

The media makes headlines with the controversial phrase: *Vive le Québec libre*, or Long Live Free Quebec. The separatist slogan is often shouted or painted on walls in Quebec, but this is the first time it's been uttered by a visiting dignitary. De Gaulle's words set the tone for an embarrassing state visit. His speech reflects the awakening nationhood in Quebec, the struggle to become a society distinct from the rest of Canada. If it means leaving the country, then so be it.

The rift parallels the awakening spirit of nationalism in some black organizations in the United States – the feeling that Blacks are downtrodden and can no longer live under white society. Already, a movement is afoot to partition five American southern states as a black homeland, a nation within a nation. The plan would split the United States into two distinct regions: one Black, the other White. There would be no integration because integration implies the subjugation of black majorities by rich white minorities. The idea corresponds to separatists in Quebec who want to partition their province and secede from the rest of Canada.

Happy fans mob de Gaulle's limo. Riding this wave of euphoria, the French president drives to Montreal. Throughout the motorcade, he talks about a pact between France and Quebec to contribute to the vigour and strength of French Canada. He's hoarse after he stops for the sixth time to address huge crowds on his way to attend France Day at Expo. Then, he's scheduled to go to Ottawa for talks with Prime Minister Lester Bowles Pearson. Already, Quebeckers are chanting "*Québec libre, de Gaulle l'a dit!*" Free Quebec, de Gaulle said it.

Quebec Premier Daniel Johnson and the President of France sing the National Anthem in Montreal, July 24, 1967, shortly after de Gaulle made his address to the Quebec people. CP/Source

In Ottawa, damage control is underway. An emergency cabinet meeting is called to examine de Gaulle's speech. External Affairs Minister Paul Martin is recalled from Montreal. He's Pearson's official representative, and he's hauled on the carpet to explain de Gaulle's address, and how it happened. Martin says he told de Gaulle that his comments weren't appropriate. Federalists complain, "It's shocking ... bloody bad manners!" They don't believe the general's comments were spur-of-the-moment. They fear that de Gaulle deliberately breached the protocol of a state visit by interfering in the country's internal politics.

Warren Allmand, a Liberal M.P. from the Montreal riding of Notre-Dame-De-Grace, sends an urgent message to Martin that the remainder of de Gaulle's visit be cancelled. Allmand notes that, throughout Canada's Centennial Year, 1,000 students from across the country are involved in exchange programs where children from one area live with children from another to learn about their culture. In Windsor, young people are twinned with their counterparts from Quebec and, over a two-week period, tour the Hiram Walker Historical Museum, *The Windsor Star*, the H.J. Heinz plant in Leamington and the University of Windsor. Allmand thinks highly of the exchange and doesn't want de Gaulle's visit to jeopardize the good it might do.

On the other side of the debate, NDP Leader T.C. Douglas says, "These are the words of an aging man at the end of a long and gruelling day." Douglas feels that hasty recriminations will serve no good purpose, and he doubts that de Gaulle is meddling in Canadian politics.

Pierre Elliott Trudeau, Liberal M.P. for the affluent Montreal riding of Mount Royal and newly appointed minister of justice and attorney general of Canada, has difficulty taking it seriously. He figures it would be like Canada questioning French sovereignty over St. Pierre and Miquelon, two French islands in the Gulf of St. Lawrence just below Newfoundland. Trudeau supports other politicians who hope that de Gaulle will apologize before he heads home.

As a result of political pressure, the prime minister cancels de Gaulle's trip to Ottawa/Hull. Obviously annoyed, Pearson tells cabinet that Canada is free, and that de Gaulle's support for those trying to destroy the country is unacceptable. W.L. Clark, columnist for *The Windsor Star*, supports the prime minister's decision. He says leaders of other countries are annoyed with de Gaulle, but just don't know how to express it. Clark applauds Pearson. "He did what a lot of them have wanted to do for a long time." Students at the Université de Montréal also support the prime minister. They greet de Gaulle with signs proclaiming, "One Canada for Canadians."

The French president is astounded by the rebukes, and decides to return to France for "urgent reasons of state." As a final slap at the feds, he calls the Quebec premier and thanks him for a magnificent reception, but sends no thanks to his federal host, Governor General Roland Michener. Lionel Chevrier, the commissioner general for Centennial state visits, and Jules Leger, the Canadian ambassador to France, escort de Gaulle to Dorval Airport. They're the only federal representatives to see the general off. It's a bad end to an unfortunate trip, the first of 60 state visits to Expo during the Centennial.

By the end of the week, de Gaulle explains his reasons for reviving links between French Canadians and France. He wants to establish a new balance of power in North America to replace the dominant position of the

United States. In 1968, during his year-end speech, de Gaulle thanks Quebeckers for their warm reception, while lamenting the unfortunate anti-Gaullist sentiment in the rest of Canada. He says France has no designs on Quebec, other than to see it as a sovereign state. He hopes that French Canadians will gain a free hand in the management of their national life and will become an international force.

De Gaulle's voice pleases Quebeckers and gives them hope. Young people are impatient, and willing to resort to violence and terrorism, if necessary. They don't believe they benefit from industry and commerce, but that their culture is under siege by rich English and Americans. De Gaulle lends credence to their beliefs and brings international attention to "the Quebec problem." It's hoped his comments will elicit intelligent discussion of the constitutional and political problems faced by Canada.

While de Gaulle is stirring the pot in Quebec, a lesser-known political figure is stirring things up within the terrorist wing of the Front de Libération du Québec. The FLQ is a political organization credited with robbing banks, and placing bombs in mailboxes and in the town hall in Greenfield Park. As an FLQ member and a French-Canadian Nationalist, Pierre Vallières feels such revolutionary actions will lead to Quebec independence or freedom. Vallières is in a Montreal jail on charges of murder, robbery and conspiracy, but he's also working on his manifesto, a book entitled *Nègres blancs d'Amérique* (*White Niggers of America*), which is published in 1968.

Vallières' book advocates the overthrow of the ruling class, and the establishment of an independent nation to liberate his fellow Québécois – the white niggers – from the bondage of capitalism. Vallières urges French Canadians to engage in terrorism to break the "shackles of colonialism and demand independence in the name of dignity." Vallières talks about three centuries of exploitation suffered by his people, initially at the hands of the French, then the English and finally the Americans. He wants compatriots to rise up and take back their country.

On May 5, 1966, Vallières and Charles Gagnon, the best known young militants, are implicated in an explosion at a shoe factory in Montreal that kills Thérèse Morin. Police arrest fifteen other FLQ members, but Vallières and Gagnon flee to the United States where they lobby for the release of their compatriots who, they say, are being held as political prisoners. The two men begin a hunger strike and picket the United Nations building in New York.

Vallières and Gagnon are arrested on September 28 for disturbing the peace and entering the United States illegally. They're picked up by New York police at the request of the Canadian government. They refuse voluntary deportation, even though they know that the U.S. will never offer them political asylum. While awaiting extradition to Canada, they're held for three months in the Manhattan House of Detention for Men, a prison known as the Tombs, where they continue their hunger strike for 29 days, living exclusively on water.

In his book, Vallières talks about a social transformation in Quebec, culminating in "the quiet revolution." He's upset by the ruling class for being responsible only for its own interests, and not the interests of 90 per cent of the population. He criticizes politicians like René Lévesque, the leader of the Parti Québécois, for deceiving the people, and he incites workers to take control over their economic and social policy.

Vallières' philosophy is echoed by author Leandre Bergeron, who fears that French Canadians are being assimilated. Bergeron says it dates back to September 13, 1759, and the battle of the Plains of Abraham. To Bergeron, when Montreal surrendered to the British, the economic colonialism of the French began. They became cheap labour, "born slaves." Bergeron says the conqueror always sees the conquered as inferior, deserving nothing better than slavery or death. He says superiority by the so-called "civilized race" leads to white racism, and he concludes that the eradication of colonialism can only be accomplished through armed struggle.

To Vallières, the problem is not that French Canadians are low paid, poorly educated or unemployed; they just have no control over their own destiny. He believes that, if French Canadians don't take charge, they'll remain "white niggers," the men with dirty hands, the working poor, the cheap labour that industry requires and, yet, tramples underfoot. Vallières means "niggers" in the most alienating and derogatory sense of the word. He defines it as sub-human. He says that people use it because it allows superiority to the lowest of the low. It reflects their own hatred and paralysis, their own fear. Vallières admits it's degrading, but he believes Quebeckers deserve it for remaining hired servants. He compares French Canadians to American Blacks: white slavery in the north, black slavery in the south; as workers become indentured, sell their labour for an hourly wage.

According to Vallières, irrational racism south of the border has done much wrong to workers both White and Black. Since there's no black problem in Quebec, French Canadians weren't aware of what was going on and yet, he says, "The liberation struggle launched by American Blacks arouses growing interest among the French-Canadian population, for the workers of Quebec are aware of their condition as 'niggers,' exploited men, second class citizens." He maintains that French Canadians were imported, like American Blacks, to serve as cheap labour in the New World. The only difference is the colour of their skin and where they originated.

To back up his claims, Vallières launches into a Quebec history lesson. He says the original settlers to Quebec were farmers, traders and artisans, *coureurs de bois*, unskilled workers or "volunteers" who could not find jobs in France. These colonists, or "Habitants," came by the thousands in the late 1600s. Seeking freedom, equality and economic independence from feudal lords and bondage in Europe, they populated and built the New World. Vallières maintains they lived under the thumb of the church and the French merchant class, in similar conditions of poverty and oppression that they left on the other side of the Atlantic.

After the French defeat, Vallières says, one ruling class merely replaced another. The English took over the economic affairs and executive power, helped by the clergy, which retained dominion over education and taxes. Bergeron suggests that the church assumed the role of "Negro King," a puppet government or tribal leader, which kept the slaves in check. Its members became "Uncle Toms," who benefitted personally, while maintaining their people in positions of authority. Worried about supremacy in English society, the church fostered French culture and language by colonizing undeveloped regions of Quebec, clearing land and planting, whether the soil was suitable or not. According to Vallières, the Habitants remained beasts of burden in a hostile country under the watchful eye of their British conquerors and the church.

The bitterness intensified, with English Canadians complaining openly about the French. Radical farmers and small businessmen, known as the

Clear Grits, were most outspoken. As Bergeron points out, their most pompous member was overheard at a dinner party: "The Negroes are the great difficulty of the States and the French Canadians of Canada." As early as 1851, the Clear Grits promoted Confederation as a larger economic unit that would prevent annexation to the United States, but that would also erode the sphere of influence of French Canadians.

During World War I, thousands of angry French Canadians took to the streets to protest conscription. The government needed troops and wanted to impose the draft across the country, but French Canadians objected because it wasn't their war. It was England's, and many refused to go. The masses smashed windows at newspapers in Montreal and Quebec in a demonstration that lasted three months and that came to a head on August 30, 1917. The police moved in and one man was killed. The wealthy home of Hugh Graham, owner of *The Montreal Star*, was dynamited. Under the rallying cry *"Vive la révolution!"* the rioters fired their rifles and waved their hats. Paris newspapers raised the possibility of Quebec's secession from the rest of Canada. The province became "Fortress Quebec," looking inward to protect itself against real or imagined attacks from the federal government. Quebec's siege mentality was complete.

In March 1918, more riots broke out in Quebec. Several thousand people sang the *Marseillaise*, set fire to the police station, sacked several newspaper buildings and burned the office of the registrar of the Military Service Act. On March 30, the army fired on the crowd. Many people revolted. They ambushed the army from rooftops, windows and balconies. Five soldiers were wounded. Four civilians died. Hundreds of workers and young people were injured; 60 were jailed. The federal government remained intransigent. On April 4, it decreed that rioters should be drafted, a decision which merely increased the rioting. Vallières says, "The disturbances ended with the close of the war, but the people's bitterness never ceased."

Throughout the Depression, social agitation increased. Strikes and demonstrations multiplied as discontent spread. In 1937, riots in Sorel, Quebec, left many dead and wounded. There were battles in the textile industry where French-Canadian labourers were treated badly. Problems intensified with conscription during World War II, but unfortunately for the rioters, their movement did not lead to any "popular, political, revolutionary organization." They were incapable of mobilizing for social reform because they were seen as sympathetic to the enemy. In 1940, the leaders of the uprising were viewed as racist supporters of Mussolini and Hitler. They lacked the support of the clergy, and all they did was establish a rude form of nationalism, a vague sense of nationhood.

In the summer of 1944, fights erupted in the streets of Montreal between French Canadians and military police. By fall, acts of violence escalated to include Chicoutimi and Rimouski, Quebec. There was more talk of independence and revolution. On November 29, several thousand French Canadians paraded through the financial district of Montreal, smashing windows in banks, federal buildings and Anglo-American businesses. An angry crowd broke windows at the Quebec residence of Louis St. Laurent, Canada's minister of justice. English Canadians recommended that machine guns be used to force the "French Pea Soups" to defend the interests of the "Free World!"

Between 1944 and '59, Vallières says, the mood of the people was suppressed under a blanket of Duplessism. Quebeckers became indifferent. No leader, no matter how stirring or passionate, could raise the masses, and they lost their ability to resist. There was only room for day-to-day living, making ends meet. "Winter had frozen the best minds." Vallières says that the Duplessis years were marked by a series of difficult struggles, lost strikes, legal tricks and censorship, but Quebec Premier Maurice Duplessis was just too much of a god. Vallières calls it the "black misery," which lasted until Duplessis' death in 1959.

"Quebec awoke only slowly from its long winter" with the unexpected victory in 1960 of the Liberals under Jean Lesage, and the coming to power of the "socialist" René Lévesque, a well-known television personality and journalist who became Lesage's resources minister. "It was as if an iron clamp had suddenly been released from French-Canadian society." Vallières says that Lévesque was like the incarnation of rediscovered freedom. The people were starting to believe they had a future, and Lévesque stimulated pride and idealism. With renewed hope, Quebeckers felt they were alive again and making progress. They also identified with Lesage, who believed in provincial autonomy and decentralization as much as

Duplessis, but who was more successful dealing with the federal government. It was "the end of the great darkness and the beginning of the quiet revolution ... the apologia of slavery was ripped up."

Vallières says that television sparked a new "national" debate, which allowed open discussion and led to political, social and economic reforms. The province surged ahead. Control over education was wrested from the Church. There were major changes in labour, economic and social policies. There was a feeling that Quebec had to modernize or risk cultural death and it gave hope to revolutionaries, like Vallières, that a new division of power was near. He says Canadian Confederation was at the point of death at the very moment it was to celebrate its Centennial. The slogan in the election of 1962 summed up the debate. Quebeckers wanted to become *"Maîtres chez nous"* (Masters in our own house).

In July 1963, many Canadians finally woke up to the problems in Quebec. Prime Minister Pearson established the Royal Commission on Bilingualism-Biculturalism to allay the seething discontent. It was recognition that "Canada, without being fully conscious of the fact, was passing through the greatest crisis in its history."

At about the same time, Pierre Elliott Trudeau rose to power as a federalist who believed in a strong central government, not based on pride of frontier, but on the desires of the people. Having travelled the world, Trudeau believed in multi-nationalism with a growing mistrust of Quebec separation. "I am against any policy based on race or religion." He was convinced that "nationalism ... can let loose unforeseen powers," including racism. Wealthy, well-educated, bilingual, he was well-suited to represent Canada's interests because he would cut no special deals with Quebec. As such, he was a perfect foil for Lévesque who was equally suited to the task of defending Quebec independence.

It has often been said of French Canadians that they are the oldest colonized people in the world with a history of 400 years. This "dubious distinction seems to indicate that men do not grow used to slavery, however long their servitude." They do not easily forget their dignity and honour. Under the threat of separation, measures have been taken to reduce discrimination, but Quebeckers still hold tenaciously to their distinctive and original character, giving more weight to culture than economics. Theirs is an increasing awareness of domination and menace. To Separatists, the province of Quebec is a great colonial power that has yet to achieve national independence and yet, federalists say, Quebec is the author of its own misfortune. If Quebeckers had become more involved in their economic development and elected fewer reactionary and defensive governments, they may have assimilated more, become more modern and enjoyed greater individual prosperity. Quebeckers reply that they don't feel that prosperity should be tied to the expense or loss of their culture.

Throughout the '6os, Vallières suggested that there was some dispute about what kind of separatism the Québécois wanted. By 1966, Daniel Johnson, the new premier, talked of equality or complete independence. Others spoke of "the two solitudes," the idea that Canada was really two nations: French and English. Still others wanted a federal system with more power and money for the provinces. To Vallières, this last idea was a constitutional miracle to save the country. Prominent federal Liberals, including Pierre Trudeau, Jean Marchand and Gérard Pelletier, supported it, but Vallières gave them little hope. There were 5,000,000 French Canadians in Quebec in 1967 out of a total population of 6,000,000. Resentful and optimistic, Vallières advocated complete separation from the dominance of English Canada, figuring it was time for the workers of Quebec to develop an independent political organization, to seize power and establish a form of security based on justice, equality and fraternity.

In the '6os, FLQ militants were convinced that America was in revolt. Housewives boycotted, union members staged wildcats, young people spoke against racism and Vietnam, staged campus sit-ins and burned their draft cards. They also burned the American president in effigy, and chose to go to jail rather than murder innocent Vietnamese. As Vallières triumphantly pointed out, they discovered that freedom was not to be found by marking an "X" on a ballot. "The poor economic health of the American people in this last third of the 20th Century leads me to believe that the American Revolution is already on the march."

Little by little, Vallières believed that racism was giving way to solidarity as class-consciousness developed. Movements, such as Black Nationalism and French-Canadian separatism, were necessary to any revolution because they allowed people to "envisage the liberation of the whole man

.... The niggers of America are one with the niggers of the entire world." Vallières equated the goals of the Québécois with those of Black Nationalism. He believed that uniting the Québécois was just the first step in developing a new, just and fraternal society for "the niggers of all other countries." It was this awareness of a collective injustice, this education, he suggested, that allowed slaves to escape. He advocated a bloody freedom, insisted that the movement become more violent as the masses overthrew the business elite. "We're going to take our affairs in hand and then, to hell with the regulations .... The sparks are going to fly! *Aux armes, aux armes Québécois!*"

In the 1960s, Blacks rediscovered pride and determination but, to Vallières, Black Power was more a philosophy than a movement. It wasn't structured, or organized. He saw Black Power as "the Afro-American equivalent of Quebec separation." By the end of the decade, Blacks were in the majority in 50 American cities and they wanted their constitutional rights respected. They wanted self-determination, armed self-defence of all American black communities, as well as control over their economic, political and social affairs, including police, schools, hospitals, jobs and playgrounds. To Vallières, it was similar to the manifesto of the FLQ in Quebec. It was black separation and it was enough to sow panic in the white ruling class.

Black Power was part of the philosophy of Malcolm X who was assassinated in 1965. It was a form of "black nationalism" where Blacks would live separately from Whites in an anti-white society. The feeling was that only Blacks could solve their problems because they were Black. As black militant, Reverend Albert Cleage Junior, put it, Blacks had to "think Black, vote Black and buy Black" to be free. Cleage believed that non-violence and mass-protest had failed and Blacks had to defend themselves against brutality. They had to seize their rights, to strike back when knocked down.

Some called it the start of the black revolution, even though most militant black leaders did not enjoy a large following, especially in the north. Self-determination was also hampered by the comparatively small percentage of the population. Comprising only 10 to 15 per cent, Blacks still required "white money" to rehabilitate housing and make improvements in the ghetto.

Despite the problems, Black Power was organized amid bombings, assassinations and riots and, to Vallières, it was a strong expression of the class struggle against, not only white capitalists, but the black middle class as well. Led by younger, more impatient and militant members of the black community, its advocates regarded the black middle class as too conservative. They were "Uncle Toms" who "played the game," told Whites what they wanted to hear and sold out to Whites in order to protect their new, more affluent lifestyle. Generally, they allied themselves with Martin Luther King Junior who advocated change, but through non-violent means. To Vallières, this conservatism was misguided. They were out of touch with their constituents, the less fortunate Blacks in the ghettos. Integration of buses, snack bars and bowling alleys no longer moved Blacks. They were motivated by riots and the disappearance of slums and ghettos. The most militant black leaders advocated organized violence and control of cities, and suggested that every black family should know how to use a gun. They were fond of pointing out that Black Power was dangerous ... to Whites.

Because the Québécois were disorganized, Vallières implored them to unite with the militant black movement in America and join the marches to Washington. He figured that working class Whites were poor in resources and weak in hope, but he was optimistic that black revolutionaries could give them the means and opportunity to revolt. He envisioned unemployed millions rising against the rich, convinced that the economic interests of workers was the same regardless of the colour of their skin. To Vallières, the black movement was valid because it was anti-capitalist, rather than racist. Blacks, he believed, could work with white students and activists to achieve their ends. They were not hostile toward absolute equality, just to the humiliation of white paternalism. Having said that, Vallières recognized that the liaison could be difficult in a society contaminated by racism. He was also afraid that the working poor aspired to be middle class and was therefore reluctant to overthrow the system. Such a goal was good for the individual, not for society as a whole.

Vallières wrote his first article in 1957. It was called "The Fear of Living" and it was an attack on the slave's philosophy. Using the image of the underground railroad and the escape of slaves from bondage in the southern

United States, Vallières referred to the philosophy of escape. All a slave had to do was search for a refuge somewhere and then flee to it, but Vallières maintained that this search for a refuge had gone on long enough. "It was time to learn how to live." He applied this idea to the Québécois and to himself. He decided that he'd buried himself in his books too long and it was time to take action.

After a trip to France, Vallières drifted from group to group until he came to the FLQ in 1966. The liberal government was trying to save the province and the Canadian confederation from the "plague" of French-Canadian nationalism. Vallières organized anti-Vietnam rallies and demonstrations and protested unemployment. It was all part of the *Révolution Québécoise*, which determined that electoral change would not cut it. Little reforms were no longer acceptable because the masses were excluded from real power. Political parties never opposed the system, just the ruling clique. "The closer they come to power, the more conservative and 'respectable' they become." He was convinced that, to be economically independent, Quebec needed to be politically independent.

After his deportation from New York to Montreal on January 13, 1967, Vallières faces a dozen charges for his part in the revolution. They range from stealing dynamite to murder. He remains in prison for a year before his trial. On April 5, 1968, he gets life, the maximum sentence for manslaughter. In a letter to friends on April 29, Vallières writes: "If we are to free ourselves completely from the slavery in which we are trapped by the present system, we must first cease to be slaves to our fears, our cowardice, our hesitations and all the little habits of men who are resigned or benumbed." He applauds General de Gaulle during Expo '67 because he gives national exposure to the cause, exposure that the movement hasn't enjoyed before.

While in prison, Vallières receives support from many groups, including the Black Panthers, the Black Power Movement, and the support of black leader, Stokely Carmichael. He's buoyed by the fact that, before 1969, there were more than 60 bombings in Montreal, as well as strikes, sit-ins and demonstrations, and he vows that he will continue the fight from behind bars. Vallières knows the struggle will be long and hard, and will mean suffering and prison for many. "We shall pay dearly for our struggle,

but it will win us a better society, one which will at last be ours." Vallières
is eventually acquitted on appeal and released from prison in 1970.
Gagnon was released months earlier. The two men are rounded up again
in the fall but, essentially, their terrorist days are over, and Vallières
becomes a teacher of political philosophy in Montreal.

Unfortunately for Vallières' revolutionary spirit, the political foment of the
'60s merely served as a wake-up call for Quebeckers and other Canadians.
In October 1969, Montreal police went on strike, while mobs rioted and
looted stores. One headline read: "Montreal is bloody and in flames." The
riot act was read as federal troops restored order, but the police strike was
soon over and the army withdrew. There were other riotous acts as the
decade drew to a close, but the day of revolution was waning. It was a
turning point in Quebec.

The FLQ's seven-year odyssey finally comes to an end during the
October Crisis of 1970. On Monday, October 5, the FLQ kidnaps the British
trade commissioner, James Richard Cross, from his home on Mount Royal
in Montreal. It immediately publishes its demands in the form of a manifesto which calls for an end to police searches, the freeing of political prisoners, safe conduct to Cuba or Algeria, and cash. When negotiations bog
down, the FLQ responds by kidnapping Pierre Laporte in front of his
Saint-Lambert home but, this time, federal reaction is swift and hard.
Unlike the response during the Detroit riot, Canadian officials clamp
down. On Thursday, October 15, the army appears in Quebec. The next
morning, the government declares martial law under the War Measures
Act, claiming that an insurrection is breaking out. Tanks and troops take
over the streets of Montreal as civil liberties are suspended. It looks like a
Canadian version of the Detroit riot except that real troops are on the
streets from the beginning and there's no question about their job or
authority.

The government makes membership in the FLQ illegal and arrests all of
its members, conducting thousands of searches of homes and offices.
Over 500 people are arrested without a warrant and are thrown into
prison. In many cases, police strike at night, breaking down doors and ter-
rorizing families. Often, no charges are laid. Detainees are not allowed to
contact their lawyers or families for up to three weeks. Under sweeping

Pierre Laporte, the victim of Canada's first political assassination in 102 years, is shown with his wife, Françoise, at the Quebec Liberal leadership convention in Quebec City in January 1970.
CP/Source

powers of the War Measures Act, the government seizes documents, over 100 weapons and about 3,000 sticks of dynamite. It's an unprecedented campaign and Separatists are furious with the suspension of civil liberties. They complain that police raids are an attempt to put Quebec in its place and stop Quebec independence. It's a tough blow against not only terrorism, but also separation. Separatists find it ironic that democratic freedoms can be suspended in the interest of protecting democracy.

On Saturday, October 17, mass hysteria reaches its highest pitch as police receive an anonymous phone call. It tells them where to find the body of Pierre Laporte. It's in the trunk of the car in which he was kidnapped, parked near Saint-Hubert air base. The news takes the country by surprise. In a weird twist, the situation gives credibility to the government and the need for dealing harshly with terrorists. The government immediately steps up the pressure. Soldiers are assigned as personal bodyguards to influential people. They're also in force at public buildings. At Laporte's funeral, extra security is called in. Soldiers train their submachine guns on the crowd. "Power becomes visible and identifiable." The government clamps down with one aim: to stamp out terrorism. For several hours, CBC TV displays a picture of Laporte, accompanied by sombre music. Vallières says a radio reporter buys into the government's message, "We have heard too much in Quebec about revolution, liberation and social justification. All that is finished now. We must support the government of Canada and do whatever we can to assure the prosperity of private enterprise in Quebec."

The government round up of terrorists takes less than two months. On November 6, Bernard Lortie is arrested as an alleged member of the Chénier Cell of the FLQ. Police offer a reward of $150,000 for information leading to the arrest of Marc Carbonneau, Jacques Lançtot, Paul Rose and Francis Simard. On December 3, police surround an apartment on the Rue des Récollets in Montréal-Nord. They negotiate the release of James Cross by offering kidnappers safe conduct to Cuba. Lançtot, Carbonneau, Yves Langlois and Jacques Cossette-Trudel, all members of the Libération Cell of the FLQ, are flown to the Caribbean on an RCAF plane. Then, on December 28, Paul and Jacques Rose and Francis Simard are arrested in a farmhouse near Saint-Jean and accused of murder in the death of Pierre Laporte. The government releases a few hundred suspects. Others are accused of conspiracy and membership in an illegal organization. Paul Rose is prevented from attending his own trial and is convicted. The drama ends. Contrary to Vallières' dreams and aspirations, there is no further guerrilla warfare in Quebec and terrorism ultimately dies with Laporte.

With the rebellion ended, the quietude wins, but not with a reaffirmation of a strong centrist government in Ottawa. Quebeckers revoke the bombs and inflamed rhetoric of the FLQ, but they also reject federalism. They recognize that they want something different in terms of socio-economic and national liberation and they start to realize the way to achieve it. They discover that, in a democracy, reforms have to come from within. Troops are never sent to crush people who vote at the polls. "Flamboyant actions and declarations seem to have given way to movements and actions which are less spectacular, but more efficient."

In essence, the spirit that spawns the FLQ survives and gives rise to the Parti Québécois in 1968 – one year after the 100th anniversary of confederation. It's a democratic movement led by René Lévesque to seek liberation through political means while maintaining some form of economic association with Canada. Lévesque wants to unite separatists under one banner. A collective consciousness has been achieved in Quebec. To many people, the word "destiny" echoes in the same air, which, in 1970, reverberated with the buzz of helicopters and the wail of sirens. The PQ gains power and popularity as a party of the people.

As Bergeron puts it, the 1960s created "an atmosphere of great festivity, of liberation, a throwing off of inhibitions." It was an awareness for Quebeckers of their own inferior social and economic status but, when it came right down to it, the armed rebellion died. It never became popular. Similar to Blacks in the U.S., conservatism kept terrorist actions in check. Quebeckers, especially the middle class, preferred to keep their heads down, to live in relative peace. As Bergeron explains, the FLQ had a lot of enthusiasm and wanted to accelerate change. They honestly thought Quebeckers would rise up and make Quebec independent and yet it didn't happen. Bergeron says the natural inclination of colonized people is fear of change, fear of violence. "But beneath this fear, complicity and some deep hope lay hidden." The problem for the FLQ was that its revolt was crushed, put down so fiercely that a lot of the fervor was quashed, like much of the revolutionary spirit of the 1960s.

Chapter 11

Post Riot: Detroit

After the riot, many black people in Detroit felt proud of having stood up for their rights. By 1969, 40 percent of them thought that riots helped, compared to only two percent in 1960. Many Blacks recognized that while riots were tragic, it was hoped that they served to wake up the white community to needed changes. They hoped the riot would act as a catalyst for the growth of an integrated city, and that Whites would finally recognize the depths of black hurt, the need for jobs, better housing and an end to police harassment. They hoped for better living conditions, but also for opportunities and dignity for black people. They recognized that riots were always crushed, but seemed to generate positive results. Riots lay problems bare for all to see and Blacks felt that, if that's what it took, then so be it. Riots made Whites feel guilty which often led to jobs or government money to solve problems. Riots "got the attention of white leadership, particularly corporate leadership, in a way that nothing else had." As one black leader suggested, "The riot was like children doing ugly, violent things to get attention."

If Whites didn't wake to conditions in Detroit, they were certainly shocked by them, finally recognizing the unrest, not apparent on the surface. As one councillor said, the city was like an iceberg "with a bright, attractive, well-publicized face, but with submerged dangers not readily seen." Ironically, in March, Detroit received an All-American City Award, which many Blacks described as a joke. Proud of its accomplishments, the city was, nonetheless, under attack from within. If those in power had opened their eyes, they would have seen that racial tensions and economic problems were in evidence before the riot. Only after the riot did those attitudes change, and then only slowly.

Even successful Blacks realized that Detroit's programs only helped "the enterprising Negro" and missed the poor and unemployed. These Blacks were more articulate and better organized and, even though the city was divided and in need of action, there was a renewed sense of optimism that Detroit would fulfill its Latin motto – *Resurgit Cineribus* – adopted in 1805 after a fire levelled the city. It means "It shall rise from the ashes" and that's what Blacks expected. The optimism was buoyed by city officials who proposed sweeping changes to municipal government. Mayor Cavanagh established a Development Team, which worked from August 3 to October 26 to come up with a 750-page report, calling for two super-agencies – one to deal with social issues and the other to grapple physical development in the city.

A result of the study was the establishment of the New Detroit Committee in September 1967. A high-profile group of government, labour, business and community leaders, it was devoted to improving the quality of life by rebuilding Detroit and responding to black grievances, analyzing what caused the riot and seeing that it didn't happen again. Headed by department store heir, Joseph L. Hudson Junior, it recruited top executives, including Henry Ford II, James Roche, the president of General Motors; and Lynn Townsend, the chairman of the Chrysler Corporation.

Touted as "speaking a new language and operating with new rules," the committee set up a centre to recruit unemployed workers at the corner of Twelfth Street and Clairmount where the riot had begun. It found jobs for 1,700 workers of whom 800 were still employed by April 1968. The Ford Motor Company also opened employment offices in the ghetto and lowered its hiring criteria to allow uneducated Blacks into the plants. Combined with on-the-job training, the idea was to increase Black/White ratios in the factory, and make them more representative of the population at large. As a result, 4,600 Blacks were hired and almost 80 percent still had jobs by April 1968. Thousands more jobs were created in 76 companies, including the Chrysler Corporation. As Henry Ford II put it, "If they want jobs, we'll give them jobs."

The committee also set a pattern for racial cooperation in other civic affairs, and got Blacks and Whites talking. It lobbied for the creation of Wayne County Community College and channelled corporate money into summer reading and recreation programs, minority business development and social research. It also looked at crime prevention and substance abuse. Fearing that many insurance policies would be cancelled 90 days after the riot, the committee even reviewed fire and property insurance in slums. Then, it established a fund-raising drive called the "Homes By Christmas" campaign, which generated $180,000 in loans to provide houses to 120 ghetto families made homeless by the riots. It also lobbied for open housing and tenant rights, but came under fire as soon as it swung into action. Conditions improved immediately, but then deteriorated as the sincerity of New Detroit came into doubt.

The Kerner Commission emphasized the need to do something about the all-white police force since fewer than four percent of the officers were Black. The New Detroit Committee recognized the severity of the problem, but struggled to deal with it. A review of the department never got off the ground. A lack of funds and the resignation of Commissioner Ray Girardin were cited as reasons, but that was not good enough for one of the main critics of the committee. U.S. Representative John Conyers, a black Democrat from Detroit, was incensed with the failure. "When a bank clerk insults you, you go to another bank. Can you go to a different police department?" Conyers felt the problem only worsened after the riot. The police tried to recruit more black officers and also required inspectors to go into the community, respond to calls in cruisers and walk part of the beat each day rather than stay at their desks. But only two of 23 inspectors were Black, and the change was criticized as lame.

New Detroit allocated $500,000 to upgrade education so that more Blacks might pass tests to become police officers. It helped improve relations with the black community, but the committee was accused of not pushing the programs fast enough. The committee also helped Blacks qualify for apprenticeship programs in skilled trades but, when Blacks still failed to make the grade, the union said it was because they were not interested in low-paid apprentice positions. The committee refused to force the issue and take the case to court or go public with the controversy. New Detroit also lobbied for $5,000,000 worth of emergency school aid and $9,000,000 for underprivileged children, but both requests were simply ignored by the state. The mayor and governor resisted, which led to more resentment.

Critics believed that New Detroit was merely set up to calm the city and appease the discontent by creating reform machinery without turning it on. It gave the appearance of doing something by studying the problem, but did not take action. Of the 39 members on the committee, 22 didn't even live in the city. Only nine were Black and three of those resigned, one in protest. Of 100 staff, only 15 were Black and most were new to ghetto conditions. Conyers conceded that committee members were intelligent, well-educated and diligent workers. He lauded the fact that they gained new-found knowledge and developed a social philosophy about the problems of inner-city poverty but, he said, "It's a little late for re-education ... Where have these people been all their lives?"

Critics said attempts to solve problems from "above" and "without" did not work. Rebuilding required involvement, not just for the people, but also with the people. To understand a problem, you had to experience it; otherwise, all the empathy in the world meant nothing. Community leaders said it required inspiration, not patronization. "You can't just throw money at a problem. You must provide special education and training to qualify for jobs, so that Blacks can be men again. New programs, and supplemented wages, is the only way to end under-employment and get rid of 'have-nots.'"

New Detroit was resolved to work with black organizations, but was unable to stop alienation between white and black communities. There was a general belief that the riot brought Whites and Blacks together around the conference table, but it actually drove them further apart in everyday life. New Detroit also failed to appeal to black leaders for help and support. The committee recognized a need to attract businessmen to invest money, develop industry and revitalize residential sections of the city, but it failed to act. It also failed to live up to its own expectations. Even its own members moved out as the evacuation of Detroit continued.

People fled Detroit in the 1960s, but the exodus accelerated following the riot. People said it was because of the establishment of freeways, which made it easier and possible. They claimed they left for free parking, clean air, lower taxes, a safer environment and shorter commutes as corporate headquarters relocated, but the real reason was the absence of racial tension. The flight to the suburbs was not unusual, but it had a traumatic effect on Detroit. It was the *coup de grace*, the final struggle, for the city.

Factories, grocery stores, restaurants, real estate developers and retailers all left, taking their money with them. J.L. Hudson especially came under fire for establishing a store at the Northland Mall as the first of two centres that moved away from downtown. Hudson had suffered 14 years of declining sales and could no longer afford it. There was one notable exception to the exodus. Farmer Jack Supermarkets, run by the Bormon family, built several stores in the city, including one on the original riot site.

The problems prompted one black group to demand that the New Detroit Committee disband and give its money to the black community. Reverend Cleage, a militant black pastor, had already established the City-Wide Citizen's Action Committee, which also dealt with community services, education, employment and redevelopment, and paralleled the work of New Detroit. The militants wanted self-help. "Black control of the black community is our goal." The action committee established a black grocery store, The Black Star Co-op Inc. and planned light industry and low-income housing projects.

Cleage found white investors to back the development, but it was Blacks who directed the businesses. The committee set up a brain trust of young professionals devoted to self-determination for black people. It provided $100,000 to hire black professionals and technicians to restore the city. In December, Cleage went to New Detroit for financial support and was offered $100,000 in grants on the condition that the group would work under the aegis of New Detroit, conduct regular audits under the auspices of Internal Revenue, and allow other groups to participate. Cleage refused to accept "whitey's terms" and that's when black members of the New Detroit committee resigned. They felt they were "showpieces." When New Detroit set up a television forum and documentary on human rights, it sent out press releases and applauded the fact that the program reached thousands. Cleage's group complained there were millions in the audience.

For a while, the business elite faithfully attended New Detroit meetings, but soon tired of it, upset with criticism from the "grassroots" that they were rich men, isolated in their ivory tower with no idea of what was going on. They were considered "honky exploiters of the poor" who paid lip service to ghettoized Blacks while continuing to move their investments out of the city. New Detroit felt it should support black efforts, but stay out of black affairs. The city was stunned and groping for answers, but the promises made in the aftermath of the riot were increasingly difficult to fulfill.

Ironically, Detroit business and labour leaders tried to accommodate black demands at the same time as the rest of the white community remained staunchly negative. Whites were increasingly more hostile toward Blacks, and the social isolation of the two groups increased. Most Whites said the riot scarred the city, caused its decline, and failed to inspire lasting solutions. They didn't believe race relations had improved and simply refused to live, or go to school, with Blacks. In nine communities from the northeast to southwest, less than half of one percent of the population was Black. The area became known as the "white noose" by people in the black ghetto.

Blue-collar communities were especially nervous, but white-collar workers also worried about how to protect themselves. Life in Detroit became uglier and more violent as the aftermath of the riot infected the city, and touched off an explosion of handgun sales by white urban housewives who had a clear case of the jitters. People also remodelled homes and businesses with fortified concrete and steel bars. There was a growing sense of alienation, separation and estrangement. Lower-class Whites were especially afraid and angry, but all Whites, even liberals, blamed Blacks for rioting. They believed teenagers, black nationalists and too much welfare instigated the riot and they'd had enough. Because of this, New Detroit never got the real financial or political backing it needed. A year after the riot, Blacks complained that no meaningful reforms had resulted, and racial conflict continued, as did the need for low-cost housing and racial integration.

As white panic increased, black citizens became bitter. Companies promised thousands more jobs, and some delivered, but the auto industry and economy declined after 1967. The war in Vietnam strained the country. Jobs were lost and black workers suffered first and worst. After eloquent promises, the federal government passed a $100,000,000 appropriation to allow police to buy tanks, armoured cars and bulletproof vests. The Detroit force joined the National Rifle Association and purchased more guns.

Ironically, the federal government had declared Macomb and Oakland County suburbs disaster areas because of torrential rains, which occurred four days before the riot. Within two days of the downpour, the areas were eligible for low-interest loans as well as federal grants and services for repairs. Smouldering, rubble-strewn Detroit made a similar request, but was refused. The White House ignored the pleas because politicians did not want to be accused of rewarding rioters. The president didn't need the flak and, a few weeks later, the request for help in Detroit was quietly withdrawn.

Lyndon Johnson established his Great Society programs to liberalize eligibility for welfare, but these did not address unemployment or poverty. The Kerner Commission recommended uniform, national welfare institutions, minimum income, job training and daycare allowances, but the ideas were ignored or left to the state.

Father Potts, at the Grace Episcopal Church, continued his work with the Virginia Park Rehabilitation Citizen's Committee, which was set up to revitalize one community. Virginia Park had been devastated by the riot but, immediately thereafter, its residents enjoyed a better relationship with politicians. They received a grant of up to $500,000 and expected more, as they worked with existing agencies to develop better street lighting, repair roads, and build new stores and quaint homes with sculptured lawns. Potts optimistically believed that the riot would unify the concerns and goals of residents. He hoped the government would improve health care and give a higher priority to housing and jobs in Virginia Park.

In his opinion, the riot was racial because Blacks demonstrated their resentment and frustration, but it was also economic. It was clear that conditions wouldn't be tolerated, and must be reversed to prevent another outburst. To Potts, it was a question of how far business leaders would go to solve problems and give Blacks a way out of the ghetto. Ominously, two years after the riot, Grace Episcopal Church was a drop-in centre with graffiti on the wall.

In January 1968, racial tensions increase as the house of a leader of a moderate black group is firebombed. In February, there are two more fire-bombings at black businesses. By March, *The London Evening Free Press* describes Detroit "as a sick city whose fear, rumour, race-prejudice and gun-buying has stretched black and white nerves to the verge of snapping." Then, on April 4, 1968, Martin Luther King Junior is assassinated. A curfew is imposed in Detroit, but only enforced in black areas. Nine thousand National Guardsmen are mobilized by the governor despite their poor showing a year earlier.

Walt McCall rushes over the border with the same feelings of trepidation that he experienced in 1967. "Here we go again," he thinks as he drives his *Windsor Star* vehicle to police headquarters at 1300 Beaubien. Shock and fear emanate through Detroit. Over the next ten days, the city reacts violently. There are fires and looting on Twelfth Street as gangs roam neighbourhoods, break windows and stone cars. Two hundred students stage a sit-in at the county building. Black workers walk out of a Chrysler plant, and force it to close. Blacks are angry and frustrated, but their actions are sporadic. McCall says the situation is kept under control by a massive imposition of force. Police realize they need to clamp down with "prompt and effective action." They've learned from the riot of '67, and will not let it happen again.

Black officers in civvies are dispatched to black areas for surveillance. When a fire truck is pelted with debris at 10:30 p.m., the afternoon shift is paid overtime to prevent a full-scale riot. The worst fire bombings occur between midnight and 2:00 a.m., but police react quickly and arrest offenders. Black and white students mix it up at Cooley High. The incident prompts vandalism and closes 20 other schools. The federal government sends advisors while black teams help preserve the peace. The Michigan State Police are also ready. Earlier in the year, the police integrate their forces and introduce a new law – the first in history – to define a riot, ban Molotov cocktails, make it illegal to block public thoroughfares and make it a felony to interfere with firefighters. Police are heavy-handed and mobilize quickly. McCall stays at police headquarters all night while other reporters cover the streets. Once again, the city is shut down with curfews and martial law but, this time, strict measures are enforced.

If someone is on the street after hours, they are immediately taken into custody. Detroit and State Police follow a new riot plan developed for just such an occurrence. Critics of the crackdown object to brute force and to convoys of armed police on the streets. Two months later, officers on horseback launch an unprovoked attack against a Poor People's March. Only two officers are disciplined. Then, in November, off-duty police beat up middle-class black students at a high school dance. Nine officers are suspended and two are charged. A month later, another police officer is suspended for pistol-whipping a young Black. Detroit police say they're being harassed. Blacks say the police are retaliating against the community. They believe the police are trying to cause another riot so they can crack down.

There is one bright spot during 1968 and that involves Detroit's beloved baseball team. Fans are concerned that the Tigers might not do well after the upheavals on their home turf and yet the team rallies to win the World Series. Skeptics are relieved. If another team had won, it could have caused a riot. While a fleeting victory, it gives the city focus. It gives Detroiters something to cheer about and celebrate. It takes their minds off civil rights violations and the crackdown over the summer.

In 1970, the most dramatic gesture for renewal is by Henry Ford II. It marks a shift from people, and New Detroit, to developments of bricks and mortar. Called Detroit Renaissance, it's a $600,000,000 hotel, office, and retail complex on Jefferson Avenue. As a personal response to the riot, Ford hopes it will live up to its name. The idea is to stop businesses leaving, and to entice new commercial development downtown. The Renaissance Center takes ten years to build, and another ten for the predicted spin-offs. It's a symbol for other developments but, unfortunately, it is a fragile renaissance.

Critics say it's another failed attempt at urban renewal. Until 2001, the centre remains a fortress. The first three floors are surrounded by brown stonewalls, which contain huge air-conditioning units, ivy and a cascading waterfall. The entrances to the compound are easily gated and, in times of trouble, can keep the rest of Detroit out. The wall is an unnatural barrier,

You can still find burned-out houses in Detroit like this one, on the corner of Winder and Brush, perhaps the result of the riot, poverty, or neglect. Ironically, it's a couple of blocks away from the new Comerica Park base- ball stadium, in an area that is slated for redevelopment.
Photo by Herb Colling.

which demonstrates the problem rather than the solution. It's like a castle, riot-proof and built too soon after 1967 when the scars are too fresh. There's a sense that, if North American cities continue to talk about convention centres and international villages to revitalize their down- town, instead of what's really needed, then decay will continue. Critics believe that revitalization can't be achieved with bricks and mortar. It can only be accomplished with people and, unless different nationalities learn to live together, racial turmoil will continue.

For five years after the riot, very little changes in Detroit. Landlords, economic and psychological oppression remain. Wooden shutters are simply nailed across the windows of gutted and ruined stores, which are abandoned. Walter Reuther, as head of the UAW, promises to mobilize 600,000 of his union members to clear the rubble, but city workers protest because volunteers are doing civil service jobs. Municipal officials also worry about lawsuits from property owners. Few UAW members

The burned-out hulks are slowly being replaced by neat and modern townhouses like Woodward Place at Brush Park. The advertising for the project simply said "It's About Time." Photo by Herb Colling.

match Reuther's enthusiasm or sympathy for the riot area and so, little is accomplished.

In a few cases, white and black groups work together to clean up debris and bulldoze unsafe walls of burned-out buildings. The Algiers Motel, for example, becomes the Desert Inn until it is finally torn down and replaced by a grassy park. A whole block of Pingree, which was reduced to ashes, is transformed into a treeless playfield. Despite these efforts, the streets that bore the brunt of the strife – Linwood, Grand River, Dexter and Mack – are lined with abandoned buildings, bricked up storefronts and gutted interiors. For two decades after the riot, they're ghostly wrecks, their doors kicked in. Some are the direct result of 1967 while others are neglected in the urban malaise that follows.

Arsons double between '67 and '68 and double again by '72, especially on Devil's Night when boarded-up buildings become popular kindling. Officials discount problems, suggesting that the increase reflects a greater percentage of investigations. Despite the controversy, a heroine craze sweeps the inner city and Detroit gains the onerous title of Murder City, USA. There's a perception by outsiders that it's a violent and irredeemable wasteland and, by 1974, there are over 700 homicides, up from 300 in 1967. The image problem speeds the departure of jobs, merchants and the white middle class.

Detroit is in a Catch 22. City fathers realize that investors won't return until something is done about crime, but the crime rate won't drop until there are jobs. Detroiters know that racism must end, so Blacks and Whites, city and suburb, can work together but, until that happens, business and industry continue to leave.

As white people bail out, Blacks become politically motivated and, six years after the riot, they finally gain political control of the city. In 1973, a black electorate sweeps militant black mayor Coleman A. Young to power. With a margin of 14,000 votes, Young defeats white police commissioner John Nichols in a campaign that centres on crime, police behaviour and reform, and results in the election of a black police chief. While the riot puts Young in the mayor's chair, it doesn't get him into the Detroit Golf Club for another 13 years. Blacks gain political, but not economic power, and that failure prevents them from changing their own social condition.

Detroit's reputation as a black city doesn't help its economic prospects. Young tries to attract new industry and jobs, but it's tough without federal funds and it's hard to coax money from other levels of government. With pure nerve and determination and, despite the limitations, the black leadership in Detroit fares better than any other black administration in the country. Young hires and promotes more black police officers and encourages a more professional attitude within the ranks, which eliminates a major grievance of 1967. The Michigan National Guard is also integrated. At the time of the riot, only one percent of the Guard are Black but, eventually, the percentage is over half.

These steps are a great leap forward in maintaining law and order. By 1978, the black vice-president of Detroit Renaissance says that Blacks look on Detroit as their city. There are more black councillors and school board officials. The exodus of white citizens escalates, which allows more Blacks to take over positions of political authority. In a show of support for their mayor, the black community in Detroit makes a conscious effort not to embarrass the administration with civil unrest.

In all, there are 59 racial disturbances in American cities in 1967. Mini-riots continue into the '70s and early '80s, but they never approach the intensity of the summer of '67. Conditions in Detroit are changing. Poverty cases, welfare rolls and unemployment rates are still higher for Blacks than Whites, but they're low for the standards of the '80s. The Civil Rights Movement has dwindled, and many young militants are gone, but Blacks are no longer excluded from city government and have better representation on the police force. With more integration, there are fewer questionable tactics. As a result, some black people feel better about themselves and their city. Police treat them with more respect and they're more in control of their own destiny. Blacks work with police to set up community stations to maintain peace. They also develop community organizations to handle drug rehabilitation, outreach and neighbourhood watch programs. Churches buy "crack houses" and rent them to reputable tenants, forcing drug dealers out.

Bob Martin and Bill McLellan are looters in 1967 but, 20 years later, they're part-time street workers with a Detroit community group. They travel with young and restless teens to demonstrate that rioting is counter-productive. They talk of their own bitterness and frustration and how it can be channelled positively. As McLellan puts it, "I'm not some white-collar dude from downtown who just sits behind a desk and smokes cigars. I'm part of the community. I'm one of them. They listen." Martin and McLellan agree that the problems of unemployment and youthful frustration persist; but they also believe that violence and looting accomplish nothing. Riots are regressive and not the answer.

There are other changes to hide the scars of 1967. Over 100,000 abandoned houses are torn down because they're dangerous. Ten percent, or 15 miles of the city, becomes vacant land, waiting to be developed. Twelfth Street is slated for renewal, but it takes ten years for the mile of gutted buildings to be cleared. Ground is eventually broken, but it takes another five before determined neighbours see the construction of a small shopping centre anchored by a supermarket.

Twelfth Street is renamed Rosa Parks Boulevard in honour of the black civil rights leader who makes her home in Detroit. On December 1, 1955, Parks refused to give up her seat to a white man on a bus in Montgomery, Alabama. She was jailed for not moving to the back of the bus, but her

On 12th Street, renamed Rosa Parks Boulevard, it's hard to believe that a riot ever took place. You have to look hard for signs of it over 35 years later. Photo by Herb Colling.

simple action resulted in a boycott that lasted more than a year and which helped eradicate segregation laws across the southern United States. Eventually, the Supreme Court ruled against segregation of public transport, opening the door for Blacks to gain equal access to public facilities.

Other black leaders see Parks' resolve as the beginning of freedom for all Blacks in the United States. It helps galvanize and unite the black community toward a non-violent social revolution as advocated by Martin Luther King. Parks takes up that cause by calling for a new kind of movement. She asks Blacks and Whites to elect candidates who serve the interests of minorities. As a symbol of her resolve, a row of modest, neat, two-storey townhouses is built to replace a block of burned-out buildings on Rosa Parks Boulevard. Underneath the street signs, however, there is still mention of Twelfth Street, a subtle reminder of the riot.

As a reporter with *The Detroit Free Press* once wrote, "The scars are still there, if you know where to find them. There are buildings that still bear the marks of the riot bullets, and people who remember how they wept that week for a wounded city. But where the worst peacetime riot in U. S. history began, there is only a tiny park with a brick walk and handful of

On the street corner where the riot started, there's a vacant lot next to an old building. It's a building that was no doubt there when the riot happened, a building that has survived the ravages of time. Photo by Herb Colling.

locust trees. On hot July days, young men lounge on pink cement benches and old men rest in the shade, and the children who play at their feet are too young to remember a city's ordeal by fire."

The changes in Detroit are a start as residents fight for a better life, a better place to live and an elimination of the city's rotten image, but there's still a long way to go. In a way, there are two Detroits. On one hand, there is the renaissance along the river with hope for new development, livable and gracious neighbourhoods, integrated, and upwardly mobile middle-class Blacks involved in corporate jobs, politics and community leadership. Then, there are slums and ghettos inhabited by poor, drug-ridden, violent and dependent people on welfare with no jobs, education or prospects. A high level of black frustration, poverty, stress and deprivation are still there with some people just waiting for the next riot. "Don't rule it out," one observer warns. "All it takes is a sufficient number of angry or disaffected people jammed into a small area, an easily defined enemy, and an incident to set them off."

Many causes of the '67 riot are still in existence and yet, while others experience riots, Detroit is virtually hassle-free. Most people believe riots are isolated because poor people are spread more thinly across the city. It's

A tribute to the first black mayor of Detroit and the new city that he helped forge. For good or ill, it rose from the ashes of the one that went before. Photo by Herb Colling,

also harder to find a target because the police department is no longer an irritation. It's more professional and over 50 percent Black. While Blacks hold political power, economic power has left the city. There's as much anger and recklessness, but not so much hope for radical change.

Former mayor Coleman Young defended his city in the '80s, saying that crowds of Whites and Blacks flood the downtown on weekends and holidays, especially for special events. Not so, in the '70s. Back then, Young said, "You could shoot a cannon through the streets without hitting anyone after 5:00 at night." To Young, people downtown was an indication that rejuvenation was working. Frustration and rage still exist but, as Young said, there was a lesson in '67. Nothing could be gained from the senseless loss of life and destruction of property. He doubts Blacks would burn their city again. Instead, the black community has turned inward on itself. The anger and frustration has transferred to drugs, homicide and suicide. Poverty, joblessness, drug addiction and hopelessness are still there, but black people are no longer against the mayor or the police, so there is no one to strike out against except themselves.

There has never been another major riot and many people doubt that

Motor City Madness will prevail, that Detroit will erupt into chaos again. They hope that enough things have changed and yet, black poverty and white racism are still facts of life. Until those conditions are eliminated, there may be little hope for inner city America. As Young pointed out, until inequities are addressed, there will continue to be problems for Blacks. Young figured that they need quality education, job training, affordable housing, fair job opportunities and as much money spent on inner-city schools as on suburban schools. He complained that Blacks weren't masters of their own house, didn't control their own destiny. As Martin Luther King once said, "... how do you expect us to pull ourselves up by the bootstraps when we don't even have boots?"

To Dino Paniccia, the Canadian director of finance at Hutzel Hospital in Detroit, many parts of the city are still disaster areas. All you have to do is board the "People Mover," a form of urban transit downtown. Paniccia says other cities demolish old buildings, get rid of slums. They practise urban renewal with new stadia, cultural and sports complexes or by enticing boutiques and shops downtown, away from suburban malls. In Detroit, they're trying to develop such facilities but, for a long time, they lacked money and it may be too late. Paniccia points to the Fox Theatre in downtown Detroit, recently renovated in the early 1990s, and suggests that it's only workable because of a police-training centre on site.

Paniccia is skeptical and, perhaps, with cause. During the riot, he remembers fur coats being sold on the streets for $100 and stray bullets going through hospital windows and lodging in walls. No one is hurt, but he remembers staying inside during the violence. He says apartment buildings around his hospital are torn down, primarily to stop snipers shooting from windows. Paniccia watches Detroit erode in the mid '60s, but the riot causes the ultimate decay. He claims that Coleman Young, Detroit's first black mayor, drives Whites out until there's so much blight it's unbelievable. "Who wants it?" Paniccia doubts Detroit will turn around in his lifetime. With automation and fewer jobs in car plants, he doesn't hold much hope for the future.

As a microbiologist at Henry Ford Hospital, Layne Katzman also views the riot as the beginning of the end. "Detroit never returned. It was a steady downhill." Prior to '67, hospital workers walk to the Fisher Building or Sachs for shopping. They go to different restaurants but after the riot, Katzman says, life in the corridor stops. Employees lock their car doors and rarely go out. Sachs, Kern's, Hudson's and Crowlie's all move out. She says her hospital withdraws from the neighbourhood and sets up satellite surgeries in suburbs. Major operations are done downtown, but others are done outside because some clients refuse to enter the city core. She says there's no trust anymore, no guarantee that there will not be another incident. Katzman still goes to the Fisher Theatre for entertainment, but she drives to Windsor to eat.

Market gardener Don Bondy also becomes more cautious. After 1967, he never walks alone at Detroit's Eastern Market and only goes to the washroom in company, for fear of being shot or mugged. Some growers even carry pistols. Prior to the riot, they use cash. After, cheques are the order of the day. In the 1960s and '70s, Bondy has to psych himself up to go to market from his home near LaSalle, just outside Windsor, but he has eight children to feed. It's his livelihood and, if something happens, it happens. Looking back, Bondy admits the market was in a dilapidated area of old slaughterhouses, but now it's better lit, there are more police. Vacant lots and alleys are being cleared. The city is making improvements and there's even a McDonald's restaurant nearby. Bondy says it's better now. The area is coming back to life, and there's hope.

Ann Bondy is Don's cousin. She was born in Michigan, but married a Canadian and lives in LaSalle. She's sad to see the decay of beautiful homes in Detroit, but she's also optimistic about the future. She doesn't think Detroit is going to die now that it has a new opera house, a revitalized Cobo Hall, new football and baseball parks. They're all improvements, which may lead to Detroit's renaissance. The plans to revitalize and rejuvenate Virginia Park led to street after street of new semi-detached houses as whole neighbourhoods were razed. Bondy says Detroit is not as volatile as it was in the 1980s, and she attributes that to Dennis Archer, the former mayor of the city.

Archer is a former teacher and lawyer who, in 1984, was named one of the 100 most powerful black Americans by *Ebony* magazine. A year later, the *National Law Journal* declared him one of the most powerful attorneys in the United States. He was the president of the national and state bar associations and, in 1985, became a Michigan Supreme Court justice. The Michigan Lawyer's weekly named him one of the most respected judges, but he surprised many when he left the bench to become a lawyer again. As Archer explained, he wanted to work on solutions to the problems in Detroit. "I got tired of reading that businesses were leaving, that people were giving up hope." He wanted to develop a working relationship between the business community and the mayor's administration, between the city and suburbs, between state and federal governments.

Initially, Archer ran an election campaign to meet people and impress his bosses about his community spirit but, within a year, he discovered that he loved politics. In a state-wide vote, he was elected to two consecutive four-year terms as mayor during which he worked to reduce crime and brought over $1,000,000,000 worth of investment by three different companies to Detroit. He learned the power of education and hard work from his father who was a caretaker in a white subdivision. In 1992, he worked with academics, hundreds of citizens, and dozens of community groups to develop a paper called *Thoughts For Greater Detroit*. A year later, he became mayor of the city.

Bondy says Dennis Archer was the mayor for the new millennium because he improved education, tried to solve the problems of low-income people, did something about drugs, and worked with people for the good of the city. Bondy criticizes Coleman Young, the previous mayor, for having no vision and being too old. She says he should have retired sooner. She also feels the people of Detroit are less tolerant of violence. They don't want their children to die, and they're less willing to live behind security gates and bars. More neighbourhood groups are policing the streets and Bondy feels the atmosphere is changing for the better.

As the mayor of Windsor in 2002, Mike Hurst agrees that Detroit is on the road to recovery, but the city hasn't reached the final destination yet, and it may never achieve that goal. Hurst says that over the past ten years there has been a resurgence of the city, its people and its image, but there's still a long way to go. Hurst says improvements have been made, primarily because of the activities of some outstanding families who are concerned about the welfare of the city. As examples he cites the Ford family and Mike Ilitch, who owns the Detroit Red Wings hockey franchise.

Also, with General Motors relocating at the Renaissance Center in down-town Detroit, Hurst feels there's a renewed confidence, optimism and jus-tifiable reason for hope that Detroit is on its way back.

Hurst says there are more business opportunities downtown and he attributes part of that success to the mayor's office. To Hurst, it began with Coleman Young who was confronted by a huge challenge, as well as circumstances that were almost insurmountable, but who convinced senior levels of government that help was needed. Hurst remembers a trip to Washington during which Young spoke firmly and eloquently to Congress about the plight of the city. Young convinced Congress to redi-rect its allocation of resources to ensure that Detroit was supported as a gateway to Canada, and the trip led to larger national government invest-ment in the north-south trade corridor.

Hurst says that when Dennis Archer became mayor he embraced the value and merit of both Detroit and Windsor working together to develop the border area. He also encouraged city government to get involved as a partner and make businesses active participants in the renewal. His efforts

Mayor Kwame Kilpatrick thinks he's the man to make positive things happen. There are signs throughout the city. In the central city area, the slogan reads "30 years of caring." Photo by Herb Colling.

led to the revitalization of the downtown core with the new theatre district, casino and two new sports stadia.

Hurst says that Archer's leadership also helped create Campus Martius, a new civic square for arts displays and music. Hurst calls it a new funky, fanciful green space, a people place, or an oasis for people coming downtown. He equates it to the greening of the riverfront, a ribbon of trees and grass on the American side, to soften the harsh concrete, glass and steel facade of the city that had been criticized for decades.

From Hurst's perspective, Archer worked hard during his two terms in office to achieve what he could to bring the city back to life. He laid the master plan for Kwami Kilpatrick, the new mayor of Detroit, an energetic young man who, Hurst says, is bound and determined to focus on grassroots issues. Hurst says Kilpatrick has a community agenda to bring back Detroit's residential neighbourhoods. Many crack and drug houses have set up in abandoned homes in certain areas of the city, and Kilpatrick says he's determined to eliminate them. He's trying to revitalize those areas and to help ordinary people reclaim their neighbourhoods.

Hurst says Kilpatrick is focussed and determined and he's launching an aggressive campaign, but he admits that the problems are huge. Hurst says, "The city has been struggling uphill for over 30 years, and still can't claim victory on the top of the mountain," but, Hurst says, the climb will continue. To Hurst, Detroit was on its knees and was threatened with being toppled over. Now, he says, the city is valiantly and proudly struggling to its feet, and he hopes it succeeds.

Sue Goerzen, the Detroit schoolteacher from Harrow, says the riot doesn't change her perceptions of Detroit or its people. She never loses faith. She believes that people are generally wonderful, and will treat you well if you get to know them. During the riot in the spring of 1968 after Martin Luther King is killed, Goerzen still goes over. She says two teachers at her school are killed and five others wounded. She's in class, a white teacher with 40 black students, when the mob breaks in. Twelve of her students jump up, surround her, and draw switchblades. "Try to get her," they say as they walk her to her car. Goerzen admits it's frightening, but she arrives home safe and sound thanks to her students, her friends. School is closed for the duration and Goerzen remains in Harrow.

The new face of Detroit. The Renaissance Center, built in 1972, is getting a face-lift. The concrete structure in the foreground – an air conditioning unit that surrounded the centre like an impenetrable fortress wall – is now coming down for what will become a more open, freer city centre.
Photo by Herb Colling.

Goertzen says that teaching in Detroit is generally a good experience, which helps her to grow, and she has no apprehension about going back. Despite that assertion, Goerzen leaves the Detroit school system in 1969 to teach home economics at the University of Windsor. She says the riots have no bearing on her decision. Goertzen believes that riots give false impressions. If some people within a race act badly, then we see all people in that race as bad but, she says, "We can't live our lives in fear. That's counterproductive." She is now in London, Ontario.

Ivy Vander Zanden probably agrees with Goerzen. During the riot, Vander Zanden is advised by police to remain in residence at Grace Hospital where she works rather than return to her apartment on Alexandrine and Third Avenue. She does what she's told, but it doesn't mean she's afraid of living in Detroit, then, or after. Vander Zanden never views the riot as racially inspired. Except for authority figures, like the police and National Guard, Blacks aren't fighting Whites. To Vander Zanden, the riot is against

The new Comerica Park baseball stadium is a symbol of Detroit's renaissance, much like The Renaissance Center was in its day. People in Detroit hope it will truly lead to a much-needed renaissance in the city, and bring people back into the downtown core.

Photo by Herb Colling.

poverty. Whites and Blacks loot stores in harmony as the poor steal from the rich.

For Vander Zanden, there's camaraderie between herself and the people in her neighbourhood. They're Black and she's White, but they go to the same stores and the same churches. They pray for each other. It's a pleasant community. Vander Zanden brings gifts from Canada, and her friends respond with canned pickles and preserves. Two different neighbours watch for Vander Zanden if she comes home late, concerned for her welfare in a big city. She remembers driving home after dark one night. Two black men are standing in front of her apartment. She has to pass them to enter her building and she's reluctant. She cruises the block a few times, but they don't leave. Eventually, she decides to chance it. As she heads toward the door, one man starts in her direction. Just as he reaches her, he turns to his friend and waves. "Good night. God Bless!" She's being cautious for no reason and it turns into another good experience.

These attitudes are an indication that the problems of race and poverty are interrelated, the fight for civil rights intertwined with economic revolution. In the United States, the battleground is the inner city and that is where the war against poverty must be engaged and won, not just for Blacks, but also for all Americans. There must be room for Blacks to live with dignity and peace, to learn, work, play, grow and participate in the community to the same extent as any other human being. The social crisis in the United States has continued and deepened with a frustration in the black community that racial problems are severe, ongoing and all pervasive. Black people are convinced that change is necessary, but they're impatient with the slow pace. There is some argument on how change should take place, but Blacks are convinced that change is necessary before the problem of racism can be solved. Simply stated, it's a problem of attitude.

Today the white majority is still in control of important institutions and, seemingly, does not sense the urgency of the black revolution. A number of Whites feel threatened by Blacks physically, and in terms of status and jobs. As a result, they flee to the suburbs and try to ignore the problem, expecting the police to act as a buffer. Despite all those years of civil rights and urban rioting, many white people still object to black freedom and want to put Blacks "in their place." Some still have an attitude that all Blacks are bad and must be kept in line. Others have a vague notion that Blacks have been wronged, but they still feel that things are getting better or are better left alone. Many neither identify, nor are disturbed by the black cause and so, do not feel that action is necessary. While those attitudes persist, the possibility of further violence will always remain. As far as the black citizens of Detroit are concerned, unless they are treated as people – fairly and without discrimination – then problems will continue.

Chapter 12

The Aftermath: Windsor

A week after the riot starts, 16-year-old Tim Burton and two friends are curious. They pile into their little black Sunbeam and cross the border for a look. The tunnel guard asks them where they're going. "Up to the mall to a bookstore." They pass customs and head for the suburbs before doubling back to the riot zone where gutted buildings still smoulder. Burned-out cars remain in the streets, a sad reminder to what has gone before.

Burton and his friends stop for a red light, and a big Buick pulls up to them. It's full of black teenagers who want to know why the Canadians are in their neighbourhood. The Blacks yell obscenities, and Burton and his friends think about running the light. Just then a military jeep pulls up on one side. The Canadians are in the middle. The Blacks fall silent. The National Guardsmen are dressed in military uniform with helmets and automatic weapons. They also want to know what's going on.

"We got lost, cutting through," Burton says.

"Get out of here. Go home," the soldiers reply as they drive off.

The Windsor boys beat it back to the border.

Burton can't believe they actually crossed. He figures they must have been crazy, but they're young. Burton feels more excited than tragic about the riot. He watches it on TV, knows it's more accessible than Vietnam and wants to check it out, but he only goes once. After six days of death and destruction, Burton's attitude toward Detroit has changed, like so many white Windsorites. He no longer feels secure about his giant neighbour.

Kevin Conrad is 13 years old in 1967 and a student at Prince Edward Public School in Windsor. There's quite a racial mix at school, but Conrad doesn't remember problems. He hangs around with black kids during recess. Some are friends, some are bullies who pick on younger kids for quarters, but it's not racially motivated. He doesn't understand what is happening in Detroit.

Ken Hull has been going over since he was eight years old. In 1967, he's finishing school at Wayne State while working as a reporter at *The Windsor Star*. He never feels uncomfortable in the Motor City and yet, he remembers covering the riot. He asks directions of a black youth who turns to him and says, "Fuck you, whitey." There is no tolerance, no understanding, no compassion. There is just a hate that he's never seen before. He can't believe the change and he thinks, "Who dropped something in the water here?" It's dramatic, sudden, complete. He never goes back.

Eileen Zuccaro says many Americans feel safe in Canada. They don't believe that we have racial conflicts, that we're more multicultural and yet, Zuccaro says, we have problems of our own. She wonders if our racial conflict is between the French and English. An editorial of the day has a similar view. "If our Indians and American Negroes compared notes on their 'have-not' positions, they might find more similarities than we Canadians would be willing to admit."

As a reporter, Walt McCall says, "Our innocence went that day. It ended very quickly and, no question, tragically." McCall says it will take time, but Detroit will heal. McCall figures the riot polarizes our attitudes. It makes us notice racial divisions and poverty. Prior to the riot, McCall believes, race was never an issue in Windsor. McCall has fond memories of Emancipation Day as a fun event. A lot of Michiganders came, and McCall says it was a badge of honour for Windsor to host it. He doubts that racial problems will ever reach the boiling point in Canada because conditions aren't bad enough, and the population size and mix isn't here. Our minority populations are smaller and he doesn't feel there is the same level of resentment or inequity. Sure, there are flare-ups in Toronto, some ugly incidents, broken windows and rioting on Yonge Street but McCall says, it fizzles quickly. "Hopefully, we'll never see anything like that." To McCall, it just isn't the Canadian way.

When asked if a riot can happen here, Laurie Smith responds face-tiously, "We're Canadian. Nothing happens here." The Windsor poet says it's part of the Canadian mentality that we're not as likely to take up arms, get involved in a mass effort. According to her, we just feel more vulnerable when there's an upheaval in Detroit because of that city's size and proximity. Smith says we're also peninsular in Windsor, more isolated from activities in Montreal and Toronto where racial outbreaks are more prevalent. Smith says Windsor is also not a transient city. It's a big city with a small town "feel," the kind of city where residents can walk the street and see people they know. Many people live here all their lives; they have a sense of roots, a sentimental attachment. There is no mass migration into Windsor and, because of its strong nucleus, Windsorites are reluctant to let their city go. They're loyal, and protect it.

An incident on a beach near Colchester shows a difference between Canadian and American Blacks. Harrow resident Kevin Gascoyne and his friends, some of whom are Black, are sitting on picnic tables at the beach. Some Blacks from Detroit drive up and start making trouble, calling Canadian Blacks names for keeping company with Whites. Nobody knows whether to respond or ignore them until one of Gascoyne's black friends stands up and says, "You're in the wrong country for that talk. Here in Canada, we're free. We never have been 'Uncle Toms.'" The Detroit youths stop, back up and drive off.

In 1967, Pat Whealan, an editorialist with *The Windsor Star* says that Canadians are proud that a race riot can't happen here, until we ask: why not? He suggests that we avoid racial turmoil more by default than by design, simply because our tradition of racial prejudice isn't as strong. Unfortunately, he concludes, prejudice exists and is growing as immigration increases.

The theme is pursued by columnist John Lindblad who suggests that, for good or ill, we follow the United States. From rock and roll to cook-outs, Canadians are just a bit slower on the draw. Nor should we be smug. There's no reason to believe that Canadians are more willing to integrate than Americans. Black, West Indian, Asian, and even European immigrants "feel alone and friendless" in what may be regarded as the Canadian wilderness. In Canada, the spark to ignite a riot may be police relations, the separatist movement or the Native question.

Dennis Hinckley came from England in 1953, and lived in Canada until his work took him to the United States in '62. He took out American citizenship and lived in Detroit, but he moved back to Canada because of the riot. For one thing, Hinckley is concerned that guns are too accessible in the United States and he likes Canada's controls. He believes in safety courses and encourages proper storage and handling to keep guns away from children. In Canada, firearms have to be kept under lock and key and separate from ammunition. Hinckley doesn't like the American idea of carrying a gun in a car unless it's in the trunk and that's why he's always apprehensive when driving in the United States. He fears highway shootings whenever he crosses the border.

When Hinckley becomes a Canadian in 1968, he feels it's the right decision, but he isn't convinced that his safety is assured. He honestly believes that Canada will soon face similar riots. Hinckley claims that racial problems have intensified in the Dominion since World War II because of what he considers lax immigration policies in this country. After all, Hinckley believes, "We're every bit as racist. Just look at how we treated the Natives."

A report published in 1967 suggests that hostility between Native Indians and Whites is at the explosive point in Western cities. Natives are pushed around by police and exploited by bootleggers and unscrupulous merchants. The study points out that 35 percent of people in jail are Native, and that there are two sets of rules: one for Whites, one for Indians. "When Indians drink heavily at carnivals and rodeos, people call them worthless drunks .... When non-Indians get drunk, people call them real swingers." The report calls for action to remove injustices, soothe racial anger and help make a better life for "Indians, Eskimos and Métis."

Hinckley admits racism is as blatant in Canada, but he feels it is also more subdued. White Canadians just aren't ready to admit it, but "It's everywhere. It's part of us. You can't separate it." He claims that Windsor residents near the casino complain to him about Blacks who litter on their way home from gambling, but they'd never make those comments publicly. To Hinckley, segregation is the only answer. To him, the races do not, and cannot, mix.

Newsman Dick Smyth echoes some of these sentiments. He says his perceptions also changed because of the riot. He's lived in Toronto since

1968 and he's seeing the same signs of what happened in Detroit. In the '60s, he says, American Blacks threw bricks at firefighters and made headline news. Now, he says, Blacks in Toronto are throwing things at police in Regent Park and the Lawrence Town Road area. The crime rate is rising and there are more racially inspired subway murders and graffiti than ever. Smyth says it's ugly and getting worse. He locks his car doors in Toronto now. "It's like watching a woman you love die of cancer."

As a director of finance at Hutzel Hospital in Detroit, Dino Paniccia disagrees. He says there are substantial differences between Toronto and Detroit. He's familiar with both, as a Canadian working in the United States. In the downtown core of Toronto, Paniccia says, ethnic groups are moving in but, unlike Detroit, they're not poverty-stricken. They have cash and the determination to maintain and improve their buildings. They renovate old Victorian houses. In Toronto, different cultures live in distinctive ethnic regions. There are Chinese, Black and Asian communities, and their ethnicity is their strength. Unlike Detroit, their homes do not degenerate into ghettos or slums. Paniccia says there's pride of ownership in Toronto. Canadian cities have a centre, but Detroit seems to have lost it.

According to newsman Pete McGarvey, a positive element comes out of the riot for the people of Chatham, Ontario, in Kent County. Many residents can't understand the racial conflict in Detroit, how it occurs, and whether it can happen in their community, which has a large population of Blacks. Shortly after Labour Day, 1967, Father Joseph Potts is invited to the United Church on Victoria Avenue in Chatham to speak about race relations to a mixed congregation. It's an unusual occurrence in the Maple City, which, McGarvey says, leads to some hard thinking and overdue changes.

A race riot is an alien concept in Chatham. To McGarvey, it's like setting up a French nation within the confines of a province of this country. McGarvey says people define their society by their own majority values, ignoring those of the minority, and that, he says, can lead to difficulties later on. He doubts that we come to grips with these things until we're confronted face-to-face and that's exactly what happened in Chatham.

In September 1967, Potts' visit to Chatham results in a forum on race relations where it's revealed that there are no Blacks employed at city hall or in municipal services. There are few Blacks in the police department and yet they constitute 30 percent of the population. There is a long history of black settlement in and around Chatham, but there is little integration. Whites in the congregation assume Blacks want it that way. Blacks say they don't.

About the same time, Fergie Jenkins is emerging as a black superhero in professional baseball. A native of Chatham, the six-foot-five, 205-pound pitcher is a strike-out leader who is becoming the city's favourite son. In 1971, the National League recognizes Jenkin's ability by presenting him with the Cy Young Award, the first Canadian ever to receive it. The 28-year-old right-hander feels he's finally getting the recognition he deserves. He wins 20 or more games every season and is the self-proclaimed best pitcher in the league. Jenkins negotiates a $100,000 salary and uses some of his earnings to set up integrated housing. Barriers are coming down in employment and attitude, but it takes time and there are a lot of things to do.

Many black people have a different perspective on race and race relations in Canada and their voice is often not heard. Kay Curtis is a registered nurse from Trinidad. She never experienced racism until she first came to Canada as a young woman in her 20s. Curtis remembers walking down the street when a little boy turned to her and called her a "nigger." She was shocked, angry and wondered, "Is this what it's all about?" She'd just come from a country where Blacks could be anything they wanted: doctors, lawyers or businessmen. They had big houses and a good living and yet, here in Canada, they felt that they didn't belong in the nice neighbourhood even if they had the means to live there.

Elise Harding-Davis, the curator of the North American Black Historical Museum in Amherstburg, was seven years old and in school when she became conscious of her race for the first time. She told the class that her father was an electrical contractor. Her teacher said, "Elise, you don't know what that means, let alone how to spell it. I'll talk to you after class." The teacher complained that Harding-Davis was "exaggerating." Harding-Davis says she was frightened, then angry, and responded by correctly spelling her father's profession. Later, her parents explained that the attitude of her teacher was a combination of ignorance and racism. It was a cruel lesson, but she learned that black people, "Have to be twice as good to get half as much."

Part of a deed for a cottage in Amherstburg. It clearly stipulates "No lot shall be sold to or occupied by any person or persons other than those of the Caucasian race."
Courtesy of Ari Varsa. Photo by Herb Colling.

Blacks often feel as if they're being marked or judged on the basis of their skin colour. They believe they receive lower grades than Whites even though the calibre of the work may be the same. Kay Curtis says she tried to get study notes for a biology exam she was about to take. When she asked for them, the librarian ignored her. She asked to speak to a supervisor, but was told to wait. Her husband, Christopher, came to see what was keeping her. He's a big man and, after he spoke to his wife, two security guards came up to him. Curtis wondered if it was school policy for security guards to escort someone to the supervisor's office, or was it because of his size and his blackness? The supervisor refused to open the door unless security guards stayed on the scene.

Clayton Talbert is with the Windsor Black Coalition. He admits black students have trouble getting study notes. Often, small cliques get together to pool their knowledge, but black students are not included. Being left out, Talbert says, they don't have the same tools or opportunities that other students have. Elise Harding-Davis picks up that suggestion. She says there's a traditional, innate belief that white people are better than black people, regardless of how well the black person has done. Frustration with that situation leads some North American black leaders to advocate a separate, but equal, solution: black teachers teaching a black curriculum in all-black schools.

When Harding-Davis graduated from her school, the principal told her that she had good marks and that she should have been the class valedictorian, but they'd never had a black valedictorian. She went home and told her mom and dad who made it clear that she'd have to deal with it, straighten it out. She did. She went back to the school to complain and, as a compromise, the school decided to have a joint valedictorian.

Rochelle Richard, a student at the University of Windsor, says, "You have to compromise yourself constantly." Richard remembers the second grade of a public school in Toronto where she scored 148 on an IQ test. She was bright and qualified to enter the gifted program, but she was denied access. The examiner felt she couldn't handle it because of her "cultural" background. Her parents were not university-educated and the officials felt that she wouldn't understand or would feel left out. Richard studied jazz, piano, ballet, African-Caribbean dancing and joined numerous sports teams to find herself, but she learned that, if you are Black, "You have to be 110 percent to show people that you're worthy." She enrolled at the University of Windsor where she became the vice-president of the Black Student Alliance.

It isn't until 1970 that the Canadian Committee on Black Studies is formed at the University of Western Ontario to delve into Ontario's black history. A year later, black studies courses are introduced at Brennan, Centennial and Patterson collegiates in Windsor, and at the Essex District High School. John Tomlinson, a teacher at Patterson, teaches the course to grade 12 students for half a year along with Asian studies for the other half. Tomlinson wants to discuss racism in world politics and approaches the board for approval. He's concerned that not many people know our black history or culture, and it isn't receiving the attention it deserves in literature and schools in Ontario.

The Windsor area is one of the first in the province to explore Canada's black heritage, and establish courses, which talk about black pioneers and how they brought little material goods with them and yet, contribute a great deal. The courses dwell on slavery, abolition, black settlement in the mid-1800s, as well as the exodus of Blacks to the United States after the American Civil War. They deal with a dramatic period in Ontario history, highlighted by interracial cooperation, as well as bitter discrimination in a strange new land.

Harding-Davis believes that racism is brought on by ignorance and intolerance from people who don't understand other cultures or are afraid of our differences. As curator of the Black Historical Museum, she hopes to create an understanding of black culture and its longevity. She wants to eliminate people's misconceptions, and thereby eradicate racism. She hopes to educate Whites about black heritage in an effort to improve race relations. "We all have to learn about each other, so we can appreciate ourselves."

Harding-Davis wonders if we're headed to where the United States was in the 1960s, but she tries not to dwell on racist incidents. She doesn't dignify them with a response. She tries to pick her fights by determining if a racial incident is just an act of ignorance or whether it is meant to hurt. As she points out, sometimes it's just better to let it go.

When Harding-Davis and her new husband are apartment hunting in Windsor in 1965, they find a nice place near Lanspeary Park after checking advertisements in the paper. Harding-Davis' husband is Black, but fair-skinned. He sees the apartment alone, but wants to bring his wife around before making a decision. Harding-Davis says, when the landlord sees her, he immediately blurts out, "It's rented. It's rented. The place is gone."

During the 1960s, a black civil rights group called the Guardian Club looks into discrimination in rental housing in Windsor in the 1960s. Many Blacks complain that they apply for apartments by phone and are accepted but, once the white landlord discovers that the applicants are Black, they are not allowed in. There's always some excuse that conditions have changed, that family members are moving in or that the landlord has made a mistake and the apartment is committed to someone else. The Guardian Club sends whites to the same apartment and often find that they are still available. The study inevitably leads to a complaint before the Ontario Human Rights Commission, and a fine against the landlord for a civil rights violation. Harding-Davis knows that others are pressing their case, but she never goes that route. "I just didn't need it."

Harding-Davis says she avoids hassles by going places where she won't be exposed to racism. She considers herself privileged because she's sheltered by a protective and loving family, but she remembers an incident involving her father in the 1940s. He was trying to get into the International Brotherhood of Electrical Workers' Union, but was told it would cost $200 for what was normally a $20 fee. Harding-Davis says, her father was told to come at night. When he did, somebody attacked him with a hammer and beat him up. Harding-Davis also remembers fellow workers stealing his tools. She says her father wanted a better life and was prepared to suffer anything to get it. As a descendant of slaves, he had immense pride in his heritage. His forebears escaped at tremendous cost and made a life and name for themselves. It took courage and fortitude, but they survived despite the odds, and he was determined to do the same.

Christopher Curtis is a black author from Amherstburg whose first novel won the Newberry Honor Award in 1996. Called *The Watsons Go To Birmingham, 1963* the book looks at racism from the perspective of a ten-year-old black boy named Kenny. It recounts the bombing of a black church in the United States in which four little girls are killed. It deals with Kenny's struggle to understand. Kenny's parents say that racists are sick and can't help themselves, but Kenny doesn't believe it. He comes to realize that they're not sick – it's just that hate eats them up and turns them into monsters. Racism is something inside, but we haven't found a way to show how wrong or bad it is.

Curtis recognizes that civil rights activists of the '60s as heroes. They're brave and special and he doesn't want them forgotten. He doesn't want their efforts to be in vain and yet, he's concerned that Blacks and Whites are no longer willing to put their lives on the line for something in which they believe. Civil rights activists accomplish a great deal, yet Curtis knows that racism still exists and is as severe as ever because it is more sophisticated, more subtle, and has merely gone underground. "When you ask somebody ... there's not a racist in this country, not one." To Curtis, racism is more blatant in larger centres like Toronto. "You know the ropes and there's no fooling around," but in Windsor, it's harder to read.

Originally from Flint, Michigan, Christopher Curtis is constantly on guard against racism. He says it can make you paranoid, but he warns young black people to be prepared and aware of it. He recognizes that some white people don't feel comfortable around Blacks and that's why he wishes that Whites could walk in a black man's shoes. Blacks, he says, in a predominantly white society, live with that uncomfortable feeling every day. Curtis often asks white friends to dinner to experience his environment if only for a couple of hours. Sometimes, people decline because they can't handle it. They don't feel comfortable around Blacks and yet, Curtis says, Blacks are always surrounded by people who are different. They can't escape. They have to adjust and they have to exist.

Curtis has developed a tough skin and, because he can anticipate derogatory remarks or actions, he is prepared. He says the comments may not be intentionally cruel or vicious, but they do seem to roll off the tongue. He complains that Whites don't see anything wrong with some of the things they say or do, perhaps because they haven't thought about it from a black person's perspective.

Blacks say they experience racism every day and yet, how should they react? They can't be filled with rage and lash out, but they have to stand up for their rights. Curtis says he picks his fights, has developed an instinct that tells him when to attack ignorance or let it pass. He's learned to take an off-hand comment with a grain of salt. Otherwise, he'd be in so many fights, he'd be worn down and wouldn't be able to cope. Curtis says Blacks must recognize and accept that they are better people for their control and dignity and yet, he admits, he can't always walk away. It's an affront to his self-esteem.

To many Blacks, racism is systemic. It exists in law enforcement, courts, business and schools, but its harder to identify and fight because of its subtlety. When it is blatant, "in your face," it's easier to handle. Sometimes Blacks have to second-guess an action or word to determine if it is racist, but they're afraid of over-reacting or being too sensitive. They also have to prove racism or catch people at it, and that's hard. Blacks can't react quickly without evidence and it takes time to get the facts. As one black woman suggested: "I consider my 17-year-old son an endangered species." He has a job and rides a brand new bike to work. He purchased it with his own money and yet, he's been stopped a number of times by police who want to know, "Where did you get that bike? Did you steal it?" It makes the boy angry, makes him want to strike out in frustration, but his parents tell him not to react, just answer the questions and don't say anything. His mother asks helplessly, "What are you going to do? Stop him from riding his bike?"

Talk to some Windsor police these days and you get the impression that there are no racial problems in the city. They see Windsor as an ethnically diverse centre that treats foreigners as people. There are a few minor incidents like stabbings, thefts, arguments and skirmishes, and police claim there are the usual "bad apples" in any crowd, but no more than any other segment of the population and certainly nothing serious. The police are generally confident that they have enough Black and empathetic officers who understand the problems and can deal with them. They're quick to point out that the first Black was hired on the police force in 1932. He was Charles Peterson and he worked in the garage.

Windsor is also the home of Alton C. Parker who served on the Windsor police force for 30 years, the most famous black cop in the city. Hired in 1942, he was Windsor's first black patrolman. He became the first black detective in 1953 and, within three years, there were two other black officers on the force, including another detective. Known as "Uncle Al, the kiddies pal" by children of all ages, Parker hosted annual parties for underprivileged children at Broadhead Park at the corner of Erie and Howard. It all started on the second Tuesday in August 1966, with 12 kids from his neighbourhood, enjoying sandwiches, cookies and lemonade. Parker wanted to help kids who had nowhere else to go, to prevent them getting into trouble and running afoul of the law. He felt he could teach them good citizenship and cooperation and, before it all came to an end 22 years later, his party had developed into a bash for 800, an elaborate affair with visiting dignitaries, parades and go-carts.

In 1976, Parker received the Ontario Medal for Good Citizenship and the Order of Canada. He was also presented with the Queen's Silver Jubilee Medal the following year. Throughout his career, he worked with recovering alcoholics, handicapped and senior citizens and, for his efforts; he received an honourary law degree from the University of Windsor in

1987, and was named "Person of the Year" in 1988 by the North American Black Historical Museum. Surprised and embarrassed by all the attention, Parker considered himself an ordinary man who was motivated to help others because of his religious beliefs. He died February 28, 1989, at which time Broadhead Park was renamed the Alton C. Park in his honour.

Barney Crichton is a white constable in Windsor's traffic division in 1967. As a police officer, he doesn't feel there are many problems between Whites and Blacks even though he admits there are only three Blacks on the force, which is below the percentage in the general population. In those days, most Blacks hired by the city are employed in the Public Works Department as garbage men. Crichton says that the job of policeman isn't as high profile and not everybody wants to be a cop. The pay is low compared to a factory job, and there aren't a lot of incentives. Canada is different too. For one thing, Crichton says, Canadian Blacks don't have to sit in the back of the bus. He remembers hanging around with black kids at school even though there are some biases. "You can never eliminate that, but Canada still isn't the same as the United States."

In his early years on the Windsor police force, Bill Jackson patrols the Old Walker House, the Frontier Club and other bars frequented by Blacks. As a white constable, he also figures that race isn't an issue. He often goes to Emancipation Day celebrations and to black churches for dinner and, he says, he's treated well by most people. In fact, Jackson is fond of saying that he's, "just a black man turned inside out." He admits that the policeman's sense of humour is crude, but that's because most officers have a lot on their minds and there are no other ways to relieve stress. Humour is just a beat-cop's way of coping. If you have a problem, you keep it to yourself. You can't even tell your partner, Jackson says, or you hear about it in the lunchroom.

Despite white assurances, Windsor Blacks have a different story about their involvement with police. Many say they share a common experience, having been picked up as robbery suspects just because they are Black, even if they don't fit the description of the thief. If a fight breaks out and police are called, they often question the first Black they see, even if they had nothing to do with the altercation. It's as if the onus is on the individual to prove his innocence. Racism, or mistaken identity? Blacks ask, "Does it happen to others, or am I the only one? The authorities rarely admit that there's a problem, but Blacks always struggle with these questions.

Police justify their actions (Blacks call it harassment) by saying that there are a lot of American Blacks coming to Windsor and causing problems. Police demand to see ID, so they can distinguish an American from a Canadian Black. Blacks say it's ridiculous and they accuse the police of playing games. Young white people come from the United States and get into mischief, but they're not handcuffed or slammed onto the hood of the car or lined up against a wall. Blacks say it's a double standard.

J. Lyle Browning is the descendant of a black family that settled in Sandwich in the mid-1800s. He fought for equal rights in the 1940s as the first black student at Assumption College, a private school for Catholic boys, with 500 students in Windsor. A well-known sports figure, Browning eventually became an engineer and, in 1951, at the age of 28, was the only Black to be vice president and general manager of a large corporation in Canada. Browning says he didn't see many black faces in positions of authority in those days, and so he helped found the Central Citizen's Association for the Advancement of Coloured People in Windsor on December 4, 1950, along with Walter Perry, Lyle Talbert and Alton Parker. It was a "coloured community group" which promoted Blacks and helped them get hired to city institutions, banks, the fire department, city hall and public buildings. The organization was set up on December 4, 1950, by Browning, Walter Perry, Lyle Talbert and Alton Parker. It made sure that Blacks could enter any restaurant, place of business or amusement park without fear of being refused service. It also made sure that black children had equal opportunities for better jobs, education and citizenship. It helped black people rent or buy properties without fear of discrimination, and made sure that Blacks were free to use Essex County beaches and recreation centres.

The Citizen's Association helped Alton Parker get a job with the police force, and helped elect H.D. Taylor to the Windsor Board of Education, a position Taylor held for 25 years, spending many as chairman. The association asked the 2,000 black residents of Windsor to get involved to make things happen by, "legislation and publicity or active pressure, if necessary." Browning believed that Italians, Polish, French Canadians and Jews had their own organizations, but he was concerned that Blacks did not. When he eventually ran for a seat on council and, later, as a provincial liberal, he never made racism an issue because he didn't want to dwell on negatives. He just kept trying to succeed.

Another prominent member of the community in Windsor, Howard McCurdy did launch a political career as a black man fighting racism. Born in London, Ontario, McCurdy's family moved to Amherstburg when he was nine. He studied at Michigan State University where he founded a chapter of the NAACP. He continued his fight against discrimination as a private citizen in the 1960s when he was an associate professor of biochemistry and microbiology at the University of Windsor and as a founder of the Guardian Club, a forerunner of the Windsor Black Coalition and the National Black Coalition of Canada. McCurdy's crusade against racism continued when he was elected in 1979 to a five-year term as a Windsor councillor, and culminated in the 1980s with his election as a federal member of the House of Commons. As the MP for Windsor/Walkerville, he was the second black man to hold such a post in Canada.

In those four decades, McCurdy fought biased reporting in *The Windsor Star*, when the paper failed to write positive stories about Blacks. He also "took up the cudgel" to attack discrimination on the Windsor Police

Howard McCurdy is a former Member of Parliament, head of the Biology Department of the University of Windsor, and a long-time proponent of Civil Rights. Courtesy of Howard McCurdy.

Commission when, in the early '80s, he agitated for an independent civil-ian review board to look into complaints of police harassment and beat-ings. The subject was heavily debated with law enforcement officers until a resolution was finally passed.

During his terms of office, McCurdy says he was sometimes harassed by police, or followed and ticketed for no apparent reason. The harassment stopped in mid-1980, after a meeting with members of the police commis-sion, but he recalls an incident in 1996 that still leaves a sour taste. He was driving to Puce, just outside Windsor, on a Sunday morning. He was going up and down different streets, looking for a friend's house, when police stopped him. The officer said he was doing 70 in an 80 zone, impeding traffic, and he demanded to see McCurdy's license. McCurdy refused, because he didn't do anything wrong and shouldn't have been stopped. He was facing arrest until he finally said, "Go ahead. Take me downtown." That's when the officer backed off and let him go, but McCurdy is still convinced that he was stopped simply because he is Black. McCurdy admits that not all cops are bad. "Some of the younger ones are pretty good guys," but he says his daughter has also been stopped for no appar-ent reason, and he's afraid that things will get worse.

In 1996, the Commission on Systemic Racism in the Criminal Justice System in Ontario criticized the way racial minorities are treated by our courts and police departments. It confirmed what many Blacks already know. They are more likely to be considered suspect by police. They are stopped, shot at, jailed and denied bail far more often than their white counterparts. "The conclusion is inescapable: some black accused who were imprisoned before trial would not have been jailed if they had been White." When convicted of a crime, they receive stiffer sentences and they're often subject to racial comments from judges and other court offi-cials. The system is unfair and discretionary. In other words, discrimina-tion is alive and well and living in Ontario.

The Commission document is particularly critical of the police. It sug-gests that, since 1978, on-duty police officers have shot at least 16 black people, ten of them fatally. In nine cases, criminal charges were laid against the officers, but none were convicted. The commission recommends extra funding for the Special Investigation Unit to carry out its statutory functions, and it supports amendments to the Police Service Act to bring the hammer down on police officers that don't cooperate with investigators. As the report states, "there is considerable suspicion of community policing, especially among Blacks and youth from other racial minorities."

The 445-page report took three years to complete, cost $5,000,000 and contained 79 recommendations. It included alternative programs to jail, better anti-racism training, jobs in the justice system for visible minorities, and getting tough with police who don't cooperate with shooting investigations. The authors said the report provided positive, cost-effective and practical solutions to a more equitable justice system, and they hoped that their recommendations would be acted upon to regain trust in the law.

The 1996 Committee on Racism proclaimed Windsor to be a tolerant city, but indicated that many individuals are not. The comment was in response to the phrase "KKK rules" spray-painted on a black history mural at a grocery store on Sandwich Street. The word "nigger" was also painted in red letters, half a metre high, on the wall of a K-Mart across from black-owned homes on Northway Avenue, right where children wait for their school bus. The manager of the store said it happened several times, but he simply painted it over as soon as it appeared. As Rick Owen put it, "We find that, if you clean it up right away, it keeps it under control. But, if you let it go, it seems to attract more graffiti." Owen wonders where all the hate comes from. He refuses to sell spray-paint to kids. "If a kid is buying spray-paint, chances are it's not for home renovation."

The police say that the incident is more vandalism than hate, but black students in Windsor's west end say they're often subject to racist taunts and graffiti. A growing number of students display White Power symbols on their clothing and are in possession of racist propaganda. Young people at bus stops have been overheard talking about "mass genocide" of immigrants as a solution to the shortage of summer jobs. Vern Mahadad as the race relations coordinator for the Windsor Board of Education says, "It's not a big thing. But we have to do something and quickly."

Subhas Ramcharan is a professor at the University of Windsor and chairman of Windsor's Race and Ethno-Cultural Relations Committee and he admits that "racism is on the increase in Windsor, Ontario and Canada." His organization was one of the first of its kind in Canada when it was formed in 1986. It blamed a resurgence of racist attitudes on the worsening economy, high unemployment and the right-wing political scene. Ramcharan says black youth bear the brunt of ethnic hatred that coincides with the downgrading of human rights and employment equity issues.

The race relations committee is worried about the trend and is wondering what to do, how it can motivate kids to solve the problem. The police hope that strengthened anti-hate laws introduced in September 1996, will help. Under Bill C-41, courts must hand out stiffer sentences for racial, religious or sexual harassment, including assault, property damage or graffiti. Jerry Pocock, a Windsor police inspector, says the public must help report on and identify people guilty of property damage and graffiti. "Say you won't tolerate it. Say you will go to court and testify."

There has been criticism of teachers for not teaching enough about race issues, and of the media for giving more coverage to white supremacists and not enough to combat their message. Minority groups also come under fire for being too divided and too apathetic. As Ramcharan says, "They think someone else will take care of it for them."

Winston Walls in front of a log cabin at the John Freeman Walls Historic Site and Underground Railroad Museum near Windsor. Photo by Herb Colling.

Despite the problems, Doctor Bryan Walls, a Windsor dentist, is still convinced that Canada is the best country in the world for visible minorities. He knows that racial conflicts are serious and remembers a black man who was beaten up on his own front lawn by Windsor police as he was putting the garbage out. Walls says he's also felt uncomfortable crossing the border with several friends, some of whom were White. In one instance, the border guard was surprised that they were all professionals. Walls says it shook his ego, having his self-worth questioned. It was an unusual experience for his friends and it made him feel uncomfortable, but it was an exception rather than the rule.

Bryan Walls speaks from the experience of a pioneering Canadian family, the great-great-grandson of John "Freeman" Walls, a carpenter and slave who escaped to freedom in 1846. Eventually, Walls amassed over 200 acres near Windsor, of which 140 are still owned by the Walls family. In 1976, their homestead became the John Freeman Walls Historical Site and Underground Railroad Museum, a private enterprise that has been described as a mecca for African Americans who are trying to reconnect with their roots. It is one of the stops on The Freedom Road, a black heritage tour which features black historical sites in southwestern Ontario, including Uncle Tom's Cabin in Dresden, the Elgin Settlement in North Buxton and the Black Historical Museum and Cultural Centre in Amherstburg.

Walls' uncles, Allen and Winston, are teachers and co-founders of the railroad museum, which promotes the equal sisterhood, and brotherhood of human kind. They refuse to dwell on the negative bitterness and resentment of slaves who were degraded and wrenched from their homes in Africa. Instead, they want to maintain an historic site that instills hard work, faith, an understanding of freedom, and pride in black heritage. Their parents have always stressed education as a means of getting ahead, and they try to develop that philosophy with people who come to their museum.

Bryan and Shannon Prince of Buxton, whose roots can also be traced back to the days of slavery, actively contribute much to building understanding and knowledge of the black heritage of that area. Responsible for the Buxton Historic Site and Museum, established as a memorial to the

Elgin Settlement of 1849 to preserve the history of fugitive slaves who found refuge there, they are frequently called upon to share their research and knowledge.

As can be seen, the problems of race may not be as desperate on the Canadian side of the border, but they are still there. To Clayton Talbert, Windsor is just as guilty of racist attitudes as any other city. He feels that Blacks should stand up and say, "I'm not going to put up with that. I'm not going to tolerate that kind of activity." He's sometimes surprised that, if a black man stands up for his rights, some white people stand up with him and support his cause. They know that what is being done is wrong, especially if it excludes Blacks in a multi-cultural society.

At a black homecoming in Windsor in 1996, Benjamin Chavis Junior called for a revival of black consciousness in North America. Chavis has been active in the Civil Rights Movement since the '60s and was one of the organizers of the Million Man March on Washington, DC in October 1995. He recommends that Canadian and American Blacks forge stronger ties to promote black pride and fight racism. As he put it, the onus is on Blacks to take a stand. "We can't have people who are ashamed they're Black. We can't have some people who pretend they aren't Black." Chavis called for unity to fight discrimination and disadvantaged black youth. "When I talk about black unity, I'm not talking about separatism or withdrawing from society ... I'm talking about people of colour around the world working together with progressive Whites to erase racism."

There are many catch phrases, concepts and buzzwords, but Elise Harding-Davis believes we should be a diverse culture, a vertical mosaic "which celebrates the differences and rejoices in the sameness," retaining our distinctness and our culture. Black student, Rochelle Richard, contends that there's a utopian world out there where everything is equal in word and deed. Some Blacks may advocate "separate, but equal," but the phrase carries a lot of baggage. Generally, it's separate, and anything but equal.

For a short while, there was employment equity in Ontario, which some Blacks felt was a good tool and at least a start until the provincial Conservatives set it aside. Instead, Premier Mike Harris introduced legislative quotas, despite the concern of some Blacks who felt that quotas were negative. Blacks said there was a problem with the way in which quotas were introduced. There was no transition period and Blacks were not asked whether employment equity should be dismantled. They complain that decisions have to be made in consultation with involvement from everyone. Decisions have to be representative while still addressing injustice and inequity.

As one sociologist points out, it would be a great loss if the drive for equality fails, not only because of the threat of racial violence and fear created, but also because of the repression of that violence. The chance to reform society, where reform is needed most, could be lost forever. As Kenneth Clark once said, in his book *Dark Ghetto: Dilemma of Social Power*, "Negroes must convince the majority, who are White, that continued oppression of the Negro minority hurts the white majority too." Of course, many Blacks know that understanding is the key, and you have to educate people to see the error of their ways and the need to make things better, but it's not enough for Blacks to look at the issues and answer the questions, Whites have to do the same thing or nothing happens. As one black Canadian suggests, "We all belong to the same race: the human race. Let's not see colour first!"

Appendix I
AN ENTERPRISING SOCIOLOGIST: BENJAMIN SINGER

A few days after the riot begins, Benjamin D. Singer and a small group of excited students from London, Ontario, pelt down highway 401 toward Detroit in a late-model station wagon. Singer drives – students in back are frantically stapling 2,000 questionnaires together.

A specialist in communication, Singer is a sociology professor at the University of Western Ontario in London, Ontario, 120 miles from Windsor. His plan is simple. His students will talk to people who've been arrested about why they got involved and what caused the riot. It's called Instant Research – a departure from traditional inquiries, which are conducted months after an event.

Singer wants first impressions: to gather information while arrests are being made, while people are in jail, while memories are fresh, and the fires still burn. To do this, he has to get in fast. He wants to avoid traditional problems where participants brag, embellish, or lie to avoid incrimination. To Singer's knowledge, this is the first time for this type of research.

Remarkably, Singer has been given *carte blanche* by Carl Heffernan, the community relations officer for the Detroit Police. By approaching Heffernan directly, Singer avoids delays from senior levels of government. He's granted access to five places of detention where his crew can talk to prisoners, one-on-one, with no guards.

Researchers, at Wayne State in Lansing, Michigan, also take part. Associate psychology professor Sheldon Lockman recruits black social workers, teachers and grad students to conduct interviews from the hastily prepared questionnaire. Lockman supervises the work from project headquarters on McMichael Street, three miles from the heart of the riot. Singer is amazed that Wayne State didn't initiate the study first. As an American, Singer grew up in Detroit and is worried about what is happening to his city. At 36, he's more concerned about his country than safety. As Singer heads for the border, he has a peculiar sense of immunity and calm. "Nothing can happen to me," he figures. "I'm from Canada." Looking back, he doubts he'd do it again.

Singer's excitement increases as he drives through Windsor to U.S. border guards who obviously think he's crazy. The guard asks if he's carrying a handgun. Singer says, "No." The guard says dryly, "Here take mine, you'll need it." Heading through the centre of Detroit, Singer sees tanks, but not many soldiers. The streets are barren and quiet and he doesn't feel the danger. He knows the area and has a false sense of security. Even when he's driving through the riot zone, looking at burned-out buildings and rubble, he doesn't feel at risk. He's working, doing what he knows best and, to him, that's important.

At the time of Singer's study, 5,750 black males and females have been arrested compared to only 780 white males and females. The ratio is 88 percent Black to only 12 percent White. The charges include petty crimes: impeding the work of firemen, possession of stolen property, breaking curfew and carrying a concealed weapon; to more serious offenses: arson, break and enter, larceny, assault (including homicide or attempted homicide), conspiracy and inciting a riot. In some cases, no charges have been laid and prisoners downplay their role. They're told that the research is independent, not related to a law enforcement agency, and will not affect their status. The interviewers are not interested in guilt or innocence and all responses are anonymous. The sole purpose is to understand the riot.

The challenge for Singer is to take a sample of arrestees in proportion to the whole population. In all, 499 black prisoners are interviewed from July 31 to August 4, which represents almost 10 percent of the total. Not all are guilty. Their answers are checked against residents of the same sex, age and race in the community who are not necessarily innocent. This is called the control sample, and those interviews continue until August 15. Only five percent of the interviewees refuse to talk.

The report profiles the average rioter using standard sociological variables: occupation, education, membership in organizations and leadership attributes. It indicates that two-thirds of the black arrestees are under 30 years of age and half of those are under 20. They've lived in Detroit less than a year compared to the average in the community. Generally, the youngest rioters are not charged with as many major offenses as detainees between 20 to 29 years of age. It's significant, because previous studies assume that rioters are displaced youngsters dissatisfied with their social position who go out of control and commit serious offenses. They're also the type of people black leaders fail to reach.

Prior to the Singer study, it's assumed that low status and rural background are the main reasons for riots, but this is not the case. Unemployment and poverty are more likely to fuel discontent and lead to violent outbursts. Rioters are most destructive in the early stages because they are impatient and believe that the American lifestyle supports violence and aggression as a way of solving problems. As one sociologist suggests, "Conditions of life for the Negro-American are not acceptable anywhere in the U.S."

The Singer study shows that most rioters are unmarried, less settled or integrated socially. They do not have wives to dissuade them from rioting, nor family responsibilities to hold them in check. The Singer study also discovers that arrestees, whose parents are dead or divorced, or who grew up in single parent families, are more likely to be arrested and are twice as likely to be charged with serious crimes than those who grew up with both parents. Generally, such isolation begins with childhood and continues into adulthood. It becomes a pattern of development.

Singer discovers that fewer than five percent of rioters are over 45 and no one over 40 is charged. Of those over 40, less than half are married compared to 72 percent in the general populace. Twice as many arrestees have been in Detroit for less than a year, which indicates they are more isolated, not integrated into the community. One-fifth have been in the community for less than ten years, whereas the control sample has lived in Detroit for over 20 years. Those who lived a short time in the city have fewer constraints on their behaviour than those who have more community ties. Those who lived less than a year in Detroit are more likely to be charged with serious crimes. Long-term residents are more likely to be charged with less serious crimes, including curfew violations.

Some sociologists believe that violence occurs when black people feel powerless to control their own institutions. They have low ownership of ghetto businesses or there's a low proportion of black policemen. Problems also arise when they can't redress grievances because the city's political structure is inaccessible to minorities. If there are no Blacks on council, then black issues are not front and centre. Blacks feel more integrated if one of their own is elected to a position of authority. It provides the feeling that their voice is being heard.

The Singer study supports this theory. One-third of the detainees have never voted and the others are less likely to vote than the rest of the community. Most arrestees, charged with serious offenses, have little contact with powerful black leaders. Their knowledge of black leadership comes from the media and so, there is a sense of alienation or lack of integration. People arrested for serious offenses are unaware that there are black congressmen, for example, and feel more isolated.

Studies suggest that riots are most likely to occur in large, older, densely populated or overcrowded areas where there's a high proportion of poor, lower-class Blacks in dilapidated rental housing. In the United States, these districts grow slowly as Blacks move in and displace a similar number of Whites who escape to the suburbs. A simmering resentment spreads because black ghetto dwellers are unhappy with their living conditions. There's high unemployment and low educational standards with few white-collar opportunities. City services are inadequate and there's a high rate of expenditure and debt. As a result, people are unable to control their own lives and institutions. Similar conditions exist in cities where riots do not take place, so those conditions may not cause riots, but they at least make conditions rife for a disturbance.

This explains why the black working class is more likely to revolt than the black middle class, which is more comfortable, has greater social control and has too much invested in the status quo to risk a riot. Most rioters have less than a grade eight education and the poorest educated come from the Deep South. They make less, work in the service industry or are unemployed. The arrestee sample is more deprived than the rest of the black community, and certainly more deprived than the white community. The group is at the bottom of the opportunity structure.

Singer determines that the longer an individual is out of work, the more apt he is to riot. About the same number of arrestees are out of work as people in the general community, but twice as many prisoners have been out of work for over nine months. Singer concludes that unemployment is the greatest single factor in determining who riots. Arrestees also have a lower occupational status than the rest of the community. Only 14 percent of the prisoners have white-collar jobs compared to 26 percent of the community with the same amount of schooling. Detainees generally have lower-skilled jobs. Twenty-nine percent of the arrestees have semi-skilled jobs and 50 percent are unskilled, whereas the reverse is true in the community sample. Advances in technology and mechanization play a role here because they remove the very jobs that those with limited education can do. Ninety-seven percent of new jobs are white-collar and technical, and will not be filled by untrained black workers.

Surprisingly, Singer discovers another correlation between scholastic achievement and criminal activity. People in their 20s, with higher education and income, aren't as likely to riot, but are more likely to be charged with serious offenses when they do. Singer says these people have blue-collar jobs where some education is needed, but the disparity between Blacks and Whites is particularly acute. More of these men are born in urban areas of Michigan than the south. Most have some high school and expect a better life, a better job, but they also face more discrimination. There are barriers to their economic and social opportunities and they may be more frustrated as a result.

Singer discovers that 18 percent of the arrestees, with grade 13 or more, are charged with a serious offense. The numbers in this category are relatively small, but this is a high percentage, and is significant. It's an indication that rioters sometimes include white-collar workers, people who strive for something better. Hope is generated, in part, through the Civil Rights Movement. Blacks have made gains, have received promises, and some barriers have been removed. They are seeing some changes and that hope brings about the possibility of revolution. "The hopeless don't revolt because revolution is an act of hope." Poverty and discrimination alone are not sufficient for rioting.

Rioters are also not necessarily the poorest of the poor, because the defeated or downtrodden become apathetic and resigned, whereas those with hope become impatient. They want to live the dream, aspire to a better life, become activists. Hope and frustration are powerful stimuli. Blacks have rising expectations that are not being realized fast enough. They can see some improvement, which gives them a sense of progress, but their expectations are frustrated as further progress is reversed, blocked or too slow.

In 1967, the government's fight against poverty and segregation stalls. The United States doesn't keep its promises because it is concentrating on the Vietnam War and the costs are escalating. The discrepancy between black aspirations and achievements becomes intolerable because Blacks are powerless to improve their lot. Impatient and angry, they can't accept the double standard that exists in America. Discontented, they become hostile. They revolt. Their spirit of rebellion comes from a demand for justice through violence, if necessary. Whites do not face up to the problem of segregation and there is no attempt to educate, train or motivate Blacks who lack the skills to get along in society.

Ironically, arrestees are more pessimistic about their own condition while feeling optimistic about the condition of their race as a whole. In fact, detainees are more optimistic about general improvements for Blacks than the community at large. Arrestees also feel that things are improving because of riots elsewhere, and not because of the Detroit riot. Singer cautions that respondents are less able to judge, and there is a limit to the optimism of detainees.

Most Blacks believe in integration and are committed to society. They want equal opportunities in jobs, housing and schools. They do not want to overthrow, but they do want to confront and modify society. They want "in" and are generally optimistic that this will happen. Only one-fifth of the respondents say the black man will never have what the white man has, and the same proportion figure that the black man will have the same as the white man in ten years. One-third feel it will take 20 years. Serious offenders feel it will take longer. There is no agreement on how Blacks will achieve what they want, but most believe that black unity, that is, Blacks working with and helping other Blacks, is the best way to achieve civil rights. Others say it can only be achieved through self-improvement, better jobs, voting and related activities. Still others believe that non-violent coercion is needed. It's possible that the hypothetical nature of the question may preclude reliable or valid data.

There are differing opinions on what might end the riot. A third of the respondents feel that the solution has to be non-violent negotiation. Twenty percent suggest that force is required. People in jail tend to blame white police for the disturbance. They resent authorities and suggest that the elimination of police brutality would solve problems. They point to the blind pig incident as the cause of violence and recommend talk and compromise rather than force to end it. They aren't as convinced that education, jobs and other social solutions will prevent riots. Community respondents prefer long-term solutions and feel the cause is the general economic and social condition. They blame some Blacks for the riot or they blame police discrimination or outside agitators, but they would also use force to end it.

The circumstances of the interview may account for the differences in attitude. Arrestees are interviewed in jail after a run-in with the law, whereas community respondents are interviewed in the comfort of their own homes. A few people believe that civil disobedience is the way to gain control, but their influence is great. In Detroit, black people don't have the skills to take control and are denied access to institutions that teach the skills. Control by Whites simply aggravates their situation and adds to their anger. Increasing social consciousness, and the drive to gain control, may have caused the riot.

Most white people believe the riot is the result of agitators, prompted by the temper of the times or an undisciplined self-interest and greed – a desire to take things. A minority thinks it occurs because of mistreatment of blacks people, abuse by police, or because of economic or social disadvantages and the inability of Blacks to do anything about it. Despite a lack of proof, two-thirds believe the riot is planned in advance. Generally, Whites believe it is negative and loses sympathy for Blacks. Ironically, they are more hostile to Blacks than Blacks are to them. The majority of white police officers believe that society favours Blacks. They fail to realize that discrimination still exists and dates back to slavery. They are not convinced that Blacks have an urgent desire for freedom, but feel they are pushing too hard, and getting too much.

Blacks have an entirely different perspective, which further demonstrates the gap. They view the riot as the direct result of police abuse, as well as economic and social disadvantages. They do not see it as planned, as the work of black nationalists, teenagers, or of welfare indolents. Nor do they blame outside agitators or the temper of the times. They do not see it as the pursuit of undisciplined self-interest and desire to take things. Half of those polled sympathize with rioters and have an increased pride in being Black, although they have mixed feelings about the riot. Few are positive about the events and don't condone looting, burning and killing. They feel that the protest is necessary, but the form is wrong and they're mixed about whether whites sympathize or not. Younger Blacks are more militant and angry with police, more positive toward the riot and militant leaders. Their anger is under control, but more sharply focussed, with the exception of those under 18 who don't have well-formed convictions about the riot, leadership or race relations. Their attitudes are more superficial and immature, not as well-informed or opinionated.

Official reports suggest there is no leader in the Detroit riot, and yet one sociologist says incidents of sniping and looting do not appear random. They are directed at symbols of coercive and economic authority in the white community, including police, firemen and their equipment. They seem designed more to prolong the riot and create confusion and fear than to inflict bodily harm. Firebombing and looting of stores, during the first day of the riot, is selective. Stores with "Soul Brother" signs are often bypassed and some chain stores, with a reputation for fair treatment, are ignored. This is not the case by the second day of rioting when whole blocks of businesses are looted and then put to the torch.

The Kerner Commission suggests that the riot is spontaneous and unplanned, but small groups may operate within the broad confusion, and contribute to the mood that intensifies and prolongs the action. How much support these leaders enjoy, where they come from, and what purpose they have, is unknown. It could be that they organize in small groups merely to loot, steal and take advantage of lawlessness, but they can be dangerous and cause a considerable amount of damage. They're often close-minded and prepared to go down fighting, convinced that rioting is the only avenue open. They can't be reasoned with in their highly intolerable, suspicious and angry state and the ultimate danger is that they attract others to their side, which increases polarization and invites a hostile counter-reaction from Whites. Generally, riots release man's baser instincts, which are usually held in check by moral codes. As people are freed from their inhibitions, the events cloud and rioters lose control.

Because of this degeneration, some sociologists discount the theory that the riot is a planned action against police harassment. They suggest that the riot is an impulsive and emotional act rather than a calculated war against Whites. It is not motivated by racism because, in a deliberate anti-white campaign, Blacks would attack Whites in all-white bastions similar to the riot in 1943. In 1967, Whites aren't the primary targets of Blacks, black properties are also destroyed along with those owned by Whites. In fact, Blacks and Whites loot together. This new pattern of rioting first emerged in 1964 when black urban dwellers engaged in violence against property and the law. It's not necessarily Blacks against Whites, so some sociologists claim the disorders are not "race riots" in the true sense of the term.

Yet another study suggests that the majority of Blacks – 85 percent – oppose and deplore the riot and say they did not participate. That study generally ignores the fact that many people are caught up in the moment and rip off stores because everybody else is doing it with impunity. Since riots appear to get results, they give legitimacy to violent and illegal acts. They appear to be effective, so people in ghettos think it's okay to riot. More people act, thinking it justified, and a snowball effect is created. The idea that most Blacks don't participate is reassuring to Whites and popular with laymen because the riot then becomes a meaningless outburst by a relative minority. The hypothesis is that riots are not collective protests designed to bring social change, but merely an example of hostility by an alienated and isolated people.

In the Singer study, the most serious offenses are not always committed by the most isolated, but by individuals who are angry at society and want to "protest." Property offenses, including break-and-enter and looting, are not relegated to a particular social rank, nor are they restricted to unmarried participants. The theory emphasizes the hope of Blacks that the riot will increase awareness of problems in the ghetto. They hope the riot has purpose, will generate sympathy, and improve their position. The chilling summation, however, is that a majority of Blacks – 60 percent – predict further rioting if the problems of poverty, unemployment and racial discrimination are not addressed.

The Singer study is mainly interested in the way the "message" spreads. It looks at the relationship of media to social pathology and determines that people watch the riot without participating or actually pick up on the idea and duplicate it. Coverage of riots throughout the United States generally raises expectations that a similar event is likely to occur in Detroit. As one resident says, "Each time they heard about one [riot] some place else, they said Detroit would be next."

Throughout the '60s, Detroit is a centre for militant black organizers, including Black Nationalist and black power groups. By 1967, student organizations, traditionally non-violent, are more vocal. Even Martin Luther King, a non-violent civil rights activist supported by the conservative middle class, talks less about non-violence and more about action. TV relays the message to compel Americans to redress wrongs toward black society.

Stokely Carmichael, national chair of the Student Non-Violent Coordinating Committee, believes that the more strident his message, the more likely he'll make it on television. He seizes every opportunity to call the American Secretary of Defense "a racist honkey" and to suggest, "fire must rage in the U.S." He also attacks civil rights organizations as buffers, and advocates force to "take what is ours." Camera crews eat it up. "America doesn't understand non-violence. America understands power."

Anyone, even contented people, can be excited and influenced to commit violent, deviant or aggressive acts during demonstrations. They're stimulated by the crowd or by sensational reports of the event. The person justifies the disobedience and joins the riot, despite the risk, simply because the media is providing coverage. Violent activity becomes legitimate if everyone else is doing it.

To give credence to this theory, 80 percent of the arrestees say they viewed the riot on TV and then went to the scene afterward. Most prisoners say they weren't even present when the riot started, or even knew about the raid on the blind pig. As a result, the reason for the riot becomes irrelevant. It isn't an important motivational event. Most people are spurred by their own curiosity, based on television reports, rumours they've heard, or their own personal experience. They enter the riot area to see the fires and theft. Some people aren't even aware that police are taking action or that a curfew has been established.

Singer concludes that many people are primed by previously televised riots. They identify with the anger and emotion, are disturbed by what they see and are "instructed" how to riot, so they are prepared for it when it finally arrives. Every time police use their truncheons to beat someone up, they are perceived as the enemy by black people watching at home. The police become agents of white aggression and give credence to black cries of brutality. Ironically, black police fall into this same category. Their uniform and gun show them as part of the establishment and, in some respects, traitors to their race. Arrestees say they expect police brutality and, since they are emotionally charged, their corresponding violence is merely a reaction or response to treatment by Whites and the police.

In Detroit's case, there is a perception of police brutality – an all-white police force beating up on black citizens. Detroit Police Commissioner Ray Girardin recognizes the difficulty and has a hard time dealing with it. He knows that strong police action triggered the event, and is afraid that further action might serve as a catalyst to stimulate and promote violence. Angry Blacks might become more aggressive because a police crackdown illustrates their original grievance. Faced with this problem, and realizing that he doesn't have the manpower to diffuse the situation, Girardin simply leaves it alone. Unfortunately, his failure to act is perceived by the public as a sign of weakness, which stimulates further aggression. The police are perceived as ineffective, unwilling, or unable to act which merely elicits scorn from riot participants.

Ironically, most arrestees indicate their general disapproval of riots and complain that they should not be shown on television because the coverage places Blacks in a poor light and does not give them a fair shake. Detainees feel there is an inherent bias in the way the news is reported. There is also a general bias in the lack of coverage of black issues and of black lifestyle. In 1967, there are no TV programs about black men, women or families, nor are black people represented in commercials. As U.S. Congressman John Conyers puts it, "You'd think Negroes don't brush their teeth or use soap."

The Singer report is one of two principal studies about the riot and its results are shared with the Kerner Commission. Critics say it is flawed because the questionnaire was not carefully developed. The study was conducted without prior testing, or a pilot survey, looks solely at sociological data and fails to analyze the psychological. It's also undertaken while prisoners are still in detention, which could influence their responses. It is, however, the most immediate study of its kind and provides valuable insight into what went wrong. As such, it was published by the U.S. Department of Labour in March 1968, and then as a book several years later.

Singer says there is a lot of paranoia in Washington after 1967. Government officials are frightened that the whole system could come crashing down. The concerns prompt Singer to be wary. He's contacted by officials with the U.S. Justice Department and warned that the Senate Investigating Committee might try to seize his research, which could be used in court to incriminate some detainees. President Johnson indicates an interest in Singer's study and the U.S. Department of Labour adds questions on employment status and indebtedness to the report. As a precaution, Singer rents a huge safe in which to keep his most sensitive material. He is prepared to cooperate and is eventually interviewed by the committee, but he makes sure that the group does not have access to any of the written material.

On a personal note, Singer does some strange things at unusual hours in Detroit. For one thing, he violates curfew regulations. While his study goes off without a hitch, it is marred by one incident, which, surprisingly, occurs several weeks after the riot. One of his students, Andrew Cameron, is afraid of going into the riot area. He is assigned to pick up unemployment statistics for both groups, and is told to stay at the Statler Hotel on Washington Boulevard in a safe and lovely area of the city. He is still apprehensive, even after Singer convinces him that the riot is over, that the danger has passed, there's no problem, and nothing can go wrong. Walking to his hotel one evening, Cameron is stabbed by a man in the street. It's yet another indication that, while the riot is finished, the problem in Detroit lingers on.

In the early '70s, "riotology" is popular in urban sociology courses in the United States and Canada. Many academic papers and textbooks are written on the subject, and professors send their students into the streets to assess the aftermath of the riot and its implications. Bob Ferguson is studying at the University of Windsor, and he remembers alleys filled with abandoned refrigerators and junk. He takes a tape deck to record the moment. "I'm standing on the corner of Twelfth and John R ..." but the angry looks of local residents force him back to his car to make his comments. The experience demonstrates the depth of feeling of this racial conflict.

Early in the 1980s, Jim Savage takes a similar course in social psychology. Students record their perceptions of the riot: what happened, what caused it, how many people died, was it a race riot? The rest of the course is devoted to debunking myths that have arisen after 15 years. Savage says nobody had a clue about how many people were killed, what colour they were, or who killed them. They weren't sure about what happened or why, didn't realize the link between socio-economic conditions and race, nor were they aware of the over-reaction of the National Guard. They knew that Whites were paranoid about Detroit, even though the riot wasn't directed at Whites generally, but at white police and white-owned businesses in its early stages. Savage is fascinated by the idea that Whites are afraid of black hostility and aggression when, in fact, most of the victims are Black and Whites do most of the killing. The course demonstrates that most student perceptions are wrong.

Appendix II
A Tribute To Lightfoot

No book about Canadian involvement in the Detroit riot would be complete without including Gordon Lightfoot, the folk singer from Orillia, Ontario, who wrote the song *Black Day In July*. Lightfoot is described as a "journalist, poet, historian, humourist and short-story teller," and his song talks about Motor City Madness touching the rest of the United States and, indirectly, perhaps even southwestern Ontario. It explains what happened, captures the feeling and mood of Detroit at that time.

As one of Lightfoot's most compelling and driven songs, *Black Day In July* reflects the panic of the riot. It refers to doors that are grimly bolted and "children locked inside" while looting and fires, "reflect upon the waters." Surprisingly, many people who've heard the song aren't aware that it's about the Detroit riot, which adds to the mystery of the piece. Subtle and understated, it's a statement, a powerful political commentary, perhaps even too powerful for Lightfoot himself.

Gordon Meredith Lightfoot released his first single album in 1965 and, during his debut in New York, was praised for his "rich, warm voice and dexterous guitar." After hearing Bob Dylan, Lightfoot wanted to write something with meaning and his songs gradually became more personal, reflecting his own identity. In 1966, he became Canada's top folksinger, followed by being recognized as top male vocalist a year later when he joined the Festival Canada tour, a train trip across the country to help celebrate Canada's yearlong birthday. The trip ended at the Ontario and Quebec Pavilions at Expo '67 in Montreal. According to Maynard Collins, Lightfoot's official biographer, the musician from Orillia was rapidly becoming part of the consciousness of the nation.

When Lightfoot played Massey Hall for the first time to sell-out crowds, Toronto papers applauded his "brilliant, creative mind." His solid reputation at home allowed him to focus on the U.S. market without losing his grip in Canada. Lightfoot's career was taking off, but it wasn't all rosy. He recorded in Nashville, but was still having trouble making it south of the border. It wasn't enough to be a hit in Canada, and he was obsessed with the American market.

Black Day In July was the tune that Lightfoot hoped would stretch his appeal across the border. He was searching for stardom, the high fame and big bucks that only an American gold could bring since it represents $1,000,000 in sales. His first album sold a disappointing 20,000 copies in the United States, perhaps because of his understated Canadian style. Lightfoot realized that he had a long way to go, and consciously set out to find the main ingredient, the subject, to create that one big hit that would make it in America.

The times were troubled. There was a lot of dissent worldwide. Lightfoot was deeply pained by the Vietnam War, as well as the street demonstrations and the destruction of inner city America to the strains of "Burn, Baby, Burn." A Canadian nationalist, Lightfoot was concerned about the deterioration of the Democratic Party in the United States and, as he watched the riots from a distance, he developed an understanding for angry, poor, unemployed Blacks, battling it out with white police and the National Guard. To him, the United States was self-destructing and turning to a firm, repressive government for protection.

Collins says *Black Day In July* is Lightfoot's only political song, his only song of protest. He wrote the bitter ballad in anger and sadness. It "was a heart-felt plea for an end to violence and a vivid description of the horrors of urban anarchy" and it was written because it touched Lightfoot deeply.

When he introduced *Black Day* in Detroit, Lightfoot said, "This is a song about your city. I'm sorry it has to be this way." Everybody applauded and the tour was a success, but the song didn't lead to a breakthrough on the American market. Lightfoot sang it in concerts and on a CBC special in March 1968. It topped the charts, but not in the United States. It failed to capture its target audience when American radio stations refused to play it for fear it would cause further riots. Even CKLW in Windsor – which pushed the song to the top of the charts in Canada – succumbed to the pressure and removed it from its play list. United Artists couldn't break the boycott and, without support from radio stations, the song was doomed. Because of the ban, Lightfoot's dream of making it in America was temporarily shattered and the cautious troubadour became bitter.

A reclusive individual, Lightfoot refuses to talk about *Black Day* even though it's one of his more famous songs. Barry Harvey is manager of Lightfoot's recording company, Early Morning Productions, in Toronto. He says Lightfoot downplays *Black Day*, doesn't discuss it with friends or fans and, when asked in his occasional interviews, offers a firm, "no comment." He hasn't performed the song since shortly after it was released in January 1968, and he refuses to sing it in concerts. The tune has never been licensed to anyone else, nor does Lightfoot perform it on any of his albums produced by other companies. Harvey says that all recordings of the song are cut from the original masters, which are owned by United Artists. Lightfoot has no rights to them even though he tried to buy them back when he established Early Morning Productions in the early 1970s. He offered $500,000, but United Artists recognized the potential market and refused.

According to Harvey, Lightfoot has always been apolitical and didn't think it right to comment about something in the United States. As a result, he turned his back on *Black Day*. He decided that it was not personally relevant, that it was not reflective of his own life and that he shouldn't get involved in another nation's politics. On the *Best of Lightfoot* album, released by United Artists, Lightfoot is quoted as saying, "I'm not a politician or a spokesperson, just a musician." He merely wanted to be "in tune." Despite this denial, the liner notes suggest that Lightfoot is indeed a spokesman, "because he says what we feel, what we think and what we need to hear." In that respect, Lightfoot is entirely Canadian. Not pretentious, he's just an honest singer who writes and sings what he feels. Uncharacteristically, though, he took a risk and it backfired.

Fortunately for Lightfoot, the setback didn't stop him totally. To his credit, he survived the end of the folk music boom in the 1960s and, because of his versatility and

Several Gordon Lightfoot album covers, which feature his earlier songs with the notable exception of Black Day In July. *It wasn't until 1972 that Lightfoot launched his career in the United States with his* Sundown *album.* Photo by Herb Colling.

range, made the transition from one generation to the next in a fickle business. By 1974, he finally made it on the American market with a tune called *Sundown* which exploded on both the pop and country charts. The tune sold over 1.5 million copies during its first year of release. It was a significant achievement, especially for Lightfoot who is described as "a cautious man who won't take chances."

In some respects, Detroit was a second home for Lightfoot. In 1965, he spent part of his summer in the Detroit walk-up of Joni and Chuck Mitchell near Wayne State. Beth Hebert, former record librarian at CBC radio in Windsor, says Lightfoot still performs at Pine Knob, the Masonic Temple or the Fox Theatre. It's almost a tradition. He seems to have a love, a kinship, with Detroit and his American audience.

Lightfoot cherishes loyalty and, perhaps, he was concerned about losing his American fans. Although not well known across the United States generally, he had a large following in Michigan and Detroit and, perhaps, he felt that he'd betrayed that audience. Perhaps it's another reason he does not want to be attached, or have his music attached, to the issue of the Detroit riot. As some observers suggest, he seems uncomfortable with his controversial ballad and has chosen to put it behind him.

Sources By Chapter

INTRODUCTION

The introduction is a somewhat personal look at the times, based on my own perceptions, many confirmed by casual comments from colleagues, friends and acquaintances. Anecdotes arise from reminiscences and personal interviews with: Tim Burton of Windsor, Katherine Clark of Windsor, Charlie and Gene Colling (deceased) of Kincardine, Jeanne Drouillard of Toronto, Garnet Fox of Amherstburg, Cheryl Garrod of Windsor, Lloyd Grahame of Leamington, Elise Harding-Davis of Amherstburg, Ruth Hirtenfeld (nee Colling) of Kincardine, Denise Kristof (nee Belisle) of Windsor, Steve Kristof of Windsor, Walt McCall of Windsor, Gail Oliver of Chatham, Rachel Parent of Tecumseh, Rosalind Peck (nee Ward) of Windsor, Laurie Smith of Windsor and Bryan Walls of Windsor.

A further sense of what life was like in the summer of 1967 came from a thorough research of various period newspapers including: *The Windsor Star, The Detroit Free Press* and the *London Evening Free Press.*

Various encyclopedia and incidental history texts and other readings provided further dates and minor details. Source books and other resources are identified chapter by chapter. Complete bibliographic information on each print source is provided in the Bibiliography.

CHAPTER 1: THE RIOTS: THE AMERICAN STORY

The general story of the Detroit riot has been well-documented, but the impact on the Canadian side, specifically Windsor, has never been told. My first chapter is primarily a review, made necessary by the fact that many people, even those who were in Windsor during the time of the riot, now well over 30 years ago, only have vague notions of what actually went on.

The most thorough and exhaustive account of the riot is Sydney Fine's *Violence In the Model City: The Cavanagh Administration, Race Relations and the Detroit Riot of 1967.* Ann Arbour; University of Michigan Press, 1989, reprinted 1992.

A more readable but, perhaps, sensational account is a book by Gordon Van Sauter and Burleigh Hines called *Nightmare in Detroit: A Rebellion and its Victims.* It was quickly published by Henry Regnery Company, Chicago, immediately after the riot in 1968.

A good backgrounder can be found in Leonard Gordon's *A City In Racial Crisis: The case of Detroit. Pre and Post the 1967 Riot.* (1971) For a sociological and psychological view point, consider Benjamin D. Singer's and Richard W. Osborn's *Black Rioters: A Study of Social Factors and Communication in the Detroit Riot* and James A. Geschwender's *Class, Race and Worker Insurgency: The League of Revolutionary Black Workers.* (1967).

Once again, *The Detroit Free Press, The Windsor Star* and *The London Evening Free Press* rounded out the general view of the riot with a day-by-day account. Pete McGarvey's *Detroit Riot Tapes,* (private collection) and a video called *Detroit Riots 20 Years Later* by

David Compton and Jim Tracey (1987), and published by CBC TV Windsor, furnished actuality clips that put me on the scene and made me feel as though I was there.

CHAPTER 2: WINDSOR FIREFIGHTERS JOIN THE BRIGADE

Historical references in this chapter came almost exclusively from Gary Percy and the document *Windsor Fire Department Archives* (1996). Patience Nauta at the Detroit Historical Museum confirmed dates and times. She also furnished an excerpt from *Our Firemen* (1894), a paper published for the Detroit Historical Museum by Robert Mercer and John McEwan.

This chapter also relies heavily on personal interviews with Inez Coxon of Leamington, Robert Ferguson of Harrow, Dave Fields of Windsor, Jack Leopold of Windsor and Walt McCall of Windsor.

Some anecdotal material came from *The Windsor Star* and *The Detroit Free Press* and attempts were made to confirm or flesh out the details through personal interviews with individuals cited in the articles.

American references and statistics came from Sydney Fine's *Violence In The Model City: The Cavanagh Administration, Race Relations and the Detroit Riot of 1967* (1989), and Leonard Gordon's *A City In Racial Crisis: The Case of Detroit. Pre and Post the 1967 Riot* (1971).

CHAPTER 3: CANADIAN NEWSMEN

This chapter was pieced together almost exclusively from first-hand accounts, personal interviews conducted with reporters and photographers of the day. They include: Spike Bell of Tecumseh, Bill Bishop of Windsor, Ken Hull (deceased) of Calgary, Les Mather of Windsor, Walt McCall of Windsor, Pete McGarvey or Orillia, Dick Smyth of Toronto, Hal Sullivan of Emeryville, and Jim Van Kuren of Windsor, with perspective, tidbits and sources provided by Bill Baker, Gino Conte and Sandra Precop from the CBC newsroom.

The Windsor Star yielded some valuable insights in the form of columns and articles, which indicated the feelings in Windsor at the time. The *Detroit Riot Tapes* of Pete McGarvey gave a sense of what reporters were dealing with in Detroit, as did the *Detroit Riots 20 Years Later*, a video report compiled by David Compton and Jim Tracey.

The American story was fleshed out from Gordon Van Sauter's and Burleigh Hines' book *Nightmare in Detroit: A Rebellion and its Victims* (1968), Sydney Fine's edition of *Violence In the Model City* (1989) and *The Detroit Free Press* (1967).

CHAPTER 4: CAUGHT BY THE RIOT

In the tradition of an oral history, personal interviews included: Vicki Bondy (nee Fox) of Amherstburg, Bernice Carlan of Windsor, Barney Crichton of Windsor, Ron DiMenna of Leamington, Ken Farrow of Amherstburg, Garnet Fox of Amherstburg, Sue Goertzen of Harrow, Layne Katzman of Windsor, Kevin Hart of Montreal, Juergen Hendel of Coldchester, Bill Jackson of Windsor, Dave Lane of Detroit, George Mooney of Essex, Ivy Vander Zanden of London, Allen Walls of Windsor, Charlie Weston of Windsor, Rick Wynants of Maidstone and Eileen Zuccaro of Windsor.

Ken Farrow also gave me complete access to his personal papers and clippings file, which he has collected over the years. The 1967 editions of newspapaers, *The Windsor Star*, *Chatham Daily News* and *London Evening Free Press*, which fleshed out the stories and allowed for some cross-referencing.

CHAPTER 5: THE BORDER IS CLOSED

The Windsor Star, Chatham Daily News and *The London Evening Free Press* (1967) newspapers provided the canvas for the colourful pictures painted during personal interviews with: Jennifer Beaudoin (nee Bondy) of LaSalle, Don Bondy of Anderdon, Grant Bowbeer of Grosse Isle, Carol Ferguson of Amherstburg, Dorothy Gascoyne of Harrow, Ken Hull (deceased) of Hull, Elise Harding-Davis of Amherstburg, Sister Immaculata of Edmonton, Phil Labelle of London, Garnet Ryan of Windsor, Bob Steele of Windsor, Joe Suchan of Windsor, Bill Taylor of Belle River, Michael Taylor of Belle River, Jim Travis of Belle River, and Pat Walker of Walkerville.

CHAPTER 6: RELIEF

Despite repeated efforts, I was unable to trace any first-hand interviews or other sources for this chapter. The story was compiled by combining elements from *The Windsor Star, The Chatham Daily News,* and *The London Evening Free Press* (1967). Connecting and corroborative details from the United States came from Sydney Fine's *Violence In the Model City* (1989).

CHAPTER 7: EMANCIPATION AND HUMAN RIGHTS

This was one of the more interesting chapters to write because it required some sleuthing that involved dredging through materials in the local municipal archives at the Windsor library, the archives at the North American Black Historical Museum and Cultural Centre in Amherstburg and the provincial archives in Toronto. An intensive search, through folders of vaguely organized personal papers of the McCurdy family – specifically George and Alvin D. McCurdy – allowed me to develop a fairly comprehensive idea of the chain of events leading to a Supreme Court challenge.

Howard McCurdy and Ken Farrow also allowed me access to their personal files of news clippings, letters and papers (1996).

Of interest were the *Minutes of Meetings of the Board of Commissioners* and The Annual Reports (1967) of the Windsor Police Department, and a publication called Progress (1948-1980) by Walter L. Perry and later Ted Powell.

The story also required an extensive perusal of *The Windsor Star* and *The Chatham Daily News* over a period of over a year from July to October (1967-1968).

Historical references to Emancipation Days come from *The Amherstburg Echo* (1886-1980) and *Radio Sketches of Periods-Events-Personalities from the History of the Essex County-*

Detroit Area from CKLW and a similar edition from the Windsor-Essex Historical Society (1963). Also of note is *Amherstburg 1796 To 1996. The New Town on the Garrison Grounds* by the Amherstburg Bicentennial Book Committee (1996).

Personal interviews with: Elise Harding-Davis of Amherstburg, Ken Farrow of Amherstburg, Bill Jackson of Windsor, and Howard McCurdy of Tecumseh also helped round out the story.

CHAPTER 8: SLAVE AND RACIAL HISTORY: WINDSOR

It is difficult to deal with the magnitude of a chapter entitled Windsor's Slave and Racial History. There are so many resources, where does one start and, equally importantly, where does one stop?

Personal interviews with Elise Harding-Davis, Curator of the North American Black History Museum and Bill Willson of Windsor helped develop a perspective. The "Archives" of Howard, Alvin and George McCurdy, and of the North American Black Historical Museum and Cultural Centre gave a critical analysis of racial tensions in Canada, as did Lyle E. Talbot's "The Distinctive Character of Racism In Canada," M.A. Thesis, University of Windsor (1982).

Tim Halford, Sister Rose-Marie Dufault and Sister LeBoeuf provided information and a paper "Hôtel-Dieu of St. Joseph – founded in 1888," about the early history of Hôtel-Dieu Hospital. The article is in the Hôtel-Dieu Archives.

I am particularly indebted to Ari Varsa of Amherstburg, Sarah Jarvis of Toronto and Bill Jarvis of Amherstburg who gave me samples of racist materials that should have been mentioned in the official history of Amherstburg, but were ignored.

General reading includes the following titles: Vincent D'Oyley's *Black Presence In Multi-Ethnic Canada* (1976), Daniel G. Hill's *The Freedom Seekers: Blacks In Early Canada* (1981), James Walker's *Identity: The Black Experience In Canada* (1979), Don Gillmor and Grant Black's magazine article "Promised Land: The Final Stop on the Underground Railroad" *Canadian Geographic* (1995), Carole Jenson's *History of the Negro Community in Essex County, 1850-1860* (1966), Fred Landon's *Abolitionist Interest In Upper Canada* (1918), *Canada's Part In Freeing The Slaves* (1919), *In An Old Ontario Cemetery* (1926), *Underground Railroad Along The Detroit River* (1955), Lewis James' *Religious Nature of Early Negro Migration To Canada and the Amherstburg Baptist Association* (1996), Alvin McCurdy's *Henry Walton Bibb* (1958), John Prince's *Personal Letter to Thomas Park* (1851), Patrick Barnard's *Ideas: Slavery In Canada: The Great Unspoken* (1975), Bob Johnstone's *Today In History: Reverend William King* (1996) and *Abolition of Slavery* (1996), Lister Sinclair's *Ideas: Slavery In Canada* (1996), Christopher P. Anderson's *The Book of People* (1981), Henry Bibb's *Narrative of the Life and Adventures of Henry Bibb, An American Slave* (1849), Linda Bramble's *Black Fugitive Slaves In Early Canada* (1988), Gena K. Gorrell's *North Star To Freedom: The Story of the Underground Railway* (1996), Joseph P. Krauter and Morris Davis' *Minority Canadians: Ethnic Groups* (1978), Carl Morgan's *Birth of A City* (1991), Neil F. Morrison's *Garden Gateway To Canada* (1954), Reverend E.A. Richardson's *Historical Sketch of the British Methodist Episcopal Church 1856-1926* (1970), Rosemary Sadlier's *Leading the Way:*

Black Women In Canada (1994), Colin A. Thomson's *Blacks In Deep Snow: Black Pioneers In Canada* (1979), and Robin W. Winks' *The Blacks In Canada: A History* (1971).

Information from *The Chatham Daily News, Amherstburg Echo* and *The Windsor Star* also helped piece the story together.

CHAPTER 9: RACIAL HISTORY: DETROIT

Once again, the American story has been well-documented, but an abbreviated version needs to be told by way of review. Robert Slogan and Tom Craig provide the most detailed account with *The Detroit Race Riot: A Study In Violence* (1964). Further background is offered in Leonard Gordon's book *A City In Racial Crisis: The Case of Detroit. Pre and Post the 1967 Riot* (1971). See also James Geschwender's *Class, Race and Worker Insurgency: The League of Revolutionary Black Workers.* (1977).

CHAPTER 10: THE QUEBEC QUESTION

This most unusual chapter in the book draws a parallel between racial problems of blacks in the United States and the Quebeçois in Canada. I stumbled across this prospective and studied it in the early 1970s as a student at Carleton University, and it has stayed with me ever since. It is interesting as a consideration of the mood of the times.

Written primarily from secondary sources, this chapter draws heavily on the works of – in descending order of importance: Pierre Vallières' *White Niggers of America* (1968); Leandre Bergeron's *The History of Quebec: A Patriote's Handbook* (1971); Marcel Rioux' *Quebec In Question* (1971); a book by Douglas Steubing, John Marshall and Gary Oake called *Trudeau: A Man For Tomorrow*; Pierre Elliott Trudeau's *Federalism and the French Canadians* (1968); R.M. Burns *One Country Or Two* (1971); J.M.S. Careless' *Canada: A Story of Challenge* (1974); a book by K.A. MacKirdy, J.S. Moir and Y.F. Zoltvany called *Changing Perspectives In Canadian History: Selected Problems* (1967); Peter C. Newman's *The Canadian Establishment* (1975); and Walter Stewart's *Shrug: Trudeau In Power* (1971).

Aforementioned newspapers also provided incidental details.

CHAPTER 11: POST RIOT: DETROIT

As a wrap-up, this chapter relies heavily on personal anecdotes from interviews with: Ann Bondy of Anderson, Don Bondy of Anderson, Sue Goertzen of Harrow, Mayor Michael Hurst of Windsor, Layne Katzman of Windsor, Walt McCall of Windsor, Pete McGarvey of Orillia, Dino Paniccia of Windsor and Ivy Vander Zanden of London.

The general information about Detroit has, once again, been well-documented and is provided primarily by way of review. Books include: Sydney Fine's *Violence In the Model City* (1989), James A. Gerschwender's *Class, Race and Worker Insurgency* (1977, Leonard Gordon's *A City In Racial Crisis: The Case of Detroit* (1971), a book by Gordon Van Sauter and Burleigh Hines *Nightmare In Detroit: A Rebellion and its Victims* (1968), Robert Slogan's and Tom Craig's *The Detroit Race Riot: A Study In Violence* (1964), as well as Benjamin Singer's and Richard Osborn's *Black Rioters: A Study of Social Factors and Communications in the Detroit Riot* (1970).

The London Evening Free Press and *The Detroit Free Press* also provided background as did David Compton's and Jim Tracey's *Detroit Riots 20 Years Later* (1987) and Pete McGarvey's *Detriot riot Tapes* (1967), always remembering that these are perceptions of people, a reflection of attitudes toward Detroit's evolution, perceptions that will also continue to evolve as we progress into the 21st century.

CHAPTER 12: THE AFTERMATH: WINDSOR

This chapter attempts to bring together attitudes about the riot, and reconcile them with the racial histories and attitudes of Windsor.

Personal interviews provide the unique insight of the following people: Tim Burton of Windsor, Jim Colling of Toronto, Kevin Conrad of Windsor, Barney Crichton of Windsor, Christopher and Kay Curtis of Windsor, Dorothy Gascoyne of Harrow, Ken Hull (deceased) of Calgary, Elise Harding-Davis of Amherstburg, Dennis Hinckley of Windsor, Bill Jackson of Windsor, Walt McCall of Windsor, Howard McCurdy of Tecumseh, Pete McGarvey of Orillia, Dino Paniccia of Windsor, Rochelle Richard of Windsor, Laurie Smith of Windsor, Dick Smyth of Toronto, Allen, Bryan and Winston Walls of Windsor and Eileen Zuccaro of Windsor.

The "Personal Archives" of Howard McCurdy, and "The Archives" of the North American Black Historical Museum and Cultural Centre provided insights that I could not have gained elsewhere.

Lyle E. Talbot's *The Distinctive Character of Racism in Canada* (1982), Paul Vasey's "Interview with Christopher Curtis" (1996) and Bob Steele's "Race Relations In Ontario: A Three Part Series" (1996) expanded my contact with unresolved racial conflicts.

Further historical attitudes were garnered from Bryan Wall's two books *Where The Underground Railway Has Its End* and *The Road That Led To Somewhere* (1980), *The Black Canadians: Their History and Contributions* (1989) by Velma Carter and Levero Lee Carter, and Roger Riendeau's *An Enduring Heritage: Black Contributions To Early Ontario* (1984).

CKLW's "Radio Sketches of Periods-Events-Personalities From the History of the Essex County-Detroit Area," and a similar edition from the Windsor and Essex County Historical Society (1963), as well as the inevitable chronicles from *The Windsor Star* and *The Chatham Daily News* allowed me to come to grips with my uncle's conundrum (see acknowledgements) that started me off on this quest.

APPENDIX I: AN ENTERPRISING SOCIOLOGIST: BENJAMIN SINGER

Without a personal interview with Benjamin D. Singer, this would have been pretty dry reading. The personal account of his activities brings his story to life.

Naturally, the chapter relies heavily on Singer's and Richard Osborne's book *Black Rioters: A Study of Social Factors and Communication in the Detroit Riot* (1970). Sydney Fine's book *Violence In the Model City* (1989) and James Geschwender's *Class, Race and Worker Insurgency: The league of Revolutionary Black Workers* (1977) provided further insight into why people riot.

Personal interviews with Jim Savage of Windsor and Bob Ferguson of Amherstburg rounded out the story and provided an insight into studies in the early 1970s.

Appendix II: A Tribute to Lightfoot

I tried unsuccessfully to talk with Gordon Lightfoot of Toronto. He declined an interview because it is not a subject that he likes to discuss. This was confirmed in personal interviews with Barry Harvey of Toronto and Beth Hebert of Windsor.

Maynard Collin's book *Lightfoot: If You Could Read His Mind* (1988) also helped me to read Lightfoot's mind, as did liner notes from his albums *The Best of Gordon Lightfoot* and *The Original Lightfoot: The United Artist Years*.

Further insights were provided by *Lillian Roxon's Rock Encyclopedia* (1971), Irwin Stambler's *Encyclopedia of Pop, Rock and Soul* (1974), and Michael L. LeBlanc's *Contemporary Musicians, Volume 3: Profiles of the People in Music* (1990).

Bibliography

BOOKS

Bergeron, Leandre, *The History of Quebec: A Patriote's Handbook*. Toronto: NC Press, 1971.

D'Oyley, Vincent, Ed., *Black Presence In Multi-Ethnic Canada*. Toronto: The Ontario Institute for Studies in Education, 1976.

Fine, Sydney, *Violence In the Model City: The Cavanagh Administration, Race Relations and the Detroit Riot of 1967*. Ann Arbour: University of Michigan Press, 1989.

Geschwender, James A., *Class, Race and Worker Insurgency: The League of Revolutionary Black Workers*. Cambridge: Cambridge University Press, 1977.

Gordon, Leonard, *A City In Racial Crisis: The Case of Detroit. Pre and Post the 1967 Riot*. Dubuque, Iowa: William C. Brown and Co. Publishers, 1971.

Hill, Daniel G., *The Freedom Seekers: Blacks In Early Canada*. Agincourt, Ontario: The Book Society of Canada Ltd., 1981.

Riendeau, Roger, *An Enduring Heritage: Black Contributions To Early Ontario*. Toronto: Dundurn Press Limited. The Ontario Ministry of Citizenship and Culture, 1984.

Rious, Marcel, *Quebec In Question*. Toronto: James Lewis and Samuel, 1971.

Sadlier, Rosemary, *Mary Ann Shadd*. Toronto: Umbrella Press, 1995.

Sauter, Van Gordon, & Burleigh Hines, *Nightmare in Detroit: A Rebellion and its Victims*. Chicago: Henry Regnery Company, 1968.

Shadd, Adrienne, Afua Coope, Karolyn Smardz-Frost, *The Underground Railroad: Next Stop, Toronto!* Toronto: Natural Heritage Books, 2002.

Singer, Benjamin D. & Richard W. Osborn, *Black Rioters: A Study of Social Factors and Communication in the Detroit Riot*. Lexington, Massachusetts: Heath Lexington Books, 1970.

Slaney, Catherine, *Family Secrets: Crossing the Colour Line*. Toronto: Natural Heritage Books, 2003.

Slogan, Robert & Tom Craig, *The Detroit Race Riot: A Study In Violence*. Philadelphia: Chilton Books, 1964.

Steubing, Douglas & John Marshall, Gary Oakes, *Trudeau: A Man For Tomorrow*. Toronto: Clarke Irwin and Company Limited, 1970.

Talbot, Lyle E., "The Distinctive Character of Racism In Canada. Windsor:" MA Thesis, Department of Religious Studies, University of Windsor, 1982.

Trudeau, Pierre Elliott. *Federalism and the French Canadians*. Toronto: Macmillan of Canada, 1968.

Vallières, Pierre. *White Niggers of America*. Toronto: McClelland & Stewart Ltd., 1968.

Walker, James. *Identity: The Black Experience In Canada*. Toronto: The Ontario Educational Communications Authority, Gage Educational Publishing Ltd., 1979.

PERIODICALS AND DOCUMENTS

Amherstburg Echo, Amherstburg: Amherstburg Echo Printing Co. Ltd. J.A. Auld, Pres. Ed., 1886-; Owner and Publisher, John A. Marsh. July 30th, 1980.

Chatham Daily News, Chatham: Thompson Newspapers Ltd. Publisher, Douglas C. Waite, 1967.

Detroit Free Press, Detroit: Knight Newspapers Inc., Publisher, Lee Hills, 1967-68.

Dufault, Rose-Marie, "Hotel-Dieu of St. Joseph – founded in 1888: Impact on Health Care and Education." Paper, Hotel-Dieu Archives.

Farrow, Ken, "Personal Archives." Amherstburg: Private Collection, 1996.

Gillmor, Don & Grant Black, "Promised Land: The Final Stop on the Underground Railroad." Toronto: Canadian Geographic Magazine, July/August 1995.

Jenson, Carole, "History of the Negro Community in Essex County, 1850-1860." Windsor: University of Windsor, Department of History, Faculty of Graduate Studies, Master of Arts Thesis, 1966.

_____ , "Abolitionist Interest in Upper Canada." Toronto: Ontario Historical Society Papers and Records, from the original, 1918.

_____ , "Canada's Part In Freeing The Slaves." Toronto: Ontario Historical Society Papers and Records, Volume XVII, from the original, 1919.

_____ , "In An Old Ontario Cemetery." Dalhousie Review. January 1926.

_____ , "Underground Railroad Along The Detroit River." London, Ontario: Michigan History. March 1955.

Lewis, James, "Religious Nature of Early Negro Migration To Canada and the Amherstburg Baptist Association." Ontario: Historical Society, Vol. LVIII, Number 2, Marsh Papers. John Marsh, Ed. 1966.

London Evening Free Press, London: Free Press Printing Company, Ltd., July 1967.

McCurdy, Alvin D., "Henry Walton Bibb." Negro History Bulletin. Address to the Association for the Study of Negro History, May 1958. "Schools 1881-1987." Archives of Ontario, Toronto.

McCurdy, George, "Resource Files;" "Genealogical Files." "Prince Hall Free Masonry." "Black Organizations;" "Scholarly and Literary Works." Archives of Ontario, Toronto.

McCurdy, Howard, "Personal Archives." Tecumseh: Private Collection, 1996.

Mercer, Robert & John McEwan, "Our Firemen." Detroit Historical Museum, 1849.

North American Black Historical Museum and Cultural Centre. "Archives." Amherstburg. 1996.

Percy, Gary, "Windsor Fire Department Archives." Windsor Fire Department: Fire Rescue Division, 1996.

Perry, Walter L., "Progress: The Oldest International Coloured Publication In The World." Windsor: Annual Emancipation Day program and magazine. 1948-1980s. Centennial Program, 1967.

Prince, John, "Personal Letter to Thomas Park." Sandwich: 12 April 1851.

Windsor Police Department, "Minutes of Meetings of the Board of Commissioners."

City of Windsor: RG 8 B1 - 1/12, Municipal Archives, Windsor Public Library, 1967.

Windsor Police Department, "Annual Report." City of Windsor: RG 8 CII /45; Municipal Archives, Windsor Public Library, 1967.

The Windsor Star, Windsor: Star Publishing Company, Ltd. July-August 1967. April-July-August 1968. July 1988.

VIDEOS AND OTHER MEDIA

Barnard, Patrick, "Ideas: Slavery In Canada: The Great Unspoken." Toronto: CBC, 1975.

CKLW, "Radio Sketches of Periods - Events - Personalities From the History of the Essex County - Detroit Area." Windsor: University of Windsor Library.

Compton, David & Jim Tracey, "Detroit Riots 20 Years Later." Half Hour Documentary. Windsor: CBC, July 1987.

Johnstone, Bob, "Today In History: Reverend William King." Toronto: CBC, January 05, 1996.

Johnstone, Bob, "Today In History: Abolition of Slavery." Toronto: CBC, July 9th, 1996.

McGarvey, Pete, "Detroit Riot Tapes." Chatham: CKCO, July 24-26, 1967.

Sinclair, Lister, "Ideas: Slavery In Canada." Toronto: CBC, January 08, 1996.

Steele, Bob, "Race Relations In Ontario: A Three Part Series." Windsor: CBC, Crosstown, 31/01/96-02/02/96.

United Artists, "Best of Gordon Lightfoot." Liner Notes.

United Artists, "Original Lightfoot: The United Artist Years" Liner Notes, September 1992.

Vasey, Paul, "Black History Month: Interview With Fred Johnstone." Windsor: CBC, Morning Watch. 22/02/96.

Vasey, Paul, "Interview: Christopher Curtis." Windsor: CBC, Morningwatch. 05/07/96.

ADDITIONAL SOURCES

Amherstburg Bicentennial Book Committee, *Amherstburg 1796 To 1996. The New Town on the Garrison Grounds*. Amherstburg: Bicentennial Project. 1996.

Anderson, Christopher P., *The Book of People*. New York: Putnam and Sons, 1981.

Bibb, Henry, *Narrative of the Life and Adventures of Henry Bibb, An American Slave*. New York, 1849.

Bramble, Linda, *Black Fugitive Slaves In Early Canada*. St. Catharines, Ontario: Vanwell Publishing Ltd., 1988.

Burns, R.M., *One Country or Two*. Toronto: McGill-Queen's University Press. 1971.

Careless, J.M.S., *Canada: A Story of Challenge*. Toronto: Macmillan of Canada, 1974.

Carter, Velma & Levero Lee Carter, *The Black Canadians: Their History and Contributions*. Edmonton, Alberta: Reidmore Books, 1989.

Collins, Maynard, Lightfoot: *If You Could Read His Mind*. Toronto: Deveau Publishers, 1988.

Gorrell, Gena K., *North Star To Freedom: The Story of the Underground Railway*. Toronto: Stoddart, 1996.

Krauter, Joseph F. & Morris Davis, *Minority Canadians: Ethnic Groups*. Toronto: Methuen Publications, 1978.

Leblanc, Michael L., *Contemporary Musicians, Volume 3: Profiles of the People in Music*. Detroit: Gale Research Inc., 1990.

Mackirdy, K.A. , J.S. Moir & Y.F. Zoltvany, *Changing Perspectives In Canadian History: Selected Problems*. Don Mills: J.M. Dent and Sons of Canada Limited, 1967.

Morgan, Carl, *Birth of A City*. Windsor: Travelife Publications Ltd., 1991.

Morrison, Neil F., *Garden Gateway to Canada: One Hundred Years of Windsor and Essex County, 1854-1954*. Windsor: Herald Press Ltd., 1954.

Newman, Peter C., *The Canadian Establishment*. Toronto: McClelland & Stewart - Baton Ltd, 1975.

Richardson, Rev. E.A., *Historical Sketch of the British Methodist Episcopal Church 1856-1926*. Owen Sound, Ontario, 1970.

Ricker, John & John Saywell, *How Are We Governed in the 1990s?* Toronto: Irwin Publishing, 1991.

Roxon, Lillian, *Lillian Roxon's Rock Encyclopedia*. New York: Grosset and Dunlop, 1971.

Sadlier, Rosemary, *Leading The Way: Black Women In Canada*. Toronto: Umbrella Press, 1994.

Stambler, Irwin, *Encyclopedia of Pop, Rock and Soul*. New York: St. Martin's Press, 1974.

Stewart, Walter, *Shrug: Trudeau In Power*. Toronto: New Press, 1971.

Thomson, Colin A., *Blacks In Deep Snow: Black Pioneers In Canada*. Don Mills, Ontario: J.M. Dent and Sons, Ltd., 1979.

Walls, Bryan E., *The Road That Led To Somewhere: A Documented Novel*. Windsor: Olive Publishing Company Ltd.

Walls, Bryan E., *Where The Underground Railroad Has Its End*. The John Freeman Walls Historic Site. 1980, reprint 1991.

Windsor, Essex County Historical Society, *Radio Sketches of Periods - Events - Personalities from the History of the Essex County - Detroit Area. Transcriptions*. Windsor: WECHA, 1963.

Winks, Robin W., *The Blacks In Canada: A History*. Montreal: McGill-Queen's, University Press, 1971.

Index

ABC (American Broadcasting Corporation), 56
Abbott, Anderson Ruffin (Dr.), 165
Abbott, Mary Ann (Casey), 165
Abolition of Slavery Act. 148
A Cappella Choir, 124
Adam Martini's Marina (Windsor), 98
Affleck, Larry, 101
Afro-American Youth Movement, 6
Airborne Division, 82nd, Third Brigade, 19
Airborne Division, 101st, Second Brigade, 19, 26
Alabama, 12, 82, 173
Alexandrine Street (Detroit), 16, 247
Alfred Street (Detroit), 184
Algiers Motel (Detroit), 31, 32, 236
Algiers Motel Incident, The, 31
All American City Award, 226
Allen, Bert, 64
Allen, Don, 99
Allmand, Warren (MP), 210, 211
Alton C. Park, 262
Ambassador Bridge (Windsor/Detroit), xvi, xvii, 54, 92
American Civil War, 154, 156, 157, 159, 179, 258
American Motors, 27
American Red Cross, 81, 82
American Revolutionary War, 141, 143
Amherstburg (ON), xii, xiii, xvii, xx, 73, 77, 78, 107, 118, 138, 147, 150, 153, 155, 162, 168, 172–175, 255, 256, 259, 264, 268
Anchor-In-Marina (Windsor), 98
Anderson, Jackie, 113
Andrew, 147, 148

Anglican Church, 110
Anti-Discrimination, Fair Accommodation Practises Act of Ontario, 170
Arbour, Doug, 67
Arbour Ambulance Service (Chatham), 68
Archer, Dennis (Mayor, Detroit), 243–246
Ariel (Ferry), 41
Arson, arsonist(s), 1, 11, 15, 22, 28, 29, 52, 61, 62, 115, 174, 236, 272
Ascon Construction (Windsor), 123
Ashby, John, 46
Ashby, ____ (Mrs. J.), 55
Ashley, Ephraim, 184
Associated Press, 19
Assumption Church (Windsor), 114
Assumption College (Windsor), 263
Assumption Parish (Windsor), 141
Atkinson Street (Detroit), 19, 42
Atlanta (GA), xv, 27, 125
Augusta, A.T. (Dr.), 165
Austin Engineering (Detroit), 101
Avenue of Fashion (Detroit), 12
Averill, ____ (Capt.), 157
Away To Canada, 145

Baby (family), 147, 148
Bagley District (Detroit), 205
Bailey, Ed, 6
Bales, D.A., (Labour Minister), 137
Baltimore (MR), 27
Baltimore Orioles (Baseball Team), 27
Banks, Roy, 26
Baptists, 159
Basilian House of Studies (Windsor), 111, 113
Bavarskis, Justinas, 19
Beatles, The, 66

Beaubien Street (Detroit), 66, 80, 84, 87, 233
Beaumont (TX), 191
Belgium, 103
Bell, B.G. "Spike," 51, 68–70
Bell Telephone Company, 95, 170
Belle Isle (Detroit), 6, 28, 64, 79, 104, 180, 183
Belle River (ON), 95, 96, 101
Belle River Surf Club, 95, 96
Bergeron, Leandre, 213–215, 225
Berry, Earl, 55
Bethune Street (Detroit), 19
Beuglet, Jeff, 78
Bibb, Henry Walton, 117, 150–152
Bibb, Mary, 117
Bill of Rights, 170
Birth of the Blues, 126
Bishop, Bill, 61, 62
Black Bottom (Detroit), 5
Black Day In July, 280, 281
Black Nationalism, 218, 219, 277
Black Panthers, 221
Black Power Movement, 11, 121, 130, 219–221
Black Pride, 269
Black Star Co-op Inc., (Detroit), 230
Black Student Alliance, 257
Blackburn, Lucie, 178
Blackburn, Thornton, 178
Blanding, Tonya, 30
Blaylock, Earl, 183
Blenheim (ON), 107
Blind Pig(s), 2–4, 25, 37, 39, 53, 106, 278
Bluewater Bridge (Sarnia), 60, 73, 97, 102, 105
Boblo Island Amusement Park (Amherstburg), 78, 172, 174, 175
Bolling, A.R. (Col.), 24
Bondy, Ann, 243, 244
Bondy, Dan, 102, 103
Bondy, Don, 102, 103, 243
Bondy, Jennifer, 101

Bondy, Mark, 101
Bonneau, Justine (Mother Superior), 164
Borders, William Holmes (Dr.), 125
Borman family, 230
Borovoy, Alan, 134, 136, 176
Bost, Gale, 89
Boston (MA), xv
Boston Boulevard (Detroit), 10
Botsford, David P., 153
Bowbeer, Norm (Dr.), 105
Bowbeer, Ruth, 105
Braithwaite, Leonard (MPP), 166
Brennan High School (Windsor), 257
Breslin, Jimmy, 44
Brezsnyak, John, 99
Briggs Stadium (Detroit), 190
Britain, 181, 207
British, 139, 140, 142, 148, 213
British Commonwealth, xviii
British Empire, 117
Broadhead Park (Windsor), 261, 262
Broderick, Al (Lt.), 96
Brogan, John, 184
Browning, J. Lyle, 263
Brown, Joseph, 3
Brush Park, 236
Brush Street (Detroit), 80, 81, 184, 235
Buffalo (NY), xv
Burnett, A.R., 169
Burton, John, 36
Burton, Tim, xvi, 250
Butler, Charles (Rev.), 202
Buxton (ON), 93, 154, 156, 268
Buxton Historic Site and Museum, 268

CBC Radio (Windsor), 65, 66, 282
CFCO Radio (Chatham), 67
CKLW Radio (Windsor), 63, 65, 281
CKLW-TV (Windsor), 56
CHUM Radio (Toronto), 65
Cadillac, Antoine de

Lamothe, 140
Cadillac Square (Detroit), 99
Caldwell's Grove (Amherstburg), 155
Calgary (AB), 60
Calgary Herald, The, 60
Cameron, Andrew, 279
Camp Dearborn (MI), 75
Campbell, Ken, 90
Campbell, William, 141
Campus Martius (Detroit), 246
Canada Customs, 122
Canada Manpower Centre, 123
Canada Mission (Amherstburg), 149
Canada West, 156
Canadian Civil Liberties Association, 134
Canadian Committee on Black Studies, 257
Canadian Council of Churches, 125
Carbonneau, Marc (FLQ), 224
Carlan, Bernice, 81, 82
Carmichael, Stokely, xiii, 221, 277
Caron Avenue (Windsor), 92
Carrol, Diahann, 99
Carter, G. Emmett Rev. (Bishop of London), 110
Cass Street (Detroit), 184
Cavanagh, Jerome Patrick (Detroit Mayor), 5, 9, 10, 14, 15, 20, 27, 28, 33, 36, 68, 103, 196–198, 201, 203, 227
Centennial (Canada), 100, 21, 217
Centennial Collegiate (Windsor), 257
Central Citizen's Association for the Advancement of Coloured People, 263
Central United Church (Windsor), 111
Charlevoix Street (Detroit), 22, 179
Chatham (ON), xi, 60, 67, 78, 93, 102, 103, 111, 113, 153, 154, 157, 158, 165, 176, 254, 255

Chatham Motors, 111
Chatham Street (Windsor), 102
Chauvin, Don, 91
Chavis, Benjamin, Jr., 269
Chene Street (Detroit), 188
Chénier Cell (FLQ), 224
Chevrier, Lionel (Commissioner General), 211
Chicago (IL), xiii, 19, 51, 97, 191, 197
Chicago Boulevard (Detroit), 10
Chicoutimi (QC), 216
Chrysler Canada, 99
Chrysler Corp., xvi, 8, 27, 172, 173, 227, 228, 233
Cincinnati (OH), xv, 2, 27, 37
Citizen's Advisory Committee (Windsor), 176
Citizen's Committee for Equal Opportunity, 202
Citizen's Complaint Bureau, 194
City-Wide Citizen's Action Committee, 230
Civil Rights, programs, leaders, 10, 11, 15, 33, 36, 259
Civil Rights Commission, 202
Civil Rights Movement, xiv, 74, 138, 194, 198, 206, 238, 269, 274
Clairmount Street (Detroit), 1, 2, 6, 7, 25, 47, 68, 227
Clark, Katherine, xxii
Clark, Kenneth, 270
Clark, Ramsay (US Attorney Gen.), 14
Clark, W.L., 120, 121, 211
Cleage, Albert Jr. (Rev.), 219, 230, 231
Clear Grits, 215
Cleary Auditorium (Windsor), 92
Cleveland (OH), 36, 51, 57, 197
Cobo Hall (Detroit), 201, 243
Coffin, Levi, 148
Colchester (ON). 94, 95, 147, 252
Collingwood (ON), 147

Collins, Maynard, 280, 281
Colonial Church and School
    Society, 163
Comerica Park (Detroit), 235,
    248
Commission on Systemic
    Racism in the Criminal
    Justice System in Ontario,
    265
Committee on Community
    Relations, 202
Committee on Racism
    (Windsor), 266
Common School Act, 161
Communists, 37, 168, 170
Confederation, 124, 215, 216
Connor Street (Detroit), 46
Conrad, Kevin, 251
Conservatives, 269
Conyers, John, Jr.
    (Congressman), 6, 8, 29,
    228, 229, 278
Cooley High School (Detroit),
    233
Cooper, Carl, 31
Coral Gables (Detroit), 76
Cossette-Trudel, Jacques
    (FLQ), 224
Coxon, Harold (Windsor Fire
    Chief), 43–46, 49, 50,
    53–55, 58
Coxon, Inez, 44
Crawford Street (Windsor), 57
Crichton, Barney, 78, 262
Criminal Investigations
    Branch, 175
Cross, James Richard (British
    Trade Commissioner), 222,
    224
Cross, Thomas (Mayor), 158
Crowlie's (Detroit), 243
Cunningham's Drugs
    (Detroit), 72
Curtis, Christopher, 256, 259,
    260
Curtis, Darryl, 12
Curtis, Kay. 255. 256
Curtis Street (Detroit), 73
Cy Young Award, 255

Dalton, Willie, 34
Dalton, Ethel, 34
Dark Ghetto: Dilemma of Social
    Power, 270
Darrow, Clarence, 180
Davenport Street (Detroit), 187
Davis, Delos Rogest, 154
Davis, Robert, 185
Day, Betty, 72
Dearborn (Detroit), 82
Dearborn Medical Centre, 13
de Bono, Spiros, 73
Defense Supplies
    Corporation (Detroit), 189
de Gaulle, Charles (Pres.,
    France), 208–212, 221
Del Rio, James (State
    Representative), 11, 29
Democrat(s), 228, 280
Densen, Henry, 22
Depression, The, 215
Desert Inn (see Algiers Motel)
Desramaux, Catherine, 113
Detroit (MI), xiii, xv, xxii, 1, 2,
    6, 7, 12, 15, 17, 20, 23, 25–28,
    30, 32–35, 37–70, 72–79,
    81–84, 86–109, 111–116,
    140, 145, 149, 170, 172, 176,
    178–182, 185–207, 208, 222,
    226, 227, 230, 232–238, 240,
    242–253, 271, 272, 275,
    276–280, 282, 283
Detroit Bar Association, 33
Detroit Benefit Fund, 53
Detroit Board of Fire
    Commissioners, 50
Detroit Commission on
    Community Relations, 131
Detroit Edison, 8
Detroit Fire Department, 40,
    43, 50, 53
Detroit Fire Department
    Band, 51
Detroit Fire Tug, 43
Detroit Free Press, The, xvii, 4,
    19, 33, 39, 51, 56, 68, 192,
    196, 201, 205, 239
Detroit General Hospital, 14
Detroit Golf Club, 237
Detroit Historical Museum, 53

Detroit Housing Authority, 181
Detroit Institute of the Arts,
    18, 97
Detroit Interfaith
    Committee, 114
Detroit Lions (football), xiv
Detroit Marine Division, 43
Detroit Memorial Hospital,
    18, 82
Detroit News, The, xvii, 56
Detroit Northwestern High
    School, 195
Detroit Olympia, xxi
Detroit Pistons (basketball),
    xvi
Detroit Police
    Commissioner's Citation, 87
Detroit Police Department,
    xvi, xxi, 4, 5, 9, 17, 87, 88,
    131, 271
Detroit Receiving Hospital,
    18, 82
Detroit Red Wings (hockey),
    xvi, 98, 244
Detroit Renaissance Center,
    xix, 234, 237, 245, 247, 248
Detroit River, 40, 79, 140,
    148, 180
Detroit Tigers (baseball), xvi,
    10, 11, 27, 234
Detroit Times, 187
Detroit Vice Squad, 2
Detroit Zoo, xxii
Dexter Street (Detroit), 47, 236
Dieppe Gardens (Windsor),
    78, 92, 100
DiMenna, Ron, 76
District Neighborhood
    Service Organization
    (Detroit), 131
Division Street (Detroit), 185
Dixie, 179
Dokx, Theofiel, 103, 104
Dorsey, Julius L., 16
Dorval Airport (Montreal), 211
Dougall Road (Windsor), 99
Douglas, T.C. (NDP Leader),
    211
Downtown Collision
    (Detroit), 101

Drake Side Road, 165
Dresden (ON), xiii, 157, 168–170, 268
Dresden, City of (Ferry), 155
Drouillard, Jeanne, xix, xx
Drouillard Road (Windsor), 82
Duchesne, E.A. (Crown Attorney), 175
Dufferin Street (Windsor), 107
Dunson, Charles, 31
Duplessis, Maurice (Quebec Premier), 216, 217
Dylan, Bob, 280

Early Morning Productions (Toronto), 281
Eastern Market (Detroit), 102
East Grand Boulevard (Detroit), 22
East Jefferson Street (Detroit), 77
Eastwood Amusement Park (Detroit), 182
Ebony, 243
Ector, Herman, 21
Edmonds, Nathaniel, 21
Edmonton (AB), 104
Edwards, George (Judge), 194
Eight Mile Road (Detroit), 38, 72
Eisenburg, Joseph, 110
Elgin Settlement, 153, 268, 269
Elliott, ____ (Col.), 148
Ellis, Curly, 78, 79
Elmwood Street (Detroit), 51
Elmwood Casino (Windsor), 99
Elmwood Cemetery (Detroit), 51
Emancipation Day, 117, 118, 120–138, 155, 251, 262
Emancipation Day Sunrise Service, 125
Emergency Measures Organization, 11
Emergency Relief Centre (Windsor), 112
Engine #2 (Windsor Fire Department), 45, 47, 49

Engine #5 (Windsor Fire Department), 49
Engine #7 (Windsor Fire Department), 45–47, 49
Engine #9 (Windsor Fire Department), 49
Engine Company #13 (Detroit Fire Department), 51
English Tavern, The (Detroit), xix
Erie Street (Windsor), 261
Esquire Clothing Store (Detroit), 5
Essex (ON), xvi, 113
Essex and Kent Scottish Regiment, 107, 131
Essex County, xvi, xxii, 109, 114, 141, 159, 163, 167, 175, 263
Essex District High School, 257
Essex East (constituency), 122
Europe, 182, 190, 214
Evans, Ronald, 24
Expo '67, xiv, 121, 207, 209, 211, 221, 280

509, The (Detroit), xix
FBI (Federal Bureau of Investigation), 37, 38, 85, 191
Fairview Street (Windsor), 104
Farmer Jack Supermarkets (Detroit), 230
Farrow, Carl (Chief), 87–89, 130
Farrow, Ken, 123
Faulkner, William, 179
"Fear of Living, The," 220
Feinberg, Abraham (Rabbi), 169
Ferguson, Carol, 105
Ferguson, Bob, 279
Ferguson, Robert (Capt.), 44–46
Ferry Street (Windsor), 40
Field Street (Detroit), 16
Fields, Dave (Windsor Fire Chief), 54
Firebombs, firebombing, 30,

47, 63, 233, 276
Fireman's Field Day, 129, 132
First Baptist Church (Chatham), 136
First Baptist Church (Windsor), 125
First Lutheran Church (Windsor), 113
Fisher Building (Detroit). 77, 242
Fisher Theatre (Detroit), 243
Flagg Brothers Shoe Store (Detroit), xviii
Flint (MI), 17, 47, 110, 260
Ford Motor Company, xviii, 27, 99, 227
Ford, Henry II, 227, 228, 234
Forest Street (Detroit), 184
Fort Custer, 189
Fort Bragg (NC), 19
Fort Campbell (KY), 19
Fort Malden (Amherstburg), 141, 159
Fort Pontchartrain d'Etroit (Detroit), 140
Fort Street (Detroit), 51
Fort Wayne Induction Centre, 28
Fox, Aaron, 183
Fox, Garnet, xx, 77
Fox, Vicki, 77
Fox Theatre (Detroit), xix, 77, 242, 282
France, 209, 211, 212, 214, 221
Franklin, Aretha, 2
Frazer Hotel (Detroit), 185
Freedman's Inquiry, 156, 157
Freedom Award, 117, 125
Freedom Road, The, 268
French, 139, 140, 190, 218
French Canadians, 207, 208, 211–217
Front de Libération du Québec (FLQ), 212, 218, 219, 221, 222, 224, 225
Frontier Club (Windsor), 262
Fry, James, 141
Fry, Mike (Dresden Councillor), 169
Fry, Thomas, 141

GM (General Motors Corporation), xviii, 27, 101, 227, 245

Gagnon, Charles (FLQ), 212, 213, 222

Garland Street (Detroit), 179

Garnet, Gurney (Lieut.), 49

Garrod, Cheryl, xxi

Gascoyne, Debbie, 94, 95

Gascoyne, Kevin, 252

Gem (ferry), 141

General Amherst High School (Amherstburg), 173

General Motors Trim Plant (Windsor), xxi, 99

George, Sheren, 14

George Street (Amherstburg), 174

Georgian Bay, xv

German, 179, 190

Gibbs, Roy (Capt.), 45

Girardin, Ray (Detroit Police Commissioner), 4, 7, 9, 23, 56, 228, 278

Gladstone Street (Detroit), 43

Glasgow Normal School, 162

Goerzen, Gerhard, 79

Goerzen, Sue, 79, 246, 247

Goethe Street (Detroit), 22

Golden Eagle, The (Detroit), xvii

Gomes, Anna, 113

Goodwin Avenue (Detroit), 21

Gore Road, 149

Goyeau Street (Windsor), 76

Grace Episcopal Church (Detroit), 6, 115, 232, 233

Grace Hospital (Detroit), 80, 247

Grahame, Lloyd, xx

Graham, Hugh, 215

Grand Boulevard (Detroit), 101, 184

Grand Circus Park (Detroit), 99, 101

Grand Rapids (MI), 17

Grand River Boulevard (Detroit), 15, 27, 44, 64, 70, 91, 104, 180, 236

Grant, Don, 57

Gratiot Street (Detroit), 22, 38

Grazanka, Walter, 14

Great Britain, 41

Greater Detroit Lutheran Council Relief Fund, 113

Great Society (U.S.), 232

Greenfield Park (QC), 212

"Greensleeves," 37

Greyhound Bus Company (Detroit), 73

Grosse Isle (MI), 100, 105, 106

Grosse Point (MI), 3, 47

Grove Cemetery (Windsor), 126

Guardian Club (Windsor), 129, 171, 258, 264

Gulf of St. Lawrence, 211

HMCS Kootenay, 100

HMCS Nipigon, 100

HMS Hampshire, 99

HMS Tidepool, 99

Haaker, Paul, 184

Hall, Helen, 32

Hall, Ken, 98

Hamilton (ON), 98

Hamilton, John, 24

Hardges, William, 185

Harding-Davis, Elise, xii, xviii, 104, 120, 160, 167, 255–259, 269

Harlan House Hotel (Detroit), 32

Harlem (NY). 191

Harris, Mike (Premier), 269

Harrow (ON), 79, 93, 94, 107, 144, 147, 149, 162, 165, 167, 246

Hart, Kevin, 72

Harvey, Barry, 281

Hastings (ferry), 40

Hastings Street (Detroit), 184, 185, 188

Haviland, Laura, 145

Hazelwood Street (Detroit), 32

Hebert, Beth, 282

Heffernan, Carl, 271

Heinz, H.J. and Company (Leamington), 210

Hendel, Juergen, 78, 79

Henry, Charles, 3

Henry Ford Hospital (Detroit), 81, 242

Hersey, John, 31, 32

Highland Park High School (Detroit), 17, 93, 195

Hill, Daniel (Dr.), 131, 133, 136, 137, 176

Hill, Dennis, 162

Hinckley, Dennis, 253

Hiram Walker Historical Museum (Windsor), 210

Hiram Walker's Distillery (Windsor), 100

Hitler, Adolph, 216

"Homes by Christmas," 228

Hood, Nicholas (Detroit Councillor), 10

Hood, Valerie, 30

Hôtel-Dieu of St. Joseph Hospital (Windsor), 49, 164, 165

Hough riot (Cleveland), 36

House, Gladys, 183

Howard Avenue (Windsor), 261

Howe, Gordie, 98

Howe, Samuel Gridley, 156

Hudson, Joseph L. Jr., 227, 239

Hudson Department Store, J.L. (Detroit), xviii, 77, 101, 104, 243

Hull, Ken, 59, 60, 251

Hull, Norm, 58–61

Humphrey, Hubert (US VP), 14

Hunter, Willie, 14

Hurner, Gordon, 106

Huron Line (Windsor), 92

Hurst, John (Rev.), 163

Hurst, Mike, 244–246

Hutzel Hospital (Detroit), 242, 254

Identification Branch (Detroit Police), 83, 84

Ilitch, Mike, 244

Immigration Act (1911), 167

Inkster (MI), 182

Institute of Applied Science, 83

Insurrection, 15, 17, 53
Interfaith Emergency Centers
(IEC) (Detroit), 114–116
International Brotherhood
of Electrical Worker's
Union, 259
International Freedom
Festival, 53, 124, 129, 138
International Human Rights
Year (1968), 176
Irish, 179

Jackson, Bill, 82–88, 122, 262
Jackson, Mahalia, 119
Jackson (MS), xiv
Jackson Park (Windsor), 55,
117, 121, 122, 125–127, 133,
137
Jackson State Prison, 28
Janes, C.E. (MPP), 170
Janisse, Roland (Rev.), 110–112
Jefferson Avenue (Detroit),
38, 180, 183, 184, 234
Jeffries, Edward, Jr. (Mayor,
Detroit), 182, 189, 193
Jenkins, Fergie, 255
Jewish Community Centre
(Windsor), 111
Jewish Community Council
(Windsor), 110
John Freeman Walls
Historical Site and
Underground Railway
Museum, 268
John Lodge Freeway
(Detroit), xix, 10, 27, 68, 75
John R. Street (Detroit),
80, 180
Johnson, ____ (Lt. Col.), 131
Johnson, Arthur, 24
Johnson, Daniel (Premier),
210, 218
Johnson, Doreen, 93
Johnson, Lyndon Baines
(Pres., U.S.), 15, 19, 22, 33,
34, 38, 232, 279
Johnson, Sam, 184
Jones, Genevieve Allen, 125
Jones, William, 24
Joseph, Joseph B., 183

Jubilee Singers, 118

Kalamazoo (MI), 17
Kapuskasing (ON), 63
Katzman, Layne, 81, 242, 243
Keane's (Marina), 98
Kee, Beverley, 78
Kelly, Harry (Gov. Michigan),
189, 192
Kelly, Irma, 125
Kennedy, John F. (Pres., U.S.),
194
Kensington riot
(Philadelphia), 36
Kent County, 74, 93, 109, 111,
141, 165, 168, 254
Kent County Medical
Association, 165
Kentucky, 146, 149, 151, 159,
178
Kercheval District (Detroit),
6, 7, 38, 197
Kerner Commission, 8, 23,
34, 37, 52, 228, 232, 276
Kern's Department Store
(Detroit), 77, 243
Kersey, Catherine, 151
Killarney Castle (Windsor), 99
Kidnew, William (Rev.), 111
Kilpatrick, Kwame (Mayor,
Detroit), 245
King, Martin Luther, Jr. (Dr.),
27, 119, 128, 129, 194, 201,
220, 233, 239, 242, 246, 277
King, William (Rev.), 153, 154
King's College Medical
School (Toronto), 165
King Street (Amherstburg), 77
Kingsville (ON). 76
Korea, 20
Kos, Eli, 114
Kos, Mark, 114
Kos, Michael, 114
Kristof, Denise, xxii
Kristof, Steve, xxi, xxii
Ku Klux Klan (KKK), 173, 175,
180, 181, 266

Labelle, Phil (Lieut. Col.), 107
Labour Progressive Party

(LPP), 168, 170
Lafayette Street (Detroit), 16,
46, 184
Lafayette Park (Detroit), 199
Lake Erie, 95, 141
Lake Huron, 78
Lake St. Clair, 79, 95, 176
Lakewood Drive, 168
Lambton County (ON), 114
Lançtot, Jacques (FLQ), 224
Lane, Dave, 75, 76
Langlois, Yves (FLQ), 224
Lansing (MI), 47, 271
Lanspeary Park (Windsor), 258
Laporte, Françoise, 223
Laporte, Pierre (Labour
Minister), xiv, 222–224
Larke, John, 58
Larkin Road (Windsor), 72
Larwill, Edwin, 154
LaSalle (ON), 107, 113, 243
Laurier, Wilfred (Sir) (Prime
Minister), 167
Lavis, John, 72
Lawrence Town Road
(Toronto), 254
Law Society of Upper
Canada, 155
Leach, Tom, 66, 67
Leamington (ON), 97, 113, 211
Lee, James Townsend, 184
Lee, William, 141
Leger, Jules (Can.
Ambassador), 211
Leopold, Jack, 48
LeRoy, John, 31
Lesage, Jean (Quebec Liberal
Leader), 216
Lévesque, René (Leader,
Parti Québécois), 213, 216,
217, 224, 225
Lewis, John, 184
Libby, ____ (Rev.), 110
Liberal(s), 216, 218
Libération Cell (FLQ), 224
Lightfoot, Gordon Meredith,
280–282
Lima (OH), 17
Lincoln, Abraham (Pres.,
U.S.), 143, 156

Lincoln Street (Detroit), 44
Lincoln Day, 118
Lindblad, John, 74, 252
Lindsay Sapphire Dancers, 99
Linwood Street (Detroit), 11, 12, 24, 43, 236
Little River (ON), 147
Livernois Street (Detroit), 10, 12, 38, 72, 75
Locke, Hubert (Rev.), 10
Lockman, Sheldon, 271
Loguen, Jermain W. (Rev.), 148
London Daily Express, The, 66
London Free Press, The, 59, 233
London (ON), 57, 60, 107, 121, 1331, 247, 264, 271
Looting, looter(s), 1, 4–6, 8, 9, 11–16, 18–21, 24, 26–30, 34, 36, 39, 48, 62, 64, 68, 72–74, 79, 80, 101, 102, 115, 116, 233, 276
Lortie, Bernard (FLQ), 224
Los Angeles (CA), 23, 36, 191
Louis, Joe, 96, 119
Lower Canada, 147
Loyalists, 158
Lust, Julius, 32
Lycaste Street (Detroit), 22, 30
Lyons, Charles "Little Willie," 183, 184
Lysander Street (Detroit), 47

Macdonald, B.J.S. (Bruce) (Judge), 88, 129–131, 137
Mack Avenue (Detroit), 22, 30, 51, 236
Mackenzie Hall (Amherstburg), 155
MacNamara, Robert (US Secretary of Defense), 20
Macomb County (MI), 232
Madigan, Robert, 187
Mahadad, Vern, 266
Malcolm X, 37, 219
Malden (ON), 148, 157
Mallett, Conrad, Jr., 4
Manhattan House of Detention for Men (NY), 213
Marble Village (ON), 147

Marchand, Jean (Liberal MP), 218
Marentette, Michael, 131, 136, 137
Mariner's Church (Detroit), xvii
Maritimes, 141
Marshall, George (Gen.), 82
Martial Law, xiv, 22, 118, 189, 222, 234
Martin, Bob, 238
Martin, Paul (MP Essex East), 122, 210
Martinello, Sedo, 122
Maryland, 145, 146
Masecar, Murray (Rev.), 111
Masonic Temple (Detroit), 77, 282
Mason (MI), 31
Massey Hall (Toronto), 280
Mather, Les, 59
Mayer, Albert (Prof.), 199
McCall, Walt, xxi, 45, 49, 53, 57–63, 233, 234, 251
McLellan, Bill, 238
McCurdy, Alvin, 160
McCurdy, George, 173
McCurdy, Howard (Prof.), 124, 129–131, 137, 138, 264, 265
McCurdy, Ralph, 129, 130, 173
McDaniels, Willie, 32
McDermott, Dennis (UAW head), 136
McGarvey, J.A. "Pete," 62, 63, 67–69, 254
McGraw, Claude, 114
McKellar, Archibald (MP), 154
McKinnon Industries (Windsor), 99
Meadows Tavern, 166
Mercer Street (Windsor), 125
Messerlion, Krikor, 11, 12
Methodists, 145, 159
Metropole Supper Club (Windsor), 99
Meyer, Walter, 12
Michener, Roland (Gov. Gen.), 211
Michigan, xiv, 23, 44, 78, 98, 102, 105, 106, 117, 124, 178,

179, 192, 203, 243, 283
Michigan Avenue (Detroit), 101
Michigan Book Exchange (Detroit), xix
Michigan Chronicle, The, 204
Michigan State Civil Rights Commission, 1, 56, 131
Michigan State Fair Grounds, 190
Michigan State Police, 10, 76, 233, 234
Michigan State University, 264
Mic Mac Park (Windsor), 137, 138
Military Police Battalions, 701st, 728th, 189
Military Service Act, 215
Miller, George, 187
Million Man March, 269
Milwaukee (WI), 125
Mimmifield, "Handsome Harry," 183
Miracles, The, 2
Mirioni, Louis C. (Mayor, Detroit), 196
Mission Schools, 164
Mississippi, 204
Missouri, 146
Mitchell, Chuck, 282
Mitchell, Joni, 282
Mitchell, Sam, 187
Mitchell's Bay Sportsman's Club, 176
Mobile (AL), 191
Mongeau, Mary Catherine, 113
Monroe (MI), 28
Montgomery (AL), 238
Montreal (QC), xiv, 32, 38, 121, 164, 207–210, 212, 213, 215, 216, 221, 222
Montreal Star, The, 215
Montrose, Georgina (Acting Mayor, Windsor), 121.,176
Mooney, George, 78, 79
Morin, Louis, 191
Morin, Thérèse, 212
Mormon Church, 15
Morrison, Irv, 57

Moscow (Russia), 22
Motown (Detroit), xvii, 2, 120, 203
Mount Clemens (MI), 17, 94
Mount Royal (Montreal), 211, 222
Moy Avenue (Windsor), 107
Murphy, Phil, 51
Music Hall (Detroit), 77
Muskegan (MI), 17
Mussolini, Benito, 216

NDP (New Democratic Party), 211
Narratives of the Life and Adventures of Henry Bibb; An American Slave, 151
National Association for the Advancement of Coloured People (NAACP), 197, 264
National Bank of Detroit, 8
National Black Coalition of Canada, 264
National Film Board, 120
National Grocers, 91
National Guard, National Guardsmen, (U.S.), xv, xvi, 10, 14–17, 19, 21–24, 26–32, 34–36, 38, 42, 48, 51, 58, 61, 62, 66, 69, 74–76, 80, 81, 97, 112, 115, 130, 189, 233, 237, 247, 250, 279, 281
National Housing Act, 171
National Law Journal, 243
National League, 255
National Rifle Association (US), 232
Naval Academy (Detroit), 183
Navy League (US), 100
Nègres blanc d'Amerique, 212
Negro Michigan Chronicle, The, 191
Newark (NJ), 10, 43
New Detroit Committee, 227–231, 234
New France, 139, 140, 207
New York (NY), 17, 51, 191, 197, 213, 221, 280
New York Times, The, 196
New York Yankees, 10

Newberry Honor Award, 259
Newfoundland, 211
Niagara Falls (ON), 102, 104
Niagara Peninsula, 145
Nichols, John (Detroit Police Commissioner), 237
Ninth Infantry Regiment, Second Division (US), 189
Noble, D.A., 95
North Africa, 182
North American Black Historical Museum and Cultural Centre (Amherstburg), xii, 150, 151, 160, 255, 258, 262, 268
North Burdick Street (Detroit), 17
North Carolina, 146
Northland Mall (Detroit), 230
Northway Avenue (Windsor), 266
Northwest Territory (US), 142
Notes On Canada West, 151

Oakland County (MI), 232
Oak Park (Detroit), 5
October Crisis (1970), 222
Ohio, 102, 117, 144, 159
Oklahoma, 79
Old Walker House (Windsor), 262
Oliver, Gail, xxi
Olshove, Jerome, 24, 32
Olympia (Detroit), 77, 91
Ontario, xvi, xvii, 102, 117, 119, 123, 136, 168, 170, 171, 257, 258, 265, 269
Ontario Human Rights Code, 171
Ontario Human Rights Commission, 117, 127, 128, 130–133, 135–137, 171, 172, 174–176, 258
Ontario Labour Committee, 176
Ontario Lacrosse Association, 94
Ontario Medal for Good Citizenship, 261
Ontario Municipal Act, 132, 136

Ontario Police College, 89
Ontario Provincial Police (OPP), 75, 89, 130, 131, 135
Operation Sundown, 10
Orangeville (ON), 94
Order of Canada, 261
Orillia (ON), 280
Osgoode Hall (Toronto), 132, 134
Osgoode, William (Chief Justice), 142
Ottawa (ON), 210, 224
Ouellette Avenue (Windsor), xvii, 72, 107, 111, 137, 138, 164
Ouellette, Wilfred, 91
Owen, John, 41
Owen, Rick, 266
Owen Sound (ON), 147
Owens, Jesse, 119

Pan Am Games, xv
Paniccia, Dino, 242, 254
Paquet, Josephine (Sister), 164, 165
Paradise Valley (Detroit), 180, 184
Parent, Rachel, xx
Paris (France), 215
Park Street United Church (Chatham), 111
Parke-Davis Pharmaceutical Company, 8
Parker, Alton C., 261–263
Parks, Rosa, 238, 239
Parti Québécois (PQ), 213, 224, 225
Patterson Collegiate (Windsor), 257
Paz, Bob, 75
Pearson, Lester Bowles (Prime Minister), 209–211, 217
Peden, Robert, 162
Pelletier, Gérard (Liberal MP), 218
Perry, Roy (Controller), 171
Perry, Walter Lawrence, 118, 121, 122, 124–126, 133, 137, 138, 263
"Person of the Year," 262

Peterson, Charles, 261
Philadelphia (PA), 36
Phillips, Mary, 17
Pine Knob (MI), 282
Pingree Street (Detroit), 236
Pitt Street (Windsor), 46, 58, 96, 111
Plains of Abraham (1759), 213
Pocock, Jerry (Insp.), 267
Poirier, Lisa, 32
Police Complaint Bureau, (Detroit), 203
Police Service Act, 266
Polke, Roger, 30
Pollard, Aubrey, 31
Pontchartrain (Detroit), 99
Pontiac (MI), 17
Poor People's March, 234
Porter Street (Detroit), 77
Port Huron (MI), 60, 73, 102, 104
Port Huron Jaycees, 114
Port Lambton (ON), 97
Positive Neighborhood Action Committee (Detroit), 21
Post, Larry, 31
Potts, Joseph (Father), 67, 68, 110, 232, 254
Powell, Edmund (Ted), 127, 128, 131–133, 135, 137, 138
Powell, Jesse, 64
Prattville (AL), xv
Presbyterian Church, 162
Preston, Gordon (Deputy Chief), 127, 130, 131
Primettes, The, 120
Prince Bryan, 268
Prince, Shannon, 268
Prince Edward Public School (Windsor), 251
Prince Road (Windsor), xxi
Prince's Grove (Sandwich), 118
Progress, 124
Progressive Conservative, 170
Provencher, Jerry, 98
Provincial Freeman, The, 150
Pryor, Clifton, 16
Public Works Department (Windsor), 262

Puce (ON), 147, 265
Puce Road, 152
Puce River Settlement School, 145

Quakers, 145
Quebec, xiv, 207–210, 212–215, 217–219, 221, 222, 224, 225
Québécois, 212, 218–221
Queen's Hotel (Windsor), 41
Queen's Rangers, 143
Queen's Silver Jubilee Medal, 261
Quickie Donut Shop, (Detroit), xix
Quinlan, Charles J. (Detroit Fire Chief), 43, 50, 54
Quinn, Al, 19

RKO General (US), 63
Race and Ethno-Cultural Relations Committee (Windsor), 266
Radio and Television News Director's Assoc. Award, 65
Radio Tokyo, 191
Ramcharan, Subhas (Prof.), 266, 267
Raymond, Frindel, 97
Reagan, Ronald (Gov. Calif.), 36
Rebellion of 1837, 149
Recorders Court (Detroit), 16, 18
Redding, Otis, 2
Refugee Home Society, (Windsor), 150, 152
Regent Park (Toronto), 254
Religious Hospitallers of Hôtel-Dieu of St. Joseph, 164
Rendezvous Tavern (Windsor), 98
Reuther, Walter (UAW Pres.), 201, 235, 236
Revolution Québécois, 221
Richard, Rochelle, 257, 269
Rimouski (QC), 216
Riot area, 25
River Canard (ON), 101, 102

Riverside Drive (Windsor), 57, 73, 104, 107, 111
Rivieria Theatre (Detroit), 105
Roberts, J., 79
Robinson, Albert, 32
Robinson, Smokey, xvii
Roche, James, 227
Romney, George (Gov., Mich.), 14, 15, 33, 50, 73, 106, 201
Roosevelt, Eleanor, 119
Roosevelt, Franklin D. (Pres., U.S.), 181, 182, 189
Roquemore, Ernest, 35
Rosa Parks Boulevard (Detroit), 238, 239
Rose, Jacques (FLQ), 224
Rose, Paul (FLQ), 224
Roselawn (Windsor), 113
Ross, Diana, xvii, 120
Rouge Park (Detroit), 204
Royal Canadian Air Force (RCAF), 224
Royal Canadian Legion, 132
Royal Canadian Navy, 100
Royal Canadian Regiment (RCR), 107
Royal Commission on Bilingualism/Biculturalism, 217
Royal Oak (MI), 47
Ruscom River, 96
Russell Street (Detroit), 180
Russell Woods (Detroit), 199
Ruter, Eugene (Supt.), 87
Ryan, Garnet (Lieut.), 107

S.S. No. 11 (School), 165, 166
Sach's (Detroit), 243
Saginaw (MI), 17
Saginaw Bay (MI), 78
Saint-Hubert (QC), 223
Saint-Jean (QC), 224
Saint-Lambert (QC), 222
St. Alphonsus Church (Windsor), 164
St. Aubin Street (Detroit), 184
St. Catharines (ON), 145
St. Clair River, 79, 97
St. Clair Shores (MI), 77
St. Clair Tavern (Windsor), 106

St. Laurent, Louis (Can. Minister of Justice), 216
St. Leonard's House (Windsor), 110
St. Paul's United Church (Detroit), 111
St. Pierre and Miquelon, 211
St. Thomas (ON), 93
St. Vincent de Paul Centre (Windsor), 111
Salsberg, J.P. (MPP), 168, 170
Sam's Department Store (Detroit), 72
Sandburg, Katherine, 27
Sanders Ice Cream Parlour (Detroit), xviii
Sandusky (OH), 97
Sandwich (ON), 42, 117, 118, 141, 147, 148, 155, 263
Sandwich Baptist Church, 160
Sandwich Street (Windsor), 266
Sarnia (ON), xx, 73, 97, 100, 102, 105
Sarnia Jaycees, 114
Saturday Night, 167
Savage, Jim, 279
Scaglione, Cec, 70
Second Street (Detroit), 101
Security Building (Windsor), 65
See America Tour, 97
Selfridge Field Air Force Base, 19, 189
Senate Investigating Committee (US), 279
Separatists (QC), 218, 223
Serrin, William, 19
Sessing, Trevor W., 167
Seven Mile Road (Detroit), 12, 73
Seymour, Arthur (Asst. Fire Chief, Detroit), 49
Shadd, Mary Ann Camberton, 150, 151
Shelton, Robert (Imperial Wizard), 173
Shively, Floyd, 13
Sicily, 182
Silverstein's Produce

(Windsor), 102
Simard, Francis (FLQ), 224
Simcoe, John Graves (Lt. Gov.), 143
Simpson, Jim, 153
Sinasac's garage, 173
Sinbad's (Detroit Marina), 98
Singer, Benjamin D. (Prof.), 271–274, 277–279
Singleton, Carl, 185
Sister Immaculata, 104
Six Mile Road (Detroit), 73, 76
Skyline Room (Windsor), 92
Smith, Bernie, 124
Smith, Carl, 22, 51, 52
Smith, Laurie, xxii, 252
Smith, Murray (Amherstburg Mayor), 174
Smyth, Dick, 63–65, 253, 254
Sniper(s), sniper fire, 13, 15–17, 20, 22–24, 26–28, 30, 34, 36, 38, 43, 45–47, 51, 61, 62, 64–66, 68, 70, 81, 94, 101, 105, 112, 115
Sojourner Truth (Detroit), 181
Sombra (ON), 97
Sorel (QC), 215
Soulliere, ____ (Mrs. Howard), 111
Soulliere, Omer, 112
Southeastern High School (Detroit), 22, 24
South Essex Citizen's Advancement Association (SECAA) (Windsor), 129, 172, 173, 175
Southfield (MI), 5
Spanish Harlem (NY), 17
Special Investigation Unit (ON), 265
Standard Airways (Detroit), 104
Stanley Street (Detroit), 91
Starbright Market (Detroit), 42
Stark, ____ (Justice), 135
State Troopers, 17
Statler-Hilton Hotel (Detroit), 67, 279
Steele, Bob, 92

Steele, Eugene, 124
Stewart, Gordon R. (Magistrate), 88, 129, 132, 137
Strasbourg (France), 97
Stroh's Brewery (Detroit), 87
Stuart, Charles (Captain), 147
Student Non-Violent Coordinating Committee (US), 277
Suchan, Joe, 104, 105
Sullivan, Hal, 65, 66
Sundown, 282
Supreme Court of Canada, 117, 132, 134, 138
Supreme Court (US), 239, 244
Supremes, The, xvii, 120
Surf Club Drive, 96
Surfside Dancehall (Detroit), 77
Sweet, Ossian (Dr.), 179, 180
Sydnor, Jack, 30

Talbert, Clayton, 256, 269
Talbert, George, 32
Talbert, Lyle, 263
Tampa (FL), xv, 9
Tass, 22
Tate, Bill, 47, 48
Taylor Street (Detroit), 32
Taylor, Bill, 95
Taylor, H.D. , 263
Taylor, Marcene, 9
Taylor, Michael, 101
Tecumseh Road, 96
Tecumseh, (ON), 113
Temple, Fred, 31
Temple Market (Detroit), 14
Tennessee, 146, 148
Tenth Precinct (Detroit), 28, 29
Third Avenue (Detroit), 247
Thirteenth Precinct (Detroit), 16
Thomas, Danny, 204
Thomas, Raymond, 183
Thoughts For Greater Detroit, 244
Throckmorton, John L. (Lieut. Gen.), 20, 26
Tiger Stadium (Detroit), 10

Timberlake, Gabriel, 149
Time, 6
Toledo (OH), xx, 17, 47, 57
Tomlinson, John, 257
Top Hat Supper Club
    (Windsor), 99
Toronto (ON), xv, 57, 66, 77,
    98, 102, 134, 135, 148, 149,
    173, 178, 251–254, 257, 259,
    280
Toronto Star, The, 59
Townsend, Lynn, 227
Township of Maidstone
    (Essex County), 73, 147
Township of Camden (Kent
    County), 157
Township of Colchester
    (Essex County), 141, 144, 165
Township of Orford (Kent
    County), 157
Township of Raleigh (Kent
    County), 153
Township of Malden (Essex
    County), 168
Travis, Jim, 96
Treaty of Versailles, 142
Trinidad, 255
Tripp, Dick, 19
Trudeau, Pierre Elliott
    (Minister of Justice/Prime
    Minister), 211, 217, 218
Trumble Street (Detroit), 47
Tubman, Harriet, 145
Tuscaloosa (AL), 173
Twelve Mile Road (Detroit),
    76
Twelfth Street (Detroit), 1–3,
    5–7, 9, 12, 15, 19, 24, 25, 32,
    42, 47, 57, 62, 64, 69, 79,
    103, 115, 200, 204, 227, 233,
    238, 239

UAW (United Auto Workers)
    (Detroit), 33, 182, 196, 199,
    201, 235
UAW Local 444 (Windsor), 110
UAW (Wayne County), 115
Ukrainian, 82
Uncle Tom's Cabin (ON), 268
Underground Railroad,

144–147, 168, 220
Union Produce Terminal
    (Detroit), 102
United Community and
    Civic Action League
    (Detroit), 2, 204
United Nations, 170, 213
United Press International
    (UPI), xviii
United Shirt Store (Detroit),
    xviii
U.S. Coast Guard, 99
U.S. Department of
    Agriculture, 110
U.S. Department of Labour,
    279
U.S. House of
    Representatives, 38
U.S. Justice Department, 279
Universal Declaration of
    Human Rights (U.N.), 170,
    176
Université de Montreal, 211
University of Toronto, 169
University of Western
    Ontario, 257, 271
University of Windsor, 98,
    124, 211, 247, 257, 261, 264,
    266, 279
Upper Canada, 139, 141–144,
    147

Vallières, Pierre (FLQ),
    212–222, 224
Vance, Cyrus, 20
Vancouver (BC), 170
Vander Zanden, Ivy, 79, 80,
    247, 248
Van Kuren, Jim (CKLW TV),
    56, 57, 64
Van Dyke Street (Detroit), 38
Vernor's Ginger Ale (Detroit),
    xviii
Veteran's Memorial Building
    (Detroit), 100
Vichy (Radio), 190
Vicksburg Street (Detroit), 24
Victoria Avenue (Chatham),
    254
Vietnam War, xv, xvi, 3, 15,

20, 26, 66, 218, 232, 250,
    274, 280
Virginia, 146, 159, 165
Virginia Park (Detroit), 2, 31,
    232, 243
Virginia Park Rehabilitation
    Citizen's Committee
    (Detroit), 232
Voice of the Fugitive, The, 118,
    150
Von Goethem, Alphonse
    (Mrs.), 103

WJR Radio (Detroit), 56, 79
WWJ-TV (Detroit), 57
WXYZ-TV (Detroit), 57
Wagner, Dean (Father), 164
Walker, John, 111
Walker, Pat, 94
Walkerville (ON), 114
Walkerville Collegiate
    (Windsor), 82
"Walk To Freedom"
    (Detroit), 201
Wallaceburg (ON), 74
Wallaceburg Police
    Department, 75
Walpole Island (ON), 97
Walls, Allen, 73, 268
Walls, Bryan (Dr.), xxi, 268
Walls, Clifford, 123
Walls, John "Freeman," 268
Walls, Winston, 267, 268
Ward, Rosalind, xxi
War Measures Act, 222, 223
War of 1812, 144
Warren (MI), 50
Washington, DC, 17, 182, 191,
    220, 245, 269, 278
Washington Boulevard
    (Detroit), 279
Washtenaw County (MI), 28
Watkins, Ethel, 205
Watkins, Howard, 123
Watson, James E. (Q.C.), 132,
    133, 171
*Watson's Go To Birmingham,
    The*, 259
Watts riot (Los Angeles), 9,
    23, 36

Waverly Street (Detroit), 47
Wayne County, 110, 115
Wayne County Community
   College, 228
Wayne State University, 18,
   186, 195, 251, 271
Weese, Walter S. (Mayor),
   168, 169
Welk, Lawrence, 19
West Bloomfield (MI), 74
Western Freight (Chatham),
   111
West Grand Boulevard
   (Detroit), 6, 10, 81, 94
West, Sandra, 12, 13
Weston, Charlie (Inspector),
   86
Wheelton, John (Mayor,
   Windsor), 121, 176
Whealan, Pat, xix, 90, 252
White, Henry, 123
White, John (Attorney
   General), 142
White House (Washington,
   DC), 232
Wilberforce, William (Prime
   Minister), 143
Williams, Fred, 21
Williams, Michael, 112
Williams, Perry, 24
Williams, Prince, 14
Willson, Bill, 165
Wilson, John (Sheriff), 178
Windsor (ON), xiii, xvi–xviii,
   xxi, xxii, 24, 40–51, 53–58,
   63, 65–69, 72, 74, 79, 81,
   82, 86–93, 95–102, 104,
   105, 106, 108–114, 117, 118,
   120–121, 132–131, 136–138,
   145, 147, 150, 152, 155, 160,
   162, 164, 170, 175, 176, 178,
   210, 245, 250–253, 257–259,
   261–269, 271
Windsor Arena, 122, 138
Windsor Black Coalition, 256,
   264
Windsor Board of Control, 171
Windsor Board of Education,
   263, 266
Windsor Castle Hotel, 41

Windsor Chamber of
   Commerce, 99, 125
Windsor City Council, 114,
   121, 126
Windsor Civic Softball
   League, 123
Windsor Clippers, 94
Windsor Council of
   Churches, 110
Windsor Fire Department,
   40, 44, 49, 50, 53, 58
Windsor Parks and
   Recreation Department,
   127
Windsor Police Commission,
   88, 127, 128, 131, 133, 136,
   264
Windsor Police Department,
   xix, 86–89, 138
Windsor Raceway, xvii
Windsor Relief Committee,
   110
Windsor Star, The, xix, xxi, 19,
   53, 57–61, 65, 70, 74, 90,
   98, 106, 108, 114, 120, 123,
   124, 127, 130, 136, 137, 210,
   211, 233, 251, 252, 264
Windsor Western Hospital,
   xxi
Winnipeg (MB), xiv
Woodrow Wilson Avenue
   (Detroit), 68
Woodward Avenue (Detroit),
   xviii, xxii, 2, 5, 14, 31, 38,
   40, 72, 81, 185–187, 190,
   192, 201
Woodward Place, 236
World Relief Fund, 110
World War I, 69, 215
World War II, xxi, 72, 167,
   181, 215, 253
Wyandotte Street East
   (Windsor), 106
Wynants, Rick, 73

York (UC), 148, 178
Young, Coleman A. (Mayor,
   Detroit), 53, 237, 241, 242,
   244, 245
Ypsilanti, (MI), 179

Zegerius, Hans (Rev.), 110
Zeni, Carol, 93
Zeni, Juliana, 93
Zuccaro, Eileen, 75, 251

Courtesy CBC Radio One, Windsor, 1550

About the Author

Herb Colling has an abiding interest in, and respect for, local history. His first two books deal with the auto industry in Windsor. He cut his teeth in 1993 on *Pioneering The Auto Age*, about Windsor as an automotive capital of Canada, and went on to write *99 Days: The Ford Strike In Windsor, 1945* which was published in 1995.

Colling graduated from Ryerson Polytechnical Institute in Toronto with a Radio and TV Arts Degree, followed by journalism studies at Carleton University, Ottawa. An announcer and reporter for CBC Radio in Windsor, he began his broadcasting career at the age of 16 at CKMP in Midland.

A former agricultural commentator for CBC, he won the Jack Cramm Memorial Trophy for excellence in farm broadcasting and, in 1986, took First Place for news reporting: Canadian Farm Writer's Federation. He was also the winner of an Award for Excellence in promoting farm safety. Most recently, he wrote and produced a CD for the 50th anniversary of CBC Radio in Windsor.

An active scuba diver, rower and sailor, Colling wrote a scuba column and sailing articles for *Waterline Magazine* in Windsor. He has also written fitness and rowing articles for *FIT* magazine, another local Windsor publication.

Colling is a consummate traveller whose travel stories have appeared in *The Ottawa Citizen*, *The Windsor Star* and *The London Free Press*. He is currently working on an anthology of his own short stories and poetry.

Since 1967, Colling has been interested in the Detroit riot, has always wondered what prompted it and how it impacted on residents in Windsor. This book is the result of that inquiry. He hopes it sheds light on the riot, its implications and on our racial development in both the United States and Canada.